Orit Kamir

Framed

WOMEN IN LAW AND FILM

Duke University Press

Durham and London 2006

© 2006 Duke University Press

All rights reserved

Printed in the United States of

America on acid-free paper ∞

Designed by Amy Ruth Buchanan

Typeset in Quadraat by Keystone

Typesetting, Inc.

Library of Congress Cataloging-

in-Publication Data appear on

the last printed page of this book.

To Nita and Rebecca—my jury of peers

Contents

Part III   WOMEN RESISTING AND SUBVERTING JUDGMENT
Beyond Conventional Feminist Jurisprudence

Acknowledgments

The materials contained in this book evolved over the course of five years, which happened to be a particularly difficult, challenging, and finally rewarding period in my personal and professional life. The writing process played a meaningful role in my analyzing and understanding the personal process, and thus in surviving it. Although the turbulence of this period hindered and slowed the creative process, it contributed to my sensitivity to and compassion for (women's) predicament and pain, and thus, I hope, to the depth of my analysis. This book holds much energy and passion inspired by various stages of a long process of injury, battle, and healing.

Many people supported me in the personal journey that coincided with the writing of this book, and I am forever grateful to them. Special thanks to Dina Wardi, John Hartman, Nita Schechet, Rachel Benziman, Batya Segal, Roni Weinstein and Dorit Lerer, Uri Sadeh, Michal Steinman, Barbara Garavaglia, Roberta Nerrison Low, Audrey Macklin, Rebecca Johnson, Pnina Lahav, Richard Lempert and Lisa Khan, James Boyd White, Omri Ben-Shachar, Yvonne, Dan, and Steve Kaplan, and, of course, my family.

I am beholden to the many fabulous students, in Israel, Michigan, and Slovenia, with whom I discussed and analyzed the films, and to friends and colleagues who graciously introduced me to films, read endless drafts, and helped with the editing. Among them are Ori Baron, Anita Bernstein, Rivka Elisha, Dror Elner, Phoebe Ellsworth, Ruth Gavison, Barbara Garavaglia, Ana Ruxandra Iacob (who graciously compiled the index), David Kretzmer, Audrey Macklin, Mariana Meisls, Hana Ovnat, Goran Selanec, Yoram Shachar, Marc Spindelman, Yofi Tirosh, and Zvika Triger. I am grateful to the forums at the University of Toronto law school, University of Victoria law school, and McGill University law school for their discussion and helpful comments, as well as to the editors of and contributors to the edited volume *Law on the Screen* (Sarat, 2005).

Parts of several chapters have been previously published separately over the years, and I am thankful for the permission to republish them here. I am also thankful to Valerie Millholland, Leah Stewart, and the staff of Duke University Press.

This book could not have been written if not for the incredibly generous, active participation and investment of Nita Schechet and Rebecca Johnson, who were with me every step of the way, and if not for the compassionate professional faith and encouragement I received from James Boyd White and Austin Sarat.

It is, as always, a pleasure to thank the University of Michigan Law School for the overwhelming generosity that facilitated the research and the writing, and in particular to thank deans Jeff Lehman and Evan Caminker.

Ever last but never least, deepest thanks to my loving family, including Pizi, who are always there for me, rain or shine.

Preface

How does law rule? In line with the optimistic worldview of earlier eras, many continue to maintain that law rules by applying equally to all; by speaking clearly and specifically; by warning before punishing; and through a systematic, institutional separation of its power, self-governed by mutual checks and balances. Others claim that all of the above are deceitful myths, opium for the masses. According to this critical view, the fictitious common notion of law's rule serves the hegemonic ruling classes in concealing their unlimited rule, feeding the false rhetoric that disguises the true social reality of power. In reality, therefore, law's rule means efficient legal preservation of existing social structures and power dynamics. In this sense, law rules through systematic concealment of its true nature and social function, achieved through the use of manipulative rhetoric of neutrality, fairness, professionalism, and equality before the law. Some believe there is some truth to each of these views, and that the specific answer depends on specific circumstances at any given time and place.

Whatever our view of the law, the fact is that, to some extent, in many parts of the world it does rule. It rules through constitutions, legislation, judicial decisions, contracts, and marriages. It rules through legal and semi-legal education, through professional rhetoric, and through authoritative images, narratives, and self-perceptions. A distinct and central means through which law rules is culture, popular culture in particular. Most people learn what they know about the law from popular culture, often without realizing they are receiving a popular-legal education and being socialized to a certain set of beliefs.

This book addresses the rule of law through (popular) culture. More specifically, it examines the ways in which popular fiction film operates as a vehicle of the rule of law. It reveals how in the course of "spreading the legal word," popular fiction film creates law, by structuring society's legal images, notions, perceptions, attitudes, sensitivities, and modes of operation; it shows how through the molding of social actors, popular film impacts the real hard core of legislation and litigation. Popular film offers interpretations and critique of juridical narratives and situations. It supplies the public with its versions of issues that concern justice, judgment, equity, affirmative action, class action, legal professionalism, and gender equality, to name but a few. It offers a central stage on which society is invited to collectively consider and practice such juridical and legally defined issues, while concurrently defining and molding itself. Popular film invites the public to actively judge situations and characters, applying the juridical notions the films present.

The study presented in this book is, therefore, an investigation of law-and-film, and thus a part of the new, growing discipline-in-the-making that goes by this name. As many are not yet familiar with this developing scholarly perspective, a few words of introduction may be in order.

Law and film are two of contemporary society's dominant discourses, two prominent vehicles for the chorus through which society narrates and creates itself. The distinction between law and film is obvious: while law is a system of organized power, commercial film is constituted by an economics of pleasure. Nevertheless, each is a discourse constituting imagined communities, to use Benedict Anderson's term. Law and film both create meaning through storytelling, performance, and ritualistic patterning, envisioning and constructing human subjects and social groups, individuals and worlds. Each invites participants—viewers, legal professionals, parties to legal proceedings, and/or members of the public—to share its vision, logic, rhetoric, and values. Law and film both demand adherence to rules and norms in exchange for order, stability, security, and significance. Each facilitates—and requires—concomitant and continuous creation of personal and collective identity, language, memory, history, mythology, and social roles, as well as a shared future.

The emerging discipline of "law and film" is a new cultural field where complex relations between these two discourses can be explored: similarities, differences, analogies, dialogue, and mutual influences on various levels.[1] Legal and cinematic structures, techniques, images, symbols, ideologies, social functions, and impact can be identified and analyzed singly and in reference to each other, inviting conceptualization and comparisons that lead to deeper understandings of the multiple perspectives of interdisciplinary analysis. This book offers a theoretical framework for reading law and film together in a socially meaningful manner.

As its subject matter, this book focuses on cultural reflections and refractions of women, femininity, judgment, honor, and dignity in the highly influential, multi-layered dialogue between law and film. A dozen influential films are closely studied, each portraying and commenting on legal treatment of women and social construction of gender, gender stereotypes, and roles; each raising issues of judgment, honor, and dignity. In this sense, all the films are popular jurisprudential texts. Additionally, they serve as social agents, constructing their own sociolegal treatment of women and gender issues even as they portray and critique existing ones. At the same time, each of the films also invites its viewers to participate in the execution of cinematic judgment. Four of the films invite viewers to judge the film's woman protagonist, pronouncing her always already guilty; they are discussed in the book's first part. Three of the films allow their women protagonists to judge others; they are analyzed in the book's second part. The last three refuse to support any judgment, transcending traditional notions both of judgment and of feminism. The readings of these films constitute the book's third part.

This book maintains that honor-based law films tend to subject sexual women protagonists to honor-based cinematic judgment, in which they are found to have always already been guilty objects responsible for the destruction of men, though themselves denied full subjecthood and agency. Offering viable alternatives, dignity-based law films tend to treat women who have been mistreated by men or social systems as victimized subjects and agents, respecting their plight as well as their survival and undefeated subjecthood. Such films refrain from subjecting their female protagonists to cinematic judgment, empowering them to pursue their own judgments, or questioning the notion of judgment altogether.

Chapter Outline

The book's chapters are organized thematically, each focusing on a single aspect of cinematic and legal constructions of women's victimization, condemnation, and/or vindication and empowerment. This clear thematic distinction facilitates systematic treatment of a complex theoretical topic. The themes discussed include cinematic judgment of women by the film's order of narration, cinematic prevention of a woman's day in court, the Hollywood hero-lawyer and the condemnation of the sexual woman, and women's judgment of legal and psychiatric institutions. Each of the chapters develops its theoretical argument through the close reading of a single film. This structure stresses my analogy between legal thinking through cases and precedents in the tradition of Anglo-American common law logic, and analysis of socio-cultural phenomena through close textual reading.

In the introduction, I present my method of analysis, which is dignity based, honor sensitive, and grounded in feminist law-and-film theory. The introduction offers a theoretical discussion of the discipline of law and film, dignity- and honor-based value systems, feminist jurisprudence, feminist film theory, feminist law-and-film theory, and their complex interrelations. Part 1, which comprises chapters 1 to 4, demonstrates cinematic judgment of women on screen. In chapter 1, I look at Akira Kurasawa's *Rashomon* (1951) to see how the very structure of the film's narrative points to its female character's guilt while denying her victimization. Chapter 2 examines G. W. Pabst's classic silent film *Pandora's Box* (1928), focusing on the judgment of sexually alluring women through stereotyping and the use of mythological archetypes, such as Pandora and Lilith. Chapter 3 presents Alfred Hitchcock's *Blackmail* (1929), examining the ironic juxtaposition between the film's status as the first British talkie and the way it silences its female character by denying her her rightful day in court. In chapter 4, I scrutinize *Anatomy of a Murder* (1959), which suppresses a woman's ongoing abuse by a violent husband, subjecting her to harsh cinematic judgment for adultery and homicide. The film also establishes the paradigmatic image of the hero-lawyer, modeled on the classic image of the western hero.

In part 2, I examine portrayals of women judging oppressive systems and individuals. Reading the popular classic *Adam's Rib* (1949), chapter 5 compares Hollywood's image of the feminist female lawyer (Katharine Hepburn) with that of the male hero-lawyer. I also briefly apply the analysis of *Adam's Rib* to two more recent Hollywood films, *Disclosure* (1994) and *Legally Blonde* (2001). In chapter 6, I study a film that invites comparison of law, film, and psychiatry as patriarchal regimes: Nuts (1987), Barbara Streisand's cinematic treatment of an abused, prostituted woman's struggle to enter the legal arena as a competent defendant in a murder case. A postscript discusses Dolores Claiborne (1995) in reference to Nuts. Chapter 7 analyzes Roman Polanski's 1994 adaptation of Ariel Dorfman's chilling play Death and the Maiden, looking at feminine and feminist notions of law and justice, women's use of law to reclaim personal memories of victimization as well as to enter collective memory, and their legal claim for social recognition. The chapter concludes with a postscript reading Jane Campion's The Piano (1993) against Death and the Maiden.

Part 3 is concerned with films that transcend both conventional judgment and feminist notions. Chapter 9 discusses Marleen Gorris's feminist Dutch film A Question of Silence (1982) together with Susan Glaspell's short story, "A Jury of Her Peers" (1916). Each of the texts concerns an emotionally abused housewife who kills a man representing oppressive patriarchy, and I read them both against feminist theories of dominance and care. In chapter 10, I return to the theoretical feminist model presented in the introduction, augmenting it with a diversity-sensitive perspective. I use this model to read Set It Off (1996) as a feminist critique of sociolegal discrimination against poor Black American women. I conclude the book on an optimistic note in chapter 11, with a look at Pedro Almodovar's postmodern, comic melodrama High Heels (1996). The film offers a new cultural image of judgment and justice that transcends gender distinctions, social roles, and judgment itself.

Reading Film: Popularity, Adaptation, Viewer Response, Implied Viewer

All but one of the films I chose for this book have received much public attention and left a significant mark both in their countries of origin and in contemporary Western culture. These films were viewed by massive audiences when first released as well as over subsequent decades, inspiring public discussion, journalistic reviews, and scholarly writing. Clearly, the popular success and durability of a film do not necessarily reflect its artistic or philosophical value, and this book does not appraise and proclaim such value. Popularity and durability do, however, attest to significance as influential social actors, and it is as such that this book reads these films.

Most films discussed in the book are cinematic adaptations of novels or plays. Some viewers—as well as some scholars—tend to overlook a story's medium and blur the distinctions between play (or novel) version and film version. In contrast, this book focuses strictly on analysis of films. I wholly agree with George Bluestone's view on adaptation of novels into films, that "the film becomes a different thing in the same sense that a historical painting becomes a different thing from the historical event which it illustrates" (1971, 5).[2] This study focuses on films' unique characteristics and modes of operation. As Bluestone rightly notes, "the spatial liberation of the cinema was its unique achievement. But film editing, combining the integrity of the shot with the visual rhythm of the sequence, gives the director his characteristic signature" (74). It is not merely the story's plotline that I focus on but the film as medium, including specific shots, editing choices, casting choices, acting styles, directing pace, atmosphere, and the viewer's familiarity with the film's genre conventions or cognizance of the director's biography and style. Comparisons between films and their source material aim solely to highlight the uniqueness of the film version.

My discussion of films does not seek to reveal or expose the films' "original" (conscious or unconscious) intent or to critique an "original" ideological agenda or the film's effectiveness in advancing it. Similarly, I do not refer to the filmmakers and their inputs (unless specifically noted). My focus is on texts and their operations, reader/viewer response, and the likely social impact of the films under discussion. Believing that a text both constitutes its reader/viewer and is simultaneously created by him or her in the process of reading/viewing, I look at both text and reader/viewer as active participants in the creative interaction that occurs at their meeting.

In the context of studying a text's construction of its reader/viewer, I look at explicit and implicit mechanisms which constitute the film's "implied reader/viewer." I borrow this term from the field of narratology and its definition of the "implied" or "constructed" reader as a "theoretical construct, implied or encoded in the text, representing the integration of data and the interpretive process 'invited' by the text . . . Such a reader is 'implied' or 'encoded' in the text 'in the very rhetoric through which he is required to 'make sense of the content' or reconstruct it 'as a world' " (Rimmon-Kennan 1983, 117).

The implied reader/viewer is thus a part of the text, distinguished from the flesh-and-blood human being actually performing the act of reading a book or viewing a film. The implied reader/viewer is the ideal reader sought and invited by the text through textual construction and manipulation. A real film viewer may be completely unresponsive, or even resistant, refusing the film's invitation, or responding to it from a different premise than that desired by the film.

I do however assume a resemblance between the films' implied viewer and at least a significant portion of their actual contemporary Western audience, a resemblance which, I believe, makes it easy for the real contemporary viewer at the beginning of the twenty-first century to assume the implied viewer's role as constructed by the film. This assumption is not scientifically substantiated in any way. It relies on the published responses of film critics and scholars to the discussed films, on random, documented audience responses, as well as my understanding of my own students' and friends' responses to the films. Given the unfounded nature of this assumption, any reference to the films' real viewers is, thus, purely speculative on my part.

Along with a film's implied and real viewer, I also refer to its community of viewers. In so doing, I allude to the work of writers such as Benedict Anderson and James Boyd White, which concentrates on the community-creating mechanisms of sociocultural regimes, such as literature and law. Whereas the implied viewer is a part of the text, the community of viewers refers to an actual, historical public that is constituted as a community by the text through the real-world process of reading/creating it. In discussing communities of readers, I usually refer to contemporary communities. Sometimes, however, I refer to a film's "original" community, that is to the audience at the time of its release.

My reference to audiences and communities of readers/viewers is further complicated by the fact that the films discussed here were released not merely at different historical periods, but also in different parts of the world and different cultural contexts. The ten films central to the book's discussion were created in countries as diverse as Japan, Germany, Britain, Holland, France, Spain, and the United States, over a sixty-eight-year period from 1928 to 1996. My choice of international films addresses the multicultural, linguistic, and national character of cinematic constructions of women in law. The book's survey of films produced in different parts of the world, in different languages and historical contexts, reveals how distinct cultures, despite their differences, perform similar social functions in parallel ways. Each film operates in its own society as well as in the global arena, and the dialogue between them constructs our contemporary universal imagined community.

Despite this clear international diversity, this book confines itself to the cultural domain of the Western world. Even a film created by a Japanese director in Japan is read strictly as a text operating within Western culture. Indian, Egyptian, Chinese, Turkish, and African cinemas, which produce and release the majority of films around the world, are not included in this discussion. I hope that experts in non-Western cultures will expand this study beyond the scope of my own capacity.

In referring to Western viewers and viewing communities, I assume their intuitive familiarity with the logic, rhythm, and basic procedural structure of the Anglo-American, adversarial, common-law legal system or, more specifically, with its Hollywood version. In their research on globalization of the Hollywood courtroom drama, German scholars Stefan Machura and Stefan Ulbrich found that audiences in the Western world are more familiar with the (Hollywood) common-law legal system than with their own respective real-world ones. This is so not merely because of the popularity of the American film industry, but also because European filmmakers imitate Hollywood's portrayal of the American legal system. Machura and Ulbrich report: "Prior to our research we operated on the assumption that courtroom films reflected the legal system more or less correctly, but we soon found this not to be so. What came to amaze us was the striking uniformity of the legal procedures that are portrayed in movies: predominantly criminal procedures. We discovered that American procedure has provided the formula for almost all cinematic legal procedures, even in films set in a country like Germany that has a different system . . . American courtroom films have created a manner of portraying legal procedure that has been followed in courtroom films set in other countries and other legal systems" (2001, 123).

Western viewers, then, are mostly familiar with the logic of (Hollywood's) common law and the basic criminal procedure of the American legal system. It is this familiarity, acquired from the movies, that they bring with them to the cinema and apply in viewing films. American law is, therefore, the natural reference point in a legal discussion of these films.

A Word on Teaching (Feminist) Law and Film

Like many good things, this book grew out of teaching. It is with great pleasure that I offer it as a textbook for classes on law and film, feminist jurisprudence, and feminist reading of law and film. Having taught feminist law-and-film courses based on materials and discussions presented in this book in four universities in three different countries, I have witnessed how effective and powerful these teaching materials can be in law schools as well as in the context of gender studies.[3] Films have a unique way of touching people's hearts and allowing them to employ their emotions in the processes of seeing, listening, understanding, discussing, and analyzing. Analysis of film from a new perspective is an exciting, intriguing, and challenging experience for students, an experience they share with families and friends, thereby continuing its work. The connection of law with film adds a personal aspect to professional legal training, making it more human, specific, and meaningful. The study of feminist jurisprudence through film makes the subject less abstract and intimidating, more concrete and intuitive. Teaching law and film is an avenue for bringing the humanities into legal studies and for integrating law with gender studies.

Introduction

Law and Film: Methodological Perspectives

There are three fundamental premises to my analytical approach: that some films' modes of social operation parallel those of the law and legal system, that some films enact viewer-engaging judgment, and that some films elicit popular jurisprudence. I suggest that study of films' performance of these functions is study of law and film. In reference to these three basic premises, law-and-film studies may be distinguished on the basis of their primary focus, and labeled accordingly as examining "film paralleling law," "film as judgment," and/or "film as jurisprudence." Each of these methodological perspectives may require the employment of various methodological tools, such as textual analysis (discussing, for example, the film's implied reader and reader response); focus on the film's composition of plot or characters; reading the film in the context of a historical survey of developments in film, society, or law; or examining or highlighting cinematic techniques (such as shots) and cinematic choices (such as casting).

Some films' interactions with law and the legal system are, of course, more significant than others. Courtroom dramas, trial films, movies featuring a lawyer or a law firm, and films that focus on social, ethical, and moral issues that are commonly associated with the legal arena (such as racial equality, abortion, affirmative action, corruption, and crime) clearly constitute this category. Further, films in which "legalistic" social or moral issues are merely a secondary subject matter may be just as meaningful in the context of their mutual relations with the legal discourse and system (*Unforgiven* and *Thelma and Louise* have given rise to more law-and-film scholarship than most courtroom dramas). At this preliminary stage in the development of law and film as a distinct discipline, I refrain from Aristotelian typology, and prefer to engage in the broad category of "law films": films that feature any type of legally oriented social or moral issue as subject matter. Many law films' interaction with the world of law is multifaceted. They often manifest two or all three of the premises presented here, thus offering a complex and powerful combination of these cinematic-legal functions.

The first premise is that law and film are two pivotal discourses that both reflect and refract the fundamental values, images, notions of identity, lifestyles, and crises of their societies and cultures, and that there exists a significant correlation between their parallel functions. Both law and film are dominant players in the construction of concepts such as subject, community, personal and collective identity, memory, gender roles, justice, and truth; they each offer major sociocultural arenas in which collective hopes, dreams, beliefs, anxieties, and frustrations are publicly portrayed, evaluated, and enacted.

Law and film often perform these functions in ways that echo and reinforce each other, inviting attentive interdisciplinary examination. Certain underlying structures and modes of operation, relevant to such functions, are sometimes more explicit, apparent, and identifiable in one discourse than in the other. An interdisciplinary comparison sheds light on the less obvious analogous structures and modes of operation of the parallel discourse. Detailed comparison of such structures can expand our understanding of both discourses, as well as the operation of broader social discourses and institutions. Most significant and intriguing of these parallel functions are the many subtle ways each field offers its reader a seductive invitation to take on a sociocultural persona and become part of an imagined (judging) community that shares the worldview constituted by law or film. (References to "readers" include "viewers" in the sense of "readers of film").

The second premise is that some films, law films in particular, perform large-scale "legal indoctrination." That is, they train audiences in the active execution of judgment, while examining—and often reinforcing—legal norms, logic, and structures. For decades, James Boyd White has been exploring and demonstrating how legal rhetoric constitutes human subjects and communities of readers, endowing them with collective visions, aspirations, and hopes, supplying them with frameworks, images, and stories with which to imagine themselves and their worlds (1973, 1984, 1999). Judicial decisions and other legal texts are inherently imbued with judgment and concerned with justice; their construction of subjects and communities are, therefore, inseparable from judgment and the search for justice. Less evidently—but no less significantly—the same can be said of many films.

Films, much like judicial decisions and legislative rhetoric, can—and do—constitute communities (of viewers) that are often engaged in judgment, pseudolegal reasoning, the pursuit of justice, and a corresponding self-fashioning. Judgment is often an activity not merely portrayed but actively performed by films, together with their (constructed and/or actual) viewers; it is often a function of film's constitution of a community of viewers and its engagement in social constitution of primary values, institutions, and concepts.

A law film can be read as passing cinematic judgment when, in addition to portraying a fictional legal system, it offers distinct normative constructions of subjects and societies, of justice and judgment, inviting a judgmental viewing process. In its cinematic judgment, a law film may echo the worldview encoded in its fictional legal system, allowing legal and cinematic mechanisms to reinforce each other in the creation of community and worldview. Alternatively, a law film may constitute a community, value system, and juridical views that criticize or undercut those supported by its fictional legal system. Moreover, as a rich, multilayered text, a law film can perform both of these functions concomitantly, through different means and on different levels, evoking complex and even contradictory responses towards social and legal issues presented on-screen.

The many and varied methods of performing cinematic judgment and engaging viewers in that judgment can be complex, subtle, and often elusive, and as a result uncritically influential. The various methods frequently involve cinematic choices regarding genre, editing, narration, plots, points of view, rhythm, and casting. Particularly frequent strategies include manipulation of viewer identification with on-screen characters and elicitation of emotional responses to powerful imagery.

The third premise of my law-and-film theory is that a law film's cinematic judgment of its on-screen legal system can offer jurisprudential commentary. Law films, therefore, often invite analysis as jurisprudential texts. Such popular jurisprudence, embedded in film, may be sophisticated, insightful, and illuminating. Associated with mass consumption and the entertainment industry, it is likely to be overlooked and dismissed; but unrestricted by conventional academic disciplines and categories, it may also be fresh, original, innovative, and imaginative, transcending familiar routes and formulas.

Films' jurisprudential input is, arguably, the most prevalent theme in law-and-film scholarship. Stressing the importance of films' jurisprudential contributions, John Denvir (1996) suggests that Frank Capra's film It's a Wonderful Life "provides an important complement, or perhaps antidote, to Chief Justice William Rehnquist's legal discussion of the reciprocal duties we owe each other as citizens. Not only do both "texts" treat the difficult legal issue of the claims of community, Capra's treatment brings out an emotional ambivalence toward community that Rehnquist's legal process ignores" (xii). Anthony Chase (1999) claims that the film A Civil Action's jurisprudential conclusion is that "if most Americans have to depend on tort law to enforce their interests against corporate capitalism they have not got a chance" (955). Austin Sarat (2000) analyzes the film The Sweet Hereafter as a jurisprudential investigation of the interconnections between law and fatherhood. Similarly pointing to films' jurisprudential impact, Rebecca Johnson and Ruth Buchanan (2002) argue that films like The Thin Blue Line, A Question of Silence, and Thelma and Louise have illustrated the tenuousness of law's claim to privileged access to truth, the troubled relationship between narrative and truth, and even the limits of language itself.

Examination of a film's underlying—and often unacknowledged—perceptions of gender roles, familial structures, and human relations can shed light on an embedded portrayal and treatment of social and normative issues that may otherwise remain effectively elusive. Similarly, the study of a film's jurisprudence and/or its cinematic judgment can reveal an underlying value system that is at odds with the film's proclaimed adherence to liberal values such as equality or dignity.

Why should one invest in reading films as popular jurisprudential texts? Why explore the cinematic judgment they perform and analyze the social values they constitute for their viewers? One answer is that films are overwhelmingly influential, playing a key role in the construction of individuals and groups in contemporary societies. They reach enormous audiences. Combining narratives and appealing characters with visual imagery and technological achievement, they can stir deep emotions and leave deep impressions. Leading viewers through cinematic judgment (and constituting notions of justice, equality, honor, and gender in the process), films can be extremely effective in molding public actions and reactions. A law film can introduce a viewer to jurisprudential issues and value systems while provoking a host of emotive responses and powerful impressions. More people are likely to be influenced by cinematic judging and jurisprudence than by theoretical legal texts or even judicial rhetoric. Additionally, since most viewers treat film as a source of entertainment and not as a jurisprudential challenge to be critically examined, a film's sociolegal influences may remain imperceptible, uncritically embraced, thereby augmenting film's influence and the need for critical, systematic investigation.

Furthermore, the study of cinematic jurisprudence may be valuable for its popular jurisprudential insight: that is, for purely real-world legal purposes. Similarly, the study of cinematic judgment may help expose structures, techniques, and mechanisms that operate in real-world legal judging, yet are more difficult to discern and identify in the less coherent texts of lived lives. The intertwined study of popular jurisprudence and cinematic judgment may also contribute to the revelation and evaluation of moral values—such as honor and human dignity—underlying social structures and the law.

Honor and Dignity: Two Antithetical Value Systems

The centrality of honor or dignity within a society's value system carries overwhelming implications and is thus deserving of strict scrutiny. While honor has been carefully studied and defined by scores of scholars over decades, dignity remains an elusive concept. A binary opposition of honor and dignity can assist in the conceptualization of dignity, which emerges as honor's antithetical adversary. Whereas honor entails a structured hierarchy and strict gender roles, encouraging violent competition among men and sexual constraint of women, human dignity aims to promote an egalitarian society, based on utmost respect for authentic, diverse individual needs and aspirations. Honor-based conceptions continue to underlie and influence significant portions of both legal and cinematic rhetoric and texts; dignity-based conceptions can increase sensitivity to honor-based attitudes, offering alternative frameworks for the creation of social meaning and legal standards. Let us turn briefly then to an examination of cultures based on honor and those based on dignity.[1]

Honor cultures differ greatly in many features, as well as in the linguistic terms they use to denote honor and shame.[2] Significant generic attributes are, nevertheless, common to many honor cultures. Whether a particular behavior is shameful may be viewed differently by different honor cultures, but the use of shame as a fundamental criterion to determine worthiness and social rank is typical of them all. Julian Pitt-Rivers suggests comparing honor "to the concept of magic in the sense that, while its principles can be detected anywhere, they are clothed in conceptions which are not exactly equivalent from one place to another" (1966, 21).

To use William Miller's words, "the well-known distinction between shame and guilt cultures, though rightly and roundly criticized, still captures a fundamental difference . . . between a culture in which reputation is all, and one in which conscience, confession and forgiveness play a central role" (1993, 116). Members of historical and contemporary honor cultures derive their social rank and sense of worthiness by measuring up to well-defined social norms of honorable behavior and avoiding or avenging behaviors and situations that are conceived as inflicting shame. Miller provides a basic definition:

> Honor is above all the keen sensitivity to the experience of humiliation and shame, a sensitivity manifested by the desire to be envied by others and the propensity to envy the successes of others. To simplify greatly, honor is that disposition which makes one act to shame others who have shamed oneself, to humiliate others who have humiliated oneself. The honorable person is one whose self-esteem and social standing is intimately dependent on the esteem or the envy he or she actually elicits in others. At root honor means "don't tread on me." But to show someone you were not to be trod upon often meant that you had to hold yourself out as one who was willing to tread on others . . . In the culture of honor, the prospect of violence inhered in virtually every social interaction between free men . . . For shame and envy are quickly reprocessed as anger, and anger often is a prelude to aggression. (1993, 84)

Honor cultures thus cultivate emotions such as shame and envy which tend to depend on relative standing in a community, rather than cultivating more internally oriented and individualistic emotions such as guilt, remorse, angst, and ennui (Miller 1993, 116). Similarly stressing honor cultures' typical linkage of social status, social rights, and self-esteem, Pitt-Rivers defines honor as "the value of a person in his own eyes, but also in the eyes of his society. It is his estimation of his own worth, his claim to pride, but it is also the acknowledgment of that claim, his excellence recognized by society, his right to pride" (Pitt-Rivers 1966, 21). Adding the "honorable impulse" expected of members of honor cultures, the formula becomes this: "The sentiment of honor inspires conduct which is honorable, the conduct receives recognition and established reputation, and reputation is finally sanctified by the bestowal of honors. Honor felt becomes honor claimed and honor claimed becomes honor paid" (22).

In honor cultures, honor serves as an effective disciplinary tool, and the behavioral code under which members achieve and maintain honor is, therefore, a structure of social power. Failure to detect an insult that taints one's honor, or failure to respond to an offense to one's honor at the right time, in the right fashion, in the right degree, results in costly consequences, i.e., in loss of honor. Such cultures are ritualistic in the sense that they demand very specific responses to offensive behaviors. Honor cultures are local and particularistic in the sense that they apply exclusively to their own members, demanding thorough mastery of the most nuanced norms and expectations. Foreigners and outcasts are honorless, and honor norms very often do not apply to them. Honor cultures are individualistic in that each member is responsible for his or her honor, and will suffer the consequences of a wrong social move. At the same time, they are collectivist in the sense that each person's honor also affects the honor of his or her clan, and sometimes that of a larger group. They are also class oriented, in the sense that a person's honor and the means of maintaining it vary greatly according to social class.

In many honor societies, the most obvious class difference is gender based.

> The honor of a man and of a woman . . . imply quite different modes of conduct. This is so in any [honor] society. A woman is dishonored . . . with the tainting of her sexual purity, but a man [is] not. While certain conduct is honorable for both sexes, honor=shame requires conduct in other spheres, which is exclusively a virtue of one sex or the other. It obliges a man to defend his honor and that of his family, a woman to conserve her purity . . . Restraint is the natural basis of sexual purity, just as masculinity is the natural basis of authority and the defense of familial honor . . . Masculinity means courage whether it is employed for moral or immoral ends . . . The honor of a man is involved . . . in the sexual purity of his mother, wife and daughters, and sisters, not in his own . . . "The honorable woman: locked in the house with a broken leg." (Pitt-Rivers 1966, 42–45).

Manly honor, thus, correlates with masculine conduct: proactive, public, courageous, assertive, and even aggressive. In contrast, a woman's honor is contingent on the suppression, restriction, and concealment of her femininity, which is reduced to her sexuality. Women are often associated not with positive honor but with its negative opposite, shame, as they are considered a potential source of dishonor to their men and families.

Despite much contemporary reference to dignity, especially in countries where it is a legally recognized value, writers typically refrain from offering precise, comprehensive definitions, sometimes claiming that it is "intuitively" self-explanatory. Often discussed from legal and legalistic perspectives, dignity tends to be treated instrumentally rather than theoretically. "When it has been invoked in concrete situations, it has been generally assumed that a violation of human dignity can be recognized even if the abstract term cannot be defined. 'I know it when I see it even if I cannot tell you what it is'" (Schachter 1983, 849). There is no standard, widely accepted, meaningful definition of dignity.

For the purposes of this discussion, human dignity is the contemporary, liberal, post–World War II, minimalist, legalistic concept. It is the fundamental, egalitarian, humanistic value celebrated in Article 1 of the 1948 Universal Declaration of Human Rights, which proclaims that "all human beings are born free and equal in dignity and rights." This dignity seems to be a descendent of the theological, Judeo-Christian notion of glory: God's absolute, universal glory is fundamental and indestructible, and, created in God's image, a fraction of that glory exists equally in all human beings. Unlike its predecessor, dignity is not theologically based, deriving its vitality and substantial contents from humanistic liberal modernism. Over the second half of the twentieth century, this value has been embraced by constitutions and legal systems in states such as Germany, South Africa, Israel, and Canada, and in international organizations such as the European Union.

Like honor in honor cultures, dignity in dignity-based cultures relates to the core of a person's worth as a human being. It is viewed as an axiomatic human quality, the source of social acknowledgment and rights and the organizing principle of humanistic value systems. Like honor, the concept of dignity confuses human nature, noble sentiment, claims to social respect and legal rights and "natural" social and legal rights. Dignity is generally treated as simultaneously empirical and normative, natural and social, absolute and tentative, both a source and a consequence.[3] In this discussion, I try to sketch a rough outline of dignity by highlighting the specific ways in which it differs from honor. I suggest that dignity can best be substantially defined through comparison with honor, constructed as an antithetical, fundamental basis of a value system. For this purpose, I use simple descriptions of both honor and dignity, avoiding ambiguity and complexity within each term and value system.

Whereas, for most members of honor cultures, honor is earned and maintained through careful, painful observance of a specific cultural code, many define dignity as an essential human quality obtained at birth. All persons are worthy of human dignity and/or possess it merely by being humans. Honor entails variable status and virtue for the few honorable persons of high social rank; dignity entails invariable, fundamental virtue for all human beings. Whereas a person's honor can be easily lost through the slightest social error, or stolen by another, many would argue that one cannot lose or be deprived of his or her human dignity under any circumstances.

Honor is socially and culturally specific, and, within a given society and culture, each person's honor varies greatly, in both type and degree, depending on his or her class and behavior. Dignity is universal, and many claim that, except in extreme cases, all human beings are entitled to and/or possess it equally. Honor dictates specific, daily (sometimes ritualistic) behavior; dignity requires no action, and merely precludes others from extreme conduct (such as torture and mutilation). Honor implies both self-esteem and social status; dignity does not convey social status. Honor demands that an individual measure him or herself against social norms and other members of the community, encouraging competition; dignity demands equal basic concern for and treatment of all. Honor encourages rivalry, antagonism, and sometimes aggression, whereas dignity fosters consideration and constraint. Honor is complimented by fear of shame and humiliation; dignity by empathy, solidarity, humanistic obligation, and perhaps disgust at the thought of human violation.

In an honor culture, an offense to one's honor burdens one with the duty to remove the stain, purify the honor, avenge the offense, and humiliate the offender. Within the logic of dignity, an attack on a person's dignity is an attack on society and its fundamental values; it does not burden the offended party, but challenges the social order. Honor (like a commodity, a valuable possession, a trophy) can be accumulated; dignity is often portrayed as the most essential human asset, which cannot be quantified or accumulated. An honor culture, therefore, offers higher stakes and higher risks, whereas dignity secures a fundamental minimum. In this sense, whereas honor promotes ambition, dignity inspires a "minimalist" social code.

Miller asserts that "the mathematics of honor usually meant that you could never be just like someone else without taking what he had, appropriating his status to yourself. For the most part, people acted as if the mechanics of honor had the structure of a zero-sum or less-than-zero-sum game" (1993, 116). Pitt-Rivers documents that, in some honor cultures, "one who gave an insult thereby took to himself the reputation of which he deprived the other" (1977, 4). Dignity, on the other hand, like a parent's love, "expands" with every newborn human being; no matter how many humans there are, there is always enough human dignity to be equally shared by all. In contrast with the logic of honor, the logic of dignity links a person's own dignity with the dignity he or she allows others. By offending another's dignity, a person offends his or her own. This dynamic motivates all humans to secure each other's dignity.

Defining an honor culture, J. K. Campbell claims that "self regard forbids any action which may be interpreted as weakness. Normally this would include any altruistic behavior to an unrelated man. Co-operation, tolerance, love, must give way to autarky, arrogance, hostility" (1966, 151). In clear contrast, dignity promotes tolerance, love, and sometimes altruism, renouncing vengeance and hostility. I, therefore, agree with Pierre Bourdieu's observation that

> the ethos of honor is fundamentally opposed to a universal and formal morality which affirms the equality in dignity of all men and consequently the equality of their rights and duties. Not only do the rules imposed upon men differ from those imposed upon women, and the duties towards men differ from those towards women, but also the dictates of honor, directly applied to the individual case and varying according to the situation, are in no way capable of being made universal. This is so much the case that a single system of values of honor establishes two opposing sets of rules of conduct—on the one hand that which governs relationships between kinsmen, and in general all personal relations that conform to the same pattern as those between kinsmen, and on the other hand, that which is valid in one's relationships with strangers. This duality of attitudes proceeds logically from the fundamental principle . . . according to which the modes of conduct of honor apply only to those who are worthy of them. (1966, 228)[4]

The constitution of honor or dignity as the basis of a society's value system, or even as one of several such bases, has profound implications and is particularly consequential to the construction of women, their cultural images, social status, and legal rights (Kamir 2003a, 2003b, 2004a). The analysis of honor and dignity as fundamental values inherently reflects feminist and feminist jurisprudential concerns. This book further suggests and demonstrates an intertwining of the honor/dignity and (jurisprudential) feminist perspectives, which, I believe, is mutually beneficial and perhaps crucial for the future of feminist thought.

An honor-sensitive feminist critique of both law and film may expose persistent patriarchal, androcentric, and sexist notions underlying our social systems, cultural images, and legal standards. A dignity-oriented feminist approach may be useful in replacing currently governing honor-based social, cultural, and legal attitudes. In this sense, this book develops a perspective that may best be described as a dignity-oriented, honor-sensitive, feminist law-and-film theory.

Feminist Law and Film

A feminist law-and-film analysis reviews the mutual interactions between law and film, assuming certain views regarding women's social status, highlighting gender-oriented constructions and implications, and critiquing underlying structures that uphold and perpetuate androcentric points of view and patriarchal social hierarchies. It also points to preferable alternatives. I believe and attempt to demonstrate that the feminist law-and-film approach developed in this book bridges the harmful gap between feminist film theory and feminist jurisprudence in a productive manner.

Feminist legal scholarship is goal-oriented, influential, and diverse (Barnet 1998; Chamallas 2003; J. Barr 1999; MacKinnon 2001; Johnson 2002). "Radical," or "dominance-focused," legal feminism has been considered to be mainstream legal feminism since the 1980s, and I thus refer to it simply as *feminist jurisprudence*. This type of feminist jurisprudence mostly targets the systematic, patriarchal domination of women, calling attention to the prevalent sexual violence against women (including rape, prostitution, child molestation, domestic murder and battery, pornography, stalking, and harassment) and demanding deep change of fundamental legal structures in order to address the endemic societal oppression of women. The expansion of antidiscrimination law to address women's discrimination through sexual harassment in the workplace is, perhaps, the most readily familiar example of real-world consequences of this line of legal feminism. In its perception of women as a subordinate class, dominance-focused legal feminism is Marxist in its fundamental logic.

Prior to the 1980s, mainstream feminist jurisprudence was of a more liberal nature. Its main goal was to overcome the law's exclusionary treatment of women, making it more gender inclusive. Liberal feminist jurisprudence assumed women's similarity to men as the basis of their right to legal equality. It did not aim to revolutionize the law, but to extend to women all legal rights enjoyed by men. Although many profeminist jurisprudential enterprises are still of this nature, they are often viewed as more liberal than feminist.

Another feminist school of thought, "cultural," or "relational," feminism, or "feminism of care," has also left its mark on feminist legal scholarship. In 1982, Carol Gilligan's groundbreaking *In a Different Voice* argued that women's unique mothering, caring, and nurturing tendencies express a unique sense of justice. Celebrating women's uniqueness, this line of thought proposes that the currently male-dominated law must be reformed to equally reflect women's sense of justice. Values such as caring and nurturing must be embraced and elevated to modify governing masculinist adversarial values of competition and rivalry. This approach, developed and theorized by prominent feminist legal scholars such as Robin West (1993, 1997), tends to focus less on the victimization of women and more on the legal implications of the celebration of womanhood. Care-centered feminist jurisprudence advocates more legal attention to feminine social functions, such as mothering, and to women's voices narrating their realities, pains, and needs. This perspective is more theoretical and less specific in targeting legal structures (such as rape law, or sexual harassment law), and is therefore less dominant in the contemporary legal reality.

The 1990s saw the birth and growth of identity-oriented critiques of mainstream feminist jurisprudence. Much of the identity-oriented critique has given voice to the perspectives of African American (P. Williams 1991) and lesbian women (Robson 1998), challenging what they consider as feminist jurisprudence's "essentialism" and "heterosexism," that is, its hidden assumptions of a privileged model of womanhood based on the life experiences of white, heterosexual, and mostly upper-class women. Concurrently, throughout the 1990s, postmodern perspectives have been very influential in academic circles, eventually making their way into legal academia and giving rise to much debate (and confusion) among legal feminists. Postmodern perspectives were much more readily embraced and integrated into feminist scholarship by feminist film theorists, who are deeply immersed in psychoanalytic rhetoric and modes of analysis.

Like feminist jurisprudence, feminist film critique is also a salient enterprise at the forefront of feminist critical and innovative scholarship. These branches of feminist scholarship have to some degree interacted separately with feminist psychological, sociological, and literary scholarship, but rarely with each other. Feminist legal discourse typically limits its interest in film to the portrayal of the female lawyer, rarely engaging in feminist film theory. Feminist film scholars occasionally refer to legal issues enacted on film and may even acknowledge, in passing, legal-feminist reference to such an issue. But they too refrain from more comprehensive attempts to establish a dialogue with feminist jurisprudence.

One consequence of this mutual lack of interest is the relative detachment and distance of many feminist legal scholars from lively, contemporary, theoretical feminist discourse. From a (post)psychoanalytic, postmodern perspective, much feminist legal work, in both content and methodology, is perceived as simplistic, overly legally analytic, solipsistic, anachronistic, and embarrassingly unreflective. At the same time, as Sue Thornham elegantly understates, "along the way, feminist film theory and criticism has become an academic subject and has become, perhaps, . . . cut off from its original sense of bold innovation and political purpose" (1999, 4). Indeed, for many feminist legal writers, a (post)psychoanalytic, postmodern perspective seems irrelevant, self-indulgent, condescending, and obscurant. Neither set of observations is wholly unfounded.

A more rigorous interdisciplinary feminist dialogue may draw feminist legal thinkers closer to the latest developments in feminist cultural studies, while reconnecting and reengaging feminist film study with real-world, politically acute issues of gender emancipation. As a feminist legal scholar, my point of departure is feminist jurisprudence. *Framed* aspires to reintroduce feminist jurisprudence to feminist film scholars—as well as to feminist legal scholars—as relevant and challenging, both in content and in methodology, in the hope of bridging the gap through a feminist law-and-film approach.

A MODEL OF FEMINIST JURISPRUDENTIAL CONSTRUCTIVE DECONSTRUCTION

This section introduces a model of the structure of a fundamental type of feminist legal analysis. I believe that many "classic" feminist legal arguments can be presented through this model, and that it is capable of facilitating many more useful theoretical developments. To avoid an overly theoretical discussion, I introduce the model by demonstrating its *modus operandi* in reference to two of the most imperative and familiar feminist legal arguments. The most familiar formulations of these arguments have been associated with Catharine MacKinnon, a dominance feminist. Despite much criticism leveled at different aspects of MacKinnon's feminist legal scholarship, it remains the standard against which many claims are evaluated. As such, it is to this body of scholarship that I refer in the demonstration of the proposed model of feminist legal operation. The first argument examines, critiques, and deconstructs the meaning and implications of the Aristotelian notion of equality in the context of gender equality; the second examines, critiques, and deconstructs the meaning and implications of the criminal definition and prohibition of rape.

Jurisprudential Constructive Deconstruction of Equality The Aristotelian formula of equality, which has been applied by many legal systems in all areas of the law, bases its notion of equality on concepts of similarity and difference. According to this definition, equality requires the similar treatment of similarly situated people, and the different treatment of differently situated people. This formula provides the framework for evaluating legal claims regarding unequal treatment, and it serves as the basis for the definition of the right to equality in specific contexts.

Like other dominance feminists, MacKinnon claims that in order to understand the Aristotelian formula in the context of "gender equality," we must expand our vision and examine this formula in conjunction with the deeply rooted sociocultural construction of woman as "other" (MacKinnon 1987, 32). This feminist legal approach combines the legal analysis of the Aristotelian notion of equality with extensive feminist literature arguing that (male-dominated) culture establishes (white, heterosexual) man as the universal, absolute standard of humanity, while constructing woman as man's negative image, i.e., as the manifestation of "difference."

Reading the Aristotelian formula of equality in conjunction with the perception of women as essentially different illuminates the full meaning of gender equality. In the context of a culture dominated by the Aristotelian formula, demanding equality for women amounts to demanding that different (or differently situated) people be treated similarly. Such a demand sharply clashes with the logic of the Aristotelian formula, constituting the notion of gender equality as an inoperative contradiction in terms (MacKinnon 1987, 33). In order to accommodate a meaningful notion of gender equality, the concept of equality must, therefore, be redefined in a manner that would facilitate the transformation of the common notion of woman's difference, and of the patriarchal social order this perception serves and reflects. MacKinnon's alternative "gender equality formula" seems to consist of a "negative" aspect as well as a "positive" one (to borrow from Isaiah Berlin's characterization of "liberty"). The negative aspect of gender equality is the project of eradicating every intrusive, systemic, social and legal mechanism that reflects, maintains, perpetuates, and reinforces the domination of women by men in any way. The positive aspect of gender equality seeks to create norms, images, institutions, laws, and other sociolegal mechanisms that establish, define, reinforce, and uphold women's identities, value systems, and needs, as defined by themselves at a time when they become sufficiently emancipated to develop a free consciousness. This new notion of women's equality would therefore imply the repudiation of anything that supports the patriarchal construction of woman and the promotion of anything that may liberate women from such construction and facilitate their self-definition.

This feminist legal deconstruction of the Aristotelian formula of equality can be structured as follows:

1. The argument's first stage is the identification of law and society's accepted, working definition of the investigated legal norm. (This stage can be called "understanding the norm.") In the specific context of equality and gender equality in particular, the definition of the norm is that similarly situated persons deserve similar treatment.

2. The second stage is the presentation of a feminist analysis of a social convention that is not commonly associated with the investigated legal norm. (This stage can be called "defining the convention.") In the specific context of gender equality, the feminist analysis of a social convention argues that law and society construct woman as inherently different (from man, the universal standard of humanity).

3. The third stage is the critical juxtaposition of the accepted definition of the investigated legal norm with the feminist analysis of the social convention. (This stage can be called "juxtaposing norm and convention.") In the specific case of gender equality, the critical juxtaposition of the Aristotelian definition of equality (similar treatment of similarly situated persons) with the feminist analysis of the social convention (women are constructed as different) leads to the understanding that in the context of contemporary society and culture, gender equality is a meaningless paradox.

4. The fourth stage is the conclusion that in light of stages one to three, the investigated definition of the legal norm must be abandoned and replaced. The new definition must acknowledge the feminist analysis of the social convention, and enable the application of the legal norm in a manner that would challenge the social convention and the value system it manifests. (This stage can be called "proposing an alternative.") In the specific case of gender equality, the proposed alternative definition of equality must establish that anything upholding the patriarchal construction of gender and gender difference is discriminatory, whereas anything that promotes women's liberation from patriarchal construction advances gender equality.

This model captures the logic of many other legal feminist arguments. As an additional example, let us consider feminist deconstruction of the criminal definition and prohibition of rape.

Jurisprudential Constructive Deconstruction of Rape Law

1. Understanding the norm. In the specific context of rape, the traditional definition offered by common law asserts that (heterosexual) intercourse is illegitimate (and thus criminal) when consisting of forced (vaginal) penetration without consent. This definition assumes and relies on a clear distinction between legitimate and illegitimate sexual intercourse.

2. Defining the convention. In the specific context of rape, the feminist analysis claims that, under patriarchy, masculine use of at least some force is considered a natural component of legitimate heterosexual intercourse. Concomitantly, women are presumed to consent to sexual intercourse (MacKinnon 1987, 85, 86, 88; 1989, 126). This is predicated on the construction of man as "hunter," "warrior," and "conqueror," and woman as one who means "yes" even when saying "no." It results in the presumption that men are always willing and women always consenting. Under patriarchy, this feminist analysis goes, women are taught to believe that sexual intercourse is something they "owe" their men and must submit to in order to please them. Women are trained to believe that men need sexual release and that it is incumbent on women to provide men with both sexual stimulation and the means for its fulfillment. Women often believe that sexual preparedness is their duty. The question they ask themselves is not whether they consent but whether the situation requires them to provide a man's sexual fulfillment. The outcome of this social indoctrination is that many women under many circumstances do not fully know whether sexual intercourse took place with or without their free consent, and are easily shaken and convinced that they must have consented. When many women under many circumstances do not know whether or not they freely consented to sexual intercourse, the question whether intercourse was consensual is almost meaningless, and it is easy to concede that all women must surely always consent to any sexual intercourse.

3. Juxtaposing norm and convention. In the specific case of rape law, the critical juxtaposition of the legal definition of rape (forced sexual intercourse without consent) with the feminist analysis of the social convention (legitimate intercourse is perceived as consisting of the use of masculine force and is not premised on the woman's free consent) leads to the understanding that in the context of contemporary society and culture, criminal law's definition of rape as distinguishable from legitimate intercourse and thus criminally punishable is practically meaningless.

4. Proposing an alternative. The existing legal definition of rape must be abandoned and replaced. The new definition must acknowledge the conventional construction of legitimate sexual intercourse, of man as conqueror and of woman as inherently consenting. It must facilitate a meaningful prohibition of rape in a way that will challenge and undermine the conventional construction of legitimate sexual intercourse, which blurs the distinction between forced sexual intercourse without consent and mutually freely consensual intercourse.

Over the last thirty years, feminist legal scholars have proposed various alternatives to the traditional common-law definition of criminal rape, and several of them have been adopted by legislators around the common-law world. Some believe that for a rape definition to be effective it must construct rape not as a sex crime but as violence, emphasizing the use of force rather than the woman's (lack of) consent. Others define rape as any sexual intercourse without consent, whether violent or not. Many believe that rape should be defined more broadly, to include sexual acts other than intercourse. I suggest that since they all attempt to resolve the predicament described by the model, they can each be evaluated against the requirements of the model's fourth stage.

The explication of the model of a feminist legal argument may have also clarified the seemingly paradoxical label I attached to it: constructive deconstruction. Unlike postmodern, apolitical deconstruction, feminist legal deconstruction is not necessarily committed to the theoretical assumption that a text's internal conflicted duality is a given or unchangeable quality. It does not assume that a text will always undercut itself or that there is nothing beyond the text. On the contrary, feminist legal deconstruction is ideologically and pragmatically motivated, and must be viewed as a methodological tool, applied not solely for its textual interest but also in pursuit of revolutionary ideological social change.

Furthermore, for feminist legal scholars, professional indoctrination may shape their perception of reality, facts, norms, and their relationships. For a legally oriented person, reality is not the inner psychological makeup of individuals described by psychoanalytic discourse, but is rather the set of governing legal orders, prohibitions, and regulations in a particular time and place. Facts are determined by judges or juries within the legal process of enforcing governing laws. Norms are commands or organizational rules that, when legitimately legislated or endorsed by a court, become legal reality, thereby influencing future determination of facts.

Legally trained people understand reality as ever changeable, facts as uncertain until determined by the authorized institution(s), and norms as inseparable from both. It is perhaps relatively easy for a feminist legal scholar to envision a new normative standard becoming law, and thus also a fact determining reality. Dramatic change, an immediate, authoritative shift in perspective, may be more comprehensible, possible, and attainable in this context than, say, within a psychoanalytic framework.

Feminist legal deconstruction is at its best when it is constructive, that is, followed by operative reconstruction aiming to furnish new legal concepts and tools more suitable—or at least less destructive than those exposed by deconstructive analysis—to the agenda of sex/gender emancipation. This, of course, requires transcending postmodern (as well as psychoanalytic) passivity and fatalism, which can content itself with playful, pleasurable exposure of the self-defeating mechanism inherent in every text. Such a feminist legal venture may be considered too analytic or theoretically naive and falsely optimistic; it is also political, revolutionary, and world changing.

INSERTING THE DIGNITY-BASED, HONOR-SENSITIVE COMPONENT

In one way or another, honor-based mentality is common to many, if not all, patriarchal societies. It is closely linked to and responsible for social conventions as well as legal norms requiring feminist jurisprudential constructive deconstruction. In spite of this, the honor-based logic of many layers, components, and manifestations of patriarchy has not received the feminist (legal) attention it deserves, perhaps because of a mistaken belief that it has lost much of its relevance. In order to remedy this gap, I propose sensitizing feminist legal argumentation to honor-based values, norms, and social conventions, as well as to the possibility of replacing them with alternative, dignity-based ones. The model of feminist legal argumentation can be so sensitized through the insertion of an "honor test," and through the explicit search for dignity-based alternatives for honor-based sociolegal norms and conventions.

The first step is expanding the argument's second stage, defining the convention, to include the investigation as to whether the analyzed social convention corresponds with an honor-based value system, and if so how and to what degree. In the specific context of the constructive deconstruction of the Aristotelian notion of (gender) equality, this honor test reveals that woman's construction as paradigmatically different often goes hand in hand with honor-based worldviews. In a culture that is, or was, honor oriented, such construction of woman may well be a manifestation of honor mentality as well as a means to preserve it.

The construction of woman as different is well suited to a world of honor, which is deeply invested in pronounced social stratification. In an honor society, hierarchy and status are the crucial social resources available for distribution based on compliance with society's norms. The categorical gender distinction is critical to the definition of social gender roles, which play a foremost function in an honor society. If masculinity is, by definition, the source of honor and a reward for honorable conduct, and femininity is the paradigmatic potential source of shame that must be oppressed and suppressed to maintain honor and prevent dishonor, then an honor society's most fundamental values depend on a rigid gender distinction. And since man is the standard of honor, woman, the potential source of dishonor and shame, is clearly different.

In the specific context of the constructive deconstruction of the criminal definition of rape, the honor test reveals that the conventional social perception of legitimate (heterosexual) intercourse, as consisting of masculine use of force and as not necessarily relying on a woman's free consent, goes hand in hand with honor-based worldviews. In a society that is, or was, honor oriented, such construction of legitimate intercourse may well be a manifestation of the honor mentality as well as a means to preserve it.

In the world of honor, the only type of sexual intercourse considered legitimate is that in which penetration is performed by a man on his wife, whose sexuality he rightfully controls. No other extramarital sexual contact is legitimate, as it fatally harms the honor of the man who controls sexual access to the woman and is responsible for guarding and protecting that access. Extramarital intercourse connotes failure on the part of the man responsible for the woman's honor, shaming and dishonoring him and his family. Such shame calls for violent vengeance, which disturbs the peace and is socially undesirable.

In an honor culture, therefore, neither consent nor force are relevant to the definition of legitimate sexual intercourse and to its distinction from illegitimate intercourse. When, according to the rules of honor, a man penetrates a woman whom he is rightfully entitled to penetrate, the intercourse is legitimate whether or not he uses force, and whether or not she conveys her freely given consent. And again, according to the rules of honor, when a man penetrates a woman who may be penetrated only by a different man (or by no man at all), the sexual intercourse is illegitimate, irrespective of either his use of force or her freely given consent. In reality, then, the critical distinction is not between "carnal knowledge of a woman against her will with the use of force" and any other form of intercourse, but between "intercourse that respects the honor code" (any marital intercourse) and intercourse that does not (any fornication or adultery).[5]

An honor mentality thus blurs the distinction between consensual, or unforced, intercourse and nonconsensual forced intercourse. In an honor-based world, the traditional common-law legal definition of rape as nonconsensual forced intercourse would clash with the honor-based conventional perception of legitimate intercourse, and render the criminal prohibition ineffective. Since contemporary Western societies are not far removed from their honor-based origins, it stands to reason that the blurring of distinctions between types of sexual intercourse may be a remnant of an honor-based era.

The significance I attach to the honor test is not merely theoretical, academic, and descriptive. Its relevance is not limited to the conceptual insight reached in the model's stage of juxtaposing norm and convention. The honor test's foremost significance lies in the context of the model's last, practical, goal-oriented stage of proposing an alternative formulation of the legal norm. The importance of identifying the honor-based component of the examined social convention is that it leads to the careful construction of an alternative definition that is free of honor mentality, replacing it with a preferred dignity-based one.

Kant's categorical imperative, which has become a pillar of modern Western culture, proclaims that one must never treat a person as merely a means to an end external to that person. Human beings must always be treated as an end in their own right. Treatment of a person as merely a means to an end offends his or her human dignity. In a dignity-based world, equality means that all persons are equal in human dignity, and thus equally entitled to be treated as ends, not means. This definition is more complex than meets the eye. Although fundamentally universalistic, it can also be the basis for specific protection of group rights. It defines gender equality as every woman's absolute right to always be treated as an end in her own right and never as merely a means, irrespective of cultural traditions, men's honor or family interests.

Human dignity prescribes the right to think, express oneself, not be enslaved, not be violently victimized, obtain an education, work in order to provide for oneself, choose one's partner, choose whether to have a family, and so forth. In a world based on human dignity, these rights are granted equally to all people, men and women, by virtue of their humanity. However, people are differently situated in social settings, often based on their chosen or enforced affiliations. For example, a certain regime (such as the Taliban) may prevent women, and only women, from obtaining an education and working to support themselves. From a dignity-based perspective, the demand that women be allowed to pursue education derives from the value of human dignity, in which the idea of gender equality is inherent. The demand, therefore, does not rely on women's similarity with men, but on every woman's equal right to be treated as an end in her own right, and not as merely a means to ends dictated by religion and custom. Human dignity can thus be the basis for the definition of equality rights that are specific to members of distinct groups. A perspective based on human dignity may add a universalistic depth to alternative feminist formulations of legal norms.

Similarly, human dignity can be the basis of a new definition of criminal rape. In a dignity-based world, the distinguishing criteria between legitimate and illegitimate sexual intercourse is whether both parties treated each other as a human end, and not merely as a means for self-gratification. In a world of human dignity, legitimate sexual contact expresses every party's recognition of the humanity and dignity of the other(s). Rape, on the other hand, is an attempt to violate the other's fundamental humanity and dignity. A person committing rape treats his victim as less than human, as an object for sexual use. Rape denies the victim's basic rights derived from his or her human dignity: to basic self-definition, self-respect, freedom from sexual aggression, and freedom from trespass across her or his most personal boundaries.[6]

Feminist legal argumentation can and should be sensitized to the deep sociolegal implications of diversity among women in a manner analogous to its sensitivization to honor and dignity. Much like the "honor test," a "diversity test" must be inserted into the model's second stage of analyzing the relevant social conventions. This test must detect distinctions applied by the social convention to diverse categories of women, mapping their implications. This analysis will, in turn, affect the alternative formulation of the governing norm, offered in stage four. This part of the argument is presented in chapter 10, together with the reading of *Set It Off*.

FEMINIST FILM THEORY

Having presented a model of feminist legal argumentation, I now present one of feminist film critique. The similarities and differences between these two models testify to the uniqueness of the feminist legal constructive deconstruction. In order to best present the second model and compare it with the first, I demonstrate its logic in reference to a substantive, classic feminist critique of cinematic pleasure, developed by Laura Mulvey, in her 1975 groundbreaking essay "Visual Pleasures and Narrative Cinema" (1999). Much like MacKinnon's scholarship, Mulvey's too has been criticized by many. Nevertheless, it remains the standard against which feminist film critique develops, and it is as such that I refer to it here.

According to film theory (in particular that of Christian Metz), an audience enjoys absolute, one-sided, controlling omnipotence regarding on-screen characters. The audience's unbounded view is empoweringly erotic. In "Visual Pleasures and Narrative Cinema," a groundbreaking essay published in 1975, Laura Mulvey aimed to read this formula of "film-viewing pleasure" in its broad context, rather than take it at its seemingly neutral face value. Her male predecessors applied psychoanalytic logic to film viewing in a way that was blind to gender; they assumed, without acknowledging, the "human," "universal" viewer's maleness. Unlike them, Mulvey reminded her readers that such psychoanalytic analysis of film viewing applies exclusively to men, as only they are privileged, in psychoanalytic discourse, with the potential of full subjecthood. Women are defined through that discourse as the male subjects' objects; the viewer's "look/gaze" is an erotic, masculine way of objectifying and controlling women. The pleasure of film viewing described by film theorists, Mulvey concluded, is the male viewer's erotic, fetishistic, sadistic pleasure of fully objectifying women on-screen through the camera's omnipotent gaze (enhanced by point-of-view shots of on-screen male characters' controlling, eroticized gazes at on-screen women). Combined with the on-screen male characters' control of women within the film's narrative, the male viewer's pleasure constitutes a male fantasy of women's submission and objectification. Female viewers were assumed to identify with on-screen women, thus accepting their objectification as a necessary means to achieve men's pleasure. It is this pleasure, therefore, that Mulvey challenged. She hoped that in its place a new language of desire would emerge.

In other words, bringing to light more of the psychoanalytic discourse underlying film theory, Mulvey showed that the promise of pleasure, omnipotence, erotic gratification, and empowered subjecthood made by film (as theorized by scholars) to its viewers was, in fact, relevant only to male viewers. Women viewers were not merely excluded from it; their objectification was the condition supporting the promise made to male viewers. No subjecthood or erotic pleasure was promised women since their objectification was the basis of film's false promise of universal subjecthood.

Following Mulvey's lead, feminist film scholars developed this critique of mainstream film theory and its social implications, expanding the feminist analyses to better scrutinize the film-viewing experience of female viewers. These viewers, they showed, were manipulated into identifying with the "to-be-looked-at" women on-screen, uncritically accepting their passive role as the object of men's gaze and the source of male erotic, controlling, sadistic pleasure. Narrative film seduced women into accepting the construction of feminine sexuality as masochistic and submissive.

Feminist film scholars further demonstrated how women viewers were simultaneously invited by film to take on the masculine identity of on-screen male characters who looked at and objectified on-screen women. This was effected through relentless cinematic manipulation of female and male viewers alike to identify with the camera's point of view which, like the on-screen men and often together with them, gazed at women and objectified them.

According to this feminist critique, women were invited by film to identify both with the voyeuristic, controlling, erotically empowered male subject, and with the female object whose submission is the source of man's sexual pleasure. Women were simultaneously seduced into participating in the erotic masculine pleasure of objectifying on-screen women, while passively accepting that, as women, their sexual pleasure was masochistic and submissive. Women were programmed to identify control, sadism, and gazing as masculine attributes; and passivity, subordination, and masochism as feminine ones. Despite the many critiques of this line of feminist film analysis, it is still a "classic" and prominent one, the standard against which much of feminist film criticism has developed. It's useful to compare this feminist film critique with the model of feminist legal argumentation.

1. The first stage of Mulvey's argument is the identification, framing, and rephrasing of the theoretical, psychoanalytic definition of cinematic pleasure, as formulated by leading film theorists. Mulvey showed that in psychoanalytic terms, these theorists (such as Christian Metz) proclaimed that narrative film enables the viewer to dominate on-screen characters with his gaze. They established that this one sided, omnipotent, dominating gaze gives the viewer erotic visual pleasure, which is, in its very nature, voyeuristic, fetishistic and sadistic. This is the essence of cinematic pleasure. Mulvey showed that the one-sided nature of film viewing renders it a particularly voyeuristic pleasure, and hence also particularly fetishized and sadistic (in the Freudian sense of these terms). This stage can be called "psychoanalytic gaze at film theory."

2. The second stage in Mulvey's argument is the presentation of a feminist critique of a psychoanalytic construction; this feminist critique is not commonly associated with the investigated theoretical definition of cinematic pleasure. Mulvey's feminist critique is of the psychoanalytic association of masculinity with potential subjecthood, and femininity with objectification. Mulvey shows that in psychoanalytic terms, man alone is capable of full subjecthood, while woman is constructed as an object for man. In the cinematic context, which focuses on the visual, this view constructs woman as man's visual object. This stage can be called "feminist gaze at psychoanalysis."

3. The third stage in Mulvey's argument is the critical juxtaposition of the theoretical, psychoanalytic definition of cinematic pleasure with the feminist critique of the psychoanalytic construction of man as subject and woman as his (visual) object. This juxtaposition makes it clear that, in describing the pleasure of film viewing, film theorists referred exclusively to the male viewer's erotic voyeuristic pleasure of fully objectifying women on screen. According to Mulvey's critique, female viewers are invited to identify with the on-screen female characters, thus passively accepting their own objectification as a necessary means to achieve men's erotic pleasure. This stage can be called "juxtaposing film and psychoanalytic theories."

4. Resting on the presumption that psychoanalysis accurately captures the essence of human existence under patriarchy, the fourth stage in Mulvey's argument is the conclusion that the only strategy possible is to use psychoanalytic rhetoric against itself in an attempt to expose, deconstruct, and undermine both it and the human reality it portrays. To use her own words:

There is an obvious interest in [Freud's] analysis for feminists, a beauty in its exact rendering of the frustration experienced under the phallocentric order. It gets us nearer to the roots of our oppression, it brings closer an articulation of the problem, it faces us with the ultimate challenge: how to fight the unconscious structured like a language (formed critically at the moment of arrival of language) while still caught within the language of the patriarchy? There is no way in which we can produce an alternative out of the blue, but we can begin to make a break by examining patriarchy with the tools it provides, of which psychoanalysis is not the only but an important one . . . At this point, psychoanalytic theory as it now stands can at least advance our understanding of the *status quo*, of the patriarchal order in which we are caught. (Mulvey 1999, 59)

Mulvey set out to expose male erotic pleasure as derived from the objectification and domination of women. She wanted to uncover the gender-oppressive nature of cinematic pleasure. She further aspired to challenge and destroy this gendered erotic cinematic pleasure and replace it with a new one. But she believed that all these goals could be pursued only from within the psychoanalytic world, using its own logic and rhetoric to expose and undermine the damaging constructions of cinematic, i.e., masculine erotic pleasure.

The comparison of Mulvey's argument with the model of legal constructive deconstruction reveals two key differences. The legal model's first stage refers to the definition of a norm (gender equality, the prohibition of rape), and its second stage refers to social convention ("Woman is different," "Legitimate sexual intercourse may contain force"). In contrast, the first two stages of Mulvey's argument ("psychoanalytic gaze at film theory" and "feminist gaze at psychoanalysis") refer to psychoanalytic(-based) constructions of human constitution (cinematic pleasure and masculine erotic pleasure). This difference leads to a second, most significant one. The legal argument's fourth stage is the replacement of the definition of the norm identified in the first stage with one that would challenge the social convention analyzed in the second stage, and the oppressive worldview it entails. In contrast, the fourth stage in Mulvey's argument ("using the master's tools") concludes that the psychoanalytic construction of human constitution presented in stages one and two is irreplaceable, as it is consistent with human reality under patriarchy. Mulvey's feminist film theory is, thus, obliged to use the psychoanalytic discourse to reveal gender biases of psychoanalytic discourse, which are also the biases of human reality under patriarchy. Feminist critique must accept the premises of psychoanalysis, and slowly use it against itself.

I suggest that these two intertwined differences highlight the efficiency of the model of feminist constructive deconstruction for social change, in contrast to Mulvey's argument, which fails to inspire reform. The model of classic feminist legal argumentation uses a Marxist outlook on and approach to human reality. But it is not committed to Marxist notions of gender and women. Mulvey's argument is committed to the premises and method of psychoanalysis, as well as to its construction of gender and women. Mulvey's potentially paradigm-shifting move did not inspire a new language of cinematic pleasure and women's agency because it was undercut and frustrated by her use of psychoanalysis as a political tool to fight sexism, by her uncritical acceptance of a subject-object dichotomy, and by her adherence to a postmodern deconstructive logic that precludes a radical break with the given text.

Mulvey assumed that, given the existing structure of our unconscious, the psychoanalytic depiction of woman is real in the sense that our unconscious mechanisms actually function in a manner that is well captured by psychoanalytic constructs. She of course did not celebrate this oppressive reality, but seemed to believe that only exposure of this system in its own terms could, perhaps, bring about slow, evolutionary change from within. There could be no other way because no other depiction captured our inner mechanisms, and there was no other language we could speak.

By starting from the belief that psychoanalysis accurately captures and portrays contemporary human reality, Mulvey's own sophisticated, self-conscious critique featured woman as a symbol of the lack of phallus, guilty of arousing male fear of castration, as a "guilty object" provoking man's justified devaluation or punishment of her, his possession, and as a mystery, prompting man's desire to demystify her. In Mulvey's critique, woman's psychoanalytic construction as the object of man's subjecting gaze and sexual pleasure is irrefutable. The meaning of woman within this framework, she explicitly asserted, is sexual difference.

Unlike Mulvey, I do not believe that psychoanalysis can supply effective tools for its own deconstruction, exposure, critique, and replacement. An ideology so openly misogynist cannot explore its own misogyny, nor can it allow a meaningful exploration of women's emancipation. An Archimedean point of view from an alternative framework is an essential precondition for such a project.

Mulvey does not seem to doubt or challenge the (psychoanalytic) "fact" that man's will and gaze can and do "objectify" woman. Neither does she doubt or challenge this objectification's (psychoanalytic) "justification" through the woman's inherent (sexual) "guilt." Nor does she doubt or challenge the possibility of a "guilty object." Yet it seems to me that any discourse that acknowledges that women can be "objectified," that such deprivation of their subjecthood can be "justified," and that there can be an inanimate "object" that is nevertheless morally responsible, hence "guilty," cannot be reconciled with a feminist worldview, with the premises of human dignity, or with other ideological sensitivities excluded by psychoanalytic theory. I suggest that the application of the distinction between honor- and dignity-based value systems can shift the sense of inescapable entrapment within psychoanalysis so eloquently articulated by Laura Mulvey, substantiating a more revolutionary feminist film critique, analogous to the feminist jurisprudence presented above.

The theory of one person's objectification of another through a viewer's gaze assumes that a person exists either as subject or as object, that one person can reduce another from one type of existence to the other, and that this reduction can be done through looking. The logic of the specific belief system underlying Mulvey's psychoanalytic discussion was perhaps best described and explained by Sartre in *Being and Nothingness*. The human look is Sartre's basic tool in his discussion of subject and object, self and other, power and shame.

Sartre defines the perceiving human subject as "being-for-itself," which means "nothingness": unbound personal freedom, countless possibilities from which to constantly choose. The essence of human existence, of subjecthood, is perpetual self-determination; the subject is one whom no exterior force can control, limit, subordinate, or determine. Subjecthood is eternal human potential of choice, self-determination, and change. An object, on the other hand, which Sartre defines as "being-in-itself," is the exact opposite: it just *is* that which it *is*. It is determined by a subject, a force exterior to itself, and exists for it, in the sense that it is a part of the perceiving subject's world as he constitutes it through his free, unbound choice, perception, and determination.

In Sartreian terminology, "the Other" is a person looking at me in a way which *objectifies* me. This objectification prevents the looked-at person's autonomous existence as "being-for-itself" and condemns him to a subordinate existence of a "being-in-itself" in the Other's world—the world the Other constitutes, as a free subject, through his look at the objectified person. In an interaction between two persons, only one can look at the other, performing the role of the free, human subject, being "the Other." The other participant in the interaction is deprived of his subjecthood, forced by the looking subject into the existence of an object in the looking subject's world, "being-in-itself." In Sartre's world, any intersubjective meeting entails an objectification of one by the other. This is so because a person cannot be both subject and object simultaneously: "We cannot perceive the world and at the same time apprehend a look fastened upon us; it must be either one or the other. This is because to perceive is to *look at*, and to apprehend a look is . . . to be conscious of *being looked at*" (Sartre 1966, 347).

The Other, therefore, undermines my subjectivity by forcing me to feel/be "looked at," like an object, rather than to look at the world and determine it as an autonomous subject. It restricts me as self in every possible way and prevents my "being-for-itself"; it overpowers and subjugates me, depriving me of my human essence (Sartre 1966, 379). In every human interaction, therefore, the Other and his look *shame* the objectified person for the loss of his freedom and mastery. "Shame" within this framework is

the recognition of the fact that I *am* indeed that object which the Other is looking at and judging . . . Shame reveals to me that I *am* this being, not in the mode of "was" or of "having to be" but *in-itself*. . . In order for me to be what I am it suffices merely that the Other look at me . . . Pure shame is not a feeling of being this or that guilty object, but in general of being *an* object; that is, of recognizing myself in this degraded, fixed and dependent being which I am, for the Other. Shame is the feeling of an *original fall*, not because of the fact that I may have committed this or that particular fault, but simply that I have "fallen" into the world in the midst of things and I need the mediation of the Other in order to be what I am . . . And yet while making me into "me-as-object" for the Other, the feeling of shame also supposes a selfness which is ashamed and which is imperfectly expressed by the "I." (350–51, 384, 385)

Sartre's linkage of the Other's objectifying gaze with the feeling of shame is not accidental. The zero-sum duel over subjecthood and objectification, in which the gaze replaces the sword, is simply a philosophical, sophisticated, bloodless rephrasing of the honor mentality. Just like honor, subjecthood, the defining social value that determines relational status and worth, can be lost or taken away by a more powerful opponent. One wrong move can cost a person his subjecthood—as it can cost one his honor. A person's loss of subjecthood to another affirms the other's subjecthood and the loser's shame and hostility, just as with honor. Just as a dishonored existence is "worse than death," so a subjectless existence is degradation to the state of an inanimate object. In other words, this portrayal of the subject-object relationship which Mulvey employs rests on a belief system rooted in an honor mentality. This honor mentality carries with it embedded gender implications.

In Mulvey's psychoanalytic terms, masculine objectification of a woman is not merely possible; it is also justified by her castration guilt. Translated into the more explicit, crude terms of honor: woman's potential ability to shame and endanger her father and/or husband (i.e., to "castrate" them) by exposing/submitting herself to another man's pleasure renders her inherently guilty, thus deserving of subordination, restriction, veiling ("objectification"). Within this value system, little significance is attached to the difference between woman's "self-exposure" and her "submission" (that is, between adultery and rape). In other words, woman's (sexual) "autonomy" is in clear contrast with the entire value system and the social order it supports.

An explicit honor terminology clearly associates "gaze" with "penetration" and "man looking at a woman" with "man penetrating a woman." "Objectifying by looking" is a variation on "possessing/conquering/defiling/shaming by penetrating." This narrative of "subject-gaze-object" reflects and perpetuates the social construction of man as "penetrating" and woman as "penetrable." Psychoanalytic definitions of man's identity, subjecthood, and film-viewing pleasure assume this narrative and depend on it. Behind the professional jargon of psychoanalytic discourse thrives a socially constructed penetration, defining man and woman by positioning them on two opposite ends of a male-defined sexual activity. Woman is thus constructed through man's self-defining criteria, and characterized as different from him in reference to his most valued and cherished characteristic. She is positioned as his inferior negative image, his lesser other. The biological connotation of penetration affords this structure a sense of natural, objective, neutral, universal, and irrefutable truth.

The same mythology underlying the conventional perception of woman as different and of legitimate sex as not precluding force or requiring a woman's free consent lurks behind psychoanalytic constructions of masculine erotic pleasure and woman's objectification by man readily adopted by film theory. Feminist legal scholars such as MacKinnon concluded that, once exposed, perceptions, constructions, and conventions tainted by such misogynistic myths must be abandoned and replaced. Feminist film scholars such as Mulvey concluded that we must continue to expose the mythology from within, having no alternative. But in fact it is a deconstruction from within that is impossible, whereas an alternative readily exists. A feminist value system based on human dignity can indeed replace the honor-based structure that is currently dominant, including its psychoanalytic versions.

"Subject looks and objectifies other" is an honor-based narrative. It reflects and perpetuates naturalized misogynistic social constructions, including the construction of man as "naturally penetrating" and woman as "naturally penetrable." It no more captures our inner mechanisms than do alternative narratives. It constructs and perpetuates such personal and collective mechanisms only if awarded a privileged position. But this is a choice, and it is ours to make. The "subject looks and objectifies other" narrative relies on determinations such as "we cannot perceive the world and at the same time apprehend a look fastened upon us; it must be either one or the other." At the risk of sounding naive, I contend that this is fundamentally false. We can, indeed, and do regularly look at another person while concomitantly enjoying the other person looking at us. Friendships, intimate relationships, professional encounters, competitions, and rivalries provide daily reminders and proof.

LAW-AND-FILM FEMINIST CONSTRUCTIVE DECONSTRUCTION

A constructive deconstructive version of Mulvey's film theory could take the following form:

1. Understanding the norm. The identification of the psychoanalytically based theoretical definition of cinematic pleasure as objectifying on-screen characters through an omnipotent gaze.

2. Defining the convention. The presentation of a feminist critical analysis of a psychoanalytic convention that constructs only man as a potential subject and woman as his object. The honor test reveals that the definition of both masculine and cinematic erotic pleasure as deriving from the objectification of women is compatible with honor-based value systems.

3. Juxtaposing norm and convention. Juxtaposing the psychoanalytic-based definition of cinematic pleasure with the feminist critique of psychoanalytic subjectification of men and objectification of women leads to the understanding that, in a psychoanalysis-influenced world, the theoretical construction of cinematic pleasure perpetuates misogynistic perceptions of woman as object for man, indoctrinating women into submissive masochism.

4. Proposing an alternative. A new conceptualization of cinematic pleasure that acknowledges the widely held interpretation of gender domination as the source of masculine erotic pleasure, and aspires to challenge it through a dignity-based value system. In a dignity-based world, objectifying the other (through a gaze) is meaningless, since a person's humanity is irreducible. An

attempt to objectify another person (through a gaze) is an attack on her or his human dignity. The construction of women as means for men's sexual gratification offends their human dignity, as it denies them the fundamental right to be treated as ends and not as means. In a dignity-based world, the attack on another person's dignity and humanity is not the source of (erotic) pleasure. Pleasure coincides with interpersonal communication premised on mutual acknowledgment, respect, empathy, compassion, care, appreciation, celebration. Cinematic pleasure may, therefore, be premised on sympathetic identification with an on-screen character, and vicarious respectful interaction with other on-screen characters. It can be associated with the potential opportunity to experience respectful identification with a vast variety of human types in incessantly changing human situations.

Had Mulvey chosen legal feminist constructive deconstruction over psychoanalysis as her political tool, her move could have triggered a paradigm shift. Films can choose to narrate dignity-based stories through dignity-based cinematic structures. Film theory can choose to read films, their cinematic effects, and their impact on their viewers through dignity-based theories. Even psychoanalytic discourse could choose to replace its underlying honor-based mythology with a dignity-based one. As in the world of law, new orders and regulations can create a new reality, which, in turn, determines new facts.

A Feminist Law-and-Film Treatment of Women's Construction as Victims and Villains

Feminist legal practitioners and writers have long attended to the systematic victimization of women, the social concealment and denial of this violence against them, and the consequential phenomenon of blaming the victim which occurs within legal systems through the use of legal tools. Such issues have always been central to feminist jurisprudence. For decades, feminist legal scholars have argued that the legal treatment of victims of sexual assault (rape in particular) constitutes a second assault on them, minimizing or denying their victimization while accentuating suspicions of guilty "contribution" and "provocation" that allegedly triggered the violent crime. Since the 1990s, some feminist legal scholars have been emphasizing the objectification that accompanies a simplistic, one-dimensional presentation of women's victimization. They argue that such objectification has influenced the legal perception of women, leading to a new type of gender blindness and discrimination. A prime example is many courts' expectation that victims of rape or domestic violence be passive and helpless; women whose conduct implies active resistance and struggle are not recognized as "reasonable victims," and their victimization is not legally acknowledged and condemned.

Feminist film scholars have focused on techniques of visual representation of women on-screen. They have shown and analyzed how women are systematically portrayed in ways that objectify them and construct them as submissive commodities for on- and off-screen male consumption and/or as deadly sexual predators (femme fatales). The analogous insights gained by these two branches of feminist scholarship are striking. My aim is to highlight these insights and combine the two perspectives to offer a fuller picture of the construction of women's victimization and culpability through observation of the significant cultural interaction between law and film.

More specifically, extending decades of feminist work in law and in film, I contend that the sociolegal construction and understanding of women's victimization, objectification, and inherent guilt is mediated to a great extent through their representation and the cultural imagery of its composition. While the conceptualization of victimization and guilt belong to the sphere of judgment and justice that we associate with legal discourse, representation and imagery are part of the lexicon of art. My exploration of the relationship between imagery and representation and judicial (or judgmental) conceptualization is an inherently feminist law-and-film project, tapping the unique, innovative potential of this new interdisciplinary field and mapping an approach to such research.

The specific unifying theme of Framed is twofold: to reveal the construction of oppressed women as "guilty objects" through cinematic judgment, silencing, stereotyping, and application of honor-based notions, and to explore their alternative construction as "victimized subjects" and performers of judgment through cinematic consciousness raising and the application of dignity-based values. The films chosen for analysis in this book present themes of women's victimization and their alleged delinquency. The victimization portrayed in the films is gender specific: it is sexual and discriminatory. Women in these films suffer abuse, rape, prostitution, sexual harassment, marginalization, humiliation, and silencing. The women protagonists' alleged delinquency is associated with men's deaths. My analysis focuses on the legal-cinematic characterization of these components, and the construction of the relationship between them.

Most films discussed in this book feature societies and legal systems that trivialize, minimize, and silence women's victimization, highlight assaults against men, and link the two by judging the women and finding them guilty. Typically, a woman is raped (or is victim of attempted rape) and a man dies (or nearly dies) following the sexual violence (whether he is the rapist or the woman's husband). The films' fictional societies and legal systems tend to focus on the men's deaths, diminishing the women's sexual victimization. Whether or not they explicitly charge the women with murder (legally or socially), most films' cinematic legal systems seem to condemn them for their own sexual plight as well as for the men's deaths. Focusing on the women and decontextualizing the men's violent deaths, each film implies that it was the woman's uncontrollable, naturally dangerous sexuality that brought about both the sexual encounter and the death.

The cinematic communities and legal systems in these films do not necessarily attribute to the women criminal *mens rea* (guilty mind) or even *actus reus* (bad act). Nor do they examine the women's specific conduct or mental state at the time of the men's deaths. The women are not treated as full legal subjects. Assuming and upholding underlying honor-based values (such as the potential shamefulness of feminine sexuality), applying sexist, misogynistic stereotypes (such as the image of the femme fatale) and prejudices (such as the belief in women's desire to be raped), these films' fictional communities and legal systems construct the women as inherently (sexually) guilty. Concomitantly, these fictional communities and cinematic legal systems suggest that the women's plights cannot be judged by legal standards, whereas the men's deaths are grave legal offenses.

Earlier, I noted that a film may echo, affirm, or undercut its own on-screen, fictional legal system. Similarly, a film may take a variety of directions in its construction of women. It may echo its fictional world's construction of women. In this, the film may offer cinematic support for the sociolegal functions it portrays. On the other hand, a film may expose and subvert its fictional social community's and legal system's treatment of women. It may renounce sexist stereotypes and avoid masculinist prejudices. In its reference to underlying genre conventions, in its choice of characters, plots, legal argumentation, and actors, in shooting and editing techniques, a film may convey different—and even contradictory—views of women, society, and law, reflecting and refracting its audience's conflicted beliefs in a changing world.

The close law-and-film reading of the films analyzed in this book shows that most of their on-screen fictional legal systems tend to construct, treat, and judge women as guilty objects. Some films adopt this construction in their presentation of women, while others reject it, offering an alternative presentation of women as victimized subjects. This law-and-film study thus reveals that women's objectification goes hand in hand with their accusation and condemnation, whereas their cultural presentation as victims of gender abuse is coherent with their construction as active agents. Films that deny women's victimization also tend to objectify them, while simultaneously prosecuting and condemning them. Films that acknowledge and emphasize women's victimization seem to have no difficulty understanding and conveying victimized women's subjecthood and agency.

Critical feminist legal analysis of an on-screen legal system, and of its logic, rituals, conventions, and protagonists, offers a convenient, challenging, and entertaining means of addressing the problematic treatment of women within real-world legal systems. Analysis of cinematic methods of constructing and judging women exposes and illuminates analogous legal methods of constructing and judging them. This concomitant reference to legal and cinematic methods reveals intersections of pleasure and power, offering unexpected feminist insights into law, film, and social functions at large.

JUDGMENT AND VILIFICATION OF VICTIMIZED WOMEN

The films presented in the first part of this book echo and uphold their fictional worlds' masculinist sociolegal treatment of women. In a multitude of subtle, transparent ways, cinematic as well as thematic, the films deny the systematic victimization of their women protagonists by men and social systems, and portray them as dangerously sexual. Decontextualizing their victimization, the films naturalize it, along with the women's inherently dangerous sexuality. Each of these films silences the female protagonist, depriving her of authentic language and the power to laugh. Secluding her, trapping her between dominating men (often her husband and a rapist), each of these films denies its woman a feminine community, support, solidarity, and empathy.

Applying and perpetuating patriarchal stereotypes and mythological feminine archetypes, these films rule their women by dividing them into familiar categories: deadly, sexually brazen Lilith women; timid, domesticated, nurturing, good, sexually subjugated, self-sacrificing Eves; saintly, completely asexual Madonnas; pathetic, manly, unnatural, and unattractive lesbians/ feminists (Kamir 2001). Alternatively, they present an allegorical woman, embodying the combination of every sexist stereotype.

Whether or not their on-screen legal systems subject the women protagonists to fictional trials, the films subject the women to cinematic judgment, inviting viewers to actively partake in the cinematic judging processes. Unbound by restrictive, statutory definitions of offenses, evidentiary rules, and the presumption of innocence, the films use the women's sexuality, as well as sexist stereotypes and prejudices, against them. Furthermore, they fill in, cinematically, judgmental functions not explicitly executed by legal systems, thus preserving archaic, moralistic notions and subverting social reform. The most significant case in point is the way the films accuse rape complainants of adultery.

As Ann Coughlin (1998) contends, societies and legal systems closely associate "rape" with "adultery." Coughlin suggests that, initially, rape was conceptually indistinguishable from adultery and all other forms of nonmarital intercourse. Intercourse was legitimate and legal only when participants were legally married to each other; any nonmarital intercourse (whether premarital fornication or extramarital adultery) was deemed sinful and strictly illegal. In practice, an unwed mother or a married woman who was caught in the act with a man who was not her husband would be charged with engaging in nonmarital intercourse. The only way for a woman to exonerate herself from such a charge was to convince a judge and/or jury that she was not the man's partner in crime, but rather, that he had imposed himself on her and compelled her to commit the offense.

Coughlin demonstrates that within the constraints of traditional criminal common law, there were three possible avenues of argument for a woman charged with fornication. "Such traditional defensive strategies would include the claim that the woman had committed no *actus reus*, that she lacked the *mens rea* for fornication or adultery, or that she had submitted to the intercourse under duress" (8). To argue that she had committed no *actus reus* (bad act) an accused woman would have to argue that the man with whom she had the illegal intercourse exercised such overwhelming power that her body was not in her command; she could not control her movements, and the man had used her body as if it were an object at his disposal. This would be an argument for lack of "voluntariness." To support this argument, the woman would have to convince the judge and/or jury that the man had used overpowering force, that she had resisted to the utmost throughout the event, and that, despite her resistance, she had not managed to regain control over her body and stop the perpetrator.

To argue that she lacked the required *mens rea* (guilty mind), an accused woman would have to claim that the man had deceived her into mistaking him for her husband, or into mistaking the sexual act for something other than intercourse (such as medical treatment). To raise the defense that she submitted to the intercourse under duress, a woman would have to argue that the man compelled her participation in the criminal conduct using credible threats of death or great bodily harm. She would need to establish that she did not place herself in a situation that resulted in the illicit intercourse.

For centuries, common law has defined rape as one of three scenarios: carnal knowledge of a woman (not the perpetrator's wife): (1) performed on her forcibly and against her will (currently phrased "without her consent"), while she resisted to the utmost (currently phrased "reasonably") throughout the event; (2) deceived by the perpetrator into mistaking him for her husband, or mistaking the nature of the sexual act; (3) who submitted in fear of the perpetrator's threats of death or severe bodily harm. Intercourse was not deemed rape if the woman willingly placed herself in a situation in which intercourse was likely to happen.

Clearly, "the elements of the rape offense (almost) are a mirror image of the defenses we would expect from women accused of fornication or adultery" (Coughlin 1998, 8). In other words, close examination of the common law reveals that its definition of rape is almost identical to the common-law defenses available to a woman accused of adultery or fornication. Within the logic and discourse of the common law, rape is symbiotically linked with other forms of nonmarital intercourse. The charges made against a man accused of rape mirror the complainant's defense arguments in her own case of nonmarital intercourse. Today, the legal procedure once used by the female defendant to defend herself against charges of committing nonmarital intercourse has evolved into the procedure used by the state prosecution to accuse a man of committing rape.

Coughlin concludes that in a society that believes that "fornication and adultery no longer should be criminalized . . . there appears to be no justification for adhering to a definition of rape that treats the rapist's victim as a lawbreaker who must plead for an excuse from criminal responsibility" (9). We should, therefore, "immediately move to reform the definition of rape so that the law enforcement officials no longer are licensed to construe rape complaints as admissions of guilt for which women alone must seek to be pardoned" (46). Coughlin does not supply sufficient historical evidence to establish the narrative she offers as more than plausible. But her construction is immensely compelling as a diachronic, deconstructive exposure of the logic and elements of common-law rape. Note also that Coughlin's arguments can be easily structured as a typical feminist legal constructive deconstruction, as defined by the model.

The films discussed in part 1 of this book portray fictional legal systems treating rape legalistically, never explicitly prosecuting or judging rape victims for adultery or fornication. Through their cinematic judgments, these films supplement their fictional legal systems' treatment of rape. Voicing and upholding rape law's suppressed subtext, they subject the women who've survived rape to cinematic judgment, constructing them as suspect and accused of adultery and sexual corruption.

In portraying sexually violated women's sexual guilt as inherent and natural, while implicitly judging and condemning them for improper, fatal, sexual conduct, these films constitute their women protagonists as both determined by their sex and responsible for the damaging consequences of their sexuality, that is, as guilty objects.

My reading of these films exposes their modes of operation not to understand or assert the underlying, misogynistic nature of humans and cinematic texts, but to unravel their hold on viewers and encourage critical rethinking of filmmaking as well as judgment. In the terminology offered by the model, part 1 offers a feminist law-and-film constructive deconstruction of four law films. This part's reading of the films finds that all four profess their commitment to the pursuit of justice and truth, defined as the thorough investigation of facts and guilt. Each of the films sets out to judge an interaction that involved a sexual encounter and the death of a man. Each of their judgments focuses on a woman character involved in the sexual encounter. But the close reading of the films also reveals that each constructs the investigated, sexually implicated woman as inherently guilty. In each film, the woman's sexuality renders her a guilty object. The juxtaposition of the films' declared norm with their conventional treatment of the women characters reveals that the cinematic judgments they conduct are paradoxical and meaningless, as they set out to investigate the guilt of a woman already constructed as inherently and irrevocably guilty.

The juxtaposition of the films' declared norm and underlying convention leads to the conclusion that a new normative, cinematic quest can and must be formulated, acknowledging and refuting films' conventional tendency to construct women as guilty objects. The films presented in parts 2 and 3 demonstrate what such alternative quests may be, and how they may be constructed. Each of the films read in part 2 pursues justice and truth not by investigating the guilt of a sexually involved woman, but by supporting her judgment of people and social institutions who would construct her as always already guilty. Refusing to investigate their heroines' potential guilt even when no known legal defense is available to them, the films read in part 3 reject and transcend judgment altogether.

In addition to a feminist law-and-film critique, my discussions in part 1 also offer a feminist reading of these texts against their grain. Whereas the feminist critique of a film exposes its sexist and misogynist modes of operations, a feminist reading against the grain brings to light existing potentially feminist textual elements, emphasizing and using them to read the text's suppressed feminist subtext. This is an additional subversive method, enabling the resistant feminist reader to defy a text's invitation to endorse its explicit androcentric belief system.

WOMEN EXECUTING JUDGMENT

Again featuring a woman's sexual violation and a man's death (or near death), each of the films discussed in part 2 explicitly addresses women's issues from a self-declared pro-feminist perspective.[7] These films make conscious, explicit efforts to offer alternative portrayals of women's sexuality, openly challenging the stereotyping, silencing, and victimization of women. Presenting multidimensional, strong female characters, they attempt to humanize, individualize, and empower them, endowing them with authentic voices and laughter, points of view, and narratives. The films address their women protagonists' sexual victimization, highlighting their pain and suffering, making a conscious effort to understand and accept, rather than suspect, judge, and condemn.

These films do not subscribe to honor-based, androcentric social values, nor do they endorse their legal systems' inherent tendency to objectify women and construct them as guilty objects. Instead of subjecting their women protagonists to cinematic judgment they let the women judge their oppressors on their own terms, inviting viewers to share the women's points of view and participate in their judgments. In their construction of their women protagonists, the films endow the abstract notion of human dignity with specific, concrete contents. Concomitantly, they combine insights associated with radical feminism, liberal feminism, and cultural feminism. In this part of the book, I examine the various feminist perspectives presented and advocated by the films, emphasizing films' unique potential to smoothly align feminist positions that are often considered irreconcilable.

The film readings that comprise part 2 present each of the films as conducting a feminist law-and-film constructive deconstruction. *Adam's Rib* tackles the semi-legal "unwritten law," used by juries to exonerate husbands who kill their wives' lovers. The film harshly critiques the social convention that views a husband's philandering more favorably than a wife's, demonstrating how it precludes an equal application of the unwritten law to women who kill their husbands' lovers. In its on-screen court, *Adam's Rib* redefines the unwritten law, expanding it to apply to women defendants. The norm investigated by *Nuts* is equality before the law, as defined by an individual's basic right to have his or her day in court, unless otherwise prevented by the authorized psychiatric and legal professionals. *Nuts* exposes the psychiatric inclination to label sexually victimized women "deviant" and incapable of standing trial, thus silencing them and depriving them of the right to have their day in court. The film supports its heroine in her struggle to secure a victimized woman's equal right to have her day in court, challenging both the accepted version of the film's investigated norm and the social reality it exposes.

Death and the Maiden calls attention to the norm ascribing to the legal system the duty to secure justice and healing in the context of a society recovering from traumatic dictatorship and civil war. This norm's official definition, presented by the film's jurist character, requires the law to turn a blind eye to crimes perpetuated by the old regime, if their legal investigation may endanger the social process of healing and reconciliation. Referring to the unspoken reality, the film reveals that under such circumstances, unprosecuted crimes would include sexual atrocities committed by officials of the old regime. Read against this, the accepted formulation of the norm implies abandonment and sacrifice of sexually victimized women. *Death and the Maiden*'s female protagonist, a rape survivor, rejects the accepted formulation of the norm. To her, the legal system's duty to secure justice and healing includes a responsibility to offer women such as herself justice and to facilitate their healing, forcing society to confront its ugly past rather than bury it together with its victims.

Taking women a step further, the films discussed in part 3 provide their female protagonists with supportive, feminine communities, emphasizing the collective nature of women's plights and the feminist project. Unlike the women characters in parts 1 and 2, these women protagonists are embraced by warm, supportive communities, expressing powerful solidarity. Within their communities, women find their voices, as well as the power to laugh together. In their refusal to judge their women, these films go beyond reversing roles and placing women in the judge's seat; they question the concept of judgment itself. They similarly question mainstream (legal) feminist perceptions from separatist, postmodern and identity-politics perspectives. Chapters 8 to 10 provide an opportunity to study the interactions between these perspectives and the feminist project.

The three films discussed in this part of the book offer their own versions of constructive deconstruction. *A Question of Silence* confronts the right to a fair judicial hearing. It exhibits both society's and the legal system's complete inability to hear women's voices, concluding that a judicial proceeding cannot conduct a hearing of defendants it is incapable of hearing. Rather than suggest a new formulation of the ruling norm, this film offers a radically different norm: women's camaraderie outside the legal domain, and civil disobedience. Similarly, *Set It Off* looks at the right to equal citizenship and the presumption of innocence, showing that poor Black women are viewed as always already guilty through association (with the Black community), and treated as second-class citizens. It too suggests loyalty and friendship among poor Black women as a total alternative to legal norms. *High Heels* questions what it means to do justice in a given case involving the death of a man at the hand of his wife. So, too, it questions the meaning of guilt itself. It finds that a killing may be the outcome of the complicated, unacknowledged victimization of the killer, herself neither more nor less guilty than others around her, including the deceased. *High Heels* (much like *Death and the Maiden*) concludes that doing justice means helping a woman recover from her traumatic past, and securing her happiness.

Part I

FEMINIST CRITIQUE OF LAW FILMS

THAT HONOR-JUDGE WOMEN

Rashomon 1

(Japan, 1950)

CONSTRUCTION OF WOMAN AS GUILTY OBJECT

Akira Kurosawa's *Rashomon* is among the most enduring and influential classic courtroom dramas. It is also "the best-known Japanese film ever made"
(Richie 1996, 79). Presenting and commenting on several testimonies relating
a criminal event, *Rashomon* offers complex, powerful insights on the human
condition, the meaning of truth, and the nature of the legal process in its
sociocultural context. "It has become one of those few films whose cultural
importance has transcended their own status as films" (Prince 1991, 128). The
film's title has become an expression used by the public and legal profession
alike in reference, among other things, to the nature of law. "*Rashomon* has
come to embody a general cultural notion of the relativity of truth" (Prince
1991, 128).

The expression *Rashomon* encapsulates a disturbingly relativistic, skeptical
view of truth, reality, humanity, and the nature of the legal process. It refers to
a situation in which, as in the film, different witnesses to an occurrence offer
completely incompatible testimonies of it, as if attesting to altogether different events. This usage implies that objective truth is unattainable and

perhaps nonexistent, and that the legal process is a place where subjective narratives can be evaluated only against each other. Additionally, the term implies that humans in general and witnesses specifically compose their versions of reality and truth in the context of self-creation through storytelling; such storytelling voices the inherent human inability to accept ourselves for what we really are and the overwhelming need for self-deception and justification (Richie 1987, 113, 116).

I suggest that the film's celebrated, manifest skepticism regarding truth and law is but one theme, disguising the film's not-so-skeptical, subtextual, popular jurisprudence and cinematic judgment. The film's implicit, underlying worldview is both theoretical and ideological; it is also inherently linked with the film's cinematic judgment, which invites the viewer to participate both in judgment and in gender construction, constituting *Rashomon* as a participant in society's self-creating process.

The theoretical component of *Rashomon*'s subtextual worldview offers a vision of the close interrelations between legal and social judging, common wisdom, culture, and nature. The ideological component is deeply conservative, androcentric, honor-based, and uncritical. The film's subtextual cinematic judgment relies on and invokes legal conventions and the implied viewer's familiarity with them. Mirroring these legal conventions in its own cinematic judgment, the film invites its viewer to participate, as both judge and jury, in the process of judging a woman and constructing her as "woman" and "guilty" simultaneously. As the film's cinematic judgment involves the uncritical upholding and nourishing of *Rashomon*'s underlying androcentric views, the implied viewer is invited to rely on and embrace these notions, as is the film's real viewing community, consisting of real-life potential judges and jury members. The nihilistic doubts about truth so vehemently presented at the film's shallowest textual level are thus revealed to be a smoke screen, allowing the complex subtextual message to operate unnoticed and hence unscrutinized.

Rashomon was created in Japan, in Japanese, by a Japanese director using a Japanese screenwriter's script. The script was based on two short stories by the Japanese author Ryunosuke Akutagawa, "Rashomon" and "In the Grove," which, in turn, rely on several eleventh-century Japanese tales (Goodwin 1994, 117). From this perspective, *Rashomon* can be viewed as a multilayered Japanese text. But its incorporation within Western culture to the degree of its title becoming a widely used expression over the course of half a century makes *Rashomon* part of Western culture as well. Significantly, the film was far more successful in the West (particularly in the Anglo-American West) than in Japan (Richie 1996, 79–80). I read *Rashomon* strictly in the context of Western culture, despite references to Japanese culture and law.

I look at the film in the context of a Western (implied and actual) viewer's familiarity with the conventions of the Anglo-American common-law legal system, with the West's cultural tradition, and with basic features of Japanese culture. I assume that while a Western viewer might not be familiar with the particular honor code portrayed by the film (a cinematic version of the Japanese Bushido code), that viewer does recognize the logic and dynamic of the film's honor culture, which is very close to those portrayed in many Western films (such as, of course, westerns).

Film Synopsis

Rashomon presents three men, a woodcutter (Takashi Shimura), a priest (Minoru Chiaki), and a commoner (Kichijiro Ueda), who, finding shelter from the rain on the decaying Rashomon gate, review testimony given earlier in a legal proceeding that took place in the police courtyard. The legal proceeding investigated the death of a samurai, which occurred after a sexual encounter between the samurai's wife and an outlaw. Both the woodcutter and the priest testified during the legal proceeding, and were deeply affected by the case.

In reply to a question from the commoner, the priest explains: "A man has been murdered," encapsulating the event to be discussed in detail throughout the film. He stresses that, even in times of famine and plague, "there's never been anything, anything as terrible as this. Never. It is worse than fires, wars, epidemics, or bandits." The woodcutter beseeches the commoner to help them understand the meaning of the event, and for lack of better entertainment, the commoner consents.

Through flashback, the woodcutter repeats the story he narrated earlier in the courtyard, describing how, three days earlier, walking through the forest in search of wood, he came upon the samurai's body in the bush, a sword still lodged in his chest. After short testimonies given by the priest and the policeman who captured Tajomaru (played by Kurosawa's frequent leading man Toshiro Mifune), the outlaw himself speaks. He is half-naked, a proud and fearsome, noble savage. "It's the truth," he declares at the outset of his testimony. "I know you will kill me sooner or later. I am not hiding anything. It was me, Tajomaru, who killed that man."

Tajomaru's testimony, the first version the film offers of its central event, is by far the longest (twenty-one minutes), most detailed, and most complex in its masterful combination of show and tell. It consists of five courtroom scenes in which the outlaw, in dramatic close-up shots of his expressive face and naked upper body, addresses the camera, (unseen fictional) judge, and viewers. These scenes are complemented by four extended flashback-within-flashback scenes. Tajomaru describes how, on a hot afternoon, he awoke to the sight of the samurai, accompanied by his wife on horseback. At that moment, the breeze lifted the woman's veil, and for a split second Tajomaru beheld her carefully made-up face, and tiny feet dangling in a childish way. Aroused, Tajomaru grasped the sword that was resting between his legs, raising it in a phallic gesture. "I thought I'd seen an angel. I decided I'd take her," he testifies.

Promising to sell him stolen swords at a bargain price, Tajomaru leads the samurai into an isolated clearing, where he attacks him and ties him up. He rushes back to the woman (gently seated by a spring) and reports that her husband was bitten by a snake. Tajomaru testifies: "She turned pale and stared as if her eyes were frozen. She looked like a child turned suddenly serious. Her look made me jealous of that man. I started to hate him. I wanted to show her how he looked tied up like that. I'd not thought of such a thing before, but now I did."

Tajomaru pulls the woman to the clearing, where, after a very long moment of silence, she grabs her dagger, and for another long minute and a half attacks the outlaw fiercely and skillfully, attempting to stab him. Bewildered, excited, amused, and engaged, he rebuffs her attacks (although not a bite), his voice-over commenting that "she was fierce, determined." Finally, realizing her defeat, sweating and breathing heavily, she sobs as Tajomaru approaches and grabs her. The outlaw laughs, looking at the samurai, as the woman continues to struggle in his arms. As this episode is central to this chapter's discussion, I include the script's description of it:

> 161 LS [Long Shot]. The woman is in the foreground, helplessly sobbing; Tajomaru in the background. He stalks up to her, she lunges yet again, but now he grabs and holds her. [Fifteen seconds.]
>
> 162 CU [Close-up] of the husband watching them; he bows his head. [Five seconds.]
>
> 163 CU. The woman claws Tajomaru's face; he wrests her head free . . . She struggles but he kisses her. [Seven seconds.]
>
> 164 The sky seen through the branches of the trees (pan). [Two seconds.]
>
> 165 CU of the bandit kissing her; she stares straight up. [Four seconds.]

166 (= [same shot as] 164). The sky seen through the overhead branches (pan). [Two seconds.]

167 cU from reverse angle; Tajomaru holding her, kissing her. [One second.]

168 (=164) The sky and trees. The camera has stopped panning; now the sun is seen shining brilliantly through the branches. Bell-like music begins. [Three seconds.]

169 ECU [Extreme close-up] from reverse angle; Tajomaru kissing the woman, as she stares blankly at the sun. [Three seconds.] (Kurasawa 1969, 73–4)

Then, the woman's lifeless hand finds Tajomaru's body, and, clutching it, scales his naked body, embracing him passionately.

Bursting with wild laughter in the courtyard, Tajomaru concludes: "And so I had her and without killing her husband. Besides, I hadn't planned to kill him." But then, he continues, the woman demanded: "Stop! One of you must die—either you or my husband. Disgraced before two men is more than I can bear. I will belong to whoever kills the other." Accepting her proposal, Tajomaru released the samurai, and the two engaged in a lengthy, professional, heroic duel that led to the samurai's honorable death.

At the Rashomon gate, the priest remarks that whereas Tajomaru stressed the woman's strength, he, the priest, found her pitiful and felt compassion for her. Through flashback to the courtyard, the priest relates to the commoner the testimony of the woman (Machiko Kyo). The woman's testimony begins: "And then, after having taken advantage of me . . ."

After Tajomaru's departure, the woman testifies, she rushed to the bound samurai, sobbing and throwing her arms around him. But, she tells the court: "Even now I remember his eyes. What I saw in them was not sorrow, not even anger. It was a cold hatred of me." Tormented by the samurai's frozen expression, the woman retreats from her husband, repeating, as if in a trance: "Don't! Don't look at me like that! Beat me! Kill me if you must, but don't look at me like that! Please don't!" Covering her face with both hands, she retreats and falls to the ground sobbing. She runs to fetch her dagger, releases the samurai, offers him the dagger, and demands: "Then kill me! Kill me quickly with one thrust!" The camera circles them both, capturing his contemptuous expression. Holding the dagger, the woman, seemingly hypnotized by his gaze, slowly retreats, then returns, constantly repeating: "Don't look at me like that!"

251 U of the woman as she moves steadily forward now; her world forever destroyed, she holds the dagger high, without seeming to be aware of it. The camera tracks with her in the direction of her husband until she suddenly lunges off screen. [Twenty-one seconds.] (Kurasawa 1969, 97–98)

According to her testimony, the woman fainted. Awaking, she saw the dagger in her dead husband's chest. She ran desperately through the forest, and, reaching a pond, tried to drown herself in it. "I tried to kill myself. But I failed. What should a poor helpless woman like me do?"

At the gate, the commoner remarks: "Women lead you on with their tears. They even fool themselves. Now, if I believed what she said I'd be really confused." The priest resumes his flashback narration, now of the testimony of the dead samurai (Masayuki Mori) as given in the prison courtyard through a female medium (Fumiko Humma). In a hollow (dead man's) voice, the medium states dramatically: "I am in darkness now! I am suffering in the darkness! Cursed be those who cast me unto this hell of darkness." Next, she delivers a narration of the events, which is presented as the dead man's on-screen flashback-within-a-flashback: "After the bandit attacked my wife," relates the samurai's voice, "he tried to console her." The voice-over continues, as we see a long shot of the woman and Tajomaru sitting in the forest clearing: "He told her that she could no longer live with her husband . . . Why didn't she go with him . . . He said he only attacked her because of his love for her."

The medium speaks in the samurai's voice: "Never, never in all our life together, had I seen her more beautiful!" In his flashback, the tormented samurai shuts his eyes in pain in view of his seduced wife. His dead voice continues to narrate: "And what was my beautiful wife's reply to the bandit, in front of her helpless husband? Kill him! As long as he is alive I cannot go with you. Kill him!" The samurai's voice laments through the medium's lips: "Kill him. I still hear those words! They are like the wind, blowing me to the bottom of this pit. Has anyone ever uttered more pitiless words? Even the bandit was shocked to hear them!"

On-screen we see the wife shouting, "Kill him! Kill him! Kill him! Kill him! Kill him!" Horrified at the woman's response, the bandit throws her to the ground, stepping on her, asking the samurai what he would like to have done with her. But the woman escapes, the bandit chasing her. The samurai remains seated, frozen, weeping, heartbroken. Then he grabs the dagger and stabs himself. The medium collapses.

At the gate, the woodcutter paces up and down, proclaiming there was no dagger, rather a sword. The commoner talks him into admitting that he did not disclose the whole truth in his first testimony, and into telling his full version. In the woodcutter's flashback narration, the woman is lying on the ground, weeping, while Tajomaru is pleading with her to come with him, promising to do anything for her and threatening to kill her if she refuses. In response, the woman finally replies: "How could I, a woman, answer a question like that?" She grabs her dagger, runs to the tied samurai, and releases him. Tajomaru understands that the men must decide the issue by fighting, but the samurai, nervously backing away, holding his hand in front of him, shouts, "Stop! Stop! I refuse to risk my life for such a woman!" He says to the woman, "You are a shameless whore! Why don't you kill yourself?" Then, to Tajomaru, "If you want her, I'll give her to you! I regret the loss of my horse more than the loss of her."

As Tajomaru reconsiders and decides to leave the scene, the horrified woman's crying turns into hysterical laughter as she rises and approaches the samurai first and then the outlaw, challenging that if either of them were a real man he would fight for her. "Just remember, a woman only loves a real man. And when she loves, she loves madly, forgetting all else. But a woman can only be won with the strength of swords."

Shamed, humiliated, confused, the men engage in a long, pathetic duel, their heavy breathing and comic falls attesting to their fear and incompetence. Having lost his sword the samurai begs: "I don't want to die! I don't want to die!" To the sound of the woman's blood-curdling scream the outlaw stabs him to death, breathing heavily.

At the gate, alerted by a baby's cry, the commoner finds the baby and strips it of its coat. To the woodcutter's shock, the commoner insists that his behavior is neither "evil" nor "terrible." He argues: "Me, evil? Then what about the parents of that baby? They had their fun, then they threw it away. That's evil!" Frustrated and outraged, the woodcutter attacks the commoner, strangling him in the fierce rain. In reply, the commoner accuses the woodcutter of stealing the woman's valuable dagger, as well as lying. He walks into the rain, leaving behind the devastated woodcutter and the weeping priest, who holds the screaming baby in his arms. Silent, the two men remain standing at the gate.

As the rain ceases, the woodcutter takes the baby from the priest's arms, saying: "I've six children of my own. Another won't make it more difficult." Emotional, moved, the priest and woodcutter thank each other for restoring their mutual faith in mankind, as the smiling woodcutter, holding the baby in his arms, leaves the gate and walks into the light of a clear day.

In *Rashomon*, judgment is passed in three distinct yet closely related contexts. The narrative presents a fictional legal proceeding, judging the event in the forest. Six of the film's seven characters (all but the commoner) testify in this proceeding. Although once removed from the implied viewer, much of this narrative is presented through on-screen flashbacks, offering the viewer the sense of firsthand experience. The viewer is thereby directly implicated in the courtroom judging. Most importantly, by placing the camera in the judge's position, and not showing an on-screen judge, the film constructs the implied viewer as the judge and so explicitly invites him or her to pass judgment.

The framing narrative (originated by the film version of the story) features three characters at the Rashomon gate engaged in reviewing, analyzing, and evaluating the testimonies given both in and out of court regarding the event in the forest. The three characters at the gate comprise a fictional lay tribunal, applying legal evidence, firsthand acquaintance with the case, common sense, and life experience. Within the framing narrative, the implied viewer is associated with the commoner (who is another one of the film's additions to Akutagawa's stories). Like the commoner, the implied viewer was not present at the court or in the forest and is therefore allegedly neutral and objective in his approach. Also, like the commoner, the implied viewer is interested in the story as a source of entertainment told to pass an evening. At the outset, justifying the film's retelling of the courtroom event, the woodcutter appeals to the commoner to make sense of the case, simultaneously addressing the implied viewer with the same request. This request asks the commoner and the implied viewer to pass judgment and reach a decision regarding the case.

Donald Richie aptly describes the commoner as the film's "chorus" (1996, 71). From a more legalistic point of view, I suggest substituting "jury" for "chorus." A jury, composed of actual, "reasonable" laypeople, is entrusted with delivering the verdict, and expected to voice the community's common sense within the common-law legal process.

The commoner is a shrewd, perceptive, insightful character. His views, sometimes highly cynical, unsettling, and painful, are accepted by both woodcutter and priest as the community's conventional wisdom, establishing the commoner as the fictional community's appropriate jury. The implied viewer is invited both to identify the commoner as the film's jury and share the decision making with him.

The judgment at the gate is clearly distinct from the courtroom proceeding. It takes place on a different narrative level, and the setting is visibly different. Yet, the courtroom proceeding triggers and structures the social process at the gate, providing testimonies to review and evaluate. The legal proceeding is portrayed as an event that is then repeated and evaluated in social contexts, supplying material to be used in the formation of common wisdom and moral views. Concomitantly, the film suggests that the social process at the gate also influences the legal courtroom proceeding. This influence is suggested through the implied viewer's construction as both judge and commoner. Sitting in as the fictional tribunal's judge, the viewer brings to the legal position the commoner's "conventional wisdom" and "common sense," and so brings the community's worldview into the professional legal world. Constructing the implied viewer as both judge and commoner, the film suggests that the community's world-view enters the professional legal world through the judge's character.

The contrast between the sunny prison courtyard of the legal trial and the rainy gate of the social one stresses the distinction between the judging contexts (Kauffmann 1987, 174). The legal proceeding in the courtyard takes place in a formal, sterile atmosphere. The courtyard is bare, the witnesses are frozen, and their speech is restrained by the norms of the legal ritual and their fear of the authorities; the weather is mild and uneventful. Unlike the formal courtyard proceeding, the judgment at the gate is not distinct and detached from the human reality it examines. In clear contrast, this judgment is inseparable from the characters' dynamic, emotional, temperamental behavior. It is passionate, personal, involved, and deeply human. Accordingly, the weather is stormy, dramatic, and expressive. In fact, the downpour is so overwhelming as to invite (in the implied Western viewer) association with the biblical flood. (If, as I suggest below, the event in the wood echoes the primal Fall, the scene at the gate seems its natural extension, taking place while heaven attempts to cleanse the earth of human evil.) In this context, the location of the social judging process acquires unique symbolic value. First, the decaying gate connotes the deterioration of social order and moral norms. It is on the verge of anarchy and chaos that the group at the gate engages in the social act of judgment.

In the face of despair, this courageous search for truth and justice is both existential and heroic. Unlike the formalistic legal proceeding, this social action is a community's struggle to maintain moral norms and so its very existence. It is an act of hope and faith. Appropriately, this act, unlike a typical legal proceeding, does not end in condemnation but rather in humble confession, sacrifice, forgiveness, redemption, reconciliation, and human bonding. These developments appease the gods; when judgment is complemented by manifestations of remorse and compassion, the rain stops and the world is renewed. The formal legal event pales in comparison. It is the little Rashomon community situated at the city gate, not the legal community in the courtyard, that is engaged in an age-old tradition of social self-creation and renewal. The formal legal proceeding is but a means to supply the men at the gate with testimony and a clear frame of reference for their social process; it is a public spectacle in the service of the social process of self-creation.

The film's third judging process, its cinematic judgment, takes place beyond the film's fictional, on-screen world. It is within this judging process, which is at the heart of this chapter's attention, that the viewer is presented with four central testimonies and is invited to rely on legal conventions and underlying familiar common wisdom to define a defendant and conduct judgment. The implied viewer's association with the film's fictional judge (combined with the legal conventions, discussed below, that the implied viewer is requested to apply within the cinematic judgment) construct the film's cinematic judgment as quasi-legal. The viewer's association with the commoner adds a social, common-sense aspect to the film's cinematic judgment.

Participating in the film's cinematic judgment, the implied viewer is associated with yet another judging image: the all-seeing God. Most of the testimonies relating the event in the forest are narrated as hearsay. But the film's use of the on-screen flashback technique to present the viewer with most of these stories undercuts the mediating effect, offering the viewer a seemingly direct impression of the narrated events. In this manner, the viewer enjoys fuller, more direct contact with the witnesses' stories than any living judge. By seeing the witnesses' stories (rather than hearing them, as a judge would), the viewer is offered a glimpse into their souls, their memories, their deepest inner selves. He is also offered the sense that his cinematic judgment is well founded, ultimate, and absolute.

Defining the Cinematic Judgment's Defendant through Legal Conventions

One of *Rashomon*'s central themes is the difficulty of knowing, understanding and judging the event in the woods that led to the man's death. At first glance, the film seems to feature four irreconcilable testimonies of the event, the inherent contradictions between them precluding any coherent, reliable knowledge of the true facts and so a responsible determination of legal and moral accountability. Yet by relying on familiar legal and cinematic conventions interwoven with conventional wisdom, the film's cinematic judgment does lead to a clear determination of the participants' accountability. The most obvious of these legal conventions is the order of storytelling in a criminal proceeding.

In any criminal common law proceeding, the prosecution is the first to present its version of the event before the court and call witnesses to narrate and support it. Thus, the first story told in any criminal case is always the prosecuting story, presenting the event in a manner that constructs the defendant's legal accountability and criminal guilt. The first witness is always for the prosecution.

In *Rashomon*, the first version of the event in the bush is narrated by Tajomaru, the film's only name-bearing character played by the cast's leading man. His is not a typical "defense version," as it does not answer to, admit, or refute any previous narration. As the first story told, Tajomaru's is the prosecutorial one, voiced by a witness for the prosecution. Intuitively familiar with this basic legal convention, the film's implied viewer is invited to view Tajomaru's account as prosecutorial within what I call the film's cinematic judgment. But if Tajomaru's testimony is prosecutorial, who is it prosecuting? In a highly convincing performance, Tajomaru offers a clear answer. He did not mean to kill the samurai. He went out of his way to do all he could to avoid the killing. Having taken the woman, he was ready to depart. But the woman tempted him to fight the samurai, soliciting the act that brought about the killing. If he committed the killing, it was despite his better judgment, with utmost fairness, honor, and honesty. It was she who wished death, suggested it, brought it about. Soliciting a killing (or even a fatal duel) is clearly a grave criminal accusation, bearing grave moral connotation.

If Tajomaru's narrative is presented as the prosecuting story, then, on the basis of legal convention, the implied viewer is invited to expect the defendant's counter version of those elements that incriminate her. A defendant need not offer a full version of the event, or prove how the crime was committed. If Tajomaru's story is a prosecuting one, then, by the legal convention, it should be followed by the woman's refutation of its incriminating elements. Indeed, immediately after Tajomaru's story, the film presents us with the woman's reply.

The woman does not provide a full narration of the samurai's death. In fact, hers is the only version that does not attempt to fully explain either the death or the disappearance of the lethal weapon. She refutes the accusation of criminal solicitation by denying any dialogue between herself and the outlaw, as well as the duel between the two men. She claims that the lethal weapon was not the outlaw's sword but her own dagger. Claiming a temporary loss of consciousness during the time of the samurai's death, she does not offer a full account of it, but implicitly suggests a plausible alternative scenario: The samurai might have used her dagger to commit honorary, traditional suicide. She explains her fainting in light of the extreme distress, shock, and despair she experienced when confronted with her husband's sudden contempt and hatred.

In the context of the film's cinematic judgment, the film's implied viewer is invited to understand the woman's testimony as a defendant's reply to an accusation. Relying on legal convention, this viewer now expects to be presented with the prosecution's reply. In the words of a treatise on courtroom criminal evidence: "The third major evidentiary presentation is the prosecution rebuttal. As of right, the prosecutor may now present evidence refuting any new matters raised during the defense case-in-chief. The prosecutor may present evidence rebutting any affirmative defenses or attacking the credibility of the defense witnesses . . . For example, suppose that the prosecutor did not discover an eyewitness until after the prosecution case-in-chief. In his or her discretion, the judge could permit the prosecutor to call the eyewitness in rebuttal" (Imwinkelried et al. 1998, 14). Thus the film permits its "prosecution" to present two new eyewitnesses, both rebutting the woman's defense and attacking her credibility. The dead man's testimony, although contradicting Tajomaru's account regarding the outlaw's own role in the fatal event, rebuts the woman's defense, strongly supporting and enhancing the accusation of her conscious, purposeful solicitation to kill, or even to murder. Whereas in Tajomaru's testimony the woman merely urges the outlaw to fight the samurai until one of them dies, in the samurai's version, she is accused of specifically demanding that the outlaw kill the samurai, and repeating that demand eight times.

In case the implied viewer remains unconvinced by the dead husband's testimony, the film adds the woodcutter's second, out-of-court testimony, which is another of the film's additions to Akutagawa's stories. It is delivered directly to the viewer. Corroborating the other prosecutorial testimonies, the only eyewitness who seems to have not been personally involved in the event claims that the woman was very much conscious when she urged the men to fight and win her by the sword. According to this testimony, the woman can be charged with and convicted for either solicitation or conspiracy (since the outlaw can be seen as plotting the samurai's killing together with the woman prior to the deadly act itself). Is the implied viewer invited to rely, as Curtis Harrington uncritically does, on the literary convention that "it is the final part that is the true story"? (1987, 144).

The underlying legal convention regarding the order of the witnesses' testimonies does not resolve the enigma of whether the man died by the outlaw's hand, his own, or the woman's, and whether it was the sword or the dagger that inflicted the mortal wound. It does, however, constitute the woman as the film's cinematic judgment's "defendant," focusing the implied viewer's attention and suspicion on her alleged behavior. It also creates the impression that the "prosecution" presented a strong case against the accused woman: Three separate eyewitnesses all testified to her guilt of solicitation to kill. Through the underlying legal conventions, the film performs a cinematic judgment in which the woman is the primary defendant and the implied viewer is invited to join the film in the real-life cultural act of judging her. The film's real-life cinematic judgment is closely linked with the fictional legal proceeding and social judgment.

Despite the construction of the woman as primary defendant, the film does not supply solid grounds for any legal determination. Each of the testimonies is compelling but suspect, and none is clearly refutable. It is hard to think of any determination that would be beyond reasonable doubt. In order to convict the woman of solicitation, it seems necessary to discredit her and her testimony. Once the woman's testimony is discredited, all three remaining testimonies point to her guilt of solicitation, and two (Tajomaru's and the woodcutter's) implicate Tajomaru in the actual killing (the woodcutter's also suggesting the woman's guilt of conspiracy). Parker Tyler captures the effect quite aptly, stating that "unless one be prejudiced for one sex or another . . . it seems almost impossible to make a really plausible choice of the truth-teller (if any)" (1987, 151). Let me disclose how the film joins its male characters in discrediting the woman, inviting the implied viewer to be prejudiced against one sex in favor of the other.

Constructing the Sexual Encounter through Underlying Social Conventions

The samurai's death is described three times in great detail, in Tajomaru's, the samurai's, and the woodcutter's testimonies. In contrast, the sexual encounter that preceded it is presented only once, in Tajomaru's first, prosecutorial version, which constructs the woman as primary defendant.[1] In Tajomaru's account, the sexual encounter was brought about by a series of natural factors: the wind, the woman's beauty (i.e., sexuality), and his own masculine nature. He saw her because the wind blew her veil (nature intervened to present her to him); she was beautiful, that is, sexually irresistible; (being the man he was) he wanted her; (being the man he was) he took her. In his narration, she was Woman in all her glory: childlike, angelic, compassionate, and yet temperamental, wild. She was fierce, ferocious, yet also weak, delicate, and helpless. She was unpredictable, full of contradictions. She was Woman: different and incomprehensible. He was attracted, intrigued, jealous; he had to have her. At first she fought him savagely, arousing his desire all the more. But then, once his lips were pressed against hers, the sun in her eyes, she gave herself to him, submitting erotically, naturally, as trees submit to sun, in passionate intercourse, a natural event.

Describing a passionate sexual conquest, a man winning a woman by overcoming her initial inhibition and sweeping her off her feet, Tajomaru's story does not portray a rape (Taslitz 1996, 411–12). The intercourse he describes does not feature a woman taken forcefully against her will and without her consent, a criminal state of mind, or legal liability.[2] As the scene features no rape, it features no rapist. In Tajomaru's narration, the woman was a natural sexual object to be desired and had, as well as a passionately consenting partner in an adulterous act. Put differently, Tajomaru's story describes how, seduced into a natural sexual encounter, a woman gives herself passionately to adultery, manifesting her deep desire to be taken against her proclaimed will. His narrative demonstrates how a woman can be and is both a (sexual) object and guilty.

Clearly, this account evokes the familiar, misogynist "conventional wisdom" of our culture that has been exposed by many writers. In its extreme form, this holds that a sexually victimized woman must have wanted the rape and brought it about, or else it wouldn't have happened. That her modest protestations and complaints must have been disingenuous, manifesting women's fundamental insincerity, designed to disguise their inherent, insatiable sexuality ("all women are potential prostitutes"). In other words: this line of thinking suggests that there is no such thing as "rape" and, consequently, that women, especially sexual women, and particularly women complaining of sexual assault, are impure, provocative, and untrustworthy. Wishing and encouraging sexual encounters, they fabricate false accusations, faking virtue and harming their sexual partners. They are unreliable witnesses.[3] Traditional, as well as contemporary, Japanese culture sustains the very same "conventional wisdom." From this perspective, a Japanese viewer and a Western one are likely to experience the film similarly.

An informed reading of *Rashomon* against Western rape myths reveals that the film echoes and perpetuates every one of them. In her summary of our culture's most common rape myths, Helen Benedict notes that the most powerful myth about rape, which underlies all others, is that rape is merely sex, and complainants of rape were no more hurt than any woman having sexual intercourse (1992, 14–17). This myth gives rise to the derivative one according to which the assailant, a hot-blooded male driven beyond self-control, is motivated by lust. "In fact, research has shown that . . . the motivation for rape stems most commonly from anger, the need to dominate and terrify" (14). Another myth is that rapists are perverted, seedy, repulsive, or crazy. This myth is used particularly when the sex crime is extremely grotesque, but is assumed to be generally true, to some extent, of all rapists. A similar myth has it that rapists are Black, or lower class, and that their victims are white women of higher classes. Statistically, most cases of rape occur between people who know each other and belong to the same social circles.

Because rape is believed to be sex, Benedict claims, rape victims are said to have lured their rapists by their looks and sexuality. In fact, rapists testify that they rarely notice their victims' looks. Similarly, "because rapists, like all men, are believed to find women irresistible, [the] myth assumes that women bring on rape by behaving carelessly prior to the crime—it was not the rapist who "caused" the rape, it was the woman who failed to prevent herself from enticing him" (16). This accusation of women goes hand in hand with the widely held view that only sluttish, bluntly sexual women get themselves raped. Accompanying myths are that a "sexual attack sullies the victim," that "rape is a punishment for past deeds," and that "women cry rape for revenge" (17).

Most of these myths are explicitly embraced by *Rashomon*'s treatment of the sexual encounter in the woods. A low-class, perverted assailant is motivated by lust; he claims that he was provoked by the woman, who deserved it (for her careless behavior), and that there was no rape, only sex. The woman's faked protestations gave way to fiery passion. The samurai later voices the opinion that the woman is loose and unworthy. The common wisdom that, having been sexually attacked, a woman is an unreliable witness, is clearly implied, though not explicitly stated, in Tajomaru's testimony and confirmed by the commoner's observations. The film offers no critical point of view regarding these manifest attitudes, which uphold each other, nor does it voice an alternative perspective. In fact, through the testimonies following Tajo-maru's, the film offers an additional, significantly damaging androcentric attitude to rape, identifying it with adultery.

Each of the testimonies following Tajomaru's refers only to events that occurred immediately after the sexual encounter. The woman begins her story at the point after Tajomaru "took advantage" of her. The dead samurai de-scribes the events that took place "after the bandit attacked my wife." The woodcutter's version starts with the outlaw sitting by the weeping woman, consoling her and asking her to join him. None offer an alternative telling of the sexual event. In other words, although none of the other characters ex-plicitly confirm Tajomaru's account, the film does not allow any of them to present a different interpretation of the intercourse, preventing the implied viewer from seeing—or even hearing—an account constructed from a point of view other than Tajomaru's.

The underlying convention that the film invites its implied viewer to apply here is both semi-legal and cinematic. Within the adversarial mentality of the Anglo-American legal world, judges and juries are not expected to conduct their own searches for the truth but rather to decide in favor of one of the parties' competing stories. Even when the law does not require it, a party may be expected by jurors to refute any contested statement made by his or her adversary. In this context, any statement made by one party that is not ex-plicitly contested by the other may be regarded by an Anglo-American viewer as accepted by the silent party, and therefore as indisputable within the legal proceeding. The viewer may regard it as an objective, neutral fact within the legal discussion. Although not necessarily proclaimed "absolute truth," it may be implicitly treated as such. Similarly, when a film offers several narra-tions of a certain event, stressing the tentative, subjective nature of each narration, but, in sharp contrast, settles for a single narration of a related event, the clear implication is that the single portrayal of the latter is un-disputed within the film or by it.

By making Tajomaru's version the exclusive account of the sexual encoun-ter, the film thus does not cast it into doubt, and, through legal and cinematic conventions, it discourages its implied viewer from doubting it. Furthermore, the film presents Tajomaru's account of the sexual intercourse as an on-screen flashback, in a "show" rather than "tell" fashion, offering the implied viewer a firsthand impression, inviting him or her to feel that he or she is watching the authentic event. Seeing, of course, even for the most sophisticated viewer, is very often believing. The unmediated vision of the scene on-screen undermines the viewer's rational knowledge that this narrated text is clearly hearsay evidence, coming from a very suspicious source. Furthermore, the film actively blurs the distinction between Tajomaru's subjective point of view and the film's "authoritative" one. In Tajomaru's flashback, the woman is shot from an angle Tajomaru could not have possibly seen her from; this confuses the viewer, linking Tajomaru's story with the camera's "objective" point of view. (The image of the woman's clutching hand, shot from a "neutral" perspective, is the most obvious case in point). As a result of the film's treatment of Tajomaru's account, it is experienced not as a possible, tentative interpretation, but as a truthful, objective, absolute portrayal.

Through its treatment of the sexual encounter, *Rashomon* thus invites its implied viewer to discredit the woman as a witness and to doubt all aspects of her testimony, both in the context of the two fictional tribunals and in the context of the film's real-life cinematic judgment. More specifically, by presenting the woman's delight in sexual intercourse with Tajomaru, the film invites its implied viewer to suspect that after that event she was not compassionate to her betrayed husband, as her own testimony indicates, but rather eager to dispense with him, as the men's accounts suggest. Furthermore, the film associates this familiar myth with yet another myth linking woman's sexuality with temptation, solicitation, and her inherent guilt for the deaths of men: the Judeo-Christian myth of original sin.

The Moral Conventions

Carrying our cultural heritage with us, we view a film through the imagery, structures, and concepts it provides. The biblical story of Adam and Eve in the Garden of Eden is a fundamental myth underlying Western culture to this day. The myth features three characters in the primordial garden: man, his wife, and the unruly, sexual snake who rebels against prevailing norms and cosmic order. The basic plotline is roughly this: snake approaches woman, who is easily tempted; through her inherently sinful, sexual weakness and soliciting nature, she sins against the law, bringing about the fall from grace, the end of the golden days in Eden, and man's death (resulting from the expulsion from Eden). The moral in a nutshell is that woman's sexual nature, combined with her weakness, untrustworthiness, and soliciting skills, bring about sin, upheaval, and man's death. In short, woman is inherently guilty. The predominance of woman's natural, innate flaws (her dangerous sexuality, weakness, and seductiveness), combined with her inherent guilt, cast her as a guilty object.

Over the last two millennia, this myth and its moral have been fundamental components of Western man's conventional wisdom. It has been familiar and obvious enough to be widely conceived as a self-evident, neutral, objective truth of human nature and reality. I suggest that, relying on this Eden myth and reaffirming it, *Rashomon* (as constituted by its Western viewer) is a modern-day miracle play. *Rashomon*'s allegorical characters—man, wife, and unruly outlaw—the primordial, isolated bush that dominates the screen and the implied viewer's imagination (associating Tajomaru's masculine sexuality with trees in the bush), and the basic plot elements (temptation, betrayal, illicit sex, and death) all conspire to recreate in the implied viewer's mind's eye the mythological Eden scene and the inseparable, conventional moral.

Above and beyond superficial contradictions in detail, all four versions presented by the film adhere to the logic of the Eden myth confirming woman's guilt. The many differences between the narratives, stressed and enhanced by the film, add to the overwhelming effect of the universal acceptance of the conventional wisdom, the moral of the Eden myth. When all else seems to be confusing, incomprehensible, and inconclusive, the film offers, at the heart of darkness, the familiar logic that seems to be the only stable ground. The implied viewer is invited to identify, apply, and embrace it, to find comfort in its consistent, solid insight. The film offers it as the only map of human nature that can make the frightening, messy reality intelligible.

Besides man, wife, and snake, the Eden myth includes a fourth character: the all-seeing, judging God. From his superior position, enabling him to see into the hearts of humans, God summons man, wife, and snake, putting all three on trial, convicting and punishing each one. As mentioned earlier, within the film's cinematic judgment, the viewer is associated with the judging God. In this position, any decision the viewer reaches becomes "natural law" and cosmic, absolute justice. Through the association with God and natural law, the film's worldview is elevated to the status of absolute truth. The association with God's judgment in the Eden trial invites the implied viewer to convict all three: the outlaw/snake of tempting, the woman of cooperating with the seducer and soliciting a crime, and the man of weakness of character.

The Mystery Convention and the Logic of Honor

According to the familiar convention prevalent in mystery narratives, cumulative testimonies that appear, at first glance, hopelessly contradictory, add up when approached with the right cognitive tools. In *Rashomon*, these cognitive tools seem to be the moral of the Eden myth (woman is inherently guilty) and the logic of honor. Reading the film against this conceptual framework, one that the implied reader is invited to embrace, reveals how the four accounts come together through the unifying theme of the woman's guilt to offer a consistent theory.

The half-naked, unshaved, brutish-looking Tajomaru is visually associated with the clouds (when he looks up at them as the policeman testifies), with open skies (when he is shown, in a quick flashback, riding the stolen horse), with the tall (phallic) trees of the forest, with the water (which he drinks passionately), and with the sun (which is in the woman's eye as Tajomaru kisses her). His actions are motivated by his own instincts (his sexual impulse implied by the telling postures of his sword) as well as by forces of nature (he explicitly states that heat caused him to rest, wind caused him to lust and kill, water brought about his illness). To this uncivilized man, the woman—in particular, the woman's sexuality—is yet another powerful, irresistible natural force.

This naturalistic portrayal of Tajomaru mitigates his moral accountability (while not depriving him of subjecthood). Responding to forces of nature, Tajomaru is acting within a realm beyond good and evil. Yet his casting of the woman as a force of nature, while denying her full human agency, does not exonerate her in an analogous manner. On the contrary, it constitutes her inherent guilt. Admittedly, her first and foremost disturbing quality—her (sexual) existence—may be beyond moral condemnation. Not so her (sexual) visibility. As long as she is properly veiled within the constraints of culture, order and peace are maintained. When she is revealed to Tajomaru, her (sexual) existence becomes the cause of misfortune. Thus it is her momentary failure to conceal herself from the world, allowing the wind to expose her dangerous (sexual) existence, that unleashes the destructive forces of Tajomaru's sexual response.

The woman's expressed fear for her husband's life is constructed in Tajomaru's story as yet another element of her inherent guilt. It was that affectionate gesture that made Tajomaru want her not merely sexually, but also emotionally. Struck by the woman's expressed compassion and capacity to love a man, the outlaw desired her emotional dedication for himself. This desire provoked his jealousy of the other man, making it necessary for him to harm her husband. Manifesting her emotions and emotional capacity, woman thus comes between men, provoking their destructive, jealous competition for her.

If the woman's sexual visibility triggered Tajomaru's desire and her expressed compassion aroused his jealousy, her voice and words unleashed his fatal violence. Had she stayed quiet after Tajomaru had his way with her, no harm would have come to her husband. Tajomaru would have gone his way peacefully, and no blood would have been shed. But rather than accepting her fate as the silent, guilty victim, the woman spoke, demanding that one of the men kill the other. Her active, vocal behavior, the sound of her voice, her words, caused the samurai's death. Additionally, the woman's willing submission to illicit adultery constitutes her as sexually guilty of ultimate betrayal and self-degradation.

In her own testimony before the court, as narrated by the priest at the gate, the woman seems tormented by an overwhelming sense of shame and guilt. The exact significance of this expressed guilt is better understood against the cultural honor norms of the film's fictional world. Samurai Japan was, and still symbolizes, a rigid honor society (R. Benedict 1989). The samurai, the warriors, were its honor-bearing class. Bushido, "the way of the warrior," was the samurai's unwritten honor code. A samurai's honor was more precious to him than his life. A samurai's wife was expected to cherish her husband's honor above all else. She was to sacrifice all (including their children) to protect that honor.

For a man to watch his wife being taken by another man is among the most devastating humiliations within any honor culture, including the samurai one. It was therefore a wife's absolute duty to ensure that such humiliation did not occur.[4] For that purpose, in samurai Japan, she was veiled, carefully educated to conceal herself, and carried a dagger, which was to be used against *herself* if necessary to prevent her sexual violation and her husband's ruin. Denis Carmody explains: "The bushido ideal for women made them a blend of Amazon and domestic slave. First they were urged to overcome female frailty and match male's fortitude. Many young girls were trained to repress their emotions and steel themselves for the possibility of using the dagger each was given when she acceded to womanhood. The occasions for such suicide seem to have abounded. Chief among them were threats to chastity. Indeed the manuals dryly discourse on teaching girls the proper point at the throat for inserting the sword, and then on how, after insertion, to tie one's lower limbs together so as to be modest even in death. Another occasion for suicide was finding that a samurai warrior's love for her was threatening his loyalty to his lord" (1989, 118).[5]

In failing to live up to her social duty, in failing to follow exemplary, legendary models of good feminine behavior, in failing to actualize her education and careful upbringing, *Rashomon's* "shameless" woman is guilty. In attempting to use the dagger in an external rather than internal fashion, she betrays her social role. In failing to sacrifice herself for the higher social good, she is selfish. In failing to die in time, before her illicit sexual compromise, she is guilty. Her choice to live, her survival, her life itself, constitute grave, offensive, rebellious sins against the social order and its most sacred values. Worst of all, in her failure to prevent her sexual violation, the woman betrays her husband's honor and reputation, bringing about his ultimate shame in a culture where honor is ranked above life. It is a stain of humiliation that no later deed can fully purify. His ultimate dishonor constitutes her ultimate unpardonable guilt.

To rephrase this in more familiar, legalist terms, if a married woman must prevent her penetration by another man *at all cost*, if, when she cannot stop him she must kill herself before he grabs her, then, conceptually, there is no such thing as rape of a married woman: any such illicit intercourse is adultery, as she did not do what she needed to do to prevent it. (The same is true for unmarried women: any "rape" is conceptually identical with "seduction.") *Rashomon's* woman, thus, is guilty of adultery.

The hatred that the woman claims to have read in her husband's eyes, the contempt that torments her until she nearly loses her mind, expresses (among other things) an accusation of this guilt. She does not try to dispute it; she admits to weakness and failure and asks to be relieved of her life, professing a strong sense of guilt and remorse.

Relying on deep, intuitive familiarity with honor norms, the film invites its implied viewer to embrace and apply such norms, which are thoroughly masculine and patriarchal. Furthermore, in combining the logic of honor with the moral of the Eden myth, the film grants this specific social ideology the universal, absolute status conventionally awarded the myth. Combining woman's status as guilty object within the logic of honor with her similar status in the Eden myth, *Rashomon* renders this status as indisputable.

The samurai's story completes the honor-oriented line of accusation implied in the woman's version. Choosing the only symbolic venue to redeem his lost honor, the samurai uses his wife's dagger to commit the suicide she should have committed. His act manifests how, when not used properly by the woman on herself, the dagger, representing the woman, becomes the vehicle of the man's death. Furthermore, as his wife failed to be a "good woman" and use her dagger properly, the samurai takes it upon himself to correct the social wrong done by her and to perform her role. In this he shames her, but also enhances his own shame, dying a woman's death (by a dagger) rather than a man's (by a sword). In this self-infliction of shame, he exhibits his ultimate "castration" by his wife's selfish, shameless behavior.

But the samurai adds yet another accusation. In his narrative (effectively voiced through another woman, who seems to be siding with him), he presents his wife's behavior as traitorous, hateful, and bloodthirsty. Having had sexual intercourse with the outlaw, thus freeing her sexuality from social and cultural restraints, the woman turns on her husband and, with a crazed hatred, demands his blood. Sexually "liberated," she betrays her loyalty, her obligation, and her love, becoming an unruly, wild threat to his very life. In the samurai's account, the woman literally becomes a femme fatale. Her sexuality unleashed, Eve becomes Lilith, heaven is destroyed, and all hell breaks loose.

Against this honor culture's ideological background, the woodcutter's story offers an interesting, critical voice. Outside the Bushido culture, the woodcutter does not hesitate to mock it and expose its presumptuousness and self-deception. The duel between the men, which Tajomaru describes as manly and heroic, is seen by the woodcutter as pathetic and clownish. While in his own version the samurai boasts of his brave, honorable suicide, the woodcutter depicts him begging for his life.

As a critic of the honor culture, the woodcutter could be expected to voice sympathy for the woman. Indeed, there is more compassion and sympathy in his version than in those of the other men. (Only the Buddhist priest, even further removed from the honor culture, expresses more compassion for the woman, if an impersonal and detached compassion.) In the woodcutter's version, the woman weeps as the outlaw demands that she marry him. Determined not to give in, she runs to her husband and releases him to fight the outlaw. And yet once both men lose interest in her and are each ready to leave her behind, she becomes more honor crazed, vengeful, manipulative, and active in soliciting their deadly duel than in any other version. Joan Mellen may be right in claiming that "in the final story, that of the woodcutter, the woman is the most demonic" (1976, 49). She suggests that accepting the men's judgment of her, the woman "flaunts her baseness . . . 'A woman can be won only by strength, by the strength of the swords you are wearing' she screeches near the end of the film. And it is with this view of her character that Kurosawa leaves us" (49–50).

From his position as an outsider to an honor-bound social class, the woodcutter sees the woman reaffirming the honor ideology and using its gender stereotypes to bring about destruction and death. The woman is therefore guilty of collaborating with a damaging social ideology and reinforcing its grip and disastrous outcomes. In so doing, she brings out the worst in the system and its warrior heroes. The samurai is reduced to a whining coward and the outlaw to a pathetic murderer. The woodcutter's version invokes the frightful image of Circe, turning men into pigs.

There is yet another layer to the woodcutter's accusation. More so than in the other men's accounts, in the woodcutter's telling the woman steps out of her self-sacrificing, feminine role. Insisting on her own honor at the expense of others, actively avenging her disgrace, she behaves in a manner that is culturally masculine. The woman is guilty of abandoning her feminine traits and acting in a masculine, honor-seeking manner. This makes her monstrous and murderous.

I claimed earlier that, despite the film's use of legal conventions to construct the woman as primary defendant, it does not supply enough "legal" evidence to convict the woman of criminal solicitation. I suggested that discrediting the woman would undermine her testimony and facilitate her conviction. The film's complex, subtextual appeal to rape myths, the Eden myth, mystery conventions, and the logic of honor does this work. Thus, by thoroughly discrediting the woman, the film assures her conviction by the viewer in the cinematic judgment. This conviction of solicitation (or conspiracy) to kill her husband is inseparable from her sexual guilt and intertwined with her dangerous visibility and expressed emotion, her illicit adultery, the sound of her voice, and her unwillingness to sacrifice herself. Significantly, whereas the on-screen, fictional legal process focuses on the samurai's death, thus investigating (and perhaps accusing) the woman only in reference to this death, the film's cinematic judgment expands the accusation, "charging" the woman with shameful sexuality, adultery, and betrayal. Whereas the widowed rape victim is portrayed as a guilty object, her rapist—the killer of her husband—enjoys the implied defense of having been overwhelmed by natural forces and bewitched by female sexuality to mitigate his culpability, maintaining both his subjecthood and his innocence.

In focusing attention and energy on courtroom and out-of-court stories and their conflicting details, the film diverts attention from the potential story that is not told in its fictional judging contexts or its cinematic judgment. Untold, "inadmissible" stories are those that do not conform to screening standards at the entrances to legal, social, and cultural discourse. Were they formulated and told, such stories could give voice to the repressed, the social "others." Their absence allows law, society, and culture to look past such social elements and neither see nor hear them. Sharing the norms of its fictional legal and social forums, *Rashomon* silences such a story.

Rashomon's untold story is the woman's, as it could have been told had she been allowed the tools to compose it, the voice to speak it, and the supportive community to share it with. If told, this could have been a story of her loneliness, seclusion, discrimination, suppression, demonization, rape, and abuse. But the film chooses not to tell the story of the woman's fear, pain, and suffering before, during, and after the sexual attack. Her hurt, denigration, violation, betrayal, despair, and loss are never given utterance. The woman may have experienced some or all of these feelings; the "facts" presented by the film give rise to such a possibility. Yet no such story is told.

The woodcutter's final testimony on the gate is an example of how the film can, when it so chooses, empower a member of a repressed class. The film allows the woodcutter to explicitly mock the ruling class and its honor-based Bushido culture. The film's readiness to allow the woodcutter a distinct class-based voice and a critical story enhances *Rashomon*'s reluctance to offer the woman point of view and voice.

On all the film's narration levels and in all its judging contexts, the main story is of a man's victimization. In the fictional legal proceeding, the questions and answers refer to the samurai's death; the witnesses are not asked to narrate the rape, as the legal tribunal is not seeking evidence that would allow a discussion of it.[6] Tajomaru is the only one who chooses to address the rape as a relevant circumstance that (proves his manliness and) explains his testimony regarding the woman's criminal solicitation.

The legal system's blindness to the rape as an offense worthy of discussion has far-reaching results. Most obviously, this attitude precludes the search for factual evidence regarding the rape, discouraging the narration of alternative versions of the sexual event. Not even the woman is permitted by the film to portray her rape as anything other than complicit adultery. Since the rape is irrelevant to the film's exclusive judicial interest in the samurai's death, the woman is precluded from refuting Tajomaru's self-serving testimony, according to which, when he kissed her, her hand seized his body in reciprocal passion. The woman could have been permitted to deny this description, substituting it with one portraying her utter exhaustion, despair, anxiety, confusion, and numbness. Physically defeated by the experienced warrior, she lay helpless in his arms, abandoning her body, prey to his savage attack.

Similarly, the film's manifest disinterest in the issue of rape precludes any discussion and consideration of the legal definition and interpretation of this offense. Clearly, the woman could have argued that, whether her hand did or did not, at that late stage, instinctively seize the outlaw's body is completely irrelevant to the definition of the event as rape. She had expressed her lack of consent as explicitly as humanly possible and her fierce, heroic struggle is the ultimate evidence that the outlaw's imposition was against her will. Yet the film chooses to leave the viewer with the unmitigated, condemning image of the woman's hand on Tajomaru's naked body, combined with the underlying androcentric, honor-based notions and misogynist myths implying her sexual guilt, betrayal, adultery.

Consequently, the woman is not construed as a victim of a criminal offense, and no attempt is made to define her victimization as a social wrong or to redress her injury. Further, within the criminal proceeding regarding the man's death, the woman is not viewed as a victim and so cannot rely on her victimization to claim a defense, such as a posttraumatic state of mind. She cannot claim that she acted in self-defense in the face of her husband's demand that she kill herself, nor can she bring forth a partial excuse against a murder charge, claiming that the samurai's abuse after the rape constituted provocation.

Additionally, the social discussion, taking its cue from the legal proceeding, dismisses the rape as well, focusing on the man's death. Accordingly, when discussing the social significance of the event, the film's most reliable character, the priest, declares: "A man has been murdered." He continues to stress the horror of this crime, unparalleled by any other, and does not dedicate a single word to the woman's rape. On the contrary, the emphasized horror of the man's death implies the woman's extreme culpability. Unseen and unheard by legal and social tribunals, the rape is easily denied by the rapist and explained through underlying misogynistic myths.

Despite its isolation of the woman in all levels of narration, despite her subjection to two tribunals composed exclusively of men, the film neutralizes the men's gender and the masculinity of the judging community. The acts of judging the woman and silencing her story constitute the men on-screen as a judging, masculine community. Yet, by neutralizing the men's gender the film prevents the viewer from considering the fact that the judging community is entirely masculine and that masculine screening norms may be silencing the woman's story, thereby luring the viewer to join the masculine community on-screen.

The man's death and the woman's guilt are judged, throughout the film, by five on-screen male characters (joined by the unseen male judge) who constitute the film's fictional community. Each of these male characters reviews and evaluates the woman's behavior and moral character. Sharing and legitimizing each other's masculine point of view, masculine life experience, and masculine common sense, their judgment of the rape, the death, and the woman is very much gender based. At the same time, neither the woman nor any of the men or events are interpreted or judged—or even narrated—by any female character from a woman's point of view. The woman is not invited to accuse or judge but merely to defend herself. No other woman except the medium exists within the film's fictional world, and she speaks with the dead samurai's voice, hatefully condemning his wife. The visual appearance of the feminine body actually makes this condemnation even more powerful, as if it were being made by both the samurai and the woman giving him voice. The only other woman who appeared in Akutagawa's story, the woman's mother, who testified to her daughter's impeccable moral character, is the only original character missing from the film. Her testimony must have been considered irrelevant, hence inadmissible.

Each of the film's male characters is portrayed as a generic, allegorical representative of a professional and social class: The samurai stands for the warriors, the woodcutter for the working class, Tajomaru for the outlaws, and the priest for the church. (The policeman stands for state officials.) Stressing their different social affiliations, the film blurs their common gender. Stressing their differing social points of view, the film does not acknowledge the predominance of their underlying bond. The men are thus never presented as a gender-based group, sharing a common interest as well as a common bias in relation to the woman, the rape, and her experience of it.

The woman, on the other hand, as a single, generic woman, does become the allegorical everywoman, Eve. Unlike the men, she is presented as "woman," a gender-based class, and "wife," a man's woman. "Woman" is in fact on trial before a community of men who share men's reason, perceptions, and anxieties regarding women and womanhood. It is this community that the implied viewer is invited to join as another judging man. Yet the film's community is presented as human rather than masculine. Just as the impact of the judging men's gender cannot be articulated before the film's court of law or judging community, and is inadmissible in both the (fictional) legal and social discourses, so it is also excluded by the film's cinematic judgment.

While depicting how the process of passing judgment (over a woman) facilitates the creation of a (masculine) community on-screen, *Rashomon* also mirrors this phenomenon, illustrating how (a judging) film similarly creates a community of men off-screen. *Rashomon*'s cinematic judgment blurs the distinction between men on- and off-screen, inviting them all to participate in a single masculine judging community. Associated with the film's fictional judge and community of "reasonable men," the viewer is seduced into sympathizing with the film's fictional judgments and actively participating in the text's cinematic judgment.

Denied the opportunity to hear the woman's untold story, the viewer is turned into an accomplice in the silencing conspiracy that reaffirms the masculine community. The viewer is trained not to hear untold, undesirable stories but rather to pass judgment based exclusively on those deemed legitimate. The film's active silencing denies the viewer the opportunity to realize the potential existence of such voices. And, as suggested by the film itself, the social significance of such a sociocultural and legal silencing is powerful indeed.

It is interesting to note that the original, medieval Japanese tale consisted only of a woman's rape and not a man's death. Having raped the woman, the outlaw leaves, and the woman, supported by the text, accuses her husband of a greed that caused her violation (Goodwin 1994, 199–200). In contrast, Richie reports the following anecdote: "Once asked why he thought that *Rashomon* had become so popular, both in Japan and abroad, [Kurosawa] answered: 'Well, you see . . . it's about this rape.' Everyone laughed." (1996, 75, ellipses in original).

Transcending the film's skeptical cynicism, the epilogue offers a reassuring confirmation of human decency and the triumph of virtue and altruism. Strikingly, in this uplifting vision of a reformed world, women are missing. As the meek, compassionate Buddhist priest replaces the honor-driven samurai, the woodcutter replaces the woman. Carrying the baby, he is the film's new improved mother image. Woman herself is not redeemed, and has no place in the film's utopian future society. Honor culture, selfishness, and cynicism are all criticized, but not so misogyny, and the viewer is not invited to rethink misogynist attitudes invoked in earlier stages of the film.

To add yet another theological allusion, Rashomon's epilogue leaves us with a vision of a masculine Trinity: Father (woodcutter), Son (baby), and Holy Priest. Accustomed to the masculinity of holy ruling trinities, we tend to be blind to their gender and its significance. Nevertheless, like the judging community at the gate, this holy community's gender is, of course, not value free. Significantly, the epilogue's holy trinity is not supplemented by a virgin mother or any other notion of femininity. Motherhood is fully appropriated and merged into the male father figure.

While restricting the discussion to Rashomon's place in Western culture, it is hard to resist a brief reference to its specific, historical context. As James Davidson (1987) notes, Rashomon was released five years after Japan's deeply traumatic defeat in World War II, as the country was struggling to repress its humiliation and readjust to its new, Americanized identity. Davidson's reading suggests that, viewed against this background, Tajomaru's powerful, savage image may be read as symbolizing the conquering West (specifically the United States), whereas the samurai and woman can be viewed as standing for traditional, defeated, devastated Japan. In this framework, I suggest that the priest, woodcutter, and commoner must be interpreted as contemporary, post–World War II Japan.

Davidson argues that Rashomon may have been viewed as expressing an accusation of both samurai and woman, stating that Japan's defeat was facilitated by the weakness of its traditional culture. In light of this chapter's discussion, the film may be read as suggesting that it was Japanese culture's "flawed femininity" that brought about the national humiliation and devastation. Had Japan fought to the bitter end, committing collective suicide, so to speak, rather than corroborating with its "violation" by the foreign, Western brute, its honorable heritage would have been spared. The samurai erred in wrongly following Tajomaru and entering into a no-win situation. But it was the woman's shameful betrayal of her cultural feminine duties that brought about the ultimate humiliation.

Not to push this too far, seen in this light, the film's epilogue's optimistic presentation of a future free of both honor and women is telling. More significantly, this historical perspective suggests that as Japan was beginning to create its new, modern identity, it embraced deep-rooted, traditional, androcentric, and misogynist notions of women and sexual guilt. This may have been viewed as cultural resistance and defiance of imposed, Western ideas of sex equality. In fact, as the film's popularity in the West clearly demonstrates, this attitude may have served as a bridge, linking traditional Japanese culture with a Western patriarchal worldview.

Postscript: Reading Against the Grain

Having offered a feminist law-and-film critique of Rashomon, I would like to conclude by suggesting an alternative feminist strategy: reading it against the grain. Reading against the grain is a subversive tactic, which does not aim to expose or critique the invitation extended by the text to its viewer through its implied reader (as this chapter has done so far). In reading against the grain, a resistant reader refuses a text's invitation, consciously choosing to impose an interpretation that although based on textual elements—undercuts the text's message and substitutes it for a distinctly different one. Such a reading uses textual elements out of context, thus performing "deconstruction," that is, a reading of the text against itself. A reading against the grain is particularly useful when the reader feels attachment or commitment to a text (which may be canonical in some respect) and rather than critique it the reader wishes to "redeem" it by creating a new meaning for it. It seems only right to conclude a discussion of Rashomon's underlying, absolute message with a counter-reading of the text, deconstructing my own reading and redeeming the film's manifest message.

Read against the grain, from the standpoint of the film's resistant viewer who refuses to accept the role of the implied viewer offered by the film, Rashomon is a story of men's weakness, selfishness, and greediness and a woman's courageous resistance and survival against all odds. In Rashomon, men are self-serving and inconsiderate of others' needs. They treat woman as property, objectifying and commodifying her. They see her value only in each other's eyes: Only at the sight of her fear for her husband does Tajomaru want her for himself, and only in the arms of Tajomaru does the samurai see his wife's beauty. Once one man expresses disinterest in her, so does the other. Woman in Rashomon is oppressed, isolated, and silenced. Yet, despite a thoroughly hostile environment, she resists and survives. Physically attacked, she fights for her life and autonomy; overpowered and violated, she does not give in but chooses to pull herself together and go on. Always emotional, well in touch with her feelings, she is thoroughly human.

Approaching her husband after her violation, she is able to forgive him, feel compassion for his suffering, and offer him intimacy and support in the depth of despair. Faced with his betrayal, she has no words to express her pain and accusation, no voice to speak her words, no community to share experiences; yet she does not surrender. Faced only with a system of meaning that dismisses and dehumanizes her, she maintains her dignity by manipulating the system and turning it against itself. Above all, in spite of her loneliness, victimization, and cruel condemnation, in spite of the explicit demand that she sacrifice herself for others, she chooses life. She refuses to die, to be silenced, and to be concealed. She resists and survives.

By using the powerful image of the medium, the film calls attention to woman's silenced voice in a male supremacist world. The medium has a woman's body, yet she speaks the samurai's words, in his own voice, presenting his point of view and serving his interests (at the expense of his wife's). In service of the system (the legal authorities judging a woman), the medium is a woman's body telling a man's story in his own voice.[7]

Although the two actresses, Machiko Kyo and Fumiko Homma, may not resemble each other physically, they are both traditionally made-up to such a degree that it is almost hard to tell them apart. Their faces are whitened, and their eyebrows are plucked, as their culture's code dictates, imposing and stressing the similarities between them—constructing each and both as "woman." And, indeed, much as the medium (a female body) speaks with a man's voice, telling his story, accepting his truth, and serving his interests (even at a woman's expense), so does the film's woman protagonist. She lends her body and mouth to the ruling social class, but this does not make either the voice she produces or the story she tells "her own."

Rashomon is a new, revolutionary retelling of the ancient Eden myth. In *Rashomon*'s tale, it is man who is easily tempted by the lurking male snake, who offers him phallic, deadly toys. Man's greed, his self-assuredness, weakness, and irresponsibility lead to his temptation and fall. Leaving woman to be victimized by another self-serving man, he refuses to accept responsibility, blaming his own misfortune, as well as the woman's, on her. Proud, he is unable to accept her compassion and forgiveness, nor offer her support, thus destroying hope for intimacy and closeness. In Kurosawa's epilogue, the samurai, representing honor-based manhood, is replaced with the asexual priest. Feminine values of love, compassion, and motherhood are portrayed as the way to a better world.

Pandora's Box 2

(Germany, 1928)

EXORCISING PANDORA-LILITH IN THE WEIMAR REPUBLIC

A distinguished member of the "classic silents" section in contemporary video stores, *Pandora's Box* is hailed by its distributors as "a masterpiece of the silent era, a momentous meeting of director [G. W. Pabst] and star . . . American actress Louise Brooks, the epitome of the modern woman of the 1920s." The videotape's back cover goes on to declare that together Pabst and Brooks "produced a startling sex tragedy and an unorthodox *femme fatale*, who is the true victim—of her own carnality and German upper-class morality." In this compelling and prevalent view of the film, "Brooks projects an animal beauty of a woman who sees the world as her sexual playground, unconscious of the havoc she wreaks on the lives of her lovers." (See also Eisner 1969).

Lulu, the unforgettable, alluring heroine of *Pandora's Box*, was created by playwright Frank Wedekind at the end of the nineteenth century and later embraced by film director Pabst (Littau 1995, 888 n. 2). In his comprehensive, insightful analysis of the film, Thomas Elsaesser accurately determines that Lulu "belongs to the traditions of the *femme fatale*, the sexually alluring but remote woman, through whom men experience the irrational, obsessional, and ultimately destructive force of female sexuality" (1986, 40). Mary Ann Doane, in an equally illuminating discussion, describes Wedekind's work as "pro-sexual" and "anti-feminist": "Influenced by Nietzsche, opposed to the women's emancipation movement because it sought to annihilate the specificity of female sexuality (which he linked to a primitive animal nature), Wedekind fought against bourgeois repression in his works and was continually pursued by censorship and accusations of pornography" (1991, 145).

Vibrant, decadent Weimar Germany was the right time and place to embrace and experiment with Wedekind's fatal Lulu.

The film version of *Pandora's Box* is a cultural product of one of the most dramatic and traumatic episodes in contemporary history. Struggling to survive in the shadow of the 1919 Versailles Peace Treaty, the Weimar Republic was haunted by a deep sense of shame and humiliation that was experienced as an unbearable stain on the national "masculinity." Whether or not this collective, honor-based sense was the main factor driving the political developments that changed the world, it was clearly a significant component (Peukert 1989, 42). (In 1945, acknowledging the horrors of its recent past, the new West German Republic was the first modern country to establish human dignity as the fundamental value at the heart of its new constitution. Four years later, the United Nations followed its lead.)

Offering a gallery of one-dimensional feminine characters, *Pandora's Box* reflects and perpetuates a host of traditional cultural stereotypes. Women, in this film, are a repressed, devoted daughter (and potentially wife), an angelic incarnation of the sexless, nurturing Madonna, a pathetic, grotesque feminist lesbian, and the dark, fatal Lulu. Portraying Lulu as the dual personification of Pandora and Lilith, the film constructs her as a guilty object that must be exterminated in defense of social order, stability, and collective survival. Despite the film's avant-garde and decadent rebelliousness, it perpetuates these traditional, honor-compatible images, along with their long-standing misogynistic implications and moralistic connotations. Concomitantly, the film mirrors and upholds its fictional, on-screen legal process, which explicitly translates the patriarchal condemnation of the sexual woman into legal guilt.

Film Synopsis

Pandora's Box opens with a visit paid by Dr. Ludwig Schoen (played by Fritz Kortne and described in the subtitle as "a prominent newspaper owner") to his young, stunningly attractive, mistress, Lulu, at her luxurious apartment.

(Among the items in Lulu's apartment, two stand out and appear in numerous shots, often behind Lulu's image: a portrait of Lulu as a weeping clown, which also appeared in the play, and a large, eight-branched menorah, which is the film's innovation). The agonizing Dr. Schoen informs Lulu that, since their scandalous relationship is ruining his career, they must break up and that he is marrying another woman. Lulu declares, "You will have to kill me if you want to get away from me." She lures Schoen to make love to her, but the scene is interrupted when he discovers the shabby Schigolch (Carl Goetz) hiding on the balcony. (The subtitle describes him as "a disreputable old man who poses as Lulu's father to exploit her.") Lulu introduces Schigolch as her "first friend," and Schoen leaves humiliated and infuriated. Lulu, unmoved, proceeds to entertain Schigolch's friend, Rodrigo, and plans an acrobatic performance with him.

In the following scene, in the Schoen office building, we learn that Dr. Schoen's son Alwa (Franz Lederer), "a young playwright," and his costume designer, Countess Geschwitz (Alice Roberts), an artist and a lesbian, are both infatuated with Lulu, who willingly flirts with them both. Appealing to his father on Lulu's behalf, Alwa is warned by Dr. Schoen: "My boy, watch out for this girl!" Still, Schoen encourages Alwa to feature Lulu in his new production and promises to support it through his newspaper.

At the opening night, as Lulu is preparing for her performance, Dr. Schoen arrives backstage with his respectable fiancée, Charlotte Marie Adelaide, the young daughter of the minister of the interior. Throwing a tantrum, Lulu refuses to perform in the presence of her successor. Schoen pulls her into a side room, attempting to force her to continue with the show. Instead, Lulu seduces him. Enter Alwa and Charlotte. They are dumbfounded. Lulu smiles victoriously and leaves for her performance. Looking like a man facing his death, Dr. Schoen says with resignation: "This is my execution."

The next scene depicts Schoen's and Lulu's wedding party in the Schoen residence. Among the distinguished guests are the notorious Schigolch, Rodrigo, and the countess, who clings to Lulu in desperate jealousy, provoking Schoen's angry intervention. Later, finding Lulu entwined on her bridal bed with Schigolch (who, together with Rodrigo, attempted to cover the bed with roses), Schoen pulls out his gun and chases Schigolch and Rodrigo out of his house in a scandalous public scene. His respectable friends attempt to comfort him, leaving the place silently. Heading back to his bedroom, Schoen finds Alwa lovingly resting his head in Lulu's lap, and chases him away.

Schoen approaches Lulu, who is admiring her reflection in the bedroom mirror. Forcing his gun into her hand, he demands: "Take it. Kill yourself . . . it is the only way to save us both" (all ellipses in quotations from the film are original). Terrified, Lulu refuses to accept the gun, and in the struggle the gun goes off, shooting Dr. Schoen. As Alwa enters the room, his father's last words are, "Beware, Alwa, you are next."[1]

In the courtroom, the defense attorney summarizes, "Honored Court: in a rapid series of pictures I have shown you a fearful destiny. Gentlemen of the Jury, look upon this woman. Have I now shown you that this woman committed no murder . . . that her husband was the victim of a disastrous chain of circumstances? No, this unfortunate is no murderess. You must acquit her, for she is innocent."[2]

In reply, the prosecutor contends: "Honored Court, Gentlemen of the Jury! The Greek Gods created a woman: Pandora. She was beautiful, enticing, well versed in the infatuating arts of flattery . . ." Taken by Lulu's irresistible smile directed at him, the prosecutor is utterly confused, and struggles to regain self-control. Looking away from her, he continues: "But the Gods also gave her a casket in which they locked up all the evil in the world. The heedless woman opened the box and disaster overcame us! The defense chooses to present the accused as a persecuted innocent . . . I call her Pandora, for through her all these evils overcame Dr. Schoen! I have nothing more to add. I demand the death penalty."

As Lulu faints, the jury leaves to deliberate and the excited audience discusses the scandalous case. The countess approaches the prosecutor, shouting: "Mr. Prosecutor, do you know what would have become of your wife if she had had to spend all the nights of her childhood in cafes and cabarets?"

The jury finds Lulu guilty of manslaughter and condemns her to five years in prison.[3] She is smuggled out of the courthouse by a crowd organized by her friends (Schigolch, Rodrigo, and the countess).[4] Back in Schoen's house, she cheerfully prepares a bath, indulging in reading fashion magazines. When a horrified Alwa reproaches her for her heartless conduct, she calls the Ministry of Justice to give herself up. Falling into the trap, Alwa stops her, succumbs to her seduction, and joins her in her journey abroad, which is made possible by the countess's self-sacrificing gesture of furnishing Lulu with her own passport.

On a gambling ship, Alwa loses his (and the countess's) money as Lulu is blackmailed and almost sold to a brothel in Egypt by "white slave" traders. Attempting to appease Rodrigo, who is also blackmailing her, Lulu begs the countess to spend the evening with him. In Rodrigo's cabin, he sexually attacks the countess, who shoots him to death and is captured by the police. Lulu escapes, and arrives in London, together with Alwa and Schigolch. Desolate, the three share a bare, frozen attic, and, prompted by Schigolch, Lulu walks the foggy streets in search of a patron and income.

It is Christmas Eve, and the Salvation Army is offering warm drinks and holiday music by a Christmas tree.[5] A young, blond woman with starry eyes gently offers a lonely, sad-looking man a warm drink and a Christmas candle. Walking away, the man passes a big poster advising women that, for some time, a man with incredibly small, unsteady eyes has been luring women to dark areas and murdering them.

Lulu encounters this man—who is Jack the Ripper—and unwittingly solicits him to come up to her room. Jack warns her that he has no money, but she insists, saying he should come anyway, since she likes him. Climbing the stairs, Jack secretly disposes of a knife he carries in his pocket. As he enters the attic with Lulu, Schigolch pulls heartbroken Alwa away. Schigolch joins a celebrating crowd in a local bar, leaving Alwa weeping on the street.

In the attic, Jack and Lulu embrace gently. Searching Jack's pockets for money, Lulu finds the Christmas candle and lights it. Jack holds her in his arms, but when his small, unsteady eyes are caught by the flickering light, he is possessed, his face stiffens, he seems to be taken over by an external power, and his hand grabs a bread knife. Still embraced in Jack's arms, we see Lulu's hand slowly loosening its grip on the man, silently drooping lifeless. As Jack leaves the building, he passes Schigolch, happily eating a Christmas pudding with a local woman, and Alwa, a broken young man, who aimlessly joins the Salvation Army's Christmas parade.

Cinematic Judgment by Archetypes

Since early Christianity, womanhood has been strictly divided into three archetypal models. As Ruether phrased it, the church fathers' "depersonalized view of sexual relations gives three basic images of the possibilities of woman . . . woman as whore, woman as wife, and woman as virgin" (1974, 163). The archetypal woman as virgin is Mary, the nonsexual, mothering Madonna; her human personifications are nuns and other holy women. The archetypal woman as wife is the ideal image of domesticated, subservient post-Eden Eve. Eve, destined by God's punishment to serve her husband and bear his sons, is the appropriate role model for all women, "Eve's daughters." The archetypal woman as whore is Lilith, "The Big Whore."

The mythological feminine archetype of Lilith grew in Jewish mythology, and was later appropriated, like Eve, by Christian European culture. In Jewish mythology, Lilith was the first woman and Adam's first wife, who left Eden refusing to surrender to Adam's sexual rule. Choosing Satan as her sexual partner, she became the queen of devils. With dark hair, fiery eyes, and magnificent beauty, she is smart, strong, free, eternally young, and sexually irresistible to men. Since the earliest of days, she has been roaming the world, luring weak men into ecstatic sexual conduct, robbing them of control over their semen, and using it to procreate her own devilish offspring. Abhorring patriarchal domesticity, Lilith comes between husband and wife, destroying their blissful matrimonial stability and murdering their young offspring.[6] Although desired by men, Lilith is feared and hated, an outcast from normative society.

The nineteenth century gave rise to a fourth archetype—"the new woman" —which developed with women's rising requests for citizenship, independence, recognition as reasonable human beings, economic autonomy, and legal rights. Breaking with traditional, patriarchal social order, "new women" were conceived as a threat to social stability, to existing social and legal norms, to family structure and values, and to men's governance in both the private and public spheres (Reynolds and Humble 1993, 6; Ireland 1989). In response to this threat, the image of the new woman was demonized and ridiculed through the creation of the familiar caricature of a brainy, unattractive woman, nonfeminine and sexually deprived. The new woman was denounced as "man hating," self-centered, antisocial, and antisexual. To explain her independence from men away as deviance, she was portrayed as a "lesbian," in the popular, demeaning sense of being uninterested in men and uninteresting to them. *Lesbianism*, in this context, also connotes castration of men. Since the nineteenth century, this image of the man-hating, castrating, nonfeminine, lesbian feminist has taken on the dimensions of a full-blown cultural archetype. She is closely linked with the ancient mythological image of Medusa, the deadly Gorgon.[7]

Clearly, these feminine archetypes reflect and perpetuate women's restrictive roles in patriarchy. The Madonna image is the ultimate ideal, reserved for the very few revered women who overcome their femininity and carnality, dedicating themselves to the superior sphere of the sacred. Failing to live up to the unachievable standards of this role model, most women are branded as fallen, carnal, and sinful. As such, the archetype of the idealized Eve offers them a "second best" role: the subservient wife and mother, meekly accepting her original sin, as well as the divine punishment that followed. The two negative archetypes, those of Lilith and the lesbian feminist, warn women of the lonely fate of women who defy their secondary, domestic role, seeking sexual autonomy or social liberation.

The close affinity between the Lilith and the lesbian feminist archetypes is not coincidental. In Jewish lore, as well as in earlier periods in Western culture, Lilith was smart, strong, independent, and unruly, as well as uninhibited, orgasmic, and irresistibly attractive to men. In mediaeval and Renaissance Europe she was associated with witches, who were perceived as both hypersexual and socially independent (Kamir 2001, chapter 3). In contemporary cultural imagery, Lilith is split in two. No longer the dangerously beguiling woman who unites strength, intelligence, and sexuality, she instead becomes either the femme fatale or the brainy man-hater. These two images warn women both against free exploration of their sexuality and against demanding social equality and power.

Rashomon features a single, allegorical everywoman, who combines a host of features stereotypically associated with women and femininity. *Pandora's Box* divides its archetypal feminine images among four characters: the Salvation Army woman, Charlotte Marie Adelaide, Countess Geschwitz, and Lulu. Significantly, while the filmmakers eliminated several of the characters from the original play, they created two of the four women characters, the Salvation Army woman and Dr. Schoen's fiancée.

The unnamed Salvation Army woman is the image of charitable pity and compassion. Blonde, modest, her eyes glowing with kindness, she offers lonely strangers warmth, unquestioning acceptance, nourishment, and hope, asking for nothing in return. Wholly good and pure, she touches even the most deviant man's heart, comforting his lost soul and bringing out the best in him. Utterly sexless and thoroughly mothering, an element of Christmas Eve, she is the personification of Mother Mary, the Madonna. Interestingly, she is a "foreigner," that is, a Londoner (presumably British), perhaps implying that spiritual salvation, as well as pure holy femininity, are qualities foreign to contemporary Germany. She is also the only woman who is present, to some extent, at the film's end. The film's end features no women; Lulu is dead, the Countess imprisoned, and Charlotte Marie Adelaide forgotten. It is Alwa, the remaining survivor, that the camera follows as he joins the Christmas Parade. The Salvation Army woman is vaguely present in the marching parade, but as an abstract spirit of holy femininity.

Charlotte Marie Adelaide is the well-bred, honorable daughter and suitable wife. Fair, quietly pretty, modest, and conservatively dressed, Charlotte Marie Adelaide treats her father, the minister of the interior, with gentle courtesy and affection. But when he slights her future husband's honor, suggesting that his unworthy behavior renders the marriage impossible, she politely but firmly sides with her future husband, manifesting her unquestioning loyalty to him without defying her devotion to her father. Tactfully and graciously she ignores her father's remark, demonstrating impeccable reservation, moderation, and due respect. Her dreamy smile, when thinking of her fiancé, testifies to her appropriate affection towards him; her refusal to stoop to petty sexual gossip elevates her beyond carnal lust, dishonorable suspicion, and base jealousy.

On the opening night of Lulu's show, she appropriately arrives on the scene with her fiancé. In sharp contrast with Lulu and the other actresses, her attire is conservative and elegant. Unobserved, she curiously but gracefully eyes Lulu, her gaze lacking any evidence of jealousy or resentment. Finding her fiancé in a compromising situation with Lulu, she maintains her poise, avoiding public scandal and refraining from manifesting her feelings. Wholesome, refined, and predictable, she is the living image of the ideal, domesticated, supportive (post-Eden) Eve.

Slightly more intriguing, Countess Geschwitz represents the modern addition to the patriarchal pantheon of feminine archetypes: the lesbian feminist. The Countess demonstrates every characteristic that portrays her as "nonfeminine" and "manly": she is strong, independent, talented, professional, economically self-reliant, opinionated, outspoken, direct, brave, loyal, and reliable. Refusing to defer to men or to cater to their desires, she is "man-hating" and a lesbian. The film's association of this image with aristocracy is notable: Countess Geschwitz is the film's single blue-blooded character. From this angle, her linkage with lower-class artists (like Rodrigo) and disreputable, low-life characters (like Schigolch) is noteworthy, especially as this "group" is posed as threatening and subverting upper-class bourgeoisie and its hegemonic morals. Particularly significant is the fact that the countess's love for Lulu is what associates her with Schigolch, Rodrigo, and their crowd. Interestingly, the countess is not judged for her deviation from the appropriate feminine role; she is merely mocked and pitied for her unattractiveness to men and blind infatuation with Lulu.[8]

Indeed, the countess is wholly devoted to her beloved Lulu. Yet her sexual infatuation with Lulu, as well as Lulu's heartless exploitation of her affections in the second part of the film, preclude the possibility of true friendship between them. This is symptomatic of the treatment of relationships between women in *Pandora's Box*. The film's apparent abundance and diversity of female characters is misleading. The film's women—more accurately its stereotypes of women—do not meet, interact, share experiences, or support each other. Not one of them has a close friend or a supportive mother. Each is isolated and confined to her archetypal realm. The countess's love and loyalty for Lulu are not reciprocated.

Cinematic Judgment by Constructing Pandora-Lilith as a Guilty Object

Lulu's moniker (in clear contrast with the respectable name the film bestowed on Charlotte Marie Adelaide) links her with a familiar tribe of feminine characters, labeled by their very names as dangerously sexual: Delilah, Lola, Lolita, Lilly, Lilah. All these sexual feminine characters are marked as affiliated with their mythological ancestor, the archetypal Lilith.[9] Indeed, like her predecessor, Lulu is dark and sexual. Her appeal, a vigorous natural force, is overpowering, irresistible, and deadly. She defies patriarchal authority, disregards social standards and norms, and disrupts tradition, rules, and regulations. Individualistic and self-centered, she pursues her needs and desires, placing them before other social values and refusing to sacrifice them for any cause. Like Lilith, she comes between man and his appropriate wife, destroying their hope for domesticity, stability, procreation, and social conformity.

Unlike Charlotte Marie Adelaide, Lulu has neither family ties nor social status (Elsaesser 1986, 41); she has no roots and belongs to no class, profession, ideology, or culture. Unlike the good daughter and potential wife, she is neither loyal nor dependable; neither decent nor trustworthy; neither respectful nor honorable. Devoid of even the slightest hint of compassion, empathy, or capacity to nurture, she lacks any feature culturally associated with good motherhood and femininity. Strikingly, Lulu cannot be tied down because she is thoroughly unattached and uncommitted in the deepest, existential sense. She does not develop genuine feelings for anyone or anything other than herself.[10] She is equally flirtatious with and utterly indifferent to everyone around her. She flirts with them, seduces them, uses them to satisfy her needs and desires, and carelessly moves on.

Read against the archetypal Lilith, Lulu lacks the powerful characteristics the film awards the countess: "manly" strength, wisdom, independence, and self-reliance. Instead, the film replaces these attributes with Lulu's instinctual manipulation of people and situations, her parasitic survival skills and her instinctive abuse of people's vulnerabilities. These unsympathetic traits are undercut by a sense of frivolous apathy and passivity. Lulu never initiates; she merely responds, spontaneously, making the most of every new situation she finds herself in.

This deterministic, passive aspect of Lulu's character is not modeled on Lilith. As the film's title suggests, Lulu inherited these qualities from another mythological character: Pandora.[11] Unlike Lilith, Pandora is neither powerful nor rebellious; she is merely a lovely, enticing vehicle sent to punish men for their hubris and disrespect for the gods. Pandora's role in the divine scheme was passive and tragic: she was set up to unwittingly carry and spread disaster. Her only relevant trait was innocent curiosity, her only action opening the box. Pandora was shrewdly devised by the vengeful gods as a Trojan horse, crafted to trigger human action that would backfire and devastate the actors. Like the Trojan horse, she was a pretty object, incapable of choice, and thus beyond the realm of good and evil or moral judgment.

By making Lulu a passive conduit of tragedy, *Pandora's Box* castrates the powerful image of Lilith, diminishing it to a Pandora-Lilith character. This paradoxical combination renders Lulu a guilty object.

This combination of archetypal images is molded, in *Pandora's Box*, into the image of a woman who "is of a certain kind," yet, at the same time, acts in defiance of the proper social place for "her kind," threatening the social order. As Dr. Schoen states at an early stage, framing the unfolding chain of events: "Men don't marry such women, it would be suicide." Lulu is "such a woman": sexual, classless, unmarriable. This is her predetermined nature, beyond good and evil; her Pandora, "object" side. But additionally, she actively steps out of the place society designated for "her kind," coming between Schoen and his appropriate fiancée, forcing him to marry her instead of the right woman. This behavior is neither passive nor Pandora-like; it is active and Lilith-like, rendering Lulu guilty of overstepping her boundaries, undermining social order, and "leading" the respectable Dr. Schoen to his predicted "suicide." The Pandora-Lilith guilty object thus takes the form of a wickedly sexual woman overstepping her proper social role.[12]

The film's unreflective and uncritical construction of Lulu as a Pandora-Lilith character constitutes, in itself, a cinematic judgment. As a Pandora-Lilith character, Lulu is inherently deadly, endangering men, matrimonial couplehood, patriarchal family, and social order. She subverts the class hierarchy and the morals of the ruling bourgeoisie. In the context of the film's social reality, Lulu is a severe threat to the fragile social order, which barely keeps anarchy and disaster at bay. She must be stopped.

Condemnation through Point of View

Up to the scene of Dr. Schoen's death, his is the film's only voice of reason and common sense, systematically introducing and interpreting Lulu to the viewer. "Men don't marry such women, it would be suicide," he teaches, warning young Alwa: "My boy, watch out for this girl!" In the backstage scene, he predicts: "This is my execution," and his dying words are: "Beware, Alwa, you are next." In every one of these scenes, Dr. Schoen offers the exclusive interpretation of events, and it is his interpretations and predictions that are consistently proven accurate. This constructs him as a reliable narrator; his is the indisputable perspective on Lulu.

In taking this stand, the film chooses to side with Schoen's worldview, while neutralizing and concealing its subjective, value-laden bias. The film could have allowed Alwa and Lulu to respond to Schoen's statements and express alternative views. Alwa could have suggested that marrying "such women" as Lulu is only "suicide" if men spinelessly give in to hypocritical social standards. He could have added that not marrying "such women" is "murder" since, once "used" and abandoned, women like Lulu have no future or hope. Lulu could have been allowed to reply (as she amply does in Wedekind's plays) that if being found out by his fiancée is Schoen's "execution," it is entirely his own doing. A man of integrity would not have kept a hidden mistress when engaged to another woman. He would have done the right and honorable thing by both women by admitting to his true desires, breaking off the engagement, rising above public gossip and spite, and marrying the mistress. And if (as the film's sharp cut from the backstage scene to the wedding scene suggests) it is marrying Lulu that he considers his "execution," or the "suicide" he mentioned earlier, Lulu could have added that this, too, is entirely Schoen's own doing. The "ruin" that he may have envisioned as resulting from marrying Lulu was entirely premised on his own weakness in the face of public opinion, and his disingenuous, hypocritical claim for an honorable reputation.

Had the film contained such alternative voices (in the form of additional subtitles), Schoen's voice would not have been so disproportionately privileged. Furthermore, the viewer would have been invited to construe the narrated events in light of competing interpretations. In *Pandora's Box*, the viewer is consistently offered a single interpretation of Schoen's death: Lulu's nature as a femme fatale and her rebellious determination to have him sealed his fate, as marrying such a woman is inherently deadly. This interpretation exonerates Schoen, his choices throughout the relationship, and his jealous, honor-driven conduct at the wedding party. An alternative perspective could have invited the viewer to consider that perhaps it was Schoen's undignified and undignifying treatment of Lulu during their relationship, and his honor-crazed behavior at the wedding party, that caused all the scandalous, humiliating scenes, drove him to chase away his own son, and finally brought him to demand his wife's suicide, leading to his own death.

In *Rashomon*, the woman's guilt lies in the combination of her alluring sexuality and her refusal to kill herself. Only in killing herself could the woman save her husband's honor and constitute her own purity and worth. Her choice to live deems her guilty. *Pandora's Box* manifests the exact same honor-based values and social expectations. Just like the samurai, Dr. Schoen demands, "Kill yourself, it is the only way to save both of us." Just like *Rashomon*, *Pandora's Box* silently agrees. Privileging Schoen's perspective and worldview, the film thus shares and upholds it, condemning Lulu as a guilty object and exonerating Schoen's hypocritical, honor-driven conduct. The film neutralizes this moral position, depicting it as exclusive and value-free. In presenting Lulu to the viewer through Schoen's eyes, the film finds her guilty of his death before its on-screen fictional legal proceedings begin. To use Doane's words: "Lulu's guilt is a guilt which is not legalistic (particularly if this is viewed as a function of individual agency), but imagistic. She exemplifies the power accorded to images which aligns them with a malignant femininity . . . Within the film as a whole, femininity constitutes a danger which must be systematically eradicated" (1991, 154).

Archetypes in the Courtroom

As the scene of Dr. Schoen's death fades out, the film cuts to a close-up of Lulu's defense attorney facing the camera and viewer, and concluding: "Honored Court: in a rapid series of pictures I have shown you a fearful destiny. Gentlemen of the Jury, look upon this woman." The viewer is thus informed that all he has seen up to that point is "a rapid series of pictures" constituting the argument for Lulu's legal defense before the film's fictional court. Simultaneously, he realizes that he is being addressed by the on-screen attorney as the fictional court's jury; he is "officially" asked to weigh the evidence and pass judgment on Lulu. In other words, the viewer learns all at once that, as he was viewing the film and semiconsciously participating in its cinematic judgment of Lulu, he has also been operating as a participant in the film's on-screen, fictional legal proceedings, acting as her jury in following Lulu's attorney's narration. As cinematic and fictional judgments merge, the viewer understands that the cinematic judgment he has been conducting up to that point, guided by the film, is taking place within a legal context and is, thus, a legal judgment.

The whole courtroom sequence, including both "substance" and "form," is purely the film's original invention and is not based on Wedekind's plays, so that the viewer manipulations discussed here are strictly cinematic.

Learning that the story narrated by the film has been Lulu's defense, the viewer becomes aware that this must be the most favorable manner of presenting the facts by the defendant. In other words, the film informs its viewer that its narration, favoring Dr. Schoen's point of view and presenting Lulu as Pandora-Lilith, is the most lenient, sympathetic manner of viewing Lulu and the events leading to Dr. Schoen's death.

As he is coming to terms with these newly provided insights, the viewer is addressed by Lulu's prosecutor. Not disputing the facts presented by the defense attorney, the prosecutor does not even refer to witnesses or evidence that have not been introduced by the defense. Defense and prosecution, it seems, agree on the facts of the case. The dispute concerns their proper interpretation and the determination of the appropriate sanction. Lulu's defense suggests that the narrated events constitute a "disastrous chain of circumstances." The prosecution, arguing that Lulu is Pandora and that "through her all these evils overcame Dr. Schoen," demands the death penalty. The legal question, as presented by the film's fictional legal proceedings, is thus whether, based on the narrated facts, Lulu is Pandora and whether, if so, she should be executed.

In constructing its fictional legal proceedings in this manner, Pandora's Box seems to suggest that legal judgment is not concerned with the specific, "legalistic" details of a crime's actus reus (bad act) and mens rea (guilty mind). Legal issues and terms such as voluntariness (Lulu's control of her hand, seized by Schoen), self-defense, negligent killing, and provocation are never raised. Had the film been interested in judging Lulu based on the specific facts of the case, Lulu's attorney would have pointed out that no evidence was brought before the court that she actually held the gun in her hand, or, if she did, that it was not Schoen himself who caused the shot to be fired, using her hand to do so. Even if it were proven that her hand did freely pull the trigger, her attorney would have argued that she acted in a state of shock, that she was defending her life against Schoen's brutal attempt to cause her death, or, at the very least, that his demand that she kill herself provoked her to the extent of losing self-control.[13] But, although it introduces a dramatic courtroom sequence, *Pandora's Box* is not interested in legalistic argumentation or in detailed criminal judgment of Lulu's specific act. Lulu's trial, the film makes clear, revolves around her dangerous nature. Offering no critique of this position, nor any alternative view, the film seems to be embracing it as its popular jurisprudence.

According to *Pandora's Box*, legal judgment of a woman should not be restricted to the narrow question of whether or not she performed a specific prohibited act, possessing a prohibited state of mind. In the film's view, the appropriate way to judge a woman is by measuring her against cultural stereotypes and archetypal images. If she is found to be an incarnation of a dangerous feminine cultural image, she is a dangerous individual and should be found guilty.

Scope of Relevance and the Untold Story of Lulu's Victimization

Another crucial point on which the film's fictional legal system agrees with, mirrors, and upholds the film's cinematic judgment is the issue of relevance, that is: the determination of which facts are relevant to the judgment, and are thus to be included in the process of judgment. More specifically: what should be the starting point of the story reviewed by the judging body?

As suggested earlier, one obvious view would be to concentrate on the time of the killing. The story would then be: finding his son kneeling at Lulu's feet, his head in her lap, Dr. Schoen forced his gun into Lulu's hand, demanding that she kill herself. As she refused, a struggle ensued, a shot was fired, and Dr. Schoen was killed. This presentation, of course, is far more favorable to Lulu than the one offered by the film, as it precludes her identification as Pandora-Lilith, portraying Schoen's death as an outcome of a tragic accident caused by his jealousy.

An alternative approach would be to narrate Lulu's full history. This approach is briefly voiced in the film by the countess when she confronts the prosecutor, challenging: "Mr. Prosecutor, do you know what would have become of your wife if she had had to spend all the nights of her childhood in cafes and cabarets?"

Framed this way, Lulu's story would be that of a girl growing up in the terrible years that followed World War I, forced by poverty and starvation into a dreadful life of child prostitution, slavery, and abuse at the hands of men such as Schigolch and Dr. Schoen.[14] Surviving their ongoing sexual exploitation the only way she knew how, Lulu became hardened and transformed into the nameless, sexual object they raised her to be. Numbing all feeling, protecting her soul by detaching it from her body and burying it where it would not be tormented, Lulu survived by taking on the role dictated to her by her abusers' sexual fantasies. Learning to survive and make the best of the unbearable, degrading situations they presented her with, she became amoral and egotistical. Given her background and situation, given her country's catastrophic economic state and social instability, her livelihood depended completely on Dr. Schoen's financial support. Had he married another woman, Lulu would have been forced to walk the streets again, selling herself to patrons. Securing her position and holding him to his moral obligation to her was the courageous act of a desperate woman choosing to live, surviving in a harsh reality using the only means society allowed her. Furthermore, on the night of their wedding, she did nothing but entertain their guests as best she could, kindly rejecting their propositions. Dr. Schoen's attack of jealousy was an honor-based rage, and his violent demand that she commit suicide to save his honor was nothing short of attempted murder. She had every right to defend herself from his jealous rage, even at the cost of his life.

The story focusing on Lulu's dignity, abuse, and survival portrays Lulu as a victimized agent, heroically fighting for her life against all odds. Based on the countess's single sentence in the courtroom, this is the story that can be constructed when reading the cinematic text against its grain. In the film's second part, this subverting, resisting reading can find a condemnation of the social and legal systems' neglect and abandonment of women. Having escaped justice, outlawed and not protected by the law, Lulu becomes a sexual object of cynical, cruel trade. Men who offer her protection from the slave traders blackmail her, demanding all she has in return for not abandoning her to the slave market. A feminist reading of the film against its grain can see this bloodcurdling portrayal of Lulu's plight as a comment on women's inherent situation in society, and on Lulu's way of surviving exploitation. The blunt, explicit reality presented in the film's second part can be read as commenting on its first part, indicating that Schoen's "relationship" with Lulu, just like Schigolch's before him, was nothing but thinly disguised sexual blackmail. From her childhood, Lulu was always an "outlaw" in the sense of existing outside the protection of the legal system. For her, as for many women, life was always a "choice" between the slave traders and blackmailing men.

This is the story of Lulu's sexual victimization that the film could have presented, but chose not to. Just as *Rashomon* does not acknowledge the woman's rape, portraying it as "sex" and "adultery," so *Pandora's Box* is willfully blind to Lulu's prostitution, exploitation, and arguably continuous rape, presenting them as manifestations of her voluptuous, deviant, excessive sexuality. From this perspective it becomes clear that the film's choice to evaluate Lulu exclusively through Dr. Schoen's comments is no different from *Rashomon*'s presentation of the sexual encounter exclusively through Tajumaro's narrative.

Silencing the story of Lulu's victimization, the film chooses the scope of relevance that portrays Lulu in the worst possible light. Ignoring her lifelong prostitution and presenting her as a femme fatale by nature and a rebel by choice, the film invites its viewer to find her a dangerous individual. The double choice of this scope, by both film and fictional legal proceedings, presents it as indisputable and neutral.

Failure of the Legal Judgment and Appeal to Natural Law

In Wedekind's plays from the end of the nineteenth century and the beginning of the twentieth, Lulu is captured by the police, judged, convicted, and imprisoned. In the cinematic text from the Weimar Republic, the legal system fails to deal with Lulu. She is smuggled out of court, escaping punishment. The existing legal system, the film implies, cannot protect the public from the fatal threat posed by Pandora-Lilith. Escaping justice, she continues to be herself, spreading death and destruction and ruining Alwa, the countess, and Rodrigo, members of the upper-class bourgeoisie, the aristocracy, and the lower, artistic class. Witnessing Lulu's heartless manipulation of Alwa and the countess, following the heartbreaking deterioration of the young, once promising Alwa, the viewer is invited to share the film's conclusion that Lulu must be stopped.

On another level, the film seems to imply that Weimar's legal system cannot protect the fragile, struggling German society from the disastrous threat posed to it by the decadent "feminine" element poisoning it from within. It must be stopped by more powerful forces than the judiciary. The film goes a long way to construct Lulu's appropriate extermination. Chasing her out of the country, the film leads her to a distant, foreign land. Here, the film recruits a mythological figure, bigger than life, like Lulu herself, to overcome her ominous power and destroy her. More than three decades after his disappearance, the film revives the mythological killer of harlots, Jack the Ripper. When Wedekind composed *Pandora's Box*, in the years 1892–1906, Jack the Ripper was, at first, a contemporary reality and later a vivid memory. His deliberate cinematic revival in 1929 takes on different dimensions. Constructing him as a man seized by seizures, endowing him with small, unsteady eyes, the film suggests that only he, the savage man of the gutters who terrorizes the streets, can enforce the natural law and order so desperately needed to save the day. Only this raw, unpretentious man, uncorrupted by contemporary decadence and unashamed to face the ugly truth, can do what needs to be done. Unlike the gory, brutal murder scene in Wedekind's play (in which the countess is murdered together with Lulu), the film's short, suggestive allusion to Lulu's killing is soft, romantic, undisturbing. Her death seems gentle and right. In this context let me mention once again that neither the Jewish Menorah in Lulu's apartment nor the Christmas motif, which endow Lulu's death with a sense of an inevitable new beginning, redemption, and hope, appear in the turn of the century plays; they are innovations of the Weimar Republic cinematic text.

3 Blackmail

(England, 1929)

"On any reading, Blackmail is a key film," determines Charles Barr (1999, 78). Blackmail is remembered and cherished above all else as Hitchcock's and England's first (fully) talking film. As such, it is, indeed, spectacular.[1] From a feminist point of view, the film offers additional points of interest. Mentioning the familiar claim that "Hitchcock's work is prototypical of the extremely violent assaults on women that make up so much of our entertainment today," feminist film scholar Tania Modleski remarks that "this first British sound film specifically foregrounds the problems of woman's speaking" (1989, 17, 21). She notes that the film's female character is "one of the first in a long line of tormented blonde heroines that Hitchcock featured throughout his career" (18). She claims that "woman's sexual guilt, a major preoccupation in Hitchcock's films, is obviously not 'transferable' to men, and until such sexual asymmetry is recognized the real complexity of the theme of guilt in the films cannot be fully grasped" (25).

Charles Barr, too, stresses that Blackmail "retain[s] its place as a canonical text" and "a film far ahead of its time" thanks to its combination of cine-

matic sound experimentation and a penetrating discussion of "sexual politics in a patriarchal society" (1999, 78). Along similar lines, Robin Wood
stresses the film's "privileged status as the first of Hitchcock's guilty woman
films, a narrative pattern not taken up again until the move to Hollywood,
where it becomes so central to his work. The pattern—and its characterizing
ambiguities—is established in Blackmail with extraordinary completeness"
(1989, 251). This influential Hitchcockian pattern, as first set in this film,
highlights woman's guilt and conceals her victimization through combined
legal and cinematic tactics. The pattern may be dubbed a systematic cinematic
judgment of mostly young, mostly blonde women. This condemning judgment relies on the association of the female protagonists' sexuality with
crime, violence, danger, and/or social transgression. It further utilizes uncritical application of traditional, patriarchal conventions and the preclu-
sion of legal (and dignity-based) discussions that could have exonerated the
women.

In Blackmail, the budding sexuality of Alice, the film's young, blonde protagonist, is linked with the deaths of two men and the disgrace and humiliation of Alice's fiancé, who is also the film's male protagonist and its image
of law and order. Based on prevalent, misogynist prejudice and underlying
honor-based attitudes, the sexual woman linked with death is presumed guilty.
Her own victimization is denied. The film perpetuates this presumed guilt by
preventing any legal examination of the woman's relevant situation and conduct. By "threatening" to turn Alice over to the law and by dramatically
"saving" her from the legal procedure and its consequences, the film increases the viewer's unfounded feeling that she would have been found legally guilty and punished severely. In fact, however, she may well have been
exonerated even by the androcentric standards of criminal common law.

Blackmail was released in Britain shortly after the release of Pandora's Box in
Germany. Despite the obvious social, cultural, and political differences between the two societies in the 1920s, the androcentric, misogynist conventions—including honor-based notions, the tactic of judging and condemning
women through the application of traditional feminine stereotypes, the bitter
resentment towards the "new woman," the conceptualization of women's
sexual guilt and their cinematic judgment—are strikingly parallel in both
films, manifesting more similarities than differences.

Film Synopsis

Blackmail opens with a long silent sequence of the police arresting a working-class suspect. Having completed his day's work, Frank Webber (John Longden), a handsome Scotland Yard detective, meets his fiancée, Alice White (Anny Ondra). She is joking and laughing with the guard at the entrance to the Yard despite her annoyance at Frank, who has kept her waiting for half an hour. At the restaurant, Alice coquettishly changes her mind as to whether or not she will go to the movies with Frank and, when he leaves in anger, she joins another man, Mr. Crewe (Cyril Richard), with whom she has been flirting even while dining with Frank.

Walking her home, Crewe, an artist, invites Alice to visit his studio, just around the corner from her parents' shop and home. In the studio, Alice comes across a newly painted portrait of a mocking jester. Together with Crewe, she playfully sketches a female nude, signing her name at the bottom, and is childishly tempted by him to try on a tutu he keeps for models, as he sings "Miss Up-to-Date," accompanying himself on the piano. Alarmed when he kisses her, Alice declares her wish to leave, but as she tries to change back into her clothes, Crewe snatches her dress, grabs her, and pulls the resisting woman to his curtained bed.

A struggle takes place behind the closed curtains. Alice's hand, reaching out from behind the curtains, finds a bread knife placed by the bed; she seizes it, the veiled struggle continues, and when Alice slowly emerges from behind the curtains, holding the knife, Crewe's arm drops out lifeless. Crewe's painting of the laughing jester seems to be mocking her, and she tears at the picture. Alice spends the night walking the streets of London, and everything she sees turns, in her traumatized mind, into reminders of the stabbing and of the dead man's arm. She arrives home just in time to get under the covers as her mother enters the room with the morning tea, and removes the cover from Alice's caged bird. The incarcerated animal fills the air with its twitter.

At the breakfast table, Alice, still in shock, hears nothing but the word knife, and drops the bread knife attempting to slice the bread. Frank arrives and, inside a phone booth in Alice's father's tobacco shop, he shows Alice one of her gloves, which he found in Crewe's apartment. Interrupting their conversation, a stranger, Mr. Tracy (Donald Calthrop), shows the couple Alice's other glove, threatening to call Scotland Yard if Frank does not buy his silence. Tracy, who had also been blackmailing Crewe, was lurking in the shadows outside Crewe's home on the night of his death, and thus witnessed

Alice entering the studio. Over a long, tense breakfast, smug Tracy indulges in humiliating Frank.

The tables are turned when Frank is informed over the telephone that, based on the testimony of Crewe's landlady, Scotland Yard is searching for Tracy as the suspect for Crewe's murder. Frank locks Tracy in the dining room while waiting for his detective friends, rejecting Tracy's pleading to let him go and repeatedly silencing Alice, who tries to intervene, protesting against Frank's plot to frame Tracy for her crime. Upon the detectives' arrival, Tracy escapes through an open window, and a chase commences, echoing the film's opening sequence. This chase is interwoven with close-up shots of Alice, sitting tensely at a table, deliberating. "What started as a sequence of police action, with some of the 'documentary' overtones of the prologue, has been pulled back, as it were, within Alice's consciousness . . . Alice seems to be summoning up images of events which are also happening 'out there.' She could be imagining the pursuit, or seeing it by form of telepathy, or willing it or fearing it" (C. Barr 1999, 96).

Tracy finds himself at the British Museum, and, having climbed to the roof with the detectives close behind, he falls through a skylight to his death, just as Alice reaches her decision to confess and take responsibility for her crime. As she physically rises (from her seat) to the occasion, a shadow covers her neck. "This evokes the hanging that she thinks she is condemning herself to, stepping into Tracy's place, but it also evokes the death of Tracy—in effect, an execution" (C. Barr 1999, 96).

At Scotland Yard, Alice is about to confess to the chief inspector, but a telephone call interrupts her hesitant, tormented speech, and the chief inspector asks Frank to deal with the young lady. Their faces frozen, woman and man walk through the corridor. At the entrance, the guard jokingly warns Frank that if Alice solves the murder, Frank may lose his job to her. As the guard laughs wholeheartedly at his own joke, Frank attempts to join in, and Alice's tormented smile is a pitiful, painful sight. As she seems to be gasping for air, her eyes rest on the painted jester, seemingly pointing at her, and the film's final shot is of the laughing image being carried away down the hall.

Encoding Woman as Pandora-Eve and Denying Her Victimization

Alice White, the shopkeeper's blonde daughter, is, as her dull name suggests, far from being a Pandora-Lilith femme fatale in the dark Lulu tradition. Although an attractive young woman, when prancing in a short tutu and long curls in the artist's studio, she is more of an Alice in Wonderland (or Shirley Temple) than a mysterious seductress. Anny Ondra's round face, big eyes, and conservative hairstyle enhance the child-woman image. Yet, unlike Lewis Carroll's mature child, Hitchcock's character is an immature adult. Donald Spoto describes Alice as "coy, flirtatious, modest but curious" (1992, 22). To this I would add infantile, silly, spoiled, naively manipulative, sexually immature and inexperienced, and innocently eager to experiment and play with fire (see Modleski 1989, 24).

Unlike Lulu, *Pandora's Box*'s dark, lower-class, streetwise survivor, who walked the streets from early childhood, Alice is the good, fair, middle-class girl, who helps her parents at the store and is destined to be Frank's devoted wife and the mother of his children. *Blackmail* portrays how, when left to her own devices, influenced by the dangerous notions of "new womanhood," her reckless curiosity and thoughtless adventurousness lead her astray, triggering the inherently catastrophic potential of her sexuality. Alice's feminine sexuality combined with her dangerous restless traits and new-woman rebelliousness attract trouble, threaten Frank's honor and status, and cause the deaths of two men.

While not a Pandora-Lilith like Lulu, Alice White is thus constructed as a curious, disastrous Pandora-Eve. Unwittingly carrying her ticking-bomb sexuality, Alice, like Pandora, is "naturally" designed to kill. Simultaneously, she is mythological Eve in all her manifestations: she is domestic and sheltered in Eden, curious and rebellious, easily tempted, sinful, guilty, and finally subdued. Alice's specific manifestation of curious, fatal rebelliousness is associated with the image of modern woman. It is her wish to step out of her traditional role, experiment independently, and improve herself that brings Alice to the artist's residence. It is to the rhythm of "Miss-Up-to-Date" that Alice is so easily seduced to take her clothes off by the man-snake. Her naive curiosity triggered, she is tempted to look into her traitorous box and taste the fruit of the forbidden tree. This leads to her fall from virtue, which entails (her) loss of innocence and (a man's) death, endangering family, honor, and the social structure.

Just as the portrayal of Lulu as a Pandora-Lilith woman conveys a judgmental attitude, rendering her a guilty object, so does the portrayal of Alice as Pandora-Eve. Furthermore, just as Lulu's stereotyping as a Pandora-Lilith precluded the perception of her as a victimized, prostituted woman, so Alice's stereotyping as a Pandora-Eve precludes the perception of her as a victim of attempted rape. Alice's dangerous, "fallen" sexuality and frivolous conduct, enhanced by her new-woman aura, frame the sexual encounter in Crewe's studio as "sex," not "attempted rape." They evoke the familiar host of misogynist rape myths presented in chapter 1, triggering the viewer's conventional knowledge that a sexually victimized woman must have encouraged the attack, that her modest protestations must have been disingenuous, that there is no such thing as rape, and, consequently, that women, especially sexual women and women who encounter sexual assault, are impure, provocative, and untrustworthy. The film does nothing to undercut the viewer's application of these conventional attitudes. On the contrary, constructing Alice as acknowledging her undeniable guilt serves to enhance and neutralize the viewer's conventional response.

Not surprisingly, when describing the sexual encounter, Donald Spoto states that Crewe "attempts to make love and in her fear she seizes a bread knife" (1992, 22). He further notes that "the stabbing of the artist that follows—in a context of violent lovemaking—becomes an ironic twist on the love motif" (23). "An attempt to make love," "violent lovemaking," and "love motif" seem to Spoto to capture the essence of the encounter, not "attempted rape," "sexual assault," and "sexual violence." Spoto's reading accords with the film's implicit "viewing instructions" and is, therefore, representative of many others.

Similarly, the cover of the videotape (which repeatedly stresses "First British Talkie"), summarizes the film's plot in the following terms: "Quarreling with her detective boyfriend, Alice White accepts the offer of escort from a handsome stranger. Allowing herself to be coaxed into his apartment, she resists his advances, and in a violent struggle, stabs him with a knife. But in her haste to leave the scene of the *crime passionelle*, she drops a glove." Once again: "coaxed," "advances," "*crime passionelle*," but no mention of rape or sexual violence. Raymond Durgnat dedicates much of his discussion of the film to the characters' liability and moral standing. He describes the sexual scene as: "He embraces her. The struggle becomes an ugly one" (1974, 85). Durgnat suggests that perhaps "the detective and his fiancée are spiritually guiltier than the rapist and blackmailer" (87; see also Modleski 1989, 22). Behind the curtain of Pandora-Eve's mythological, sexual, fallen guilt, Alice's sexual victimization is completely denied.

Far less allegorical than *Rashomon*, *Blackmail* nevertheless features a single woman surrounded by a host of men. Much like in *Rashomon*, the men are of different social classes; they have different educational backgrounds and occupations, and manifest unique combinations of personal characteristics. Some men are members of the working class, some are outlaws; Mr. White is a shopkeeper, Crewe is an artist, and Frank and his colleagues are detectives. Some of the men are naive while others are shrewd; some are aggressive and others forthcoming. Alice, the film's focal protagonist, is also its Woman. (Alice's stern mother, the gossiping neighbor, and Crewe's comic landlady make very brief appearances, induce comic relief, and are not developed characters.) As the primary representative of her sex, Alice's character takes on allegorical dimensions. Her characteristics, the stereotypical images associated with her, and the judgmental attitudes she is constructed to evoke all become allegorically feminine. Alice's portrayal as a curious, disastrous, guilty-object Pandora-Eve thus becomes a portrayal of Woman, specifically young, new women.

Unlike the male characters, Alice is not a member of any social class in her own right. Not defined by education or occupation, Alice (like the woman in *Rashomon* and Lulu in *Pandora's Box*) is defined by her sex and gender, while her social position is determined by the men she is connected with. She is a shopkeeper's daughter, but also a detective's wife-to be; for a short while she is an artist's companion (leading a would-be bohemian life), but also on the verge of becoming a fallen, outcast woman. *Blackmail* suggests that, when not securely fastened to a man, when freely "floating" among men and social classes, woman's instability renders her not merely different, but threatening to the system and to men's lives and honor.

In *Rashomon*, the Eve-Lilith woman who defied her prescribed wifely role, turning into a monstrous murderess, had to be removed in order to secure a new, all-male, stable society. Lulu, the Pandora-Lilith, had to die to set Alwa free, and allow his possible future redemption and marital union with an appropriate woman (such as his father's fair, timid, upper-class fiancée). Alice, Pandora-Eve, must be socialized, domesticated, and disciplined by a strong man. She must be trained to be a proper wife and mother, and severely guarded against her own dangerous nature, as well as distracting social trends. No ending could be more appropriate than marrying her off to Frank, representative of patriarchal law. In Selim Eyuboglu's words, "we can see the narrative structure of Blackmail as the confrontation between order and disorder. Disorder is Alice's assignation, the murder and, finally, the blackmail. Order is the elimination of the blackmailer at any cost, as well as the return of Alice as a silenced object" (1991, 69). Free birds, in Hitchcock's fictional world, represent chaos, danger, and disaster; the caged songbird in Alice's room is a source of domestic joy, beauty, and cheerful sound.

Yet Alice does not remain the silly child-woman the film presents at the outset. In fact, she is the only character in the film that undergoes fundamental growth, change, and development. After her traumatic experience in Crewe's studio, Alice sobers and matures. Searching her soul, she finds an embryonic conscience, responsibility, will, and voice. Reviewing her actions, she decides to assume responsibility. She is determined to decide for herself, develop her unique voice, tell her story, and have her day in court.

Indeed, her remarkable progression could have led Alice to independence and full personhood. But, actively supported by the film, Frank successfully denies Alice the voice, story, independence, responsibility, and day in court she seeks. Frank and the film seal Alice's uncontested guilt and secure social order and stability by stifling her timid, newly found voice and placing her in the (matrimonial) care of the law. Eve's attempt to break out of her stereotypical role is successfully suppressed, and she is confined to her familiar, caged space of subservient, guilty domesticity.

Cinematic Sound and Silencing Woman's Voice

England's first "talkie," "Blackmail remains, over sixty years later, an astonishing achievement technically" (Spoto 22). The film's famous breakfast scene, in which the recurring word knife is dramatically emphasized, while the rest of the speech is blurred into a background noise, uses sound to confine the viewer to Alice's consciousness, thus securing viewer identification with Alice, while enhancing her sense of guilt. In a similar—if less dramatic—scene, the viewer identifies with Mr. White as they both attempt to overhear Frank's phone conversation with Scotland Yard, which takes place in a closed phone booth in Mr. White's shop. Here the sound effect enhances the tension as, together with Mr. White, the viewer fails to make out the content of the dramatic news Frank is receiving. As she wanders the streets, Alice stumbles on a sleeping beggar, mistakes him for a corpse, and lets out a bloodcurdling scream—which metamorphoses into the landlady's scream as she is seen finding the dead Crewe. Alice is thus, once again, cinematically associated with the death of the man by use of the soundtrack.

But despite its commitment to sound, *Blackmail* does not award woman a voice of her own. Donald Spoto mentions that, due to her pronounced Polish-Czech accent, Anny Ondra's voice had to be replaced by that of another woman (Joan Barry), who spoke Ondra's lines off camera "while Ondra silently moved her lips" (1992, 22). Anny Ondra's voice was, therefore, excluded from England's first talking film. One actress's voice was replaced with another's, proclaiming the interchangeability of women's voices. Alice White, England's first cinematic image of a speaking woman, manifests "silently moving lips," representing an artificial patching of a severed woman's body and a severed woman's voice.

Further, the film continuously reinforces its leading male character's effective silencing of Alice. When she attempts to speak her mind, assume responsibility for her actions, and prevent Frank from framing Tracy, Alice is repeatedly hushed by Frank, who demands that she let him handle the situation. Conveniently sending Tracy to his death, the film confirms that Frank's handling of the situation *was* for the best, and that Alice's silencing was fortunate. Later, when Alice attempts to confess to the chief inspector at Scotland Yard, Frank once again manages to "save her from herself" and prevent her testimony. The film facilitates Frank's intervention by having the phone ring in the chief inspector's office. The viewer's inevitable relief at the resolution of the dramatic tension results in the viewer's intuitive perception that Frank's successful silencing of Alice was opportune.

Alice finds it hard to articulate her experience, trauma, and pain; she struggles to collect her thoughts and make sense of them, to verbally express her hurt, shame, fear, and shock. In front of the chief inspector she stutters and hesitates, unable to compose a coherent statement. The presence of another woman could have aided Alice in formulating, expressing, and sharing her feelings. In the company of a close girlfriend, a sister, a compassionate mother, she could have succeeded in communicating her emotions. She could have wept, allowing herself to be hugged by an understanding and accepting peer. In a supportive, understanding, feminine environment, she could have found her voice, words, line of thought, and learned to make sense of them for herself as well as for others. But the film denies Alice the company of another woman, leaving her lonely and thus speechless. She is condemned to helplessly confront the experienced, self-assured Frank, who, literally, speaks his native tongue in the domain of Scotland Yard. In her single attempt to articulate her story and convey it to Frank in the film's closing sequence, all she can do is whisper: "You don't know. I can't tell you. It's too dreadful. He tried . . . I was defending myself. I didn't know what I was doing. And then . . ."

Going a step further, the film does not merely prevent the emergence and manifestation of Alice's feminine voice and speech, but also constructs her inner voice as a masculine one. This is most blatant in the long sequence of Alice's nocturnal wandering. When she comes across a policeman, his gloved arm reminds her of the dead man she left behind; a neon sign portraying a rocking bottle reminds her of her hand holding the knife and stabbing Crewe's body; every dummy in every window reminds her of the corpse. *Blackmail*'s traumatized woman can see nothing but the murder she has just committed and the death she brought about.

Had Alice been given a woman's consciousness and inner voice, she might have also been reminded of her own victimization, pain, and shock. Had she spoken to herself as a woman would, she might have remembered the unwelcome touch, the violent hands assaulting her vulnerable body, shattering her privacy, ripping her cloths. She might have felt her paralysis, helplessness, and terror.[2] Strangers' eyes might have reminded her of the rapists' eyes staring into hers. Strangers' hands might have seemed to be coming at her to harm and attack. Every man might have seemed threatening. She might have wanted to cleanse her body, ridding herself of the rapist's odor.

Yet Alice remembers only her own crime and feels only her guilt, just as a man would likely expect her to think. Suffering no postrape trauma, she instead suffers from a "postmurder trauma," much like *Rashomon*'s woman. Replacing her stifled feminine voice with a masculine one, *Blackmail* commits the ultimate silencing, as well as the ultimate denial of Alice's victimization, all the while accentuating her guilt.

Laughter and Cinematic Judgment

Blackmail further robs Alice of yet another powerful vocal expression she once possessed: her laughter. Early in the film, Alice laughs with the men at their jokes. Her laughter expresses her sense of subjectivity, freedom, and self-assurance. After Crewe's attempted rape, Alice ceases to laugh. Her pale face is sober and tense, and her eyes wide open. She can no longer relax and express the optimism and confidence that underlie laughter. In the film's final scene, Alice attempts to laugh with the joking men, but no longer the sheltered child-woman, she finds that she cannot. Having become the sexual, guilty, fallen woman, Alice cannot laugh with the men because she is the object of their jokes. As Modleski describes: "Here the woman literally and figuratively occupies precisely that place that Freud assigned to women in the structure of the obscene joke: the place of the object between two male subjects. It might be argued that one of the main projects of the film is to wrest power from the woman, in particular the power of laughter, and to give the men the last laugh, thereby defusing the threat of woman's infidelity, her refusal to treat with proper seriousness patriarchal law and authority" (1989, 19). The sound of Alice's laughter is replaced with the image of her face, distorted with a tormented, futile attempt to reclaim the laughter she once owned. As the last scene fades out, we are left with the sound of two men's laughter and the mute, mocking glee of Crewe's jester. And the memory of the twitter of Alice's caged bird.

Much more than joyous amusement, the jester's visual, haunting laughter denotes society's watchful eye, its moral judgment, and its shame-inducing condemnation. The jester is the film's "chorus" and "reasonable man," as well as Alice's judgmental all-male jury. (Selim Eyuboglu's suggestion that, structurally speaking, the jester stands in for Hitchcock himself, is particularly telling in this context [1991, 6].) When, entering the artist's studio, Alice first encounters the jester's watchful laughter (and his pointing finger), she is startled, responding like a person taken by surprise at being found out. Filming the reaction shot of Alice's confused, distressed face from the jester's point of view associates the viewer with the snarling image. (Similarly, the shot of the jester's portrait from Alice's point of view bonds the viewer with Alice.) This encounter with the jester puts Alice on notice, warning her against her unseemly, potentially dangerous conduct. More specifically, the jester seems to be mocking Alice's arrogance in thinking she can handle the situation she has gotten herself into; that she can really play the part of the new woman.

Choosing to overcome her distress at the jester's gaze and assume a carefree posture, Alice ignores the portrait, dismissing its warning message. She next encounters his mocking laughter as she gets out of Crewe's curtained bed. As Alice trembles, the jester's I-told-you-so laughter marks the outcome of her wrongful conduct, her presence in the man's room. Rebelling against his condemnation, Alice tears at the portrait, but cannot stop the laughter. Once again, a very long, emphasized reaction shot of Alice's face from the jester's point of view links the viewer with the jester. The camera is then placed on Alice's other side, trapping her between jester and viewer, implying that there is no room for her to hide from the condemning public eye. In Alice's last encounter with the jester, when it passes her as she and Frank walk together out of the chief inspector's office and into their future, it seems to be informing Alice of her punishment.

Mirroring both Alice and the viewer, the jester thus exposes Alice's wrongful conduct, its deadly outcome, and the consequent penalty, pronouncing her shameful guilt and justified domestic incarceration as Frank's hostage-wife. Its merciless all-seeing look and all-condemning mockery signal to Alice and the viewer alike the conventional, common-sense perception and condemnation of her behavior. The jester's judgment and denunciation of Alice represents the film's cinematic judgment, which is presented to the viewer as the reasonable person's common-sense view.

The jester's judgment is visually linked with patriarchal law through the image of Frank's portrait in Alice's room. The morning following the fatal sexual encounter, Alice is startled by the firm, judgmental gaze she sees in the portrait of Frank in his police uniform that looks down on her from her bedroom wall. The portrait's penetrating look and Alice's anxious response associate Frank's stern gaze with the jester's mocking laughter. Patriarchal law and social conventions mirror each other, dominating, judging, and condemning Alice even in her most private spaces. No portrait is offered by the film to encourage or comfort her with an accepting, compassionate look. Alice's own portrait, which she allows Crewe to draw using her own hand, presents her as a naked object for male gaze and desire. Her smiling face is generic, childish, and expressionless.

The Legal Question That is Not Posed

Blackmail is not a law film in the obvious sense of portraying a courtroom drama, but rather in focusing on a vital legal issue. Following Alice through an attempted rape, allowing the viewer to witness (at least partially) the circumstances that led to her killing of the assailant, the film poses the following legal question: Does and should an attempted rape constitute a "self-defense" argument for a woman who kills her assailant, attempting to prevent the rape?

Self-defense is a legal defense that negates a defendant's criminal accountability for a killing s/he committed. Legally speaking, once accorded such a defense, the defendant's killing is not defined as criminal, and the defendant is acquitted of all criminal charges. Self-defense exonerates the killer from the most severe social stigma and criminal penalty. It signals that the defendant's life and bodily safety are valuable and cherished enough for the law to acknowledge an exception to the rules banning the killing of others, and that society recognizes the defendant's right to save his or her own life or bodily integrity even at the cost of another person's life. Does and should this defense apply to Alice in the situation portrayed in Blackmail?

Blackmail poses this legal question while providing its viewer with a detailed, panoramic view that can serve as a solid basis for viewer understanding and evaluation of the situation: the characters, the chain of events that led to the fatal act, Alice's curiosity and inexperience, Crewe's manipulation, their clashing perspectives on the encounter, Crewe's use of force, Alice's despair and panic. The film's viewer is supplied with every piece of information needed to consider Alice's responsibility for entering a dangerous situation, the issue of her "consent" to the sexual encounter, the seriousness of the threat she was facing, her likely perception of it, Crewe's criminal accountability for the forced sexual encounter, and the "reasonableness" of Alice's reaction under the specific circumstances. Blackmail's viewer is placed in a good position to follow an on-screen legal discussion of attempted rape as self-defense in a homicide charge brought against Alice, as well as to consider the legal issue in the context of the film's cinematic judgment.

Yet, despite the film's seemingly meticulous preparations, the question of attempted rape as a self-defense argument in a criminal charge is avoided: It is *not* brought before a fictional, on-screen court of law, nor presented to the viewer by the cinematic text. Instead, it is quickly replaced with a set of alternative moral dilemmas, all focusing on Alice's duty to turn herself in and admit to her criminal culpability for the crime. Blackmail secures these dramatic shifts of attention away from the question of rape as a basis for an argument of self-defense by introducing Tracy and advancing the conflict between him and Frank, by then killing Tracy, and finally by placing Frank in the chief inspector's office as Alice attempts to give her testimony.

Up to Tracy's appearance on the scene, Blackmail leads it characters and viewers alike to concentrate on Alice's presentation of her self-defense case to Frank, her husband-to-be and a representative of the law. But with Tracy's entrance, attention shifts to a set of choices that must be made by Alice and Frank. The first of the choices is whether to buy Tracy's silence or to allow

Alice's case to come before the court. Once Scotland Yard identifies Tracy as a key suspect, Alice and Frank are faced with a new choice: whether to turn Alice in, or to allow the unfortunate Tracy, a blackmailer with a criminal record, to take the fall for the killing she committed. With Tracy's untimely death, the characters' and viewers' attention is once again shifted to the final dilemma: should Alice sacrifice her freedom and Frank's honor in order to clear her conscience and set the record straight?

Whereas the legal question regarding attempted rape as a valid self-defense argument in a criminal homicide case *questions* Alice's guilt, suggesting that she may have been justified in her action and thus innocent, all three subsequent choices that arise with Tracy's appearance on the scene *assume* Alice's guilt, questioning merely whether or not she should assume responsibility for it. All three begin with the assumption that Alice committed murder, and distract viewer attention to three derivative concerns: Given her culpability, should Frank buy her freedom? Should she allow Tracy to take the fall for the crime she committed? Should she admit to a crime the authorities are no longer concerned with?

The stereotypical portrayal of Alice as Pandora-Eve presumes her mythological, sexual guilt. The series of moral questions presented by the film through Tracy's blackmail presume Alice's legal guilt. Thus, Tracy's blackmail attempt allows the film to silence the question and potential legally based discussion of the relevant legal question, robbing Alice of her day in cinematic court. Faced with Tracy's blackmail, the viewer is invited to join Frank in the chivalrous impulse to protect Alice and buy her freedom. Realizing Frank's brutal, vengeful, honor-driven willingness to sacrifice an innocent man and have him pay for a crime he did not commit, the viewer is invited to rethink the situation, identify with Alice, and support her desire to assume responsibility and confess to her actions. Tracy's death once again shifts the pendulum, inviting the viewer to take Frank's pragmatic position that there is no point in reopening a closed case. Together with Frank, the viewer is relieved when the deus ex machina sound of a telephone ring interrupts Alice's tormented attempt to confess to the chief inspector in the shadow of Frank's threatening, prohibiting presence. When Frank takes her arm and escorts Alice out of the office, the film's viewer cannot but feel relief that Frank has saved Alice from making yet another wrong choice that would have, once again, cost them both dearly. Concentrating on the urgent need to preserve Alice's liberty and Frank's honor, viewer and fictional characters alike forsake the issue of Alice's justification. Her victimization, the basis for her self-defense argument, is neglected and her presumed guilt enhanced. Similarly, viewers and characters are encouraged to dismiss the significance of allowing Alice to have a day in court. Seen from Frank's point of view, as he anxiously participates in Alice's meeting with the chief inspector, Alice's attempt to relate her story to the chief inspector is nothing but an irresponsible mistake. The film leaves no room for the possibility that such a narration may enable Alice to display her subjectivity, manifest her voice, constitute her point of view as significant and meaningful, and perhaps even secure a legal exoneration that would set her free.

What would a court of law have decided had Alice succeeded in bringing her case before the film's fictional common-law legal system? Generally, the criminal-law definition of self-defense is phrased along these lines: "One who is not the aggressor in an encounter is justified in using a reasonable amount of force against his adversary when he reasonably believes (a) that he is in immediate danger of unlawful bodily harm and (b) that the use of such force is necessary to avoid this danger" (LaFave 2000, 491).[3]

Most treatises on the doctrine of self-defense do not address the specific situation of killing in self-defense against rape.[4] Some offer general, applicable standards, occasionally touching briefly on this specific issue. One such treatise, "Corpus Juris Secundum: A Contemporary Statement of American Law as Derived from Reported Cases and Legislation," includes the following relevant standards and considerations: "A homicide is justifiable when committed by necessity and in good faith in order to prevent a felony attempted by force or surprise, such as murder, robbery, burglary, arson, rape, sodomy and the like" (496). Additionally,

> Excusable homicide in self-defense occurs when a person, in the course of a sudden affray or combat in which he has become engaged with another, necessarily or under a reasonable apprehension of danger kills the other to save himself from death or great bodily harm . . . According to some authorities, fault or freedom from fault on the part of the accused in bringing on the difficulty determines whether a homicide in self-defense is excusable or justifiable; if accused was without fault the homicide may be justifiable, but if he was originally at fault but abandoned the conflict and retreated as far as he safely could, the homicide may be excusable, but it cannot be justifiable . . . Where one has taken the life of another human being, and thereafter contends that he did so in self-defense, he can only be successful in his conten-

tion if he was in a place where he had a right to be . . . Generally, the use of a deadly weapon . . . in self-defense is justified or excusable when, and only when, it is necessary, or reasonably or apparently necessary to defend against death or great bodily harm. (514–15, 519)

More specifically: "The use of deadly force may be justifiable if the actor believes such force is necessary to protect himself against sexual intercourse compelled by force or threat" (535).

According to these formulations of the criminal doctrine, the relevant questions regarding Alice's case are these: Does rape constitute "unlawful, great bodily harm"? Was Alice "at fault in bringing on the difficulty"? Did she "have a right to be" in Crewe's studio? Was the sexual encounter in Crewe's studio "attempted rape," or was it merely "violent lovemaking"? (This last question would require exploration of the common-law definition of rape, which, historically, was "the carnal knowledge of a woman forcefully and against her will." Traditionally, rape charges were not brought against a man if the complaining woman placed herself in the dangerous situation that resulted in the sexual encounter.)

The legal, common-law discussion of Alice's self-defense against rape would have required probing into deep social conceptions, and wrestling with stereotypes, misconceptions, prejudices, biases, anxieties, and long-standing legal notions. Judging by the cited legal standards and attitudes, it is reasonably likely that Alice would have been exonerated on the basis of self-defense.

Interestingly, there are practically no reported cases dealing with a situation such as Alice's. In three contemporary, American cases in which defendants raised self-defense arguments based on attempted, forced sexual advances made towards them, the defendants were all men, defending themselves against same-sex sexual attacks or perceived attacks.[5] Nevertheless, at least one contemporary, predominant criminal-law scholar, George Fletcher, seems to believe that Alice would have very likely prevailed: "Of course if [a woman] were threatened with rape, she could use every necessary means at her disposal to protect herself. No legal system in the Western world would expect a woman to endure a rape if her only means of defense required that she risk the death of her aggressor . . . As the innocent party in the fray, a woman defending against a rape has interests that weigh more than those of the aggressor. She may kill to ward off a threat to her sexual autonomy" (1996, 560).[6]

This real-world legal perspective sheds new light on *Blackmail*'s systematic prevention of Alice's day in court. Had the film allowed her to come before a court of law, Alice might have been legally justified (or at least excused) and exonerated. Officially vindicated, she might have ceased to be the guilty woman, at least from a legal perspective. She might have been transformed from "fornicator" to "rape victim and survivor." She might have gained freedom and independence. She, as well as the film's viewer, might have learned that a woman is legally justified in fighting a sexual assailant, and perhaps even in taking his life while protecting her dignity and bodily integrity. Alice, as well as the film's female viewers, might have felt empowered by the knowledge; some male viewers might have felt threatened. Alice might have been set free to reconsider her future, making it harder on Frank and the film to marry her off to the law, forever guilty, afraid, and dependent on Frank's good will.

This real-world legal perspective exposes the full significance of the film's choice to introduce Tracy and distract viewer attention from Alice's self-defense. Had the film allowed Alice her day in court, rape could have been distinguished from fornication, and she might have been found innocent of both fornication and manslaughter.

The Scope of Alice's Guilt

Other than being Pandora-Eve, what, exactly, is Alice guilty of? She is guilty of flirting with another man, humiliating Frank, and staining his honor by entering Crewe's studio. She is guilty of greedily aspiring for more than she is socially entitled to and of acting independently. She is guilty of teasing Crewe and asking for his sexual attack, of misjudging the situation she has gotten herself into, while presumptuously thinking she could assess and handle it. Alice is guilty of bringing about both Crewe's and Tracy's deaths, and of placing Frank in immoral situations regarding Tracy and his employer. She is guilty of being sexually active (fornication) and not protecting herself and the world from the hazardous potential of her sexuality; she is guilty of not protecting Frank's honor, his reputation, and his integrity; she is guilty of throwing Frank and Tracy at each other, bringing out the worst in them. Alice's guilt bears striking resemblance to that of *Rashomon*'s woman and that of *Pandora's Box*'s Lulu.

In order to fully realize the extent of the guilt the film places on Alice's shoulders, let us consider an alternative possible ending, in fact the ending of the play by Charles Bennet on which the film is based: "The play ends with the revelation that the artist had a heart condition, and died of a heart attack; the stab wound was only superficial and is attributed by the police doctor to his falling on the knife as he died. Both Tracy and Alice therefore go free" (C. Barr 1999, 80). In the play, therefore, Alice is not guilty of either death, a construction which greatly diminishes our condemnation of her social and sexual conduct. The film could have followed the play's construction or presented any number of changes. It could have, for instance, chosen to keep Crewe alive, putting him on trial for attempted rape, while putting Alice on trial for assault. This way, the film could have explored Crewe's guilt, and the extent of Alice's right to self-defense. But the film chose to exonerate Crewe and spare him moral and legal scrutiny, constructing Alice as the film's single defendant, responsible for the deaths of two men, and thus also for her sexuality and improper social misconduct that led to those deaths.

Film Paralleling Society and Law

This reading of the film, in turn, may also shed light on real-world dynamics and explain the surprisingly small number of cases dealing with situations such as Alice's, and the equally surprising lack of legal attention paid to the question of sexual assault as justifying killing in self-defense. Blackmail offers a telling explanation for why cases such as Alice's do not come before the law, illuminating the law's disdain to develop a comprehensive doctrine for such cases.

Alice's case did not come before the film's fictional court because Frank, Scotland Yard, and the film all had a vested interest in preventing the legal discussion and in penalizing Alice outside the scope of the legal system, through patriarchal matrimony. Real-world cases such as Alice's give rise to similar social dynamics. Alice, like real women, might be the sole beneficiary of a legal proceeding that may proclaim her innocence. But she does not fully realize this. Alice is isolated and secluded from other women, denied a voice to express her story and realize her innocence. Her sole point of reference is Frank. Furthermore, Alice's legal exoneration would not guarantee her social exoneration. In fact, the public exposure that is inherent to a legal proceeding is more likely to guarantee her social condemnation. Whether legally guilty or innocent, Alice is socially guilty from the first moment she flirts with Crewe while dining with Frank. Entering the artist's studio and trying on the tutu justify, according to public norms, any behavior on Crewe's part since "she asked for it" and "should have known better." Alice's social verdict is sealed long before any court of law reaches its legal determination. She is socially condemned, as are her relatives, including Frank.

Bringing Alice's case to court might have been a building stone in changing public opinion and norms. It might have contributed to the advancement of women's social status. A public discussion of Alice's case would at least have broken the silence and allowed for the formulation of women's voices. Such voices might then unite, and perhaps pave the way to significant, fundamental change. But for the silence to be broken, for the public discussion to begin, Alice must pay the price of her reputation and social status. She must sacrifice herself, as well as her loved ones, for the sake of the feminist revolution. The reappearing jester, cruelly pointing at Alice, exposing and laughing at her, is a powerful, effective, disciplining reminder. His forceful image is the film's realistic explanation of why cases such as Alice's do not have their day in court.

Silencing and Minimizing in Historical Context

The year of Blackmail's release, 1929, was the year the British public first encountered talking movies. It was also the year in which British women were granted the right to vote. More specifically: young British women aged 21–30 were enfranchised; women over 30 had already obtained the right ten years earlier, in 1918. Suffragist claims regarding women's rationality, intelligence, and equal status with men were very familiar to Blackmail's original audience, as were women's demands for participation in public life and the job market. The joking remark made in the film by the Scotland Yard guard, regarding women detectives who would rob Frank of his position, was a timely joke indeed.

Read in its historical context, Blackmail may thus be the first backlash law film ever produced, (predating both Rashomon and Anatomy of a Murder by nearly three decades). Alice White, England's young new woman eager to leave her parents' shop and experiment (by discovering the unfamiliar world, learning to paint, taking moral responsibility, making her own decisions) is the image of the young woman awarded the right to participate in public life. Blackmail presents her as an infantile, irresponsible person, whose social instability and personal independence wreak havoc and cause death. Liberated from parents and husband, Alice turns, literally, into a femme fatale. Her choices are immature and disastrous, and the thought of allowing her to participate in the job market is a dangerous joke. The only solution that guarantees social order and security is marrying her off to Frank, representing patriarchy and the law.

Furthermore, Alice may think that by gaining the right to vote she has entered the legal world, where she will be treated as a subject. In fact, *Blackmail* demonstrates, the legal world is as exclusive as it ever was, and Alice's guilt remains a social, rather than a legal, issue. Social norms do not change with women's legal achievements: the jester continues to laugh just as he did before. In short, formal legal rights are all very well, but Alice shouldn't confuse them with real-world power relations, and patriarchal practices. Androcentric social practices and institutions including family, rape, police, and film, are as secure as ever. Frank, Crewe, the jester, and *Blackmail* all come together, securing order and tradition. The film's viewers may rest assured: 1929 is the year of the talking movie, not of the talking woman.

Cinematic Judgment and Hitchcock's Guilty Women

Blackmail is an exemplary case of a film that features both cinematic judgment and Hitchcock's theme of the guilty woman. Many of Hitchcock's films deal with crimes that invite discussion of legal, jurisprudential, and social issues. Many feature the guilty woman. The concept of cinematic judgment, as presented in this book, may be useful in framing and discussing some of these films. Obvious Hitchcock films that can be read as performing cinematic judgment of a woman protagonist include *The Paradine Case, Stage Fright, To Catch a Thief, Vertigo, North by Northwest, Psycho, The Birds,* and above all, *Marnie.* A brief look at *Marnie* reveals its close resemblance to *Blackmail* and its cinematic judgment of a guilty woman. Rather than allow Marnie her day in court, where she could have argued that her repetitive thefts were—at least partially— redeemed by trauma caused by childhood sexual victimization, Hitchcock prefers to marry the young blonde off to the man who threatens to turn her in to the authorities, thus literally blackmailing her into matrimony. Marnie's presumed legal guilt, combined with implicit sexual guilt (her "frigidity"), are thus maintained through the denial of legal discussion coupled with her subjection to patriarchal matrimony. At the same time, Marnie's rape at the hands of her disciplining husband is thoroughly denied by the film, and her rejection of his lawful "love" is attributed to her sexual deficiency and troubled mental state.[7] The only factors distinguishing *Marnie* from *Blackmail* seem to be the three decades that passed between the making of the two films, and the crossing of the Atlantic Ocean.

Blackmail *Read Against the Grain*

I have, so far, offered a one-sided presentation of *Blackmail* as a backlash film. Such a reading is, of course, always merely one possible option. Robin Wood, clearly aware of the film's misogynistic potential, suggests that a deeper reading reveals its critical view of women's oppression: "Our continued identification with Alice—as, by this point, the film's conscience, a conscience that is denied a voice by the male authority figures, the constable who won't take her seriously, the commissioner who doesn't want to listen, Frank who wants to silence her—is decisive here: it is precisely this identification that enables us to experience the film's dominant male figure as oppressive and invalidated" (1989, 273–74).

Tania Modleski acknowledges the film's obvious misogyny, as well as most critics' and reviewers' willing, uncritical acceptance of its misogynistic premises (1989, 22–23). Nevertheless, she chooses to read *Blackmail* as a text that exposes misogynistic social structures:

> While on the surface *Blackmail* seems to offer an exemplary instance of Hitchcock's misogyny, his need to convict and punish women for their sexuality, the film, like so many of his other works, actually allows for a critique of the structure it exploits and for a sympathetic view of the heroine trapped within that structure. This means that the female spectator need not occupy either of the two viewing places typically assigned her in feminist film theory: the place of the female masochist, identifying with the passive female character, or the place of the 'transvestite,' identifying with the active male hero . . . Women are undoubtedly prevented from indulging in the same unreflecting laughter enjoyed by male spectators, but this deprivation is of course hardly a loss and, in any case, other pleasures remain possible. First of all pleasure is involved in analysis itself, in understanding how the joke works even when it works against women . . . Secondly, one can find pleasure in acknowledging and working through one's anger, especially when that anger has long been denied or repressed. This is a pleasure Hitchcock's films repeatedly make available to women. (1989, 25, 27)

As with any rich text, *Blackmail* can and should be read against itself. A feminist reading of the film against its grain may stress that, despite Hitchcock's own reading of the film as focusing on Frank, torn between love and duty (Spoto 1992, 23; Modleski 1989, 29), Alice, in fact, is clearly the film's main protagonist, "the spectator's primary identification figure throughout most of the film" (Wood 1989, 257), and the film's single growing, evolving character who reaches maturity, responsibility, depth, and moral solidity. Alice's quick development suggests that she may have always been a more complex personality than her social image revealed. Inside every dumb blonde, the film can be read to imply, lives a real person. The men surrounding Alice, on the other hand, are portrayed as greedy, manipulative, dishonest, honor driven, dominating, and exploiting. Despite the superficial differences between the honorable Frank and the dishonorable Crewe, the film can be read to reveal the deep similarity between them, constructing both as oppressive agents of patriarchy (Wood 1989, 262).

As Modleski suggests, the film portrays woman as trapped "between a figure of law and one of lawlessness" (1989, 28), while she herself is inherently and radically outside the law. This portrayal offers an effective critical tool, exposing law's role in the service of oppressive patriarchy. Similarly, Modleski goes on to argue, the film criticizes the patriarchal family, hinting "that the [matrimonial] union is founded on the man's ability to blackmail the woman sexually" (30). And if the film does not allow Alice her day in court, nor a voice to articulate her truth, it does allow her to say "I was defending myself. I didn't know what I was doing." A sensitive viewer is invited to further articulate the potential argument.

The film's ending clearly invites a deep identification with Alice, and a painful reaction to her entrapment. It is not a happy ending. It is a difficult, disturbing one, enhanced by the jester's cruel laughter at Alice and the viewer alike (Wood 1989, 274; Modleski 1989, 30). Alice's development and growth throughout the film make her final oppression even more painful, bringing back to mind the sad image of Alice's twittering, caged bird.

4 Anatomy of a Murder

(U.S.A., 1959)

HOLLYWOOD'S HERO-LAWYER REVIVES THE UNWRITTEN LAW

Much like *Rashomon, Pandora's Box,* and *Blackmail, Anatomy of a Murder* features a fatal triangle: a woman, her husband, and her seducer/rapist. In *Rashomon,* the rapist seems to kill the husband; in *Blackmail* the woman kills the rapist; in *Pandora's Box* the woman kills the husband. In *Anatomy* we encounter a fourth possible option: the husband kills the rapist.

In *Rashomon*'s fictional legal process, the rape—although partially shown on-screen—is neither investigated nor tried, and the law concerns itself solely with the man's death. In the film's cinematic judgment, the rape, undistinguished from adultery, is constructed as constituting the woman's guilt regarding her husband's shame and death. In *Blackmail,* the rape, which takes place on-screen behind a closed curtain and is portrayed as violent seduction, does not receive legal or cinematic treatment. The woman, Alice, is denied the opportunity to stand trial before an on-screen court and is thus prevented from claiming that her rape justified—or at least excused—the killing she committed. Saving her fiancé's honor, the film chooses to silence her and leave her, together with the viewer, convinced of her guilt and shame. In *Pandora's Box*, no sexual assault of Lulu is brought before an on-screen court of law, nor does the film allow its viewer to consider her a victim of continuous sexual abuse. Catching her in what he perceives as potential adultery, her husband attempts to save his honor by demanding that she kill herself. The incident results in his own death. An on-screen court, as well as the film, finds Lulu guilty of being a dangerous Pandora-Lilith woman, and therefore of the husband's ruin and death.

At first glance, *Anatomy* seems to differ dramatically. Despite the rapist's death, the film's lawyer-protagonist does everything in his power to bring the rape into the on-screen courtroom and into full view. In fact, this legal battle is, arguably, the film's central theme, and is awarded full attention. Nevertheless, the film's explicit focus on the rape does not lead to the construction of the woman, Laura, as a victim of sexual assault. On the contrary, in a subtle and complex manner, the film's legal treatment of the rape merely grounds the cinematic judgment and conviction of the woman.

In order to secure the hero-lawyer's inevitable triumph, the film revives the old legal tactic, particularly popular in mid-nineteenth-century America, of disguising an unwritten-law argument made to the jury with an official insanity plea. This tactic invokes the underlying judgment and condemnation of a rape victim as an adulteress, guilty of risking her husband's honor and life. It is, thus, once again the raped woman who stands cinematic trial, and is found guilty of dishonor and death. I suggest that the film's formula of bolstering the hero-lawyer's stature by establishing the victimized woman's guilt is particularly significant given *Anatomy*'s eminent and influential role as a model for later Hollywood hero-lawyer films and television series.

Film Synopsis

Anatomy of a Murder's Paul Biegler (James Stewart) is an aging, small-town lawyer in Michigan's Upper Peninsula. Having lost his public position as district attorney, a disappointed Biegler spends all of his time fishing, and his secluded life begins to resemble that of his best (and only) close friend, Parnell (Arthur O'Connell), an older lawyer-turned-drunk. Returning from a long fishing excursion one night, Biegler is contacted by Laura Manion (Lee Remick), whose husband, Army Lieutenant Frederick Manion (Ben Gazzara), has been arrested for killing a bar owner, Barney Quill. Manion shot Quill in his crowded bar, manifesting determination and deliberation. The killing is said to have taken place an hour after Laura told her husband that Quill had raped her.

Manion is a difficult client. "He is cool, aloof, cerebral and close to un-cooperative with his lawyer. Throughout the film both he and his wife seem less than wholly devoted to one another. She is a voluptuous flirt and he has tired of her company" (Hoff 2000, 661–62). Reviewing the legal options potentially available for Manion's defense, Biegler and Manion decide to base the defense on an insanity plea, as there seems to be neither legal justification nor legal excuse for his fatal action. An army psychiatrist, having examined Manion, testifies that he was seized by an irresistible impulse, and therefore committed the killing in a trance. A fierce legal battle is fought over the status of the irresistible impulse as a full insanity defense and over the validity of the army psychiatrist's professional testimony. Ardent professional work leads Biegler and Parnell to an old, forgotten Michigan Supreme Court decision that serves as relevant precedent, substantiating their legal stand.

An even fiercer legal battle revolves around the relevance of Laura Manion's alleged rape by the deceased Quill. Biegler and Parnell, aided by Biegler's devoted helper, Maida, struggle to bring Laura's rape before the jury, while the prosecution team wrestles furiously to undermine the endeavor and to prevent the rape from entering the legal arena. Prosecution and defense both realize that the jury's sentiment regarding the rape may determine the final outcome. Although Laura's testimony seems truthful, her overtly sexual appearance and behavior seem to generate reasonable doubt regarding her reliability.

In a dramatic, last-minute development, the deceased man's daughter, Mary Pilant, overcomes her admirable loyalty to her dead father, appears in court, and produces Laura's torn panties, which are treated as proof that Quill did indeed rape her and tried to dispose of her condemning underwear in his own home. Biegler's and Parnell's ceaseless, futile-seeming efforts to recruit Mary to their side have finally paid off.

Biegler and Parnell win their case, but Manion flees without paying the bill, leaving a note stating that he was seized by an irresistible impulse to move on. An eyewitness tells Biegler and Parnell that Laura was crying as they left; this testimony confirms the strong suspicion actively cultivated by the film that Laura was a battered wife. The defense team is hardly surprised by Manion's betrayal, and finds comfort in Mary's decision to hire their services to manage the estate she has inherited from her father, Laura's rapist and

Manion's victim. As they leave the vacant lot previously occupied by the Manions' trailer, and head to meet their new client, Biegler drops a woman's extravagant high-heeled slipper into the trash and Parnell concludes: "That's what I call poetic justice for everybody."

The Hollywood Hero-Lawyer

Timothy Hoff begins his essay on *Anatomy of a Murder* by asserting that it "is regarded as one of the best trial movies ever made" (2000, 661). He concludes by stating that a "superb story, a splendid cast and an artful direction might well have been enough to have made *Anatomy of a Murder* a cinema classic. But added to all this is a magnificent and unusual score by Duke Ellington who makes a cameo appearance" (665). Michael Asimov further declares that "the film *Anatomy of a Murder* (Columbia, 1959) is probably the finest pure trial movie ever made," adding that "the film is based on a powerful 1958 novel by Robert Traver" (1996, 1131). Likewise, in her survey of the typically American literary genre of "legal thriller," Marlyn Robinson confirms that in the 1950s and 1960s "best selling authors continued to profit from the public's love-hate relationship with lawyers . . . Outselling all of them was the first of the truly realistic American courtroom dramas, *Anatomy of a Murder*, published in 1958. This marvelous and indeed literary who-done-it came from the pen of a future Michigan Supreme Court Justice, John D. Voelker, writing under the pseudonym 'Robert Traver'" (1998, 31). In a similar vein, Richard Griffith notes that "appearing on the best-seller lists for 65 weeks, it was also a Book-of-the-Month Club selection" (1959, 12–13).

There seems to be a consensus that book and film alike are classic, beloved exemplars of the American legal suspense drama. This dramatic type's most distinctive—and most taken for granted—feature is its focus on its protagonist, the American hero-lawyer. Referring to the golden age of hero-lawyer film, Asimov claims that: "In older trial movies, lawyers were often described in glowing terms. Although there were a few scoundrels . . . most film attorneys seemed oblivious to the need to make a living. Untroubled by ethical conflicts, they fought hard but fair in court. We find them springing to the defense of the downtrodden, battling for civil liberties, or single-handedly preventing injustice" (1996, 1132). As Rennard Strickland points out, these legal classics tended to cast as their leading men "actors whose screen ethos has made them ideal cinematic lawyers: [Louis Calhen,] Spencer Tracy, Henry Fonda, James Stewart, Gregory Peck, Paul Newman and Robert Redford"

(1997, 16). In this context, *Anatomy* marks the beginning of the hero-lawyer's golden age. Perfecting the cinematic good-lawyer character of previous years, it may have inspired the mythological celluloid lawyers to come.

Paul Biegler, *Anatomy*'s hero-lawyer, is a trustworthy, modest man, an honorable gentleman, pure-hearted, and a loyal friend. Underrated by his ungrateful community, he is, nevertheless, a first-rate legal professional. He is also a man of nature, silence, and seclusion—features that resonate with the purity of the American frontier. The sharp contrast with the slick big-city lawyer sent from Lansing to assist in the prosecution of the case emphasizes Biegler's endearing country-bumpkin image and underdog position.

As an exemplary hero-lawyer, Biegler combines professional legalism with a manly commitment to natural law. In so doing, he embodies Hollywood's resolution of the jurisprudential dilemma posed by the inherent disparity between positive law and natural law. Hollywood's hero-lawyer transcends this age-old tension between law and justice, reconciling them both in his unique, legal-professional, American manhood. (I discuss this theme in the context of comparing the hero-lawyer with the classic western hero in great detail elsewhere; see Kamir 2005b.) Biegler's mythological role as the physical embodiment of law and justice, highly skilled professional lawyerism, and manly commitment to intuitive natural law has been the ideal model for many of Hollywood's hero-lawyers (Al Pacino in the 1979 . . . *And Justice For All* is a prominent case in point).

Anatomy's viewer is invited to identify with the film's hero-lawyer in a variety of ways. The film identifies Biegler and Parnell as "heroes" by portraying them as sympathetic characters, while their opponents are shown to be unfriendly, unattractive, slick, and less competent. Additionally, as in Traver's novel, the viewer is strictly restricted to Biegler's perspective and point of view. The novel's first-person narration, though not literally mimicked, is thus faithfully maintained. Casting James Stewart as the hero-lawyer is yet another powerful means of securing viewer sympathy and identification.

But Paul Biegler cannot be perceived and admired as a hero if all he does is defend an unsympathetic, cynical, bad-tempered murderer like Manion, while struggling to redeem his own honor and professional standing. If the cinematic *Anatomy* is to construct and uphold Biegler's heroism, it must furnish him with a worthy moral mission in defense of justice and natural law. In this context, no mission is more manly and equitable than the honorable, chivalrous adherence to the American "unwritten law."

Having carefully studied the history of America's unwritten law in its courts, Robert M. Ireland (1988) reports that the years 1843–85 saw a significant number of highly publicized trials involving the unwritten law. Most cases were of enraged husbands who killed their wives' paramours. They all pleaded insanity, sometimes as an exclusive defense, while alluding to the unwritten law that "a libertine deserved assassination." Most of the cases resulted in jury acquittal on the grounds of insanity. The insanity plea allowed the defendants to introduce proof of seduction or adultery, which they would have otherwise been precluded from presenting to the court. (For the most part, the written criminal law partially excuses a husband's fatal response only when he catches the victim in the sexual act with his wife; in all other situations the sexual event is considered irrelevant to the legal consideration of the killing. Arguing insanity, the defendant could refer to the sexual misconduct that drove him insane.) Attempting to enrage the juries, the press, and the public, the lawyers conducting these cases highly dramatized them, turning them into show trials (if not in the usual sense of the term) (Ireland 1988, 157–59).

After 1834 (when Ohio's Supreme Court first ruled on the issue), it was particularly popular to combine a killing husband's unwritten-law defense with professional testimony that the defendant was seized by a specific kind of insanity: the irresistible impulse. The appeal of this insanity defense lay in that it "embrace[d] the notion that a person could be rational and yet insane" (Ireland 1988, 165). This construction nicely bridged the gap between the rationality attributed to the defendant by the logic of the unwritten-law defense and the insanity attributed to him through psychiatric testimony. It freed the defense from having to prove the defendant could not tell right from wrong, the prevailing standard in the United States since at least the early nineteenth century (Ireland 1988, 165).

The unwritten law was situated precisely at the intersection of positive law and nineteenth-century America's natural law. Advocates of the unwritten law fully acknowledged and accepted the authority of law, in general, and by no means attempted to reject or undermine it. They merely argued that its application in specific cases would cause great injustice. To use Martha Umphrey's words: "in court its advocates cast it as a kind of transcendent principle emerging out of a man's natural right to protect the boundaries of his domestic sphere when formal law could or would not do so. The attorneys asked a jury to nullify not the authority of the state in general, but the application of generally beneficial formal rules in a very particular circumstance in order to avoid a moral injustice. Moreover, as a matter of legal process, attorneys, because they could not plead the unwritten law, entered a plea of insanity on behalf of their clients; and thus the unwritten law was inexorably bound up with formal legal rules governing the 'madman's' excuse from criminal responsibility" (Umphrey forthcoming).

The unwritten law, acknowledging a husband's right to avenge himself and take the life of any man who has a sexual relationship with his wife, has been rooted at the very core of the honor-based value system for centuries. Jeremy Weinstein (1986) contends that somewhere between the first and the fifth centuries, when Britain became monogamous, adultery was recognized as a grave wrong that infringed a husband's rights in his wife. "Adultery, considered a private wrong, was remedied by the self-help of the husband and his kinship group—that is, by *vendetta*. Failure of the kin to fulfill their solemn duty to take vengeance resulted in dishonor" (202–3).

Weinstein's masterful account of the eventful history of written and unwritten law's relationship with adultery in England and the United States demonstrates how, through countless intricate developments over the course of thousands of years, adultery has maintained its unique status as the most serious offense to a husband's honor. In sixth-century England, under Ethelbert's Dooms, the state's attempt to encourage the dishonored husband to relinquish his right to kill an adulterer illustrates the severity of a husband's dishonor. The state prescribed that, if a husband were willing to accept compensation instead of pursuing a vendetta, the adulterer would have to take the woman he had defiled off her husband's hands, pay the husband the great sum of a free man's life, "and procure a second wife and bring her to the other man's home" (Weinstein 1986, 206).

In the early twelfth century, adultery was considered such a grave wrong that it remained the only one for which compensation was not obligatory (Weinstein 1986, 210). The Normans, powerful and centralist, suppressed vendettas and private vengeance with the exception of adultery, the single offense not taken over by state law (210). Due to the sinful nature of the conduct, "adultery became an offense punishable by the Church at a time when the state began to win acceptance for its exclusive right to mete out punishments by co-option of private vengeance" (211). The result was that "the state, having failed to provide an adequate remedy, did not punish the cuckold's vengeance, and thus institutionalized it through permission" (212). In one form or another, this has remained the case throughout Anglo-American legal history.

The Puritan period, in both England and the American colonies, was exceptional in making a married woman's adultery a capital offense (Weinstein 1986, 225). But even when this offense was taken off the books, a husband's right to avenge his honor remained justified, excused, overlooked, or sanctioned at least to some degree under certain circumstances. In some American states, a husband's vengeance found legal justification if he caught "the other man" in the act. So, for example, in the state of Texas, in the years 1857–1974, an explicit statute provided that "homicide is justifiable when committed by the husband upon one taken in the act of adultery with his wife, provided the killing take place before the parties to the act have separated" (230).

By reviving, supporting, and glorifying the unwritten law, *Anatomy of a Murder* reinforces the honor-based value system, with its blunt, overwhelming implications regarding gender roles and women's sexuality. Further still, the unwritten law was historically used in times of potential women's liberation to fortify the patriarchal social order. By resorting to the unwritten law, *Anatomy* regresses to nineteenth-century conservative attempts to curb women's nascent rights.

Robert Ireland (1989) and Hendrik Hartog (1997) each contend that nineteenth-century America's sensational adultery honor-killing trials signaled a reactionary move in the face of women's potential emancipation. Hartog asserts that "in 1859, in 1867, and again in 1869–1870, Americans were transfixed by the trials of men who had murdered their wives' lovers," and further analyzes: "These trials reveal a profound male disquiet about lost or changing rights and traditions, and the cases themselves were used by the defense lawyers and by parts of the media to create a new legal understanding designed to restore male honor and property rights in women" (69). In his account, the intense language of male honor in these trials resulted from and responded to the challenge posed to traditional conceptions of male honor by new, popular notions of "companionate marriage" and contractual freedom within marriage (95).

The honor-killing husbands were universally acquitted, Hartog explains, in response to a feeling that male authority was being contested, "because wives were understood as having gained public rights that necessarily meant losses of rights for husbands" (1997, 77). Calling on all-male juries to restore the social order despite even the law, the attorneys in each of these trials offered a simple story: an "ordinary honorable man" acted in "self-defense" as any man would have, by right, done in his place (80–81). The husband's right to self-defense was widely perceived as countering the threatening rights "to separate, to divorce, to keep custody of their children, to earn an income, to live an independent life—of wives in the mid-nineteenth-century United States" (92). Hartog rightly notes that "reform may have been for the most part symbolic. Yet, the symbols had potency" (95). Although little actually changed in women's rights and lives, "defense counsels' narrative assumed the existence of an increasingly alien legal culture that threatened male honor and husbandly identity" (95).

Further still, since some of the defendants were openly known to have been abusive husbands, their public glorification and acquittal belittled the issue of domestic violence and denied battered wives' victimization. "Drawing upon the realities of such cases critics of the unwritten law submitted that its vindication of paramouricide . . . condoned and even encouraged wife abuse" (Ireland 1989, 35).[1]

The outbreak of "moral panic" regarding libertines, adultery, and the liberation of women, which reached its peak in the years 1859–70, slowly waned over the last three decades of the nineteenth century. Juries, less and less enchanted with the unwritten law, abandoned it, and state supreme courts limited or abolished the doctrines of legal insanity that had enabled the acquittal of the violent retaliators of their sexual dishonor. At the same time, "more and more state legislatures eliminated the need for private vengeance by enacting statutes that punished adultery as well as seduction" (Ireland 1989, 38).

Decades went by, and during World War II, women once again gained new independence as they entered the workplace in substantial numbers, taking over positions abandoned by men drafted to serve in the war. Following the war, adultery laws, enacted in the second half of the nineteenth century and at the beginning of the twentieth century, fell into disuse, as society displayed tolerance for much more relaxed sexual norms. Concurrently, divorce laws became a more common vehicle to deal with "sexual dishonor" (Ireland 1989, 38). Further still, in its 1955 Model Penal Code, the American Law Institute recommended that adultery be decriminalized; many states immediately embraced the recommendation (Weinstein 1986, 226).

Yet, as ever, women's slow advancement was perceived as threatening to undermine the patriarchal social order, and a conservative backlash was quick to follow. As American soldiers returned from the war, women were told to go back home, return the labor market to their men, and devote themselves to mothering and homemaking. In the 1950s, the iconic Donna Reed was fully satisfied and content filling the role of the perfect, traditional housewife. And in 1957–59, just as the American Law Institute recommended the decriminalization of adultery and states began to implement this liberal recommendation, *Anatomy of a Murder* revived the unwritten law, constructing its hero-lawyer as the victorious defender of an abusive husband who avenged his honor by killing the man who defiled his right to exclusive sexual access to his wife.

In the years 1859–70, in the face of women's symbolic advancement, lawyers, juries, and the media combined to revive the unwritten law and reinforce patriarchy and manly honor through sensational show trials. Exactly one hundred years later, just as the last vestiges of the unwritten law were fading away, a successful Hollywood law film, based on a best-selling novel, once again revived the legal phoenix, in the face of threatening liberal attitudes towards "family values" and gender roles. Once again, domestic violence is overlooked as a husband's honor takes precedent, associated with natural law, "true manhood," and American values.

Further still, *Anatomy* carefully presents a jury consisting of women, signaling that they too partake in the "commonsensical" revival of the unwritten law. In the nineteenth century, well aware of the deep social implications, many women strongly objected to the jury acquittals of honor killers, and "to woman's rights activists, the success of the defense demonstrated the corruption of male-only juries" (Hartog 1997, 87). Some were conscious enough to tell "a newspaper reporter that had there been females on the jury that tried [one of the honor-killing husbands] he might have been convicted of the murder" (Ireland 1989, 36). In *Anatomy*, women are co-opted into the moral panic about endangered honor and thus denied a dissenting voice.

Interestingly, in 1959 it is *Anatomy*, a law film, which replaces the nineteenth-century show trials, and fills their sensational, conservative, backlash social function. Novel and film together may have reached as many Americans as did the nineteenth-century trials, replacing, with their literary and cinematic law, the legal system and judgment—the real courts, lawyers, and juries.

The Unwritten Law and the Distinction between Rape and Adultery

A closer look at the doctrine reveals that the unwritten law regarding a man's right to kill a man in retaliation for a sexual encounter with a kin woman applied only to two types of sexual acts: "adultery," i.e., consensual sexual relations between a married woman and a third-party male; and "seduction," i.e., sexual relations between an unmarried female and a male (Ireland 1989, 27). There was no specific reference in the unwritten law permitting a husband to kill his wife's rapist.

In his revealing 1906 treatise, Thomas J. Kernan lists and carefully analyzes "the decalogue of the system" of the unwritten law, which, he states, "has its basic foundations in the public opinion of the communities in which it prevails, and has all the certainty and sanction that constitutions or statutes could give it" (451–52). The "ten commandments" he articulates and reviews refer to a wider scope of issues than merely husbands' rights, including issues of dueling and employment. For the purpose of this discussion, it suffices to review Kernan's formulation of the first two "cardinal laws": "Law I. Any man who commits *rape upon a woman of chaste character* shall, without trial of hearing of any kind, be instantly put to death by his captors or other body of respectable citizens *not less than three* in number . . . Law II. Any man who commits *adultery* may be put to death with impunity by the *injured husband*" (451–52, my emphasis). Kernan notes that "the strongest one of [the unwritten rules] is the first . . . This seems to be a law of almost universal application everywhere" (454). Indeed, Law I is an exclusive category in itself, pronouncing the acceptance of the dangerous "lynch law" by the many who sympathized with the lynchers of rapists. (This sympathy, of course, carried deep racial implications that are beyond the scope of this discussion).

The relevant unwritten law in Frederick Manion's case is the second one, which allows a husband to kill a man who has intercourse with his wife. The rule, however, specifically refers to a wife's *adultery*, and not her *rape*. This makes historical sense. A husband's private revenge was not co-opted by the state because adultery was not criminalized by the state. Rape, on the other hand, remained a criminal offense at all times, sometimes even a capital offense. Therefore Law II did not cover a wife's rape.

One could argue that if adultery furnished a husband with the right to avenge his stained honor, then the same must have been true of rape. The only difference between the two was the wife's consent to the sexual conduct at issue, and consent did not affect the damage to a husband's honor. Indeed, in the context of the discourse of Law II, a wife's consent to an adulterous relationship was of no consequence. What mattered was the defiling of the husband's absolute right to his wife's body and sexuality and the desecration of his manly honor.

Historically, "because the action belonged to the husband for his loss, the wife's consent was immaterial" (Weinstein 1986, 219). Similarly, in nineteenth-century America, "in the rhetoric of the unwritten law, wives were barely relevant. The struggle was one between men . . . 'The person or body of the wife is the property of the husband, and the wife cannot consent away her own purity . . .' Their seduction dishonored their husbands, robbed their husbands" (Hartog 1997, 79). Or, as phrased by the leading lawyer who defended honor-killing husbands, John Graham: "The wife's consent cannot shield the adulterer, she being incapable by law of consenting to any infraction of her husband's marital rights" (Umphrey forthcoming, 146).

According to this line of thought, the question of whether the interaction between Laura Manion and Barney Quill was rape is, at best, irrelevant to the application of Law II to Frederick Manion's violent act. A more conservative view would be that only adultery would constitute Manion's husband's right, whereas rape would not. In any event, all that is required for the application of the unwritten-law defense is that the defendant *believed* (or, in some jurisdictions at some periods, that he *reasonably* believed) that the other man had sexual intercourse with his wife. It is the defendant's mental state, his mens rea, and *not* the actual events that took place that constitute the relevant basis for the defense. Even if he were completely mistaken in his belief, even if nothing whatsoever occurred outside his own mind, he may still use the defense. Legally speaking, the focus must be strictly on his cognition, and not at all on objective reality. Thus, Frederick Manion's state of mind should have been at the center of *Anatomy*'s attention, whereas Laura's actual conduct should have been irrelevant or, at most, in the background.

Nevertheless, a major part of the film revolves exactly around these legally irrelevant issues: whether the sexual act at hand actually occurred, and whether it was rape or adultery. The film further insists that Biegler's legal triumph depends on a determination that the sexual event did indeed occur and that it constituted rape, not adultery. The film thus unnecessarily shifts its viewer's attention from Frederick Manion's state of mind to Laura Manion's sexual conduct, and to the construction of that conduct as rape or adultery.

Anatomy of a Murder, therefore, implicitly rephrases the unwritten law to condone a husband's killing of his wife's *actual rapist*, rather than her (reasonably) *suspected lover*. (This is one of its most significant popular-jurisprudential contributions). The obvious reason for this shift seems to be the film's justified sense that in 1959 the original version of the unwritten law was less likely to win jurors' and viewers' sympathy than the new, more liberal version, which does not so bluntly deny a woman's right to sexual autonomy and self-determination (as well as a man's right not to be killed unless he actually committed a wrong). It can be argued that this literary-cinematic version of the unwritten law channels public rage and vengeance in a far more progressive direction than the original unwritten law. This new formulation seems to condone a husband's outraged vigilantism only when his wife's will was brutally ignored and her body abused, and not when he fears that she may have freely exercised her will in choosing an extramarital sexual partner.

But in the cinematic *Anatomy*, the central issue is not the mere introduction of the uncontested rape into the legal proceeding, but rather the determination of whether the sexual event took place at all, and whether it was rape or adultery. This emphasis has very different social implications, and they are not in the least progressive. In this context, the cinematic *Anatomy* departs from the literary counterpart in three complementary ways: First, it attempts to prove that intercourse did occur (a fact denied by the prosecution and its witnesses), thus shifting attention from Manion to his wife. Second, it significantly emphasizes the need for the sexual event to have been rape and not adultery in order for Biegler to win the case, thus dramatically enhancing the centrality of the rape-versus-adultery determination. Simultaneously, it undermines Laura's credibility, introducing serious doubts as to the truth of her story (on both counts: the occurrence of the event, and its characterization as rape).

The literary Laura is described by Biegler as a "Hollywood tigress," a fantasy come true. "Her femaleness was blatant to the point of flamboyance; there was something steamily tropical about her; she was, there was no other word for it, shockingly desirable" (82). And he continues: "I remembered something Parnell McCarthy had once said. 'Some women radiate sex,' he said. 'All the others merely trade in it.'" But this Laura is, nevertheless, a decent, honest person, a completely reliable witness, and the novel offers no reason to doubt her or her narration of the rape. The cinematic Laura is not merely sexual, but also, as Hoff justly describes her, "a voluptuous flirt." Her vulgar, continuous flirtation with Biegler, as well as with every other man the film throws her way, begs the suspicion that she may have been just as provocatively inciting in her dealings with Barney Quill, and/or that she may be lying about the whole encounter.

In a striking break with the novel, the film portrays Laura as surprised, undermined, and "found out" by the prosecutor's cross-examination. Whereas in the novel her testimony regarding the rape is straightforward, believable, and unchallenged by the prosecution, in the film it is vehemently and effectively challenged. For example, when asked by the prosecutor whether she has ever been a passenger in Barney's car before, the cinematic Laura, bewildered, shaken, and stuttering, is unable to offer an answer. The effect of Laura's lack of credibility is further magnified by the film's choice to remain faithful to the spirit of the novel's first-person narration, and its restriction of the viewer's scope of knowledge to that of Biegler's. In atypical fashion, the film refrains from giving Laura flashback recollections that would present the sexual encounter on-screen. The film thus denies the viewer what could have been a natural, visual confirmation of Laura's testimony.

Laura's vilification, the focus on her conduct, and the questioning of her rape story clearly enhance the dramatic tension so crucial to a cinematic drama, and may be explained on these grounds. But they also imply an obsessive focus on the rape victim (instead of on her victimizer) and on the differentiation of rape from adultery. The familiar feminist claim that by focusing on a rape victim the legal system subjects her to undermining, accusatory scrutiny is just as relevant to film as it is to law. *Anatomy* certainly subjects Laura to such scrutiny. In this context, law and film perform analogous socio-ideological functions in parallel fashion; the feminist-jurisprudential critique sheds light on the film's cinematic choices. Analysis of the film, in turn, sheds light on the operation of the legal system.

The film's differentiation between rape and adultery may, of course, coincide with progressive, egalitarian, and liberating social agendas. But this is so when the differentiation highlights the harmful coercion inherent in rape, contrasting it with the variety of legitimate, consensual sexual relations, including adultery. *Anatomy*, however, contextualizes the rape-adultery distinction very differently.

Due to the film's transformation of the unwritten law, Manion's freedom and, more importantly, Biegler's success and status as a hero-lawyer all depend on the sexual encounter's having been rape and not adultery. But Laura's flirtatious nature and her unreliable testimony give rise to the strong suspicion—if not presumption—that it was, in fact, adultery. In order to secure her husband's acquittal, Laura is thus required to defend herself and convince the on-screen jury that she is not guilty of adultery, but was indeed raped. More importantly, she must similarly convince the film's viewer, in order to secure the construction of Biegler's mission as noble, and his character as heroic. Thus, while in the film's fictional on-screen trial Frederick Manion is the single official defendant, in the film's cinematic judgment (as well as in the fictional trial's subtext), it is Laura Manion who is on trial. The cinematic-legal question at stake is whether the sexual encounter in which she participated was indeed adulterous, as suspected, or whether she can prove that she was raped and thus is not guilty.

In short, in *Anatomy*, the burden of proof regarding the responsibility for a man's violent death shifts (from the prosecutors in Frederick Manion's fictional case) to Laura (in the film's cinematic judgment), and she becomes the character burdened with the duty to prove her (fundamentally sexual) innocence.

Thus the film's rape victim is constructed and treated as the defendant in the film's cinematic judgment. She is accused of committing adultery. The sole defense offered to her by the film is that she was raped, and therefore did not willingly participate in the adulterous relationship. In the process of this cinematic judgment, the viewer is presented with evidence regarding Laura's forceful attack, her lack of consent and utmost resistance, her sexual/moral character and history, and the question of whether she freely placed herself in a potentially dangerous situation (which would deny her the status of a rape victim). It is noteworthy that Manion, who stands trial in the film's fictional legal proceeding, has the best legal representation the film can supply him with: its own hero-lawyer. Laura, not officially on trial in the fictional proceeding, but very much so in the cinematic judgment, has no attorney, counselor, or even friend to represent, support, believe, or care for her. The viewer is certainly not invited to fill this role. The film isolates her almost completely, with the exception of her little dog, who serves as her only companion.

What *Anatomy* does is revive and give voice to the suppressed sociolegal narrative underlying contemporary rape law, as described by Anne Coughlin (1998). As presented in detail in the introduction to this book, Coughlin's analysis reveals that the subtext of contemporary rape law constructs the raped woman as inherently suspect of committing adultery. Demonstrating this analysis, the film voices rape law's underlying accusation of the raped woman in its cinematic judgment, calling on the viewer to be judge and jury in this legal procedure. As such, it supplements the legal system's treatment of rape, maintaining and supporting rape law's suppressed subtext, which constructs rape as a defense to be used by a woman accused of adultery.

In *Anatomy*'s cinematic judgment, Laura Manion is finally found not guilty, but only by reason of reasonable doubt. Her testimony is not fully believed and embraced; her sexual character remains dubious, and, at the end of the deliberations, she is strongly suspected to have, at the very least, placed herself in danger of rape. Thus, her shame as an adulterous woman is not fully redeemed, nor is her guilt in tainting Biegler's mission, as well as his status as a hero-lawyer, with a shadow of doubt and dishonor. Having failed to fully exonerate herself, remaining the dangerous "voluptuous flirt" that threatens social order, her husband's honor and freedom, and men's lives, Laura is punished by the film. It effectively incarcerates her by subjecting her to matrimonial confinement, in which she will be battered and restricted by her violent, jealous husband "'til kingdom come," as Manion promises. Since the legal system is incapable of punishing her properly for her "voluptuous" nature, since it cannot protect society, her husband, and men at large from the severe threat her sexuality poses, an abusive marriage seems to be the perfect patriarchal solution. Voicing the film's view, Parnell concludes: "This is what I call poetic justice for everyone."

Anatomy's Discarding of Rape and Domestic Violence

Despite *Anatomy of a Murder*'s concentration on Laura's rape, the film denies her sexual victimization. She is not recognized as a rape victim nor as a battered wife. Both rape and domestic violence are systematically understated to the degree that they become devoid of any significance. *Anatomy* treats Laura's rape as no more than sexual intercourse that may not have been fully desired. Despite what she has just endured, Laura is not portrayed as in any way traumatized; she is as cheerful, flirtatious, and light-headed as ever. The mention of her "panties" as an element of the legal investigation of her rape is introduced as a comic matter. Nothing about her portrayal by the film elicits any sense of horror or sympathy. The only aspect of the rape that is presented as unpleasant is her black eye: evidence of a brutal physical assault. Even this brutality, however, is taken lightly by all, including Laura.

Speaking to one of the prosecution's witnesses, Biegler charges that the community was happy to overlook Barney Quill's "little fault" of "raping *other men's wives*" (emphasis added). This utterance perfectly conveys the film's attitude that it is Laura's marital status that makes Barney's sexual conduct unacceptable. Despite the film's insistence on differentiation between rape and adultery in the context of constructing Laura as suspect and guilty, it seems to obscure this distinction when constructing the meaning of rape and the rapist's accountability. The criminality of rape is thus explicitly associated with the offense to the raped woman's husband.

In a similar vein, referring to Laura's torn panties, which play a key role in substantiating her account of the rape, *Anatomy*'s judge declares that "there isn't anything comic about a pair of panties which figure in the violent death of one man and the possible incarceration of another." In the film's world-view, even the panties are only related to the two major events at hand: one man's death, and the other's potential incarceration. The woman's rape is completely obliterated. This statement echoes the nineteenth-century public perception of Evelyn Nesbit Thaw (wife of Harry Thaw, who killed her "se-ducer"). Martha Umphrey (1999–2000) claims that the public obsession with Nesbit's photographs—and not with her husband's or his victim's—during the long course of Harry Thaw's trial "replicated and reinforced a cultural logic both implicitly and explicitly articulated throughout its coverage: that her 'beautiful face' had lead 'one man to his death, another to the grim prospect of the electric chair'" (729). This "cultural logic" constructs Nes-bit's beautiful face and Laura's torn panties as inspiring, triggering, and causing the tragic events that brought about men's death and ruin. Com-pletely overlooked are the women's abuse, victimization, and pain. *Anatomy*'s judge's statement also echoes the Buddhist priest's dramatic announcement at the film's opening that constitutes *Rashomon*'s frame of reference: "A man has been murdered." No reference is made to the woman who was raped in the course of the same event.

The film similarly raises Laura's domestic abuse only to reinforce patri-archal values, while overlooking its significance as a severe social phenome-non that renders Laura a victim. The theme seems to be introduced to fulfill two functions: First, to undermine Laura's credibility regarding the rape, suggesting that perhaps she was beaten by her own husband and not by Barney Quill. This enhances the dramatic tension mentioned earlier, while using Laura's character to reinforce the prevalent perception of alleged rape victims as unreliable witnesses. The second function is the enhancement of yet another dramatic tension. Knowing that Laura is battered by her husband, Biegler fears that she may not provide the testimony necessary for Manion's acquittal and his own triumph. In one instance, Laura explicitly considers the freedom she would gain if her oppressive husband were convicted and incar-cerated for life. Identifying with Biegler, the viewer worries that the domestic violence may undermine his heroic mission, anxiously hoping that Laura will overcome her "selfish" concerns and faithfully sacrifice herself to support her abusive husband. Engendering deep viewer identification with the hero-lawyer and his point of view, the film encourages an active hope for Laura to choose the path of silence regarding her domestic abuse. We become accom-plices to the silencing of the battered woman.

From a slightly different perspective, the film offers Laura a choice between two options. She can admit that it was Manion, not Quill, who physically assaulted her, suspecting that her encounter with Quill was adultery and not rape. This choice would lead to Manion's conviction in the fictional legal proceeding, Biegler's professional failure, Laura's self-implication, in the film's cinematic judgment, as a bad wife, as having failed the hero-lawyer, and as an immoral woman (who probably did have a consensual adulterous relationship). It would also liberate Laura from Manion's hold. The alternative option is for Laura to stand by her man and his lawyer, and deny the abuse, testifying that only Quill battered and bruised her. This would lead to Manion's acquittal in the film's on-screen legal procedure, Biegler's success, Laura's exoneration in the film's cinematic judgment, but her entrapment with her batterer.

The film, thus, constructs Laura's "choice" as one between self-damnation but freedom from abuse on the one hand, and self-exoneration but eternal imprisonment on the other. The film chooses for Laura the worst possible combination. Her stuttering, unconvincing testimony suffices to supply the jury with the sought-after excuse to exonerate Manion in the fictional legal proceeding, but not Laura in the cinematic judgment. Manion is released, Biegler redeemed, and Laura condemned by the viewer and entrapped with her batterer. Like rape, domestic violence is thus introduced by the film in the context of promoting conservative "family values" and perceptions of the dutiful, self-sacrificing wife. *Anatomy*'s portrayal of Laura's victimization at Manion's hands does not elicit horror, sympathy, or an understanding of her situation as a victim of domestic abuse. On the contrary, the film presents Manion's violence as a natural, deserved response to Laura's voluptuous flirtation. The overly sexual woman and the overly jealous, violent man constitute a match made in heaven, well deserving of each other.

Last but not least, Laura's vilification and the denial of her victimization go hand in hand with the variety of female role models offered by *Anatomy*. Laura is the "voluptuous flirt," the "army slut," the "dumb blond," the second rate femme fatale, a diluted version of the already diluted Pandora-Lilith we encountered in *Pandora's Box*. The film's Maida, on the other hand, is Biegler's helper: the obedient, asexual, nurturing woman. Wife, secretary, mother, and nurse all rolled into one, Maida is the ultimate transparent facilitator. Mary, as her name clearly indicates, is the virginal good daughter: loyal, dutiful, and hard working. As an obedient daughter she is completely devoted to her father, but on realizing the truth, she sacrifices her own reputation and best interests and supports the right cause and the film's male hero. The film's casting choices perfectly accommodate these images. Lee Remick's stunning figure in tight pants is unforgettable, whereas the other two actresses are indistinct. It would have been hard to structure more stereotypical, allegorically simplistic, one-dimensional female characters. The perfect domestic ("Good Post-Eden Eve") archetypal feminine image is split into the older nurturing, motherly wife and the younger, dutiful, virginal daughter characters, both contrasted with a diluted version of the dangerously sexual ("Lilith"), the uncontrollable, nondomestic woman.

I suggested earlier that Anatomy is one of the classic hero-lawyer films on which later law films and television series were modeled. Anatomy's treatment of women, their victimization, and judgment, is, therefore, an integral part of what came to be the model of hero-lawyer law films. The pattern can also be seen in the antihero-lawyer films which gradually became predominant over the last two decades of the twentieth century. Interestingly, even as the hero-lawyer's image declined, and Hollywood's lawyers lost their virtue and innocence, law films' female protagonists seem to have remained overly sexual women, denied cinematic recognition as sexual victims while judged and condemned as shameful and guilty. Further, the more fallen the lawyers, the more dangerously sexual their feminine counterparts became. William Hurt's *Body Heat* (1981), Paul Newman's *The Verdict* (1982), and Tom Cruise's *The Firm* (1993) are cases in point. In these films the fallen lawyer protagonist is ruined (or almost ruined) by his deceitful, sexual female client/partner/seducer, whose own victimization the film denies. In these films, the lawyers seem to be punished for their uncontrolled sexual attraction to the fatal women, their failure to maintain Biegler's sexual innocence. It appears that as long as he held his ground, resisting the sexual woman's temptation, the cinematic lawyer maintained his heroic status. Having succumbed to the temptress, he fell from grace, losing his magic (even if in some cases repentance and overcoming the sexual attraction redeem the fallen lawyer).

Richard Gere's lawyer character in *Chicago* (2003) is an interesting contemporary variation on the familiar theme. Here, a self-serving, shrewd, utterly cynical lawyer's successful career is inseparable from his dangerously sexual, male-murdering, greedy female clients, whose own abuse is, of course, ignored. It seems that whether hero, fallen hero, or villainous antihero, Hollywood's protagonist lawyer is often intertwined with the character of the sexually guilty woman.

Postscript: A Feminist Reading Against the Grain

As in previous chapters, let me end on a positive, constructive, feminist note. It seems a stretch to read *Anatomy of a Murder* as a feminist text. Nevertheless, several underlying seeds can be used to read it against itself.

Lee Remick's Laura, "voluptuous flirt" as she may be, is also a vulnerable, heart-wrenching, lonely character, and a frustrated, confined housewife. All alone in her tiny, isolated trailer, this lively woman is the image of youth wasting away in the shadow of the oppressive Donna Reed icon. Her exaggerated, slightly ridiculous voluptuous persona is a manifestation of the deadening boredom imposed on her, the lack of alternative avenues available to her to express herself, as well as her husband's and other men's sexual fantasies. If she is an "army slut," it is because her husband likes to "show her off" as a sexual object, and because she is denied any alternative, meaningful lifestyle. If she offers herself to men as a plaything, it is because the lifestyle of an army wife denies her the company of other women, as well as any other social context. At the same time, playing out his sexist wishes subjects her to her husband's violent rages of jealousy. Laura's sad, lonely, wasted life can evoke sympathy as well as a harsh critique of the gender roles imposed on her.

Just as significantly, Eve Arden's Maida is the film's sober common sense, the reasonable person, the film's chorus and jury. (This is one of the film's innovations in comparison with the novel). Although not offering Laura a supportive feminine community, Maida defines her as "soft, easy—the kind of woman men like to take advantage of, and do." Maida does see Laura as product and victim of male society, and it is as such that she constructs her for the film's characters as well as the viewer. In the following decades, in the 1960s and 1970s, Maida would grow with the second feminist wave, further developing her embryonic compassion for her "fallen sister" and her criticism of the men who like to take advantage of her—and do.

Part II

CINEMATIC WOMEN DEMANDING JUDGMENT

From Liberal Attitudes to Radical Feminist Jurisprudence

and the Ethics of Care

Adam's Rib 5

(U.S.A., 1949)

HOLLYWOOD'S FEMALE LAWYER AND FAMILY VALUES

(READ WITH *DISCLOSURE* AND *LEGALLY BLONDE*)

Adam's Rib is a classic courtroom comedy, released in 1949. Featuring a female lawyer representing a female defendant and arguing the case for women's equal rights, it is often read and remembered as a radical challenge to traditional, patriarchal hegemony. Relying on audience familiarity with legal and cinematic conventions, the film opens up new possibilities for the public perception of relations between women, law, and judgment. Presenting a powerful female lawyer who wins what she defines as a feminist case, takes an active part in constructing the judgment of a woman defendant, and succeeds in maintaining her supportive, egalitarian marital relationship, the film is groundbreaking. The film's feminist woman protagonist restructures both legal and social judgment of women in the film's fictional world. She "has it all" personally and professionally: a role typically reserved by Hollywood for male protagonists. Nevertheless, the film ultimately upholds conventional, patriarchal social order and its stereotyping of women. The fictional legal system and the film per se reinforce each other in precluding the possibility of triumphant feminist legal argumentation and the existence of a community of women. The film's cinematic judgment scrutinizes its female lawyer, finding her guilty of disrespecting the law, fighting for the wrong legal theory, and threatening her domestic bliss.

Film Synopsis

A young woman follows her unfaithful spouse from his office to his lover's home, where she pulls a gun and, both eyes shut, shoots at the embracing couple, causing the man a minor injury. In the next scene, a married couple, Amanda Bonner (Katharine Hepburn) and Adam Bonner (Spencer Tracy), wake to reports of the shooting in their morning papers. Amanda expresses sympathy for the woman. As she drives herself and her husband to town, she argues passionately that were the defendant a man he would have enjoyed a sympathetic public, benefiting from the unwritten law allowing a man to protect his home. A desperate wife resorting to violence to save her marriage, she argues, deserves similar treatment. "As she questions the fairness of society's view, she becomes excited and emotional, her driving becomes erratic and she almost has an accident" (Graham and Maschio 1995– 96, 1036). Entering his office, Adam, an assistant district attorney, is assigned to prosecute the attempted murder, to which Amanda, a private attorney, responds by volunteering to represent the defendant, Doris Attinger (Judy Holliday).

Rejecting Adam's repeated attempts to convince her to abandon the case, Amanda explains how important women's rights are to her, insisting that Adam himself shares her ideological convictions: "Listen, Adam—she says—I know that deep down you agree with me—with all I believe and want and hope for. We couldn't be so close if you didn't. If I didn't feel you did" (Gordon and Kanin 1949, 55). Amanda's legal argument is that because women are equal to men in their skills and talents, women are entitled to equality before the law; like men, women should—and do—have the right to defend their homes against home wreckers. "Amanda's strategy is to show that women are equal to men. She fills the courtroom with prospective women witnesses who she hopes will testify to their accomplishments. A chemist testifies about her scientific accomplishments. An acrobat demonstrates her athletic ability, at one point hoisting Adam aloft and subjecting him to ridicule" (Tushnet 1996, 247–48).

Each courtroom scene in which Adam and Amanda battle over the Attinger case is followed by a domestic scene at the Bonner home after work. As the legal battle intensifies, the marital relationship grows stormier. We witness the Bonners hosting a dinner party and viewing a home movie of their newly acquired country house, cooking dinner together, and massaging each other. But as the legal battle progresses, their evenings together gradually grow more tense, and their loving, lively dialogue is replaced by long, awkward silences. After the acrobat demonstrates her strength by lifting Adam up in the air, Adam accuses Amanda of disrespecting both the law and himself. "I'm old fashioned," he continues. "I like two sexes. Another thing. All of a sudden I don't like being married to what's known as the *new* woman. I want a wife, not a competitor! *Competitor! Competitor!* If you want to be a big he-woman go ahead and be it—but not with me!!" (Gordon and Kanin 1949, 85). Suitcase in hand, he leaves home, slamming the door behind him.

Amanda wins her case, as the jury finds Doris Attinger not guilty. That evening, with a flirting neighbor, Amanda exclaims, "Be something, won't it? Win the case and lose my husband" (Gordon and Kanin 1949, 102). Soon after, Adam walks in, finding Amanda and the neighbor in a posture that could easily be mistaken as romantic. As Adam pulls a gun, Amanda calls out, "Stop it, Adam, stop it! You've no right! You can't do what you're doing. *You've no right!* No one has a right to—" (105). Adam, content, replies: "That's all, sister. That's all I wanted to hear. Music to my tin ear . . . I'll never forget that no matter what you think you think—you really think the same as I do. That I've no right. That *no one has a right*—to break the law. That your client had no right. That I'm right. That you're wrong" (106). He puts the muzzle in his mouth, and biting it off explains to the horrified Amanda: "Licorice. If I'm a sucker for anything it's for licorice" (106).

In the next scene, at their tax consultant's office, Adam and Amanda are gravely and reluctantly dividing their property. When Adam bursts into tears, Amanda stops the meeting and supports him as they leave together for their country house. That night, in their bedroom, Adam announces that he has been asked by the Republicans to run for judge, to which Amanda responds by asking whether the Democratic candidate had been nominated. Adam replies that if she competed against him he would cry, revealing that his earlier tears were a trick to win Amanda back, and Amanda concludes that this "shows what I say is true. No difference between the sexes. None. Men, women. The same . . . Well, maybe there *is* a difference. But it is a *little* difference."

"*Vive la difference!*" responds Adam triumphantly, as he climbs into bed and pulls the curtains (118).

A First View: Feminist Optimism

Critical academic writers and lay audiences alike are engaged by *Adam's Rib*, hailing it as feminist and uniquely progressive. Scholars analyzing the female-attorney subgenre find that the film's feminist theme and positive portrayal of the female attorney are unique and unprecedented, not only in the context of the 1930s and 1940s but also in comparison with late-twentieth-century cinema.[1] Indeed, in some respects relevant to this book's themes, the film is a bright lighthouse. Reading *Adam's Rib* against the films presented in part 1 illuminates this film's alternative, feminist treatment of the judgment of women and women's guilt.

Adam's Rib opens with a long, detailed scene of Doris Attinger's attack on her husband and his lover. The film leaves no room for ambiguity: Warren Attinger was embracing his lover, and, using a gun she had just bought, Doris shot in their direction, but with both her eyes shut. Her accurate description of the event coincides with the viewer's firsthand impression, thus characterizing her as a credible witness who can be trusted when she painfully describes her ongoing abuse at the hands of her husband. In contrast, Warren Attinger's credibility is undermined when he accuses his slim, delicate wife of being fat.

When Amanda Bonner takes Doris Attinger's case it is precisely and explicitly to challenge the conventional condemnation of women. Amanda's passionate argument is that patriarchal gender-based social standards, conventions, and stereotypes undermine the egalitarian application of gender-blind legal norms. (In other words, she offers a feminist constructive deconstruction of the equality norm.) The gendered judging mechanisms quietly employed and embraced by the films presented in part 1 are openly confronted by *Adam's Rib* feminist lawyer protagonist. Shifting attention away from the assault on Attinger's life, Amanda focuses it on Doris Attinger's victimization at the hands of her husband, as well as on the legal system's biased treatment of Doris as defendant. She demands that the legal system acknowledge its gender-based discrimination and treat Doris as it would any male defendant, consequently finding her action justifiable, or at least excusable.

Going beyond a refusal to isolate and silence Doris Attinger, *Adam's Rib* provides her with the support of an articulate feminist lawyer. Amanda is committed to winning Doris's case and zealous in the pursuit of her acquittal, securing Doris's right to her day in court. Further, Amanda's line of argument defies the legal isolation of her client by framing her judgment as an offense to all women. Supported by the film, Amanda fights and prevents the prosecution's conventional attempt to concentrate on Doris as a deviant individual. On the contrary, Amanda argues that Doris is judged as a woman, and that her judgment therefore constitutes class discrimination. Filling the courtroom with women and putting accomplished women on the witness stand, Amanda emphasizes the collective, gender-based nature of her client's trial. In a classic feminist move she thus exposes the private as public and turns the personal into the political. In the discussion of the films in part 1, I argued that while women characters are found guilty, they are also deprived of both the status of victims and that of agents. In contrast, Amanda portrays Doris as a woman victimized by her husband, and as a potential victim of a discriminatory legal system. At the same time she does not attribute Doris's behavior to her "nature," nor does she portray it as an instinctual response to her victimization. Stressing Doris's remarkable conduct as an exemplary mother, as well as the difficult situation her husband placed her in, Amanda awards her full agency, justifying—or at least excusing—her chosen course of action. Rather than a guilty object, Amanda constructs a victimized agent.

I believe that a major factor in the film's feminist reputation is the confident, optimistic tone with which it portrays an egalitarian social reality. Women, in the film's fictional world, are fully integrated in both the labor force and the legal system; they assertively voice their values, present their point of view in the public sphere, and are heard by both men and the legal system. In this fictional world, women respect themselves and are respected by men and society; they can and do influence the law from within, succeeding in advancing their social status and achieving these heroic accomplishments at a very low personal price. Where there is a will, there is surely a way, the film promises, cheerfully presenting utopia as reality and encouraging women to dare. Such an optimistic feminist portrayal of reality is indeed fresh and highly unusual. Furthermore, in Adam's Rib, man and woman, Adam and Eve, are constantly engaged in intense dialogue. In the public sphere of the courtroom, as well as in the private sphere of home, they are always together, occupying the same space. They speak the same language of law and justice, listening to each other respectfully, seeing each other's point of view, and sharing values, concerns, and ideals. Partners in intimacy and profession alike, they create the world together, struggling to make it fit and just for both. In Adam's Rib, law is the arena where man and woman struggle together to acknowledge and accept each other and to bravely confront social reality and restate social norms from an inclusive, egalitarian perspective. The film's energetic pace and witty dialogue rejoice in this vision, sweeping viewers up in the celebration. In this, the film is truly outstanding.

A Second Look

Adam's Rib's optimistic tone is dramatically emphasized by the film's screwball-comedy temperament (Everson 1994). Extroverted and dominant, the film's tone overshadows other, more subtle tendencies. But a closer look at the film's choices, on both legal and cinematic levels, reveals a different, less obvious—yet no less powerful—tendency.

THE FILM'S LEGAL FEMINIST ARGUMENT AND STEREOTYPING OF WOMEN

In the film's fictional legal world, Amanda Bonner, champion of women's rights, defends Doris by fiercely pursuing a liberal, feminist legal approach, demanding to extend the unwritten law to women. According to Amanda, Doris never meant to hurt her husband, merely to scare away his lover, who was shattering Doris's family. Under the unwritten law, a man shooting at his wife's lover would be viewed as rightly defending his home, Amanda argues. The law, echoing and reinforcing public opinion, would sympathize with his anger and pain, objecting to the violence but ultimately condoning it. A woman, claims Amanda, deserves the exact same treatment. Convicting a woman for attempted murder where a man in her shoes would walk free amounts to sexual discrimination. The highlight of this argument is Amanda's plea to the jury and viewers to see in Doris Attinger a wronged husband, in Attinger an unfaithful wife, and in Beryl Caighn, the third party, a "slick home-wrecker" in "a pin-stripe suit" (Graham and Kanin 1949, 89). "Now you have it, Judge it so," exclaims Amanda. "An unwritten law stands back of a man who fights to defend his home. Apply the same to the maltreated wife and neglected mother. We ask you no more. Equality!" (89).

Dramatic and extravagant as it may be, this line of feminist legal argument fails not merely because the film's grotesque visualization of the characters in drag renders it ridiculous and unconvincing. It fails because it undermines itself while zealously upholding the worst manifestation of patriarchal oppression of women. As I discussed in chapter 4, a man's traditional unwritten "right" to take the life of the man who violates his matrimonial rights (and perhaps also of the woman who sexually betrays him) is the most extreme manifestation of patriarchal, honor-based mentality. Within this worldview, a woman's sexual availability is a commodity owned and controlled by her husband. A woman's "indecency," i.e., exposure of her sexuality, shames and humiliates the man who owns it, by willing "submission" to another man at the expense of the rightful owner. A woman's adultery, therefore, constitutes a devastating attack on her husband's honor, entitling him to "self-defense," i.e., to prove and restore his manliness and manly entitlement by cleansing his stained honor and eliminating the invading male opponent (and perhaps also the guilty wife).[2] The unwritten law was very popular in the American legal reality in the mid-nineteenth century, but lost its appeal and standing at the beginning of the twentieth century, and has not been used since.

Within the film's legal world, feminist legal thought is equated with the explicit demand not merely to uphold this honor culture, but to revive it in 1949, render it legal support, and expand it by extending to wives honor rights heretofore reserved (almost) exclusively for husbands.[3] Sex equality Amanda-style means that women, too, should be legally entitled to possess honor, and that men's adulterous behavior should be constructed as shameful, just like women's. This supposedly feminist stand elicits little sympathy. It stands in clear contrast to every humane and liberal notion of the value of human life, human autonomy, dignity, liberty, free choice, and the rule of law. Rather than undermine the legal support of patriarchal ideology and practice, this line of argument serves only to reinforce such support, and is therefore all but feminist. Practically speaking, when it was still in use, the unwritten law benefited almost exclusively men, since, statistically, women never tended—and do not tend today—to kill their husband's lovers.[4] Hence extending this defense to women offers no practical advantage that would justify the consequent reinforcement of patriarchal values.

The dangerously androcentric nature of the unwritten law was familiar to women, and to feminist women in particular, as early as the nineteenth century. Robert Ireland notes that "the unwritten law represented an extreme reflection of Victorian America's preoccupation with strict sexual probity. The doctrine incorporated many of the myths and hypocrisies of that era, including the notion of female sexual passionlessness and the double standard of sexual conduct" (1989, 38). He reports that American women seem to have been "significantly less enthusiastic about it than men who were much more its direct beneficiaries" (37). Feminist women (such as Elizabeth Cady Stanton) opposed it strongly and vocally (Hartog 1997, 70).

Women's rights activists viewed the acquittals of murdering husbands as "barbaric and designed to ensure male control over marriages and sexual conduct" (Ireland 1989, 37). Attorneys advocating the unwritten law on behalf of their clients, in turn, linked the "dangerous libertines" who violated men's matrimonial rights with social reformers, including women's rights activists (Hartog 1997, 75). It is clear that lawyers propagating the unwritten law and feminists were on two sides of the public battle. Women's rights activists did not and would not support any expansion of the unwritten law, even by extending it to women. Presenting Amanda's promotion of the unwritten law as a feminist move is thus misleading.

Furthermore, Amanda's line of argument strongly reinforces patriarchal stereotypes of women. In her attempt to secure sympathy for the defendant, Amanda positions her in sharp binary opposition to her rival, the unmarried home wrecker. Assisted by the film's casting, Amanda constitutes the good woman as a fair, dependent wife and devoted mother. Her opponent, the evil woman, is a dark, unattached woman, a shameless temptress, and an inherent threat to society's sacred family values. The film's seemingly feminist legal argument divides women into Eve and Lilith, pitting the domestic against the whore in a struggle over a man.

Within this traditional metaphoric realm, clearly condoned by the film and its legal feminist protagonist, Amanda herself is a stereotypical new woman, as clearly stated by Adam. The powerful female attorney has taken over "wearing the pants" in her family, humiliating her husband into a secondary, "feminized" role. She is the articulate Yale graduate who runs an aggressive private practice, while he is a gentle, easygoing, stuttering public servant. She drives them both to work, while he cooks, wearing an apron. Her picture is on the front page, while he cries. Instead of mothering children, Amanda raises dogs.

Unlike the countess in *Pandora's Box*, Amanda's masculinity is not explicitly translated into "man-hating" lesbianism. Nevertheless, despite her obvious good looks and extravagant wardrobe, Amanda is not feminine, sexual, or attractive in conventional, heterosexual terms. On the contrary, there is something boyish about her appearance and movement. Her "masculinity" is mirrored by the comically feminized character of the admiring neighbor who writes her love songs and declares he is so thoroughly convinced by her arguments that he would be willing to become a woman. The manly Amanda attracts the effeminate man, threatening to castrate the "real" man and undermine the institution of marriage, social order, and the rule of law (as Adam states when he packs his things and leaves). A feminine bonnet is another symbol used by the film to emphasize the difference between Doris's "feminine" image and Amanda's "unfeminine" one. Buying his wife a flowery bonnet, Adam tries to feminize her. But the bonnet is totally wrong for Amanda, and she uses it to dress Doris for the trial and emphasize her feminine image. In the film's last scene, Amanda jokingly decides to wear the bonnet, which merely highlights her unfeminine looks. Amanda, the new-woman attorney, is thus not a role model for ordinary women on- and off-screen, but rather a (comic) transcendent exception; an anomaly.

Amanda's witnesses, a chemist, an acrobat, and a forewoman carefully selected to represent the power and worth of womanhood, are caricatures as well. These women are neither typical of real women, nor "feminine" in any way. Each excels in a man's world by outdoing men at their own game, playing by men's rules. Not one challenges masculine norms and conventions or manifests any characteristic that could be viewed as uniquely "feminine." Much like Amanda, they are exaggerated, unconvincing "he-women," to use Adam's derogatory term. In order to be successful women, they signal, women must and do fully adjust to the masculine world and learn to be better men than men. Those who possess outstanding "manly" skills may succeed. Such images of women are no more realistic or less damaging than the traditional Eve and Lilith ones.

By dividing the female characters into Eve, Lilith, and he-woman types, the film's feminist legal argument precludes the possibility of a feminine community within the law. This effect is strengthened by the obvious class distinction between Amanda and the other central female characters. The woman lawyer's elitism is taken to the extreme, almost to the point of ridicule. Real contact between her and the other women (defendant, witnesses, secretaries), or, for that matter, contact among any of the women, seems impossible. The film's fictional female characters are thus separated in their distinct patriarchal categories, and women viewers are offered no feminine community to emulate. Accordingly, the film's women do not share a unique, distinctive feminine culture. Amanda's treatment of her female client is not caring, compassionate, and empathetic in any way that could be considered as a feminine alternative to masculine standards. On the contrary, her relationship with Doris is purely professional in a traditional patriarchal mode: cold and dry. Amanda's logic of sameness between the sexes is embraced, enhanced, and taken to its limits by the film.

In its treatment of Amanda's liberal feminist argument, is the film pushing the unwritten-law argument *ad absurdum*? Does it subversively invite its viewer to see through its extreme presentation of Amanda's argument, thus exposing the danger of a legal upholding of the honor code? I have no doubt that resistant viewers may read the film's depiction of Amanda's argument this way. However, rather than leave the viewer to struggle with the difficulties of the liberal feminist jurisprudence it presents, the film offers an attractive, easy alternative. This alternative is not an improved feminist argument, but rather a gender-blind liberal one, offered by the film as Adam's superior jurisprudence.

In *Adam's Rib*, it is Adam's liberal legal position that, in stark contrast with Amanda's line of reasoning, both advances women's interests and invites viewers' sympathy. Within the specific legal situation as constituted by the film, Adam's uncompromisingly positivistic stand that "the law is the law" and no one has a right to break it, accords with his enlightened, gender-blind liberal argument that no one has the right to shoot at a spouse, as well as with deep respect for the rule of law. Significantly, this legal stand is depicted by the film as nonfeminist. Clearly, the legal attitude that is both enlightened and most desirable for women is the commonsensical, supposedly nonfeminist stand advanced by the mainstream male protagonist. Unlike the film's feminist, subversive legal argument, which separates men from women, women from women, the rule of law from feminist causes, ideology from the interests of real-life women, Adam's commonsense attitude to the law offers the just and enlightened solution for men and women alike, and for society at large. The pervasiveness of this legal argument's appeal is such that, in a moment of truth, at gunpoint, Amanda herself instinctively embraces it.

Adam may have lost the battle in the film's fictional courtroom, but that serves only to enhance the dramatic effect of his winning the war within the film's social reality and in the realm of common sense. Amanda's feminist jurisprudence may have fooled the film's fictional jury, but not the film's viewers, its real-life jury. It is Adam's inclusive perception of law that invites the viewer to join a community of liberal, law-abiding citizens. This enlightened community, created in the shadow of the film's "real," "good" law, believes in human life, liberty, equality, and the rule of law. Although not feminist, this gender-blind community of men and women, united around the figure of a nonfeminist male attorney, offers the best solutions for women's predicaments.

Let me stress that both the facts of the fictional case and the legal arguments as presented by the parties manifest a series of cinematic choices, and could have been constructed differently. Much like the text of an appeal court's legal decision, Adam's Rib opens with a report of "the facts of the case." As in a legal text, these "facts" are presented and perceived as the given, objective framework dictating the legal discussion and much of its outcome. Even more than in a legal text, such facts are products of an ideological-rhetorical process manifesting a series of choices.

In Adam's Rib, the case at hand is clearly as sensational and unusual as that of a man biting a dog. The film could easily have depicted a more plausible, realistic case, such as that of a battered woman attacking her abusive spouse. (Clearly, public awareness of this phenomenon was not then what it is today, yet "A Jury of Her Peers," discussed in chapter 8, addressed domestic violence as early as 1916.) In fact, the film's Doris Attinger is a battered, abused wife. Yet this fact is almost lost in the sensational context of a violent "love triangle." Amanda reveals the fact in her cross-examination of the husband, but does not mention it in her summary. The film chooses to present legal arguments that all but ignore this aspect of the case. Rather than concentrate on Warren Attinger's abusive behavior as that which provoked his wife's violent act, the case is presented as a reversed story of familiar, patriarchal jealousy and honor. (In fact, the film's choice to open with an "objective" presentation of Doris Attinger's criminal act is, in itself, telling. As discussed in chapter 8, in "A Jury of Her Peers," Susan Glaspell chooses to present the details of the female defendant's crime through the sympathetic point of view of a female acquaintance. Clearly, in its "objective" tone, and in the choice to present the facts before offering a frame of reference, the film is far less sympathetic to the female defendant.)

The film's presentation of the facts of the case is complimented by its choice of feminist legal argument. Amanda's gender-blind, liberal feminist perspective not only undercuts itself, but also deprives the defendant of more coherent, effective arguments that would stress the uniqueness of her predicament. A genuine feminist legal argument, focusing on Doris Attinger's unique situation, would have prohibited the film's equation of her predicament to that of Adam's in the licorice scene. It would have made clear the inherent difference between the situation of a successful lawyer finding the wife he left behind in the arms of another man (homosexual or not), and that of an abused, dependent housewife, fearful of losing her sole income and support for her three children. Whereas the first is indulging in patriarchal honor and jealousy, the latter is a victim, desperately responding to ongoing abuse that undermines her existence. A compassionate feminist legal argument could have, further, brought the film's fictional female characters together, inviting the viewer to join their feminine community. In other words, a legal argument containing insights of radical feminism, cultural feminism, or both, would have been compelling in the context of the film's legal case's facts.

Clearly, in 1949, feminist legal theories of dominance had not yet been fully articulated. Nevertheless, in her summary before the jury, Amanda does present what could have been developed into a dominance type of feminist legal argument. "Deep in the interior of South America, there thrives a people known as the Lorcananos, descended from the Amazons. In this vast tribe, members of the female sex rule and govern and systematically deny equal rights to the men—made weak and puny by years of subservience. Too weak to revolt. And yet, how long have we lived in the shadow of a like injustice?" (Graham and Kanin 1949, 89). Had the film allowed her, Amanda could have defended Doris along this feminist line of argument. She could have presented Doris as a battered, abused, and neglected wife, driven to despair by her inability to support her family. This would have been a dominance-type feminist legal argument. Amanda's victory would have then been convincing and powerful. As it is, her short "anthropological" remark clashes with Amanda's liberal sameness argument and makes little sense.

The film's choice to apply a liberal feminist legal argument to a narrative of an abused wife who attempts to kills her husband's lover (or the betraying husband himself) undermines the feminist argument's success. A different feminist legal strategy applied to facts supplied by the film, and/or a choice of a different story (such as a story of employment discrimination) could have allowed for a triumphant feminist legal argumentation.

GENRE CONVENTIONS OFFER CINEMATIC SUPPORT
TO THE LEGAL ARGUMENTS

Discussing *Anatomy of a Murder* in chapter 4, I argue that a classic court-room drama of the hero-lawyer type features a heroic protagonist in pursuit of an idealistic social mission. Elsewhere, I present the argument that such cinematic hero-lawyers are modeled on the hero of the classic western (Kamir 2005b). They are powerful, charismatic loners who courageously and pro-fessionally uphold the community's fundamental values, doing what needs to be done to protect the social order from external enemies and internal weak-ness. Often outsiders to the communities they struggle to save, cinematic lawyers stand for the justice, courage, integrity, and equity at the heart of the idea of law. At times frustrated and weary, they are nevertheless devoted to worthwhile social causes as well as to the rule of law, struggling to maintain them against all odds. Like its predecessor, the western hero, the cinematic lawyer is not an upper-class man of words from the East Coast, but a small-town man of action. His biography is often mysterious, and at times he leads a bitter, lonely life in the shadow of a tragic past. His antagonist is the cynical, articulate, big-city lawyer, ruthlessly representing money and specific, often elitist, interests. The cinematic lawyer is shy and slightly awkward, especially around women, like his gunfighter predecessor.

Anatomy of a Murder's Paul Biegler was masterfully crafted a decade after the release of *Adam's Rib*, and Amanda could not have been modeled on him. But the prototype of the western hero was well established and deeply cherished in 1949, even more so than in 1959. Amanda Bonner is a lawyer fighting for a social cause and is thus a natural candidate to be portrayed as a hero-lawyer. The film could have constructed her character along the familiar lines of the small-town, underdog loner, inviting the viewer's sympathy and identification. Yet the film chose to cast the majestic Katharine Hepburn, and characterize her Amanda as a sharp, cold, "not mothering," articulate, upper-class Yale graduate. Amanda dresses better than any other character in the film's fictional world, and speaks more, and far more eloquently, than the rest of the characters. Overly aggressive, militant, and self-assured, she is a ruthless warrior, lacking any of the endearing characteristics Jimmy Stewart has in his role as Paul Biegler. This undermines not merely her femininity, as mentioned in the previous section, but also her position as the film's point of identification. Decades of western viewing have trained viewers to recognize, cherish, and identify with unassuming heroes fighting for the just cause. Amanda does not resonate with that familiar image. Biegler does.

Moreover, the classic western hero, the "true man," stands for "natural law," which includes the unwritten law and the traditional honor code. But he combines this instinctive sense of "equity" with respect for the positive, state law. Biegler, his descendant hero-lawyer, goes further, perfecting the symbiosis of "justice" and legalistic professionalism. Like a true man, Amanda fights for the natural law embodied in the unwritten law and its underlying honor mentality. But she is portrayed, through Adam's perspective, as disrespectful of the positive law, mocking and "outsmarting" it (to use his term). Adam's perception of her attitude towards the law, upheld by the film, undercuts Amanda's standing as an excellent professional (since as a lawyer, excellence entails excellence in upholding the law), as well as a true man. Of course, her sex may also come between her and a perfect embodiment of a true man . . .

It is Adam, Amanda's antagonist, whom the film portrays as the small-time, lovable underdog, fighting for an unpopular but just social cause: the rule of law. The defeat and humiliation Adam suffers at Amanda's hands (highlighted by the insult of the flirting neighbor) further invite sympathy and identification. Interestingly, Spencer Tracy's subsequent cinematic legal career bloomed, casting him, among other roles, as the memorable attorney in *Inherit the Wind* and the judge in *Judgment at Nuremberg*. Indeed, Rennard Strickland claims that of all the "actors whose screen ethos has made them ideal cinematic lawyers . . . Spencer Tracy deserves to hold the screen-lawyer prize for sustained service at the bar" (1997, 16). Not surprisingly, *Adam's Rib* was Hepburn's last appearance as an attorney of law.[5]

To complicate things further, *Adam's Rib* is not merely a courtroom drama. It is a classic romantic comedy of the type Stanley Cavell defined as "the Hollywood comedy of remarriage" (Cavell 1981). In films of this genre, a couple encounters an obstacle, breaks up, overcomes the obstacle, and reunites, forming a stronger, more mature marital unit. It is the woman, Cavell argues, who is the film's protagonist, and it is she who must undergo symbolic death and rebirth to enable the revival of the relationship. Read against these conventions, Amanda's legal feminist "crusade" is clearly the obstacle to overcome on the road to happily ever after, a youthful folly the couple needs to endure and transcend.

Pressing this point, I suggest that in addition to the genres already mentioned, *Adam's Rib* belongs to the exclusive Tracy-Hepburn genre.[6] At the heart of this distinct group of nine films is the unique, captivating chemistry and intimacy that characterized this on- and off-screen Hollywood couple. Enchanted by the authentic closeness between the Tracy and Hepburn characters, a viewer cannot but perceive anything that comes between them as a temporary hurdle on the path to true love.

Immediately after the film's initial, violent scene, the viewer is shown the Bonners' warm, loving intimacy. Breakfasting in their bedroom, Tracy and Hepburn are the perfect couple. Anything that threatens this perfection must be inherently wrong. Against this point of departure, Amanda's feminist cause and legal activism are too risky. A male film lawyer's professional activity typically increases his manliness. In films presenting a feminist agenda (think of *Thelma and Louise* and *A Question of Silence*) women's bonding

replaces—or at least supplements—unfulfilling, abusive male-female relationships. Unlike either of these types of films, *Adam's Rib* chooses to construct Amanda's professional activity as threatening to undermine the film's
most cherished (family) value: the Tracy-Hepburn relationship. In this context, feminist lawyering and a community of women cannot be but temporary
comic diversions. Supported by its legal and cinematic conventions, the only
community the film allows is the Tracy-Hepburn fan club.

As I discussed earlier, *Adam's Rib* supports Amanda in her quest to prevent
gender-based judgment and condemnation of Doris. In other words, the text
does not actively invite its viewer to judge Doris, nor does it lead the viewer to
find her (inherently) guilty. Yet, while sparing Doris Attinger, the film puts
her feminist, new-woman attorney on trial, inviting the viewer to judge her
together with her feminist quest. Adam's sympathetically convincing liberal
argument, Amanda's retreat in the licorice scene, the grotesque impression
of Amanda's reversal stunt, her failure to fit a familiar hero role, her public
humiliation of Adam, and above all, the threat her behavior poses to the film's
family values—all invite the viewer to judge Amanda and her feminist legal
crusade, and find them dangerous.

Splitting the woman protagonist in two, *Adam's Rib* is compassionately
accepting of Doris, its Eve, even as it judges Amanda, its new woman,
finding her extreme, threatening, and obstructive to family, society, and the
law. Amanda is "redeemed" only by the film's happy ending in the form of
Adam's return, the couple's reconciliation, and the closing scene's implication that in the future Amanda will be more careful in challenging her husband. But the cinematic judgment's cautionary message is unambiguous, just
like its condemnation of the film's third woman, the sexual, seductress Lilith,
who, like Amanda, is not a defendant in the film's fictional legal proceeding,
yet is found guilty by the cinematic judgment. The dignifying, nonjudgmental
treatment of Doris, the film's official defendant and, conveniently, the good
mother, is, thus, a smoke screen. *Adam's Rib*'s cinematic judgment of its
woman lawyer is typical of later films portraying women lawyers, and may be
seen as setting the stage for this problematic subgenre.

A Third View: Applying Hollywood's "No-Choice" Policy to Women

In his study of structures and conventions underlying Hollywood's classic
films and their contemporary descendants, Robert Ray (1985) argues that
these films' basic paradigm and major source of attraction is their comforting

promise that deep contradictions can be reconciled and that no hard, painful choices between America's fundamental values must ever be made. The viewer is repeatedly reassured that he can, in fact, have his cake and eat it too. Hollywood's viewer, according to Ray, is invited to identify with both an on-screen "outlaw hero" (the lone rider with the shady past) and an "official" one (the courageous sheriff), or with a character combining both functions. Either way, the viewer is allowed to transcend the choice between individuality and loyalty to community. The "reluctant hero" is a case in point: He is the individualistic loner, who reluctantly joins a community in need, because a man's got to do what a man's got to do. His conduct, although courageous and honorable, is not always by the book. His communitarian life is short and target oriented, and upon victory, he withdraws to his private life. Applying Ray's terminology, Hollywood's hero-lawyer may be defined as a reluctant hero, combining characteristics of an official hero with those of an outlaw hero, thus satisfying the American dream of overcoming the need to choose.

In fact, it is male viewers who, in Ray's theory, are invited to see themselves, simultaneously, in both types of Hollywood's male heroes. In the Hollywood classics discussed by Ray, good women are avoided by outlaw heroes and married by official heroes; identifying with both types of on-screen male heroes, the male viewer needn't choose between family values and freedom. On-screen women are not, themselves, heroes of either type. Female viewers must identify either with the male heroes, taking on the androgynous identity Laura Mulvey has described, and/or with the on-screen female objects of male desire.

In the "woman's movie," on the other hand, where female characters are the protagonists, the underlying conventions are dramatically different. "According to Haskell, the main themes of the woman's movie are sacrifice, choice, affliction or competition . . . Even when the featured woman was a professional, she would have to sacrifice her career for her marriage, choose between her career or her children, compete with another woman for a man's love, or die on the heels of a professional triumph" (Caplow 1999, 60). In fact, these conventions are apparent even outside the woman's movie: Hollywood's women characters typically confront choice, sacrifice, and pain, while male heroes and viewers are often freed of them by the powerful underlying structures depicted by Ray.

Let me illustrate this point with a familiar example. Ray's most compelling case study is the film that brings Hollywood's conventions to perfection:

Casablanca (Ray 1985, 89–112). Rick (Humphrey Bogart) and Laszlo (Paul Henreid) epitomize the complex relationship between outlaw and official hero, and Rick is the ultimate reluctant hero. The classic blurring of differences between them is manifested, among many ways, in their common love of a single (good) woman whom one marries and the other leaves behind. Adding Haskell's perspective to Ray's, it becomes apparent that, throughout the film, Ilsa (Ingrid Bergman), the film's single female character, role model, and point of identification for women viewers, suffers choice, sacrifice, and pain. The (male) viewer, on the other hand, deeply identifying with both Rick and Laszlo, has it all: both the girl and the freedom he so cherishes. Ilsa's sacrifice is both obvious and transparent; even Ray himself, concentrating on the male characters and viewer, does not seem to notice it.

These underlying conventions, feminist writers convincingly show, were typically applied to woman-lawyer films: "Surprisingly, there were a notable number of movies made during the 1930s and 1940s that featured women lawyers . . . These were largely woman's movies in a legal setting with sacrifice themes that frequently highlighted their heroines' flaws, moral lapses, or failures as women . . . Typically, the women lawyers were forced to admit their hubris for wanting it all at the expense of their more feminine duties of wife or mother. Like other woman's films of that period they were melodramas" (Caplow 1999, 61). In their discussions of contemporary female-lawyer films, Caplow (1999), Graham and Maschio (1995–96), Miller (1994), Sheffield (1993), and Shapiro (1995) argue that little has changed. "Female attorneys in film have been presented as an oxymoron; they have two identities—'female' and 'attorney'—which cannot logically coexist" (Miller 1994, 205).

If we accept Ray's thesis, it seems that Hollywood's most appealing promise is that the male viewer, identifying with cinematic male heroes, can have it all and pay no painful price. At the same time, as Haskell claims, Hollywood illustrates how women must make painful choices at great cost. The gender roles mirrored and affirmed by Hollywood are thus defined by the necessity to choose, pay, and sacrifice: what distinguishes man from woman is man's freedom from difficult choices. This panoramic view of Hollywood conventions sheds new light on *Adam's Rib*. Clearly not adhering to the conventions of the woman's melodrama, it does not force its female lawyer to choose, sacrifice, and pay. On the contrary, the explicit risk of losing her husband does not prevent her from pursuing her professional, ideological mission, nor does it undermine her confidence. She stands her ground, and, although the price and pain of his choice are mitigated by the film's comic tone, it is he who is forced to choose between the woman he loves and his traditional views of family and gender roles.

Applying both Ray's and Haskell's perspectives, it becomes apparent that despite Adam's choice, the film offers its viewer Hollywood's seductive dream: a reconciliation of contradictory fundamental American myths. Justice in a particular, difficult case ("equity") is reconciled with the rule of law, as is the sacred status of family with the notion of equality for all, including women. Cast in Ray's terms, Adam is the official hero, standing for community, stability, and the rule of law, while Amanda is the outlaw, reluctant hero, who takes action only when she feels forced into it by Adam's condescension, does what needs to be done, and retreats to personal life. Not the superhuman, Herculean image combining natural law with positive law, she is, arguably, a more realistic character, and an equal part in the combined image of outlaw and official heroism.

The bold casting of a woman in the sacred role of outlaw hero is striking. This role, notably filled by John Wayne and Humphrey Bogart, is the bastion of masculinity. Additionally, in *Adam's Rib*, the blurring of boundaries between official and outlaw heroes is also the blurring of boundaries between Adam and Eve. Hollywood's formula merging the two paradigmatic heroes typically brings together the Bogart type with the Henreid type; i.e., the John Wayne and the James Stewart characters of *The Man Who Shot Liberty Valence*. The association of these two types of masculinity enables the male viewer to identify with both, leaving the woman as the film's "other": the prize, gift, object. In *Adam's Rib*, the convention of merging official and outlaw heroes is subversively used to bring together man and woman, both on- and off-screen. The ancient notion of "couple" takes on a new dimension when, in the context of Hollywood's conventions, the viewer is invited to identify with a symbiotic pair of male-female heroes. Gender roles—both on- and off-screen— are transcended when the man-woman couple is posed as the fundamental unity reconciling contradictory myths. Viewers, men and women alike, are invited to perform the revolutionary experiment and identify with a transgendered couple, combining masculinity and femininity while blurring the rigid boundaries between them.

The film's choice to construct this subversive, revolutionary reconciliation is enhanced by its selection of the courtroom as its arena. The adversarial American legal system epitomizes the idea of binary rivalry, intuitively associated with manly, zero-sum war games. The film's positioning of male and female attorneys as adversaries could have had the exclusive effect of subjecting the woman attorney to the masculine conventions of the legal world, thus reinforcing them. But in the context of the previously discussed Hollywood conventions it can be argued that by co-opting the adversarial legal system into transcending society's deepest binary distinction, that between man and woman, Adam's Rib fundamentally "demasculinizes" it, suggesting that, like other realms of life, the law must be rethought to accommodate women and men alike. In this, the film echoes Amanda's demand within the fictional legal system for equality between the sexes, lending her legal argument cinematic support. Better yet, the film in fact improves Amanda's feminist argument, substituting a more subversive demasculinization of the legal system for the problematic liberal notion of the sexes' sameness. If Amanda's legal argument only goes so far as demanding for women the same rights created for and enjoyed by men, the cinematic subtext further suggests a fundamental reconceptualization of the legal system to accommodate femininity and masculinity alike.

There is yet another perspective. Read from the perspective of Hollywood's conventions of reconciliation and choice, Adam's Rib lends Amanda's legal struggle further, more straightforward support in demanding for the film's women characters and viewers what Amanda demands for women within its legal system. Amanda demands that rights given exclusively to men be equally extended to women: if man is justified or excused when violently protecting his home, woman must enjoy that right as well, she claims. Similarly, the film insists that if male viewers are offered the dream of reconciled contradictory myths at no painful cost, the same dream should be extended to women. In freeing Amanda from the need to choose between husband and career, in freeing the viewer—and the woman viewer in particular—from the need to choose between Adam and Amanda, between family and women's rights, the film echoes Amanda's campaign to offer Doris Attinger, and all women, the same provocation defense traditionally reserved for men.

But, like Amanda's quest, the film's strategy is not free from feminist doubt. Discussing Amanda's legal argument, I suggested that the provocation defense is inseparable from patriarchal ideology and that, rather than extending it to women, it should be confronted. I further noted that in reality it is men who commit violent jealousy crimes, hence extension of the provocation defense to women is not of great practical significance. Is a life free of choice and sacrifice a man's dream? Does the vision of painless reconciliation of contradictory myths serve the ruling patriarchal ideology?

Clearly, it offers a way of accepting reality without rebellion, of settling for personal solutions that avoid ideological clashes. Just as clearly, in contemporary social reality, most women are still required to make both choices and sacrifices, and to pay painful prices for any deviance from traditional gender roles. Professional life still requires of women choices and compromises most men needn't face.

Should women be offered participation in the dream of choice-free reconciliation, or is it in women's best interest to confront that dream and expose its conservative, constraining effects? Which is more empowering for women: *Adam's Rib*'s optimistic extension of men's legal rights and cinematic dreams to women, or the bleak, realistic vision of law and life offered in feminist texts such as "A Jury of Her Peers," *Thelma and Louise*, *Set It Off*, and *A Question of Silence* (discussed in chapters 8 and 9)?

In *Adam's Rib* women on- and off-screen are not faced with a choice because the film does not represent a community of women and does not offer it as a possible option. There is no pain in Amanda's return to Adam, because the film fails to imagine an alternative for her; in the absence of a real option, her union with Adam is made to seem free of choice, pain, and sacrifice. It is constructed as natural and unavoidable. Over fifty years later, a film envisioning a realistic reconciliation of a community of women with meaningful couplehood is still unrealized. Are women better off with the unresolved choice?

Postscript: Disclosure and Legally Blonde

This chapter's reading of *Adam's Rib* can help decipher other female-lawyer "feminist" law films, revealing a recurrent structure. *Disclosure*, Barry Levinson's 1994 box-office hit, portrays the sexy Demi Moore character, Meredith Johnson, sexually harassing her helpless employee, whose long-deserved managerial job she has snatched through affirmative action. Years earlier, that same employee, Michael Douglas's lovable Tom Sanders, left her brokenhearted, and this is her opportunity to take her revenge on the playboy reformed into a devoted family man. When this scorned woman proceeds to falsely accuse him of sexually harassing her, Tom is forced to press countercharges, represented by the bold feminist attorney Catherine Alvarez (Roma Maffia), renowned for her long, relentless battle against sexual harassment. During the hearing, Tom learns that his devoted secretary has always felt awkward by his physical closeness to her, that his female colleague has always felt discriminated against, and that his ever supportive wife, herself a lawyer, has experienced plenty of sexual harassment, never making a "federal case" of it. He also learns, together with the viewer, that an employee complaining of sexual harassment is blamed, undermined, and shunned by employer, colleagues, and friends, losing job, self-esteem, and faith in the system. The painful experience humbles him and changes his sensitivities as well as his behavior. Finally all ends well: he is redeemed, Meredith is forced to leave, and her place is filled by Tom's friend and supporter, the older, highly professional Stephanie Kaplan (Rosemary Forsyth).

At first glance, the film's profeminist reading appears self-evident. Much like in *Adam's Rib*, a powerful feminist female lawyer in pursuit of a feminist legal cause takes a difficult case to court and triumphs against all odds. Like Amanda, Alvarez is both professionally successful and happily married to another lawyer (who, she admits, first approached her when she was working under him). As in Amanda's feminist strategy, gender-role reversal is central to Catherine Alvarez's line of argument as well. Defending Tom while accusing Meredith, she zealously argues that the feminist struggle to secure the right to say no applies to men as much as it applies to women. Furthermore, focusing on the phenomenon of sexual harassment, defined and challenged by radical feminism, the film invites male viewers to identify with the male protagonist as a means of changing their perspective on sexual harassment and invoking their sympathy for victims of sexual harassment, who in real life are mostly women. Tom experiences the horrors of sexual harassment first-hand, and, transformed by the insight, can truly empathize with women's narration of their own painful experiences. He will be a changed man in his sensitivity to the women surrounding him, wife, female colleagues, and secretary. The sexual harasser is promptly punished, and another woman, this time a deserving one, is promoted to the managerial position once coveted by Tom. Acknowledging her qualities, he gladly accepts her leadership. Relationships between men and women are restored and improved. Last but not least, the film offers a variety of female characters, exploring their struggles to succeed in a man's world.

But a second view reveals an underlying current, which accounts for the film's reputation as a backlash text. Catherine Alvarez's feminist argument is as liberal as Amanda's, and as ineffective in the specific context of sexual harassment as Amanda's was in the defense of an abused woman shooting at her husband (and his lover). Defined and developed within the logic of radical feminism, the concept of sexual harassment is inseparable from the view of gender as a hierarchy and contemporary society as exhibiting male suprem-acy. Within the logic of radical feminism, sexual harassment is sex discrimi-nation, and a manifestation of patriarchal dominance of women by men. It terrorizes women, threatening their safety and dignity, undermines their pro-fessional status, and reduces them to accessible sexual objects. It thus rein-forces patriarchal values and social structure. A man, too, can be sexually harassed, by either a man or a woman, but, in the framework of radical feminism, even such harassment contains more than mere workplace abuse of power: it reinforces gender as hierarchy, thus upholding the existing power structure and contributing to the ongoing gender subordination of women. Portraying Catherine Alvarez as a fictional Catharine MacKinnon, the film neutralizes the legal feminist philosopher and activist, transforming her radi-cal feminism into a liberal manifesto.

The most obvious flaw of the liberal argument in the specific context of the film's "facts" stems from the improbability that male viewers would read the Douglas character as deeply threatened and traumatized by the sexual ad-vances of Demi Moore's character. The film's argument that men and women are equally affected by (heterosexual) sexual harassment and require equal protection suggests that a sexually harassed woman is in a similar situation to Tom when Meredith kneels at his feet and insists on performing oral sex on him. The analogy belittles many women's grave experience of sexual harass-ment. By presenting this liberal, gender-blind argument as the feminist stand on sexual harassment, the film does feminism a disservice, much as *Adam's Rib* does to the demand for sex equality. Further, what male viewers are likely to take seriously is the threat posed to male employees by vengeful ex-lovers who can easily steal their jobs and falsely accuse them of sexual harassment.

Disclosure's liberal feminism, much like *Adam's Rib*'s, is complimented by a stereotypical, archetypal portrayal of the film's female characters. Meredith Johnson, the dark, unattached, ambitious career woman with an enormous sexual appetite and no scruples, threatens family values by being actively irresistible to men. She is a modern-day Lilith character. Tom's wife, Susan (Caroline Goodall), is the ultimate modern good Eve: a fair, asexual, selfless, reliable, loving mother and wife, who puts her marital and maternal duties before her career, and supports her man unconditionally. Stephanie is the older, gray, unassuming, asexual, hard-working woman, a devoted single mother and Tom's guardian angel throughout the film. It is to this modern-day Mother Mary the film awards the desired managerial position, explicitly stating that she deserves it "on the merit," regardless of gender considerations. The disastrous affirmative action that brought on the fatal Meredith at the film's opening is corrected by the gender-blind decision at the film's end, as the dangerous, sexual woman is replaced with the good, asexual one. The fair Susan regains her husband, the dark Meredith is outcast, the virtually ungendered, nonthreatening, gray Stephanie is successfully integrated in the workplace, and patriarchal peace and order are restored and secured.

Seven years later, on the threshold of the new millennium, *Legally Blonde* offers a very different vision of the female lawyer and feminist legal strategy. Elle Woods (Reese Witherspoon) is a drop-dead gorgeous blonde from California, eagerly preparing to fill the role of wife and homemaker to Warner Huntington III. When Warner (Mathew Davis) drops her on becoming a Harvard law student, stating that as a future senator he needs a Jackie and not a Marilyn, Elle, supported by her bewildered sorority sisters, enrolls at Harvard Law School to win him back. Humiliated and outcast by students and professors alike for her over-the-top girlie dress, grooming, and mannerisms, Elle sets out to succeed by the standards of the East Coast law school. Persecuted by Warner's bitchy, upper-class new fiancée, Elle finds consolation in the friendship of her manicurist, and in the support of a young lawyer, Emmet.

Proving herself in classroom performance, Elle wins a summer position in her criminal-law professor's prestigious law firm, where she is assigned (together with Emmet, Warner, and the fiancée) to a sensational murder case. Elle's client is a blonde California fitness queen, Brook, accused of murdering her rich husband, who was thirty years her senior. Elle bonds with the defendant, supports her, and gains her trust, but when sexually harassed by the sleazy law professor, she realizes he hired her only for his sexual pleasure, and decides to leave law school. In response, Brook fires the law professor and hires Elle in his place. Despite her apparent inexperience, Elle uses her "Cosmo-girl" knowledge about perms and designer shoes to expose two of the prosecution's witnesses, provoking one of them, the deceased man's daughter, to admit that it was she who shot him, mistaking him for Brook, her stepmother. Two years later, graduating at the top of her class, Elle delivers the graduation speech. Viewers are informed through subtitles that Warner graduated with no honors, no job offers, and no girlfriend, whereas Elle is joining a prestigious Boston law firm, and Emmet is about to propose to her that same night.

In stark contrast with *Adam's Rib*'s hard-core "sameness" feminism, *Legally Blonde* promotes an extreme version of "difference" feminism. Elle Woods, whose signature color is pink, epitomizes everything that is stereotypically girlie, celebrating high heels, fitness exercise, and sexy maneuvers that capture men's attention and guarantee dinner invitations. Unlike Amanda, Elle is surrounded by women and bonds with them in a highly "feminine" fashion, celebrating the gift of feminine community. The mutual support the women offer each other empowers them all, enabling Brook's acquittal, Elle's success in law school, and the manicurist's success in winning her dog back from an ex-partner.

Yet, much like *Adam's Rib*, *Legally Blonde* is a wild, over-the-top comedy. Its merry, optimistic feminism is alluring and uplifting, especially attractive for young audiences. Like Amanda, Elle Woods is allowed by the film to have it all: good looks, a good mind, a good career, and a good man who appreciates her for what she is. She is allowed to wear her flowing blonde hair and pink dress and heels, while also winning her case in court, saving a woman falsely accused of killing a man, and graduating at the top of her Harvard Law School class. Brook, falsely accused because of her sexual, blonde image, is publicly redeemed thanks to Elle, while the sexually harassing professor is disgraced. Warner is punished for casting Elle as a Marilyn type, stereotyping her as a dumb blonde, and refusing to see her true worth. His snobbish fiancée is transformed, drops him, and becomes Elle's best friend, joining the supportive manicurist, the sorority sisters, Brook, and even a once-condescending female law professor. The manicurist regains her self-esteem, finds a good man, and has a baby girl she calls Elle. Feminine women who allow themselves to be themselves can have it all, at no significant cost or personal sacrifice. Little wonder young women (such as many of my students) cheer this film, grateful for its hopeful, reassuring, contemporary vision of triumphant womanhood.

But does the film convey an optimistic, young vision of "difference" feminism, or a postfeminist vision, depoliticizing young women through an addictive, misleading fantasy? Radical feminism is embodied in the film's ridiculed, militant lesbian character, who is openly hostile to Elle, and whose feminist struggle consists of a campaign to replace the male-oriented term *semester* with *ovester*. Her ungroomed hair and nails are portrayed as nonfeminine and unattractive. Not redeemed until the film's very end, this stereotypical, unattractive, lesbian feminist is clearly not offered as a role model. But Elle's "difference feminism" is not presented as a serious philosophy or a real alternative to existing social values either. Elle's feminine legal "strategy," solely relying on hair-care expertise, wins her case, but can hardly be viewed as a serious, systematic, feminist theory or legal methodology. Cute and funny it is, but hardly a coherent worldview. Not surprisingly, it is complimented by Elle's contempt of dark hair and brunettes, a dismay fully supported by the film. Sexy blondes are fully redeemed, portrayed as smart, good, and honest.[7] But brunettes are bitches, lesbians, or murderesses.

Focusing attention on the alleged discrimination against and hardship of the overly attractive, overly "feminine" Elle, the film distracts viewers' attention from the real discrimination and hardship of real women. Few women have Reese Witherspoon's figure, and no woman can go through law school investing her energy in nail salons, tanning parlors, boutiques, and fitness centers. The film's false promise that any woman can be a triumphant Elle Woods if she is bravely true to the girlie woman within suggests that the existing system is benign, and that a woman's failure to have it all is her own private, personal fault. *Legally Blonde*'s guilty women are not on-screen but in the audience.

6 *Nuts*

(U.S.A., 1987)

THE MAD WOMAN'S DAY IN COURT

For better or worse, Nuts is conceived, above all, as a Barbra Streisand film; it is as such that it received much public and critical attention, meeting with both rave and contemptuous reviews. A typical pro-Streisand review declared that:

> Nuts is most definitely a Barbra Streisand movie, and a quite wonderful Barbra Streisand movie at that . . . At the center of it all, holding the film together with a singularly riveting performance, there is Barbra Streisand in the role of . . . well, it doesn't really matter, does it? . . . And therein lies the magic of Nuts. Not only do we get La Streisand in an incredible, all-out Oscar-bait movie-star performance—she laughs, she cries, she hits 'em in the eye—we also have all these fine actors around to react to it . . . You never forget that it is Barbra Streisand that you are watching on the screen, and not just some hooker with an attitude problem. Which is just as it should be, this being a Barbra Streisand movie. A wonderful Barbra Streisand movie. (Salem 1987)

Similarly, another critic announced that "*Nuts* [is] an enormous personal triumph for its producer, Barbra Streisand, who gives the performance of her career . . . She has hardly made a wrong choice . . . Deeply moving and rudely funny, it's impossible to take your eyes off her for a second. This is real Oscar stuff" (Lumenick 1987).[1] On the other extreme, straightforward anti-Streisand critics gleefully complained that *Nuts* was "an intolerably smug film which decks out a tear-jerking psychiatric case history with a load of kooky flummery, the whole thing tied up in pink bows as a crudely tailored vehicle for Barbra Streisand's egotistical talents" (Milne 1987; see also Maslin 1987, Kehr 1987).

Most typically, critics proclaimed that "*Nuts* is another situation in which La Streisand has done almost everything—produce, star, write music, even (as some stories go) help Martin Ritt direct and edit. *The Washington Post*'s Desson Howe put it into a new verb—'Streisanded'" (Broeske 1987). It is hardly surprising that a reader responded to this review by writing: "In reading your recent summary of reviews on the new Barbra Streisand film, *Nuts*, it became clear to me that most of the negative reviews were not based on her acting, or on the film itself, but on the fact that Streisand is a powerful woman who has control over all aspects of her projects . . . If she were a man, she would be called a 'genius,' but because she is a woman, she is simply labeled 'la Streisand'" (Cooke 1987).[2]

Perhaps the most telling review was John Levensque's praise of Streisand's 1991 *The Prince of Tides*: "Moviegoers who are wary of another Streisand-fixated project can relax; although she also produced and directed *The Prince of Tides*, Streisand willingly plays second fiddle to Nolte in this story . . . *The Prince of Tides* is a much more convincing movie than Streisand's last outing, *Nuts*, which she produced and starred in. Part of the reason for Streisand's success this time out is that she seems to have learned the fine art of taking the back seat" (Levensque 1991).

Nuts did not succeed at the box office. It did not receive a single nomination for an Academy Award, having been "pretty much ignored in the New York and Los Angeles Film Critics' rosters of top films of '87" (Beck 1997). Some critics concluded that "*Nuts* raises questions about the continuing appeal of its star, Barbra Streisand, or at least of her appeal in a non-singing role" (Mathews 1988). Similarly, the film was all but ignored in the academic literature on film. Tom Topor, on the other hand, received much praise for the screenplay (as he later did for his 1988 *The Accused*). This, despite some critics' accurate observation that "Streisand is hampered by a heavy-handed screen-play that leaves nothing to the imagination" (Walters 1987), and that she "throws us a life preserver: she brings such ferocity to her role . . . that she transforms the film's scabrous, delinquent dramaturgy into something re-sembling real life . . . She stares down the script's inadequacies and burns them to a cinder" (Rainer 1987).

I leave this intriguing story of Nuts's reception to my reader's considera-tion. One simple point made clear by the quoted reviews is that, despite its obvious qualities, once it was classified as a Streisand product, Nuts was completely overlooked as a film and as a law film. In this chapter, while fully acknowledging the significant role played by its female producer and leading actress, I read and analyze it as a law film in the thematic context of other such films. As in previous chapters, my analysis refers strictly to the film and not to the earlier play version. Tom Topor's 1980 play in three acts narrates a similar plot, yet constructs different characters, emphasizing different themes.

Like the other two films presented in this part of the book, Nuts features a powerful woman protagonist who, facing a biased, discriminatory legal sys-tem, openly challenges it, demanding fair judgment and justice. Like Adam's Rib's Amanda and Death and the Maiden's Paulina, Nuts's Claudia is a smart, independent, articulate, unconventional woman who thinks for herself, voices her views, looks with eyes wide open, and actively judges, applying her own standards. Depicting her as an unruly, uncontrollable, uncompromising woman, the film celebrates her power and freedom while acknowledging her vulnerability and respecting her dignity. Tough and unpleasant as she may be, the film does not stereotype, judge, or condemn her, but instead accepts and supports her.

Film Synopsis

Nuts is a courtroom drama, closely following one woman's struggle in a com-petency hearing to be pronounced sane and capable of standing trial for the killing of an upright man who was her client (john). Having collapsed after the fatal event, exhibiting catatonic symptoms, Streisand's Claudia Draper was diagnosed by two psychiatrists as being incapable of standing trial. One of these psychiatrists, Dr. Herbert A. Morrison (Eli Wallach), the aging head of the psychiatric department of the New York County Prison Hospital, plays a central role in the legal proceedings, repeatedly testifying to his patient's acute situation which, in his professional opinion, precludes the possibility of a criminal proceeding. She is ill, he determines, and belongs not in a prison cell but in the psychiatric department, where she can be cared for and helped despite herself.

Claudia's elderly, grieving parents, Rose and Arthur Kirk (Maureen Stapleton and Karl Malden), hire the services of a distinguished, silver-headed, high-priced lawyer. Explaining to the judge that his client is "impossible to talk to," the prominent lawyer attempts to concede, on her behalf, to the plea of the attorney general (silver-haired Robert Webber) that she be declared incapable of standing trial. Repeatedly ignored, distanced, and silenced by her own lawyer as well as by the judge, precluded from expressing her own view and giving sound to her voice, a frustrated Claudia finally attacks her patronizing lawyer, breaks his nose, and is carried out of the courtroom. The judge mockingly assigns the case to Aaron Levinsky (Richard Dreyfuss), a reluctant, shabby, public defender who happens to be present in the courtroom.[3] Humiliated by the judge's blunt attempt to rush him into conceding to the prosecution's case, Levinsky refuses to adopt his predecessor's line of defense, insisting on his duty to consult with his client. In retaliation, the judge schedules a timetable that thwarts the proper preparation of a defense.

In the state prison psychiatric facility, Claudia refuses to cooperate with her court-appointed lawyer, testing and challenging him by prying crudely and provocatively into his privacy ("Does the missus give you good head?" she asks), as well as flashing him. Claudia consents to consult with him only after accepting him as her lawyer on her own terms, clarifying his status as her representative and saying, "You pretend that I am sane, and I will do the same for you." She notifies him that she is perfectly competent to stand trial, bluntly rejecting his solid legal advice to present the court with a professional psychiatric opinion supporting her position. "I am my case," she states, confident in her ability to convince the court of her sanity. She falls silent only when he asks, "Why is all this happening to you?"

In the course of the legal proceedings, we learn of Claudia's troubled history. Having been deserted by her biological father at an early age, she was adopted by Kirk, her mother's second husband. After her own divorce (preceded by an abortion), Claudia, a young woman from an upper middle-class background, began to prostitute herself. Establishing herself as an upper-class, high-priced "professional," Claudia would interview her affluent potential clients before agreeing to offer them her sexual services. Addressing the court, Claudia takes great pride in her professional, successful autonomy, her exercise of free, honest, responsible choice and the thorough control she has over her life. Through one of her nightmares, we learn that the deceased client (the silver-haired Leslie Nielsen) refused to leave her apartment at the end of his session. He demanded that she "bathe" with him, becoming violent when firmly turned down. Grabbing hold of her in a murderous rage, he attempted to strangle Claudia to death on her bathroom floor. On her back, choking, desperately grasping a piece of broken mirror, she managed to stab him and save herself.[4]

As Levinsky proves himself committed, trustworthy, caring, and honest, Claudia gradually comes to respect and even feel some warmth towards him. Nevertheless, she does not yield, and refuses to be examined by a psychiatrist for the defense. Similarly, she forbids Levinsky to cross-examine her parents, who testify for the prosecution. Her responses to them are cold, sarcastic, and hostile. She bitterly and cruelly mocks their repeated manifestations of love, expressing disgust and annoyance at their presence in the courtroom. From their testimonies for the prosecution we learn that this hostile aliena- tion started at an early age, and that Claudia has refused to have any com- munication with them for many years. Despite Levinsky's desperate requests, Claudia refuses to disclose any relevant information to her lawyer.

Levinsky grudgingly obeys his client's instructions and waives cross- examination of her mother, but refuses to do the same for her stepfather, ignoring Claudia's repeated reminders. Breaching Claudia's specific instruc- tions, in a dramatic line of questioning he reveals that for many years young Claudia was molested by her stepfather, who habitually joined her in the bathroom, later buying her silent "consent."[5] (A short flashback, convey- ing Claudia's memories, portrays her giving in and opening the bathroom door to her pleading father. Another flashback portrays her battering hus- band similarly pleading for forgiveness behind a closed bathroom door.) To her mother's emotional cry that she did not know, Claudia replies, "You didn't want to know, Mama." (Another short flashback shows her mother's shadow holding a glass of alcohol and shutting the door on a young, weeping Claudia.)[6] Collapsing, Claudia is taken away, and Levinsky spends the night comforting her in the psychiatric department. He sincerely apologizes for getting carried away and acting like a "damn lawyer," and she forgives him.

The next day, despite her psychiatrist's fierce insistence to the contrary, Claudia convinces the judge (silver-haired James Whitmore) of her total understanding of the allegations brought against her, as well as of her ability to contribute to her own defense. She wins the right to stand trial, and, after a painful first step towards reconciliation with her mother, she leaves the courtroom still wearing her inmate robe. The film's last shot leaves her strolling the busy streets of New York City, joyously cherishing her newly gained freedom. A subtitle concludes that Levinsky represented Claudia in her murder case, and that she was acquitted on the basis of her self-defense argument.

Law, Psychology, and Film in Nuts:
Woman between Law and Psychology

The films discussed in chapters 1 to 4 present women protagonists trapped between two men: an oppressive husband (or fiancé) and a sexual offender. Nuts's Claudia is positioned between a lawyer and a psychiatrist and, more generally, between psychiatry and law.

Much like feminist legal academics, feminist psychoanalysts have been offering fundamental, systematic critique of psychoanalysis's treatment of women since the early 1970s. In a recent publication, Fiona E. Raitt and M. Suzanne Zeedyk (2002), a psychoanalyst and a legal scholar, put forward a comprehensive, interdisciplinary, feminist critique of the implicit relationship between psychology and law. (They use the term *psychology* to refer to both psychology and psychiatry, and I do the same). The core of their argument is that, underlying the explicit, uneasy, competitive interaction between law and psychology, there is a deep implicit bond that connects the two disciplines through their most essential premises. They argue that "the implicit relation comprises three key characteristics: the tenet of objectivity, a male normative standard against which human behavior is evaluated, and an individualistic model of human behavior. These characteristics are central both to psychology and to law; when the two join forces, the characteristics are reinforced and further empowered . . . They shape the development and the operation of syndrome evidence" (Raitt and Zeedyk 2002, 6).

In their attempt to establish themselves as scientific, both law and psychology value objectivity above all else, regarding it as the exclusive path to truth and knowledge. Rationality, reason, and logic are considered by both disciplines as closely related to objectivity, and are thus highly valued. This self-deceptive image pushes both disciplines to privilege factual evidence and quantitative, experimental data. In truth, both disciplines are dominated by a male point of view, which is mistaken as an objective one. Their denied androcentrism, falsely presented as neutral, scientific objectivity, is thus at the very heart of both disciplines. Additionally, both disciplines are deeply committed to individualistic models of explaining human behavior. The problem with this commitment is its denial of contextual influences on behavior, implying that behaviors can be explained merely by the analysis of their internal features (8).

Yet, the authors claim, human behavior cannot possibly be explained unless fully contextualized. Human conduct is always embedded in a sociohistorical-personal context, and it is in such context that it must be viewed in order to be understood. They embrace the argument that " 'context stripping' is particularly marginalizing to women because the issues that are of most importance to them are 'by their very nature, complex, contextually grounded concerns': interpersonal and familial relationships, institutional issues such as sexism, societal issues such as violence against women" (56).

Raitt and Zeedyk suggest that law and psychology are invested in their mutual, implicit relationship because they both benefit greatly from it. Psychology supplies law with "scientific," "objective" explanations of human behavior, which may transform vague, uncertain facts into "hard evidence." On the other hand, psychology also uses its connection with the law to test its own theories, and above all to gain prestige, power, and recognition as a privileged social science. Psychology, they feel, is intoxicated with the distinction it believes its mutual relationship with the law imparts, and is thus all too eager to supply the law with its needs. "Ultimately, though, despite the appearance of mutuality, science comes to law *on law's* terms" (27).

The authors believe that analysis of psychological syndromes that have been accepted by legal systems and are regularly used in legal proceedings can best expose the aforementioned implicit relationship and its detrimental effects on women. They thus offer a detailed analysis of such syndromes, including Battered Woman's Syndrome (BWS) and Rape Trauma Syndrome (RTS). They suggest that feminist scholars (such as Lenore Walker) initially developed and presented such syndromes in an attempt to explain patterns of victimized women's responses. The syndromes were meant to supply the courts with systematic explanations that would facilitate the perception of a victimized woman's conduct as "normal" and common and her testimony as reliable. Syndromes were designed to describe, define, and explain victimized women's typical emotional responses, so that when faced with a battered woman accused of killing her abusive husband, or a rape victim testifying for the prosecution against her rapist, a court could take into account the deep and relevant implications of the woman's victimization.

Law's and psychology's combined privileging of objectivity, their unacknowledged male perspective and their decontextualizing individuation of defendants and witnesses disfigured the syndromes, transforming them into "scientific" means of medicalizing (that is objectifying) victimized women, subjecting them to the graces of the "professional expertise" of masculine psychology, and depicting them as deviant, disturbed, insane, and unreliable. Thus constructed, the syndromes may occasionally help some women receive slightly better legal treatment than they would have otherwise, but they have failed to transform law's basic misunderstanding and misconceptualization of women and their lives.

RTS was intended to contextualize the conduct of a rape victim, maintaining that following a rape, "a woman may experience a wide range of emotions, including shock, disbelief, anger, fear and anxiety, while in the later aftermath, a woman's feelings might range from fear, humiliation and embarrassment to anger, revulsion and self-blame. Not every woman experiences the same symptoms in the sequence, although very few show a complete absence of symptoms" (90). When RTS was presented to courts in the mid-1980s, it was designed to educate judges and juries about women's typical reactions to rape and to augment a complainant's evidence, "providing some degree of corroboration that the alleged attack occurred" (92). The logic was that "if a woman claims that she has been raped, and then behaves in a way that exemplifies the typical behavior and emotional reactions of women suffering from RTS, it is highly suggestive of the veracity of her allegation that she has indeed been raped" (98).

But the "objective," androcentric, decontextualizing nature of law and psychology hijacked the syndrome. Rape victims manifesting RTS were viewed as mentally damaged and unstable, and thus as unreliable witnesses. Complainants were subjected to strict scrutiny regarding their manifestation of RTS, treated as suspect defendants rather than victims. Complainants who did not manifest RTS were found to have not been raped, since they could not corroborate their complaint with the appropriate mental response.

Similarly, some psychologists believe that women may recover their memories of childhood sexual abuse only at a late stage in their lives, often in the context of a new trauma or a therapeutic process. Psychologists document that the confrontation of such memories of childhood sexual abuse is likely to result in immense emotional difficulties. "At worst, the result is severe, chronic psychological and/or psychiatric dysfunction; at best, survivors are likely to experience continuing bouts of low self-esteem, guilt, anxiety, and depression" (138). This data was presented in order to contextualize the confused, distressed state of women who testify to childhood abuse. It has, however, resulted in the definition of the so-called "False Memory Syndrome," suggesting that women do not "recover" memories of childhood abuse, but that such memories are, rather, cultivated by irresponsible psychotherapists. Lacking "objective," male-centered, individualized appeal, recovered memories of childhood sexual abuse have not been acknowledged by legal systems.

Raitt's and Zeedyk's description of the implicit relation between law and psychology implies that legal usage of psychological-syndrome data regarding women is likely to perpetuate the described trends unless a major, revolutionary shift of basic paradigms takes place. Read against this law-and-psychology perspective, Nuts may be viewed as a popular-culture feminist treatise voicing a critique that is very similar to the one articulated by Raitt and Zeedyk.

Standing before the law as a defendant, Claudia is initially defined by the system as a deviant, mentally ill survivor of both prostitution and a traumatic sexual and violent incident, thus incapable to stand trial. (Although not specifically mentioned in this context, her abortion is also viewed as a damaging experience, both manifesting and perpetuating her illness.) Learning of her childhood sexual abuse, the system (urged by Dr. Morrison) tends to view it as yet another traumatic experience, which similarly contributed to Claudia's mental illness. Much like Raitt and Zeedyk, Nuts exposes the underlying premise that is so highly valued by both law and psychology at Claudia's expense: androcentric, decontextualized "objectivity." Two psychiatrists, three lawyers, and two judges treat Claudia as an object of scientific observation and categorization. Claudia is subjected by the psycho-legal system to supposed objective, professional, scientific scrutiny, which is, in truth, conducted from a thoroughly denied male perspective, treating her as a deeply disturbed, ill woman stripped of any social context. In response to this institutional treatment, Nuts empowers Claudia to expose the system's false claim to objectivity, its androcentric perspective and its biased lack of contextualization.

Throughout the film Claudia consciously and explicitly prevents the legal and psychiatric professionals from objectifying and medicalizing her. Bluntly refusing to cooperate with their would-be scientific, detached, patronizing questioning, she asserts her subjectivity and humanity by defying their authority and subverting it through mockery, improper sexual jokes, and disrespectful laughter (as defined by Dr. Morrison). Preventing them from invading her personal, mental domain and from dictating the conceptual framework through which she would be discussed and defined, she thus preserves her privacy, liberty, and dignity.

Eluding their attempted objectification of her, Claudia turns the spotlight on them, reciprocating their treatment of her, demonstrating to them how it feels to be on the receiving end of "objective," "professional" objectification and decontextualized individuation. As Dr. Morrison and Aaron Levinsky inquire about her personal life, she responds by posing extremely personal, offensive, and humiliating questions to them, suggesting that, as she is a human being just like them, their "professional," "objective" treatment of her is, in fact, just as personal, subjective, and invasive as her treatment of them. It is the singling out, she implies, the subjection of an isolated individual to heightened scrutiny, that constructs her as guilty until proven otherwise.

Undermining their pretense of professional, objective detachment, Claudia bluntly addresses the psychiatrists' and jurists' masculinity, inquiring after and commenting about their sex lives and provocatively flashing them. In so doing she exposes the denied underlying sexual difference, as well as the dynamics of male supremacy that are at play in her attempted medicalization and incarceration. Blatantly stating that she knows what they look like "with their pants down," when their insecurities, weaknesses, and sexual "deviance" are revealed, she notifies them that she will not be fooled into cooperating with her own oppression by overlooking the gendered, socially structured, highly subjective context of her interactions with them.

Claudia furthermore contextualizes her situation by comparing her chosen lifestyle with other women's. All women live under patriarchal oppression, she suggests. In order to survive, they all sell themselves to men. Some marry men they despise and others "peddle their daughters" to maintain their marriages. The only differences lie in the degrees of self-deception and avoidance of responsibility. Claudia proudly compares her choice to other women's, declaring that hers is free of self-deception, dignified with full responsibility and control.

In specific reference to the psychological syndromes mentioned by Raitt and Zeedyk, Nuts does not allow its fictional, on-screen, psycho-judicial system to label Claudia as mentally ill due to childhood sexual abuse, domestic battering, prostitution, or attempted rape. It leaves no room for doubt that

Claudia has, indeed, survived all these types of abuse and victimization. (The film uses short flashbacks to fully support Claudia's testimony, and reassure the viewer that she was in fact subjected to all these forms of sexual victimization. The possibility that Claudia may be suffering from False Memory Syndrome, or simply lying, is thus explicitly precluded, leaving the viewer no leeway to avoid the issue of women's sexual abuse.)[7] The film similarly states that Claudia has indeed been deeply wounded by the systematic abuse, and that the different abusive episodes in her life may be connected and may all reenact her childhood trauma. This preliminary sexual molestation may have made her more vulnerable to sexual abuse in her adult life and may underlie the bad choices she has made. Nevertheless, Nuts presents Claudia as a fully capable, sane subject, possessing dignity and entitled to full human rights. Preceding Raitt's and Zeedyk's critique, the film uses psychological knowledge to contextualize Claudia's situation and explain how her conduct should be constructed as sane and even reasonable.

But Nuts does not agree with Raitt and Zeedyk on the issue of the similarity and difference between law and psychology, offering an alternative view. Raitt and Zeedyk find law and psychology equally guilty of false objectivity, androcentrism, and decontextualization. In fact, in their account, law seems to be the more powerful of the two, and thus more morally responsible. Nuts proposes that, whereas the psychiatric institution is inherently invested in these dangerous premises, the legal system may avoid stepping into their misogynist trap if it remains true to its authentic, liberal worldview. Nuts portrays Dr. Morrison as representing the misogynistic psychiatric social institution. But whereas some lawyers and judges are clearly willing to follow Dr. Morrison's lead, Aaron Levinsky and Judge Murdoch stand their ground and refuse to cooperate with Dr. Morrison and his patronizing labeling.

Dr. Morrison's professional training authorizes and requires him to view his patients from a superior point of view, which assumes his better understanding of them than their own and his superior ability to analyze their motivations, including those bluntly refuted by the patients. Such motivations are defined as unacknowledged, suppressed, or denied. Once labeled by Dr. Morrison, a patient has no grounds to challenge his professional determination: Her arguments will be interpreted by the doctor according to his own theory as supporting his analysis. Anything she says will be used against her.

Acknowledging the threatening possibility of psycho-legal cooperation, Nuts expresses a surprisingly optimistic faith in the legal system. According to Nuts, the essential distinction between the legal system and the psychiatric one is law's fundamental commitment to the vision of the autonomous, rational, free subject, best qualified to determine his or her ends, means, identity, and happiness. Innocent until proven guilty, sane until proven mentally ill, responsible until proven otherwise, the legal agent is presumed fully human, and must be treated by the legal system accordingly. Within this conceptual framework, Levinsky is committed to representing Claudia according to her best judgment, whether or not he approves of her choices. He must fully accept and respect her chosen line of self-presentation and defense, and convey it to the court with his utmost professional skill. Similarly, Judge Murdoch must listen to Claudia and presume her sanity and reasonableness unless he is absolutely convinced to the contrary beyond reasonable doubt. As long as attorney Levinsky and Judge Murdoch remain faithful to the fundamental values of their profession, Claudia will be heard, will enjoy the benefit of the doubt, will be recognized as a victim and a sane agent and will have her day in court.

Optimistic and reassuring, this liberal stand is troubling from a feminist point of view. Does it imply that the legal system is, in fact, satisfactory as it is and need not be transformed, or even reformed, to meet women's needs? If so, can this optimistic message be considered feminist?

Claudia between Law, Psychiatry, and Film

Self-reflectively, Nuts calls attention to cinema's own singling-out treatment of its characters, which is often androcentric and decontextualizing. Claudia's critique of the singling out conducted by the legal and psychiatric systems similarly targets and exposes films and their viewers. This point is made most effectively in a single, memorable scene. Attempting to get acquainted with his client, Levinsky enters Claudia's apartment, gently going through her photographs (of her parents), books, dolls. He listens to her voice messages, and thoughtfully picks appropriate clothes and underwear for her court appearance. In a pronounced manner, the camera joins Levinsky, sharing his point of view, shifting from one item to the next, lingering and focusing on some. As Levinsky admires some photographs of Claudia in sexy postures which he finds in her closet, the camera is positioned over his shoulder.

In the following scene Claudia, shocked to learn of Levinsky's visit to her apartment, accuses him of taking advantage of her situation as the inspected specimen and invading her privacy. Had she not been singled out, she accuses, he would never have dreamt of going through her underwear as if he were entitled to do so. Taken by surprise, the viewer realizes that his own vicarious visit to Claudia's apartment *as a film viewer* was just as invasive, patronizing, disrespectful, and objectifying as Levinsky's, and that he, too, was taking advantage of Claudia's singling out without questioning it. The viewer realizes that by going through Claudia's apartment, he shared Levinsky's pronounced masculine perspective on her. He notices that in focusing on the individual circumstances of her life, he overlooked the wider context: that she is a human being who deserves the right to privacy just like any person who is not hospitalized in a mental ward.

Ashamed and uncomfortable, the viewer realizes that every time Claudia turns the tables on the film's fictional characters, jurists and psychiatrists, suggesting that they, too, would have seemed crazy and guilty had they been scrutinized like her, she is also addressing the film viewer. The film's cut from Claudia's accusation of Levinsky and the viewer to her nightmarish recollection of the murderous client going through her underwear enhances the severity of Claudia's accusation.

Cinematic singling out—exposing a character to viewer scrutiny—is commonly perceived as natural and neutral treatment of characters and plots. Calling attention to its own objectification and penetration of Claudia in the described scene, Nuts exposes cinema's systematic singling out of characters and its implications. Sharing law's and psychology's implicit premises, film, too, is at risk of joining in psychiatry's self-sustaining, patronizing, indisputable labeling. But Nuts suggests that, like law, film can avoid this pitfall by remaining true to its own underlying values. Like law, film can and must afford its characters a fair opportunity to present themselves at their best. It must treat them with humanity and respect, and give them the full benefit of doubt. In its treatment of Claudia, Nuts demonstrates this idealized vision. The film denies the psychologist such treatment, just as he denies it of Claudia in the film's fictional world.

Nuts Contextualized

WOMEN AND JUDGMENT

The discussions in chapters 1 to 5 revealed how in each of the analyzed law films a woman protagonist, whether or not brought before the film's fictional on-screen court, is subjected to cinematic judgment in relation to the death of a man. The films' judgment of the women is inseparable from their devaluation and dismissal of women's sexual oppression and abuse, their condemnation of female sexuality, and their unacknowledged upholding of an honor-based value system.

Read against this background, Nuts almost seems to confront these films' treatment of women and judgment, responding to them and posing an alternative approach. Claudia clearly kills a distinguished man. Yet unlike other women protagonists, she does not merely have her day in court, but also wins her case. Furthermore, and far more significantly, unlike the other women protagonists, Claudia is not subjected to the film's cinematic judgment. In fact, she may be the single on-screen character whom the film refrains from judging. In Nuts, while the film's on-screen fictional legal system charges a woman with the death of a man, it is her stepfather whom the film subjects to cinematic judgment and condemnation. In Nuts, it is not the woman's sexuality that brings about havoc and death; it is man's sexual abuse of woman that causes pain and tragedy, resulting, among other calamities, in death. The stepfather's passive, cooperating wife, as well as law and psychiatry, the patriarchal social institutions that attempt to shield and protect him from exposure, are cinematically judged to be accomplices.

STEREOTYPING WOMEN

Unlike the women in the previously discussed films, Claudia is a fully developed, three-dimensional human being. She can be angry and stormy, but also vulnerable and caring. She manifests self-confidence but also self-doubt ("Maybe I am crazy," she discloses her fear to Levinsky). She is blatantly sexual, but is also her mother's little girl ("I love you all the way to the moon and back again," she weeps). She is strong and fragile, assertive, sharp, and outspoken, yet completely silent and discreet about her innermost truth: her traumatic past and her parents' guilt. She is manifestly proud of her professional success as a prostitute, and deeply ashamed of not having been able to stand up to her stepfather and refuse his advances. She puts on a glamorous act, and is desperately lonely. She is a person, not a good Eve, dangerous Lilith, or grotesque "new woman." It is as a person that the viewer is called on to relate to her.

SILENCING AND BREAKING THE SILENCE IN *BLACKMAIL* AND *NUTS*

Structurally, Claudia's situation most closely resembles that of Alice White in Hitchcock's Blackmail. A closer look at the two law films' cinematic treatment of analogous themes illustrates and emphasizes the differences between them. Like Alice, Claudia kills a man while he is attempting to rape her. Like Alice, Claudia "placed herself" in the dangerous situation through socially unacceptable sexual behavior. Like Alice, Claudia wishes to convey her story to a court of law, although such an exposition would stain the honor and social position of the significant man in her life (in Alice's case her fiancé, in Claudia's her stepfather). But whereas Alice, accepting the social condemnation of her inappropriate behavior, feels thoroughly shamed and guilty, wishing to turn herself in and take responsibility for the man's death, Claudia defies social sexual norms, openly denouncing them as hypocritical and discriminatory. She manifests neither shame nor guilt, and demands her day in court to prove her innocence.

Unlike Alice, who sees only her own guilt, Claudia sees herself as having been victimized, understanding her violence as justifiable self-defense. Significantly, *Blackmail* constructs Alice as seeing her murderous act reflected in every object she encounters (a shop-window dummy, a neon sign, a policeman's arm, a bread knife). Claudia, on the other hand, dreams of her victimization by the deceased, reliving the horror of his attack, not guilt for her fatal response. Whereas *Blackmail* (like *Rashomon*, *Pandora's Box*, and *Anatomy*) focuses on the man's death and the woman's responsibility, disregarding the woman's sexual violation, *Nuts* focuses on the woman's victimization, hardly referring to her fatal conduct.

Had *Blackmail* allowed Alice her desired day in court, she might have had the opportunity to articulate a self-defense argument, and perhaps even prevail. A legal acquittal might have helped her forgive herself, as well as face her fiancé and the rest of society. But, collaborating with her policeman-fiancé's honor-based self-interest, *Blackmail* prevents Alice from approaching the law, distracting the viewer from the question of her moral responsibility, as well as from her right to be heard by the law. Instead of allowing Alice her day in court, the film chooses to discipline and silence her through patriarchal matrimony.

Nuts, in contrast, focuses specifically on Claudia's right to her day in court. The whole legal proceeding portrayed throughout the film deals precisely with this issue. Further, securing her right to stand trial, the film allows Claudia to succeed in convincing the court that her fatal conduct was in self-defense. Applauded by the film, its fictional legal system thus determines that a woman is justified in killing a man who, in his attempt to rape her, becomes dangerously violent. This is so even though she has entered the dangerous situation willingly, manifesting blunt sexuality. Little wonder that unlike Alice

White, Claudia smiles joyously at the film's end (for discussion of women's laughter and smiling see chapter 8).

In *Nuts*, a woman's no means no, under any and all circumstances, and a woman's right to sexuality and sexual autonomy justifies, in the extreme, the taking of a man's life. In this cinematic legal decision Claudia is publicly and officially pronounced innocent. All that *Blackmail* denies Alice, *Nuts* bestows on Claudia generously, consciously, and deliberately. Where Hitchcock chose avoidance and denial, Streisand chose overt recognition and acceptance.

A comparison of *Nuts* with *Blackmail* similarly calls attention to the two films' diverse treatment of woman's silence. Alice is a woman silenced by her sexual victimization and the sense of shame and guilt it instills in her. From a cheerfully talkative, self-assured, adventurous young woman, Alice is transformed into Frank's domesticated wife-to-be, harboring a terrible secret too shameful to articulate. Streisand's Claudia, on the other hand, is liberated by the film from her deadening silence, in which she had imprisoned herself all her life. The film's legal proceeding, supported by the film, empowers Claudia to break the suffocating silence, find her voice, and speak her truth.

Attempting to leave the unbearable past behind, Claudia spent her life avoiding her parents and locking her poisonous secret in the depth of her soul. Unable to forgive herself and come to terms with her childhood silence, she responded with denial, suppression, and more silence, masterfully veiling her wounds with an eloquent façade of brazen self-assuredness. To compensate for her sense of utter lack of control, she constructed herself as exercising full control over her life and sexuality. To compensate for the feeling of humiliating sexual victimization and objectification, she convinced herself that she willingly sold her company and sexuality; they were not taken away from her against her will or with her passive collaboration, but rationally exchanged in the free market. In response to the ever tormenting secret, she prostituted herself openly and publicly, constructing herself as one who has nothing to hide. Shielding the vulnerable child hidden within, she cultivated the self-image of a bold, unashamed woman, who sees through any pretense and self-deceit, pointedly, courageously, and mockingly looking truth in the eye and unmasking any weakness and anxiety.

Seeing through her false-conscience, the film does not judge Claudia, offering her instead compassionate, unconditional acceptance. Supplying her with a supportive environment, the film empowers Claudia to break the silence that has poisoned her life, underlying her self-destructive courses of action. The film facilitates the relatively safe breakdown of the walls of denial and pretense with which Claudia has protected and imprisoned herself. Furthermore, the film provides her with a fictional, on-screen legal system which, like the film itself, encourages and allows her to confront her traumatic past, self-hatred, guilt, and shame and begin her journey to emancipation.

PROSTITUTES AS VICTIMS AND PREDATORS
IN *PANDORA'S BOX* AND *NUTS*

As in *Pandora's Box*, *Nuts*'s protagonist is a young, highly attractive woman who earns her living by openly and willingly selling sex to male clients. Nevertheless, a closer look reveals the fundamental differences in their approaches, which are far greater than these similarities. As chapter 2 points out, *Pandora's Box* portrays Lulu as a Pandora-Lilith woman, i.e., an irresistibly attractive woman, reeking with wild, uncontrollable sexuality, whose overwhelming threat to men and society is inherent to her nature. In the words of the ancient fable, she can't help it—it is in her nature. Both the film's fictional legal proceedings and its cinematic judgment ignore Lulu's brutal social background, deeming it irrelevant and leaving it outside the scope of consideration.

In contrast with *Pandora's Box*, *Nuts* expands the relevant time frame beyond the present, basing both its fictional judgment and its cinematic evaluation on Claudia's traumatic past. Starting off by presenting a violent, unpleasant woman who makes a living off of her sexual allure, the film explores further, finding that it is not by nature or completely free choice that Claudia is the cynically sexual woman she is. Her molestation at the hands of her stepfather, later followed by her abuse at the hands of her husband, her mother's indifference, and society's failure to protect and save her compose the social reality underlying Claudia's choices and lifestyle. Against this background, her choices must be read with great sensitivity and compassion.

PLEADING INSANITY IN *ANATOMY OF A MURDER* AND *NUTS*

As a courtroom drama, *Nuts* portrays a single preliminary part of the legal process: the competency hearing, evaluating and determining Claudia's sanity and ability to stand criminal trial. Sanity is similarly a central theme in *Anatomy of a Murder*. Charged with the murder of his wife's alleged rapist, Lieutenant Frederick Manion, the defendant in the film's fictional legal proceeding, claims that he acted under the influence of an irresistible impulse, and is thus not legally responsible for the outcome of his actions. Manion's insanity plea is meant to allow the jury to set him free for committing a killing that, although officially illegal, is perceived as moral and just according to the unwritten honor norm.

Despite obvious differences, both films portray two sides of the same ideological coin. As Levinsky and *Nuts* discover and disclose, the state's efforts to declare Claudia insane and prevent the legal proceeding is motivated by the desire to shield and protect Claudia's stepfather from humiliating public exposure. In other words, the state attempts to uphold Kirk's unwritten social right to preserve his honor and silence any damaging evidence that may put him to shame. (At first, the state believes that his daughter's shameful lifestyle is the potentially damaging truth to be hushed for Kirk's benefit. As the legal proceeding divulges, far more is revealed to be at stake.) Perhaps unconsciously, the state's stand similarly shields Claudia's deceased client, as well as the whole social class of silver-haired, affluent, well-connected men, a class that includes the prosecutor, the psychiatrist, Claudia's first lawyer, and the judge. All these men share in the unwritten privilege to privacy, which sustains and secures their honorable status. (Significantly, Levinsky is not a member of this club, being a public defense attorney who takes the subway home to Brooklyn at the end of the day.) Lieutenant Manion's insanity plea and the state's insistence on Claudia's insanity, therefore, both serve the same social purpose of upholding the honor code and shielding honorable men.

The difference lies in the films' differing responses to the analogous pleas made on behalf of the honor code. Whereas *Anatomy* accepts the defense's plea of insanity, and with it the argument to uphold the honor code, *Nuts* rejects the state's analogous argument, exposing it as a self-interested attempt to secure ruling class men's immunity from public and legal scrutiny. Rejecting this patriarchal attempt, *Nuts* chooses instead Claudia's dignity and human worth, as well as her right to equality before the law.

From an additional perspective, that of feminist critique of psychoanalytic conventions, both films' insanity pleas reflect and respond to the status quo in which men, even those who committed heinous crimes, are presumed to be sane and freely choosing agents, whereas nonconforming women are presumed mad unless proven otherwise (Raitt and Zeedyk 2002, 49). Claudia's sanity plea, like Manion's insanity plea, is an uphill struggle.

Both *Anatomy*'s and *Nuts*'s on-screen, fictional legal systems accept the untypical, subversive gender conceptions manifested in the man's insanity plea and the woman's insistence on her sanity. But *Anatomy* does not doubt Manion's sanity, suggesting that neither did the jurors who accepted his plea, honoring the unwritten law. Despite the defense's legal victory, *Anatomy* perpetuates the common view that a man is sane, rational, and responsible, even when guilty of murder and acquitted on the grounds of temporary insanity. *Nuts*, on the other hand, embraces its legal system's finding that despite the killing she committed, her status as a prostitute, her belligerent, "unfeminine" behavior, and professional opinions testifying to her mental illness, Claudia is sane and perfectly capable of standing trial.

HOLLYWOOD'S HERO-LAWYER IN *ANATOMY* AND *NUTS*

Like *Anatomy*'s Paul Biegler, Levinsky is modeled on the classic western hero.[8] He is the highly skilled warrior, the underappreciated outsider, who reluctantly takes on the worthy social cause of protecting and empowering the cinematic personification of the film's social cause. Underrated and ridiculed, he remains stoically faithful to his quest, proving his integrity, professional skill, and courage and earning the respect and gratitude of the film's worthy characters and viewers. But this is where the similarities end.

In clear contrast with *Anatomy* and other Hollywood lawyer films, *Nuts*'s woman protagonist is the film's main character, whereas the lawyer figure merely represents and supports her. The film's lawyer is *not* its focal point, and his best interests do not dictate viewer conceptualization of the female character and thematic issues concerning her. Claudia repeatedly reminds both her lawyer and the viewer that her attorney's function is not to patronize, discipline, overpower, or outshine her, but merely to translate *her* chosen line of defense into legal terminology. *Nuts* fully accepts this perception, restricting its lawyer to a supportive, secondary role. Furthermore, Levinsky's client is a dirty-mouthed, troubled prostitute who clearly killed a distinguished man. This Hollywood lawyer must earn his heroic status through compassionate acceptance, support, and redemption of a "fallen woman" under her own terms. This extreme deviation from standard, generic norms may explain critics' discomfort and annoyance.[9]

This feminist edge takes on an interesting significance in the context of the cinematic lawyer's commitment to both law and justice. As discussed in chapter 4, Hollywood's hero-lawyer reconciles two incompatible loyalties: to natural law and to positive law; to justice and to state law. In *Nuts*, this Herculean task is translated into Levinsky's dilemma between his noble inclination to give the best possible fight to exonerate the innocent Claudia, and his professional duty to obey his client even against his best professional judgment. Obeying Claudia entails not supplying the court with a sympathetic psychiatric evaluation and not cross-examining her parents. The dilemma results from Levinsky's belief that he cannot secure her victory (and consequent acquittal) without breaching Claudia's instructions.

Levinsky's lose-lose dilemma is inherent to the radical feminist treatment of women viewed as sexually abused, who do not consider themselves as such or who reject intervention in their lives. Viewing consciousness-raising as the par excellence feminist method of getting at women's realities, truths, and needs, a feminist perspective must respect a woman's self-determination as a fundamental and irreplaceable source of insight into her condition. At the same time, battering and prostitution, among other evils, are considered abusive and oppressive means of domination and discrimination that must be confronted and fought—even if a victim is intimidated or conditioned by her abuser to cooperate in her own victimization. As demonstrated by John Stuart Mill's liberal condemnation of slavery disregarding the slave's own perception of it, this paternalistic dilemma is at the heart of any humanistic ideology, which considers certain fundamental truths regarding the human condition as self-evident and absolute.

Unable to resolve this irresolvable dilemma, Nuts does all that a feminist text can do: portray it with utmost respect and painful awareness of the cost and loss inherent in any choice made. But in posing the dilemma as Levinsky's, Nuts goes further, equating Hollywood's hero-lawyer's classic law-and-justice dilemma with the feminist dilemma of paternalistic intervention. This is an innovative feminist twist on the classic law-and-justice conflict, as well as on the hero-lawyer's fundamental constitution.

From an additional perspective, Levinsky's dilemma is how to best respect, cherish, and implement his client's dignity: by dignifying her expressed wish, or by dignifying her humanity, even if it requires paternalistically ignoring her expressed wish, which is distorted by years of abuse and victimization. This formulation defines justice as the most nurturing, respectful, humanistic translation of a woman's dignity into the legal language of rights. This formulation is the film's feminist, dignity-oriented popular jurisprudence.

To use the matrimonial metaphor I employ in the discussion of other films, if Claudia's relationship with Levinsky is her "marriage" to the law, then in Nuts this marriage is a bond that links two equally worthy perspectives, and is designed to dignify both to the utmost. Nuts grounds the happy marriage between lawyer and client in a remarkable on-screen chemistry between its leading man and woman.[10]

Discussing *Adam's Rib* in chapter 5, I suggested that Amanda's liberal feminist jurisprudence cannot, by definition, offer a coherent, convincing treatment of the specific, highly unusual case chosen by the film, of a woman shooting her unfaithful husband and his lover. Consequently, the film portrays a liberal feminist argument that promotes honor-based values and is incapable of eliciting viewer sympathy. *Nuts* offers a very different treatment of an analogous theme. *Nuts* presents a case tying together incest, prostitution, (attempted) rape of a prostituted woman, and homicide (with a side story of domestic battering). To be effectively treated, this combination requires a radical feminist perspective. *Nuts* meets the challenge, offering a unique technique that succeeds in avoiding a one-dimensional treatment, and in highlighting diverse angles and layers.

Claudia, the film's single woman protagonist, does not voice a radical feminist agenda; hers is a strictly liberal point of view, demanding to be treated as a man would have been treated in her shoes. Claudia views herself as an autonomous, rational individual, practicing free choice and taking great pride in her control over her life and responsibility for her choices. Claudia is greatly invested in this self-perception, and vehemently refuses to be portrayed as anything but a fully self-determining agent. She presents her prostitution as a career she is proud to have chosen: it represents her rational, unsentimental confrontation and acceptance of the human condition. Unlike other women, who deceive themselves and the world, pretending to love men they sell themselves to, Claudia is well aware of the commercial nature of her sexual encounters and is in full control of them.

Nuts offers Claudia a respectful, accommodating, compassionate stage to present her self-perception. It does not, however, share her liberal perspective. *Nuts* clearly suggests that beneath Claudia's rational, independent choice lurks a horrible, repressed, traumatic past of childhood abuse which, denied and untreated, poisons Claudia's life, directing her to self-destructive choices and causing her to repeat the traumatic experience and its damaging effects. This view could have simply been a psychoanalytic one. But linking Claudia's circumstances with incest, domestic violence, prostitution, (attempted) rape, a killing, and a social attempt to silence her by committal to a psychiatric hospital implies a radical feminist perspective, focusing on women's systematic sexual oppression in a male-dominated social order.

Nuts, thus, offers a dual perspective on Claudia's situation: one emphasizing her agency and subjectivity, the other her victimization. The two perspectives do not undermine and discredit each other, but rather integrate into a coherent, multilayered portrayal of Claudia as a victimized agent.[11] The abuse she has suffered all her life has imprisoned her in an existence dominated by trauma, fear, anger, and vulnerability. It has greatly limited her options, influencing her personality, behavior, and the course of her life. But it has not deprived her of subjectivity, agency, humanity, and dignity. It has not diminished her to being a passive victim, determined merely by the victimization and trauma she has undergone. She remains a fully capable person, despite her injuries and wounds. An androcentric, or honor-based, film would have portrayed Claudia as a guilty object; Nuts portrays her as a victimized agent.

Nuts' portrayal of Claudia demonstrates the meaning of a film's dignifying treatment of its female protagonist. Acknowledging her victimization and contextualizing it, the film does not deprive her of her humanity, subjecthood, and agency. Accepting the ambivalent, tragic reality of human existence, it cherishes the strength of the human spirit under the most painful and challenging of circumstances. Refraining from judgment, the film admires Claudia's survival in the face of repeated attempts to break her spirit and dehumanize and objectify her, offering her a respectful, supportive shoulder and ear. In its warm embrace of Claudia, Nuts further demonstrates the deep, inherent linkage between a dignifying treatment and a compassionate, caring feminist perspective. Further, Nuts constructs its hero-lawyer as offering Claudia tender, "mothering" lawyering.[12] This on-screen empathetic legal representation, together with the film's own compassionate, nonjudgmental treatment of Claudia, links cultural feminism with legal theory, as well as with jurisprudential liberal and radical feminisms presented by the film. The film's feminist popular jurisprudence coherently advocates the combination of diverse feminist perspectives with a dignity-based value system.

Levinsky's role in the film's ideological advocacy is crucial. Free of any predetermined ideological commitment, Levinsky is devoted to the pursuit of truth and justice. It is as such that he encounters Claudia's liberal self-perception, gradually revealing, realizing, and acknowledging the complimentary radical feminist conceptualization of her situation. He responds with acceptance, respect, and compassion. The film's viewer is invited to join Levinsky in this process and proceed with him step by step. Although, through flashbacks, the viewer is offered privileged access to certain memories Claudia does not share with her lawyer, on the whole the viewer is invited to identify with Levinsky through a shared point of view. Like Levinsky, the film's implied viewer considers himself a reasonable, decent man, bewildered, taken aback, yet intrigued by Claudia's situation and behavior. This viewer is invited to join Levinsky's gradual process of learning to see Claudia both through her own perspective and through the radical feminist one suggested by the film.

Levinsky's character and his development seem to manifest the film's belief that a decent, just, and truth-seeking legal system can and must embrace a dignifying, sympathetic, feminist treatment of Claudia, and do her justice. Nevertheless, Nuts's faith in the legal system does not subvert its radical feminist vision of women's systematic oppression. The film offers an intriguing combination of a highly critical perception of women's social condition with a fundamental faith in the ability of the existing legal system to awaken, acknowledge the reality of women's lives, and bravely join the struggle to empower them and set them free. Death and the Maiden, A Question of Silence, "A Jury of Her Peers," Set It Off, and High Heels, discussed in the following chapters, offer very different (far less optimistic and arguably less naive) perspectives on this point.

The most significant point on which Nuts does not differ from the other films discussed in this book's previous chapters is Claudia's seclusion from other women and isolation from a feminine community. Throughout the film, Claudia is never allowed the company of a woman friend. The female inmates in prison and in the psychiatric ward are never considered as potential company for Claudia. As in Adam's Rib, Claudia's closest and most successful on-screen relationship is with her male lawyer/partner. Against all odds, this heterosexual couple manages to communicate, to develop mutual respect, understanding, and compassion, to win Claudia's just case and to secure justice. A male-female dialogue is possible, the film reassures us, and when successful it is sufficient to secure a just solution to women's plight. A collective feminine struggle is not considered as an option. The single small step toward feminine bonding is hinted at in the budding, emotional reconciliation between Claudia and Rose, her repentant mother.

Postscript: Dolores Claiborne: Taking Nuts's Feminist
Jurisprudence a Step Further

Dolores Claiborne is the surprising 1995 adaptation of a Stephen King novel. A painful psychological drama starring Kathy Bates (supported by Jennifer Jason Leigh and Judy Parfitt), this film patiently follows a troubled young woman's awakening to the devastating memory of paternal sexual childhood abuse. As she emerges from fifteen years of repression, denial, and systematic escape from the traumatic memory and from herself, the film's belligerent, unpleasant young woman, Selena, realizes, together with the sympathetic viewer, how the repressed childhood trauma has all but dictated her "freely chosen" lifestyle as a driven, individualistic, autonomous, successful legal reporter. She further realizes how her mode of survival resulted in the cruel judgment and condemnation of her mother, Bates's Dolores, who, in a desperate attempt to save her daughter, killed the molesting father, her alcoholic, battering husband.

Arriving in her childhood town in time to take an active part in her mother's indictment for a later, related killing, Selena is impelled by the film to confront her past, her means of survival, and the devastating consequences of her penalizing of the tormented Dolores. Accepting herself and her past, Selena lets go of her judgmental condemnation of her mother, demanding that the legal system follow her example and do the same. Using her professional expertise to expose the personal, honor-based motivation underlying her mother's persecution by the local law-enforcement authorities, Selena forces the law to adopt her own newly gained, mature, empathetic, dignifying acceptance of her mother. The system is reluctant, but the professional, emotionally empowered, uncompromising Selena prevails.

Dolores does not think of herself as a feminist or an oppressed woman, but as an uneducated, unsuccessful woman who would do anything to secure a better future for her daughter. Selena refuses to see herself as a victim, preferring to believe herself a rational, independent free agent. The film gently accepts the women's self-perceptions, simultaneously offering a wider, radical perspective. It thus establishes both women as victimized agents. Significantly, this film does not need a mediating male character such as Levinsky, inviting its viewer to gradually identify with its two unpleasant women protagonists. The honor-driven, vengeance-seeking, law-enforcing authority is exposed and defeated and the legal system is disarmed through Selena's professional use of legal logic and argumentation.

In *Dolores Claiborne*, both mother and daughter receive compassionate, dignifying, and nonjudgmental treatment. Further, the film does not merely celebrate the miracle of women's survival, but also the strength and beauty of a feminine community. The film suggests that it is the deeply committed, twenty-two-year love-hate relationship of mutual support with another tormented woman (her upper-class employer) that facilitated Dolores's survival.

Similarly, it is her mother's lifelong unconditional love and caring that facilitated Selena's. The three women's complete understanding and acceptance of themselves and each other is captured by the film's unforgettable line, conveyed by each of the women to the others: "Sometimes being a bitch is all a woman has to hold on to."

Death and the Maiden 7

(U.S.A., 1994)

CHALLENGING TRAUMA WITH FEMININE JUDGMENT AND JUSTICE

(READ WITH *THE PIANO*)

What *Death and the Maiden* helps us understand is that the very fact of being a victim of rape and torture (ironically) makes Paulina an 'outsider' to the legal process ostensibly in place to redress such injuries . . . The [film] could be read as her attempt to impose her outsider justice by continuously reacting against linguistic and procedural barriers set up by traditional forces.—ROBERT F. BARSKY

Featuring a painful, familiar encounter between wife, husband, and rapist confined together in a secluded setting, presenting the viewer with contrasting versions of the parties' guilt, Roman Polanski's *Death and the Maiden* offers alternative narration and judgment to *Rashomon*'s theme. As in *Rashomon*, where samurai and bandit shared the Bushido warrior ethics, *Death and the Maiden*'s male protagonists (one a lawyer, the other a medical doctor) share a distinguished professional status. As in *Rashomon*, the woman attempts to pit the men against each other, demanding that her husband kill the rapist. But

Death and the Maiden does not feature a man's death, and instead devotes its full attention to the woman's rape, the issue evaded by *Rashomon*. Not constructing Woman as a manifestation of misogynist stereotypes, *Death and the Maiden* portrays its woman protagonist as an active and impressive human being and a survivor of abuse.

Whereas in *Rashomon*'s cinematic judgment the woman is accused, judged, and found guilty in relation to the man's death, *Death and the Maiden* facilitates and supports its woman protagonist's private, semi-legal accusation and condemnation of both men. Placed by the film simultaneously in both wife's and husband's perspectives, the viewer is initially invited to sympathize with both their points of view, then to side with the woman, judging both men, and finally to embrace the film's condemnation of the lawyer husband. Most significantly, this film's cinematic judgment also targets the unsuspecting viewer.

Married to her country's leading jurist, the woman is "married to the law." But her husband is no hero-lawyer, nor the film's focal point. Refusing to harness the law of the land to do his wife justice, the lawyer-husband pronounces the deep truth of her status as "outlaw": not protected by the rule of law. (On this point, *Death and the Maiden*'s woman protagonist experiences the legal system very differently than the women in *Nuts* and *Adam's Rib*.) In response to her exclusion from the official legal system, taking the law into her own hands, the woman conducts her private legal process, formulating her unique, feminine notion of law and justice that derives from her needs as a rape victim. In so doing, she is portrayed by the film as a victimized agent, manifesting her dignity and exposing the men's false honor by enforcing her sense of justice through a semi-legal process.

Death and the Maiden explores the issue rebuffed by *Rashomon*: a couple's struggle to transcend judgment and restore an intimate relationship devastated by a traumatic event of victimization and failure. The film locates this intimate struggle in the social context of a society recovering from a traumatic past of dictatorship and massive violation of human rights, striving to forge the basis for a new future. Victims of the old regime, their victimizers, and bystanders find themselves forced to cooperate in the making of this fresh start.

At this critical time of reorganization, when social and cultural paradigms are caught between a traumatic past and an unclear future, how do victims cope with their victimization and recover from painful personal trauma? How can and should the legal system be used to reconcile present and past, victims and victimizers, society and individuals, private memories and collective memory? What are the goals and duties of law and the legal system regarding individuals and the collective at such difficult times, and how should they be prioritized? How should a legal system respond when legitimate demands of an individual for law and justice conflict with social needs for stability and reconciliation? How can justice be done, for whom, at what cost, and what can justice mean in such painful circumstances? Focusing on a sexually victimized woman, Death and the Maiden asks how law does—and should do—justice, locating a victimized woman's personal memory within a collective history in the fragile moment when a conflicted society struggles with its unbearable past and intimidating future.

Death and the Maiden is based on a powerful play written by Ariel Dorfman, who also cowrote the screenplay with Polanski and Rafael Yglesias. The film is distinct from the play just as the play is distinct from Franz Schubert's Death and the Maiden Quartet, different in turn from the song of the same title, composed by Schubert seven years later, based on an earlier poem by Mattias Claudius.[1] In this discussion it is the Dorfman-Polanski film that I read, as a film.[2]

Film Synopsis

Death and the Maiden's protagonist, Paulina Lorka (Sigourney Weaver), endured severe, continuous, and prolonged torture, including repeated rape, perpetrated by a totalitarian, South American regime, now overthrown.[3] She survived the abuse without betraying the identity of her spouse, then a leader of the resistance movement, only to find, on her release, that he had given up on her and was involved with another woman. Fifteen years later, under the new regime, her spouse, Gerardo Escobar (Stuart Wilson), a celebrated human-rights attorney, is nominated to head the public commission investigating the old regime's violations of human rights.

Striving to ensure national solidarity while avoiding dangerous political pitfalls, the president authorizes the commission to investigate only crimes that resulted in fatalities. Paulina challenges and condemns her spouse's consent to head such a commission, calling his decision a betrayal. As she confronts him on a stormy night in their secluded oceanfront home, they are unexpectedly joined by a stranger (Ben Kingsley) who helped Gerardo earlier in the evening when his car broke down and who was now arriving to return the tire Gerardo had left behind. Paulina recognizes the stranger as one of her rapists; in fact, the doctor who raped her brutally, fourteen times, while tending to her wounds and playing Schubert's Death and the Maiden.[4] Recognizing his voice and bodily odor, his laughter, and characteristic phrases of his speech, she challenges the state's decision (and her spouse's consent) not to investigate her torture and rape. She is determined to take the law into her own hands, conduct a private proceeding, establish the truth, and do justice. She demands her resisting spouse's full support and active participation in this private legal proceeding.

During a long, dark night, at the outskirts of a city and on the margins of society, Paulina judges her rapist, as well as her spouse. Using brutal force, she coerces the rapist, Dr. Roberto Miranda, to confirm her accusation, admit to his inhumanity, and assume moral responsibility for his actions. Threatening her spouse with a gun, she repeatedly prevents him from releasing the accused man, forcing him to confront her victimization and sacrifice and his own weakness. On the edge of a cliff above a stormy ocean, having pushed the two men to admit their crimes against her, she chooses not to impose a death sentence on her rapist and releases him. Later, in the film's final scene, Paulina's eyes meet Roberto's as the story's three characters, trapped together forever, meet by chance in the civilized, elegant world of a concert hall.

Cinematic Jurisprudence: Two Concepts of Law and Justice

Gerardo Escobar is the leading jurist of a society in limbo: no longer under the tyrannical rule of dictators, Gerardo's country is not yet fully secure of and in its democratic identity and strength. Gerardo is confronted with the existential question of how the law of the land can best serve his country at this crucial, delicate time. Gerardo's rational, pragmatic resolution is that the law must facilitate a much needed social transformation, securing that transformation with as little risk as possible to public stability and everyday "normalcy." If the price to be paid for a safe future is that aggressors responsible for human-rights violations under the old regime are not prosecuted and not condemned, then so it must be. Law is but the means, and the end is a smooth social transformation, necessitating unity and internal concord.

Representing the country's authoritative legal system, Gerardo refuses to harness the law to Paulina's case. His manifest, ideological arguments refer to the unreasonable threat posed by the prosecution of such a case to the fragile sense of unity and harmony the new government is struggling to create. On a positivistic legal level, Gerardo's stand is that Paulina, who was tied and blindfolded during her rape and torture, cannot provide conclusive evidence to support her accusation, and that due to her shaky mental state she is an unreliable witness. Like any potential defendant, Roberto is entitled to a fair trial, which cannot be conducted based on Paulina's testimony. Legal truth and legal guilt can be determined only on the basis of hard evidence beyond reasonable doubt, which Paulina cannot supply.

A more general perspective reveals that victims of systematic torture are often prevented from seeing their victimizers, and often suffer severe post-traumatic mental injury, which makes them "emotionally unstable" (Herman 1992, 35, 56). Gerardo, therefore, determines that victims such as Paulina, brutalized by a powerful regime which left few fingerprints and which damaged the victims' mental state, cannot support legal actions against alleged perpetrators. Aggressors, therefore, cannot be legally prosecuted and convicted, and the crimes committed against these damaged victims cannot be legally exposed and condemned. The law is not an appropriate instrument to cope with such aggression and victimization, and hence not an appropriate platform for telling the stories of human-rights violations to facilitate the integration of victims' individual memories into the country's collective memory.[5]

Paulina's starting point is not society's need for stable normalization, but rather her own personal needs as a victim. During the long night depicted in the film, Paulina, awakening from her fifteen-year retreat and self-inflicted incarceration, gradually comes to identify and articulate her needs as victim and survivor for the first time.[6] For the first time since her victimization, she feels the urge to regain herself, her life, identity, dignity, self-respect, and place in society. She even wants to reclaim her beloved Schubert, whose music she has been unable to bear all these years. To pursue these goals, she gradually realizes her need for explicit public acknowledgment, recognition, and compassion. In order to live once again, she must be seen, heard, accepted, validated, and embraced by her community, embodied at this crucial moment in Gerardo.

Paulina needs to tell her story, to give her testimony of the abuse and dehumanization she endured, and to be believed. She needs empathy. She needs to be exonerated from the guilt she feels for her helplessness while her tormentors denied her subjectivity and human worth.[7] She needs to break free from the shame that has silenced her and caused her withdrawal.[8] For Paulina, the demand that her needs be met is a demand not merely for recovery and empowerment but also for justice, and the device which can achieve that justice is the legal process. Conducting her private process, Paulina discovers and demonstrates the specific characteristics of law and the legal process that make this vehicle most suitable for her needs.

Healing through the Legal Process

Law consists of clear, familiar, ritualistic moves, structuring and normalizing processes of confrontation and testimony. Almost automatically, Paulina reads her accusation against Roberto, charging him with rape and torture, and then offers him the floor for his defense. The painful, chaotic, highly charged meeting between victim and aggressor is thus smoothly translated by these orderly legal moves into a manageable, well-organized procedure. The familiarity of the ritualistic moves offers Paulina consolation, some security, and a sense of sanity and control in the face of haunting memories of brutal savagery that threaten to flood her fragile existence. In addition to its ritualistic nature, the legal process inherently and ineluctably repeats elements of the traumatic experience. Such repetition seems crucial for Paulina: to return to the horror, contact her loss, pain, and rage, and finally transcend them and proceed with her life. Death-in-life had become a safe, familiar hideaway, and only the law's counterforce is compelling enough to extricate Paulina and bring her back to the scene of the crime.

In the process of articulating her accusation, the law allows and obliges Paulina to narrate her story, and to do so facing her abuser, coercing him to acknowledge her and listen to her construction of his guilt and her victimization. The legal process thereby enables Paulina to satisfy her need to narrate her memory, imposing it on the man who used his superior power to violate and objectify her. Paulina's insistence on her truth, on her very self, defies her abuser's attempt to deprive her of the basic human capacity of assigning meaning to her own life and to his conduct toward her. This is in itself a victory. Confronting him as an equal member of society, unafraid, she celebrates her humanity and subjectivity, her survival and his defeat (Herman 1992, 11).

For Paulina's truth to be fully realized, the narration and confrontation must be shared with her community and sanctioned by it. She needs approving witnesses. Describing the role of the community in the therapeutic process of trauma victims, Judith Herman, author of the definitive *Trauma and Recovery*, specifies: "Sharing the traumatic experience with others is a precondition for the restitution of a sense of a meaningful world. In this process, the survivor seeks assistance not only from those closest to her, but also from the wider community. The response of the community has a powerful influence on the ultimate resolution of the trauma. Restoration of the breach between the traumatized person and community depends, first, upon public acknowledgment of the traumatic event, and, second, upon some form of community action" (1992, 70). Paulina believes the legal process is the appropriate vehicle for this purpose as well: it can and must restore her to her community, and, through recognition and restitution, offer her justice.

Initially, Paulina believes that the legal proceeding can induce Roberto to admit to her truth, assume responsibility, and express remorse. "I want him to confess," she insists. As the night progresses, Paulina discovers that not even the law can force the truth out of her abuser. But perhaps she also realizes that her existence and recovery do not depend on his confession. It is not the transformation of the aggressor, but the mere process of publicly confronting him with the narration of her memory that sets her free. This, perhaps, is the essence of the legal process she seeks.

Scholarship on testimony offers additional perspective for discussion of Paulina's need for a legal process. In an interdisciplinary study of testimony, Shoshana Felman and Dori Laub offer illuminating insights. Dr. Laub explains the aspatial and atemporal nature of the traumatic experience and the crucial role of testimony in the healing process:

> The traumatic event, although real, took place outside the parameters of "normal" reality, such as causality, sequence, place and time. The trauma is thus an event that has no beginning, no ending, no before, no during and no after. Trauma survivors live not with memories of the past, but with an event that could not and did not proceed through to its completion, has no ending, attained no closure, and therefore, as far as its survivors are concerned, continues into the present and is current in every respect. The survivor, indeed, is not truly in touch either with the core of his traumatic reality or with the fatedness of its reenactments, and thereby remains entrapped in both.
>
> To undo this entrapment in a fate that cannot be known, cannot be told, but can only be repeated, a therapeutic process—a process of constructing a narrative, of reconstructing a history and essentially, of re-externalizing the event—has to be set in motion. This re-externalization of the event can occur and take effect only when one can articulate and transmit the story, literally transfer it to another outside oneself and then take it back again, inside. Telling thus entails a reassertion of the hegemony of reality and a re-

externalization of the evil that affected and contaminated the trauma victim. (Felman and Laub 1992, 69)

The therapeutic process of narration, constitution, and reclaiming of the traumatic memory, Dr. Laub asserts, manifests itself in testimony. To testify is to narrate and create a memory, thus framing the traumatic experience within a distinct time and place and escaping its totality. Testimony, Laub stresses, is not a private, solitary process; it requires audience, community, a human reality that is external to the testifying victim. "Bearing witness to a trauma is, in fact, a process that includes the listener. For the testimonial process to take place, there needs to be a bonding, the intimate and total presence of an other—in the position of one who hears . . . Testimony is the narrative's address to hearing; for only when the survivor knows he is being heard, will he stop to hear—and listen to—himself" (Felman and Laub 1992, 70–71).

Judith Herman elaborates further:

> In the telling, the trauma story becomes a testimony. Inger Agger and Soren Jensen, in their work with refugee survivors of political persecution, note the universality of testimony as a ritual of healing. Testimony has both a private dimension, which is confessional and spiritual, and a public aspect, which is political and judicial. The use of the word testimony links both meanings, giving a new and larger dimension to the patient's individual experience. Richard Mollica describes the transformed trauma story as simply a "new story," which is "no longer about shame and humiliation" but rather "about dignity and virtue." Through their storytelling, his refugee patients "regain the world they have lost." (Herman 1992, 181)

Paulina believes that only the legal process can facilitate her testimony, that is, supply her with the presence of the listening other, which would enable her to listen to herself and reconstitute her trauma as a memory of an event of the past rather than an endlessly present presence. Only the legal scene, as a site of sanctioned testimony, can set in motion the therapeutic process of constructing a narrative and a history and establishing a trauma-free present.

Gendering Concepts of Law and Political Victimization

Death and the Maiden demonstrates how, when a society haunted by a traumatic past struggles to mold a new future, a victim's demand for public remembrance and recognition through legal discourse can clash with a wider social longing to forget and reconcile. Simultaneously, the film portrays this conflict from an additional perspective, as one between a woman and her man. The woman demands that her story of sexual victimization and resistance be acknowledged within both marital and legal domains. Her partner, on the other hand, needs to forget his own weakness in the face of her heroic self-sacrifice, and desires to make a name for himself in a new, happier era. The narrative's double vision suggests a deep linkage between victims' struggle for voice and memory within a legal system serving a community that wishes to forget and deny its skeletons, and women's struggle for legal recognition within patriarchal, often misogynistic law. Victims' need to transform their abuse into collective history is closely associated with women's demand for justice through law, or, in other words, with a feminine concept of justice.

Death and the Maiden's explicit association of a formalistic, positivistic notion of law with a male character, while linking a more compassionate, humanistic notion with a female character, clearly genders these two concepts along familiar lines, invoking a jurisprudence featuring a feminist ethics of compassion and care. Gerardo's "masculine" perception claims to be objective, pragmatic, and free of emotional biases. In comparison, Paulina's law is one through which a wronged person can claim and regain her personhood and dignity. Further, it is law that employs and applies intuition, compassion, trust, and personal commitment. In order for law to be good and just it must demonstrate empathy, it must convey and facilitate faith, and encourage and empower Paulina to speak her truth. For Paulina, a "good" future cannot deny its "bad" past. Society must use its legal system to confront its past and to come to terms with its legacy of pain and ugliness; this is how law must do justice.

Love, compassion, and personal commitment are the primary qualities Paulina demands of her attorney-spouse, all of which he fails to offer her. Only through deeply felt empathy and devotion, she believes, can he clearly intuit the truth of her testimony and deliver a just decision, thus being both a good partner and a representative of a just law. A neutral, unfeeling, "objective" stand amounts to impotent cowardice, she accuses. To her, Gerardo's failure as jurist and husband are one and the same: he fails to feel enough to be able to see right from wrong, as well as to supply her with the emotional support she requires. In the absence of empathy, compassion, and commitment, human reality cannot be fully grasped and interpreted; no side can ever be taken and no substantial judgment reached, as there will always be "reasonable doubt."

Interestingly, Paulina's notion of a compassionate law does not seem to entail an empathetic treatment of Roberto Miranda, the defendant, nor does it exclude the law's judgmental aspect or undercut its inherent violence. Paulina's perceptions of law and justice do not imply indiscriminate acceptance. On the contrary, it seems to apply compassion only to those who "deserve" it, in the sense of having demonstrated their own compassion and commitment to others, or at least not having actively and brutally violated human dignity. In Paulina's feminine book, justice does not entitle Roberto to compassionate judgment. Or does her decision to spare his life indicate otherwise?

The dialogue, or confrontation, between the competing masculine and feminine concepts is clearly a challenge posed to the traditional, masculine concept of law by feminist jurisprudence of care. But the film does not privilege feminist jurisprudence of care over more radical feminist legal analysis. On the contrary, its presentation of the community of men exposes the doctor and the attorney as mutually collaborating in the perpetuation of Paulina's sexual victimization.

In raping her repeatedly, objectifying her, and robbing her of dignity, self-respect, and a sense of autonomy, Roberto transformed Paulina from a beautiful young woman, promising medical student, and brave underground activist to a dependent, fearful housewife. When we meet her, she has cut her long red hair short in order not to remind herself of who she used to be; she has given up medicine together with all other activity, and she cringes in fear at the sound of anything that enters her secluded, domestic sphere. From a promising, energetic person, eager to fulfill herself as a human being, she has become Gerardo's housewife, waiting for him in their ocean-side home, cooking his meals, supporting his career, and loving him. Her life is dedicated to him, and she does nothing more. Gerardo owes this full-time, obedient, traditional wife to Roberto's brutal rape, which effectively domesticated her as Gerardo's meek helper.

In turn, Gerardo's stereotypical, sexist conviction that Paulina, a rape victim, is crazy—that she is not a reliable witness, that her testimony cannot be trusted, and that her memory cannot be the basis for the legal accusation and conviction of her rapist—secures Roberto's dignity and freedom. Gerardo's misogynous view of Paulina obstructs the prosecution of Roberto, the exposure of his conduct, his public shaming, and incarceration. Just as Roberto's rape secures Gerardo's patriarchal family life as Paulina's husband, so Gerardo's chauvinistic perception of a raped woman, in his position of jurist, ensures Paulina's rapist amnesty. Rapist and patriarch-jurist empower and shield each other from the threat of the "castrating" woman through a shared misogynous worldview, perpetuating patriarchy and its domination of women. The law, embodied in Gerardo, shares rapists' vision of women, silencing the raped woman and preventing exposure of the crime committed against her.

Bonding through their joint profit from her silenced subjugation, they erect their camaraderie and sociolegal order on the shambles of her violated dignity and personhood. This perception of the patriarchal social order as maintaining women's systematic oppression through, among other means, legally condoned sexual violence, is at the core of any radical feminist jurisprudence focusing on domination, oppression, and abuse. *Death and the Maiden* seems to seamlessly integrate the two voices of feminist jurisprudence—an achievement rarely found in academic scholarship.

Rape and Political Atrocities

Political atrocities committed by tyrannical regimes often include sexual abuse. The mass, systematic rapes committed by Serbs in the former Yugoslavia remind us that mass rape can reach monstrous dimensions.[9] In the context of Paulina's confrontation of her rapist and her husband, the film—like the play—presents rape not only as one form of torture, but also as deeply analogous to all forms of political atrocity.

Unable to rely on her husband's unconditional support, Paulina faces a masculine wall of mistrust.[10] The men are united in treating her, the raped woman, as unreliable and crazy. Both men look at her with utter disbelief, communally denying her memory, her knowledge, her testimony, and her sexual victimization. Their collective mistrust undermines not merely her ability to bring her rapist to trial, but also her self-perception and self-respect. Lacking a mirror willing to reflect her as a sane, sexually abused subject, she is doomed to remain a raging, neurotic woman. The men's treatment of Paulina over the long night constitutes a second rape.

The analogy between rape and political atrocities suggested by *Death and the Maiden* implies that victims of tyrannical regimes face an impasse similar to that experienced by victims of sexual abuse. Like abused women, victims of totalitarian regimes face a wall of sophisticated, eloquent "doctors" and "lawyers" like Miranda and Escobar, powerful agents who doubt their sanity, are suspicious of their memories and testimonies, and have vested interests in mistrusting them. Like raped women, victims of dictatorial regimes are considered unpleasant "damaged goods," and are expected to remain concealed and silent, out of the public eye. Legal systems of democratic, liberal new regimes consider these victims untrustworthy, and proclaim that their memories and stories cannot support prosecutions and convictions. This is especially true of radical, rebellious civil-rights activists, who are often feared by new, liberal regimes almost as much as by old, tyrannical ones.

Death and the Maiden suggests that, just as husbands and rapists, abusers and jurists often share worldviews and interests, so old and new regimes, dictators and liberal legal systems have more in common than is immediately apparent. Victims of tyrannical regimes are likely to suffer a second rape perpetrated by new legal systems—much like rape victims. It may thus be useful to study patriarchy, its networks and self-perpetuation mechanisms, to better understand the abuse of victims at the hands of "progressive" legal systems that rise after dictatorships. The study of thousands of years of patriarchal subjection of women may shed much light on other forms of abuse. At the same time, feminine concepts of law and justice, developed in the context of sexual abuse of women, may be useful in ameliorating the plight of victims of political atrocities.

A corresponding, complementary reading of Death and the Maiden is similarly powerful. Death and the Maiden presents rape victims as victims of oppressive, tyrannical regimes. A rape victim is likened to a freedom fighter, ideologically oppressed by a totalitarian regime. Women raped under patriarchy, this logic seems to imply, are no different from citizens abused under dictatorship. Further, women attempting to use the legal system to expose their rapists and secure their convictions find themselves in a situation similar to that of victims of a tyrannical regime, demanding justice when their country seeks nothing but reconciliation and amnesia. Just as a new, liberal government wishes to leave the horrors of dictatorship behind and unite victims, aggressors, and bystanders in the making of a new future, so any legal system under patriarchy prefers a peaceful unity of rapists, victims, and bystanders to the unsettling demand of raped women to expose and condemn their rapists. As Death and the Maiden demonstrates, bystanders and legal systems—like Gerardo—have much in common with rapists, feel much sympathy for them, and have much to gain from their brutal aggression.

National recovery from the terror of a tyrannical regime is a unique, extreme phase in the life of a nation. But some of the evils bluntly evident in such unsettled situations are common and widespread in more routine situations, if much less apparent. Scrutiny of the extreme situation can shed light on transparent everyday mechanisms that go unnoticed. The communal wish to forgive and forget, to silence victims of a tyrannical regime and maintain unity and stability at their expense, can be seen as an allegory of the norm, exposing the everyday situation of raped women denied access to legal justice. This allegory forcefully asserts that a raped woman is a member of a discriminated group; that raped women are a part of a terrorized, subjected population; that rape is a political crime, perpetrated under patriarchal regimes; that legal systems are inherently reluctant to acknowledge rape, its victims, and aggressors, to prosecute and to expose the system and interests behind the individuals. Study of reluctant legal systems following tyrannical dictatorship is, thus, also study of legal systems' treatment of rape victims.

Cinematic Judgment through Construction of (Implied) Viewer Identification

Through the cinematic technique of split identification, *Death and the Maiden* places its viewer in Paulina's position as sole possessor of the power to look and judge, while, at the same time, subjecting the viewer, together with the men on the screen, to Paulina's penetrating scrutiny and demand for feminine justice. Roberto is the sole defendant in the film's on-screen judging process. In this fictional judgment, Paulina is the prosecutor, and Gerardo the judge (although Paulina nominates him to represent Roberto). But in the film's cinematic judgment, both men, together with the implied viewer, are judged by Paulina. This casting of both (professional, semi-allegorical) male characters as "defendants" in the film's cinematic judgment reinforces the sense of their inherent association. This association invokes dominance-feminist social perceptions. Paulina, on the other hand, is closely and severely scrutinized by the film and its implied viewer from Gerardo's perspective, yet she is not fully judged.

Gerardo is a respectable, hard-working, successful lawyer, a devoted family man, honest and reasonable. Stuart Wilson's character is pleasant looking, friendly, chubby. He is an appealingly contemporary everyman. Despite his distinguished social status, Gerardo treats his aggressive, unpleasant wife patiently and respectfully, even when she attacks him and trashes his dinner as he arrives home wet and tired at the end of a long day.[11] The viewer's urge to identify Gerardo as a good guy and side with him is fostered from his first appearance on-screen. It is maintained and complemented by the film's choice to have Gerardo wear a homey robe and clumsy slippers throughout most of the film. As the film unfolds, viewer identification with Gerardo becomes structural, as the viewer, like Gerardo and together with him, is limited to Gerardo's partial point of view regarding the disputed past, and invited to examine and judge the other characters' testimonies of it.

Paulina and Roberto each know the truth of their alleged encounter fifteen years earlier. Paulina knows, or at least believes she knows, whether it was Roberto who raped and tortured her. Roberto, too, must know whether his denial of her accusations is truthful. Gerardo is the unknowing bystander, just as he was when the events occurred. Moreover, both Paulina and Roberto are actively competing for recognition; they are parties to a conflict, each desperately trying to convince, seeking approval and belief. Each of the two claims to be an innocent victim, accusing the other of brutal, inhuman aggression. Gerardo is in the position of the judge: hearing both sides, weighing the evidence, applying his common sense and knowledge of the world, he must determine who is telling the truth and which of the two is the aggressor. So must the viewer.

The film's viewer is inherently a bystander with no knowledge of the occurrences of the past other than that provided by the testimonies of Paulina and Roberto. The viewer is also the disinterested judge, invited by the film to use common sense and wisdom to weigh the evidence and decide between the contesting parties on screen. Responding to Paulina and Roberto, the viewer develops emotions towards both parties that influence his or her understanding of the situation, evaluation of the testimonies, intuition, and inclinations. Restricted to the same knowledge of the disputed past and positioned in the same judging position, Gerardo and the viewer are similarly situated, Gerardo representing the viewer's on-screen self in regard to the claims concerning the past. Together with Gerardo, the viewer is torn between love and compassion for the powerful, suffering Paulina, and repulsion at her crude, aggressive behavior;[12] between sympathy for the humiliated Roberto and suspicion that he may be concealing horrible guilt.[13] Together with Gerardo the viewer finds it hard to believe that a normal-looking doctor could be the monster Paulina claims he is, and together with him also longs for society to be able to move on, to leave its troubled past behind and enter a normal stage, where one needn't constantly check one's conscience and confront guilt.

Viewer identification with Gerardo is clearly an element of Dorfman's play, but the Dorfman-Polanski film takes this bond a step further. Comparison of play and film on this point demonstrates cinematic choice and its consequences. In Dorfman's play, the viewer's point of view regarding the past is restricted to Gerardo's. An adaptation of the play to film would typically widen the viewer's scope by using flashback to portray the contested past. (Nuts is a case in point: Claudia's flashback memories are the film's reassurance that her version of the contested past is reliable. The flashbacks place the viewer in a privileged position in comparison with Levinsky.) Free from stage unities of time and place, a film version of Death and the Maiden can reasonably be expected to present the viewer with scenes of Paulina's captivity. The film's striking choice not to deviate from Dorfman's play can be read as an active, deliberate choice to restrict the viewer's point of view to Gerardo's, tightening identification with the on-screen character. This is particularly noticeable as "Polanski's films usually allow us to assume the position of an omniscient spectator of the film's characters. As such, we are granted a very unrealistic, and privileged, position . . . Polanski's Death and the Maiden constructs a very different viewer's position: following Ariel Dorfman's play, the film restricts the spectator's knowledge" (Crnkovic 1997, 40; see also Weschler 1994, 90).

To enhance the effect, the film chooses, just as actively, to deviate from the play by acquainting Gerardo with a crucial, dramatic element of Paulina's past only during the night portrayed by the film. In the play, Gerardo has known all along of Paulina's rape during her captivity; he may not have been able and willing to fully confront it and verbalize that knowledge, but he knows. In the film, Gerardo learns of Paulina's rape on-screen, together with the viewer. Just as in the case of the choice not to deviate from the play through flashback shots, here the cinematic choice to deviate from the play version secures viewer identification with Gerardo at the dramatic moment of their mutual realization of the terrible fact of rape.

Throughout the scene in which Paulina explicitly reveals the truth, the film presents the viewer with Gerardo's shocked and horrified face through long reaction close-up shots. Paulina, emotional, fragile, is presented through point-of-view shots from Gerardo's perspective. These shooting choices establish a powerful cinematic bonding between viewer and Gerardo. Significantly, Gerardo wears heavy, square glasses. Shot from a low angle, in the dark of the scene, Gerardo's glasses cast dark shadows over his face, enhancing the dramatic expression of shock and bewilderment while illustrating the shadows entrapping the character. These editing choices are maintained throughout much of the film, attracting viewer attention to Gerardo and maintaining identification with him.

Whereas Gerardo invites viewer identification through a shared judging position and limitation on knowledge, it is Paulina who clearly dominates the screen, inviting viewers' substantial identification. Sigourney Weaver's mesmerizing character is by far the most charismatic, powerful, and impressive on-screen, all highlighted by the choice to award her more screen time and close-up (as well as middle-range and point-of-view) shots than the other characters. (Many of the point-of-view and over-the-shoulder shots are also from Paulina's perspective.) She is the film's uncontested hero (in the male-gendered sense, as I discuss below). Unlike the two men, hesitant, stuttering, impotent, Weaver's Paulina is a confident, determined woman, completely secure in her moral position, admirable in her ability to hold her ground in the face of the men's suspicion, distrust, and manipulations. Further and very significantly, Paulina is the film's exclusive owner of an on-screen gaze: she is the character subjecting all others to her fierce, penetrating look.

Despite her fear, pain, and shame, Paulina looks relentlessly at the men, all the while accusing, judging, and condemning them according to her own notions of law and justice. Her brave, relentless gaze exposes the inhumanity of the aggressor, the weakness of the legal official, and the underlying solidarity that unites them. Her words and actions prosecute them—together with the patriarchal world they represent—from her own feminine perspective. Despite the men's separate and combined efforts, the film does not allow them to subject Paulina to their gaze, power, and accusations. Those days, it states, are over, ended with the dictatorship. In the bad old days, Paulina lay blindfolded as men interrogated and raped her; now it is she who gags them, puts words in their mouths, videotapes their confessions, and holds a gun to their heads. She is a woman acting freely and forcefully as only men once could, while cherishing and enforcing her unique feminine voice and convictions. Refusing to play the passive role of the blindfolded goddess of justice, she pursues her feminine justice with eyes wide open. Through identification with Paulina, the film invites its viewer to share not merely her rage, but, more importantly, her empowerment: her bold, brave gaze as well as her condemnation of patriarchal failure.

If Paulina's determined action identifies her as the film's hero, her crudeness and aggression threaten to undermine this position.[14] But Weaver's Paulina is not merely crude and aggressive, but also fragile and hurt. We see her lead a lonely life with the radio as sole companion. We see her mourn her inability to bear children, as she sobs when Gerardo makes love to her. We witness her cringe in fear in her lonely bed, panic at the sound of Roberto's voice and at the smell of his body, and escape in anxiety into the stormy night. Paulina's visible vulnerability enables us to overlook her aggression, to see it in context as a scar of her victimization, attesting to the monstrosity of what she was forced to undergo. Significantly, the viewer's point of view regarding Paulina's present sorry condition is broader than Gerardo's, who seems almost oblivious to her loneliness, pain, and fragility. This superior point of view afforded viewers by the film brings them closer to Paulina while distancing them from Gerardo.

Viewer identification with Paulina is enhanced by the film in comparison with the play, as is identification with Gerardo. Camera and viewer bonding with Paulina, in Gerardo's absence, is constituted as early as the film's third shot (after a shot of a quartet playing Schubert's *Death and the Maiden*, and another of the turbulent ocean). Situated outside an open window in Paulina's dining room, the camera dollies around the house, stops by another open window, hesitates, and slowly enters the room. Paulina, unaware and unsuspecting of the stalking camera and viewer, seems lonely and vulnerable in the big, empty house by the stormy ocean. Entering her home, joining her in her space, we watch Paulina set the dinner table for two, and together with her we listen to the radio as it announces Gerardo Escobar's nomination as head of the commission assigned to investigate only those incarcerations that resulted in death. (The radio further mentions that Escobar is on the president's short list of candidates for the office of minister of justice.) Not yet realizing the context, we witness the disturbing effect of the news on Paulina, as she smokes on the balcony in the pouring rain and sits on the floor in the dark, nervously gulping her meal. When Gerardo arrives, we realize together with Paulina that he means to conceal the truth from her. His dishonesty is our first impression of him and, together with Paulina, we respond with disappointment and disrespect.

This scene sets the foundation for viewer identification with Paulina and suspicion of Gerardo, which linger throughout the film. In comparison, it is noteworthy to mention that Dorfman's play begins with Paulina alone onstage, sitting, drinking wine, on the terrace of her beach house. At the sound of an approaching car she escapes, terrified, into the bedroom, where she hides behind the curtain. Gerardo's voice is heard from backstage, thanking the car's driver and inviting him to come another day. Gerardo enters, and a dialogue between Gerardo and Paulina ensues.

Clearly, in the play version there is no camera paternalistically leading the viewer through the open window to slowly join Paulina in her domain, nor can Paulina's agonized face be shown in a long close-up shot. Other differences are not so obviously functions of the different media, and express the film's choices in contrast with those of the play. Unlike the film, the play does not secure our bonding with the lonely, hurt Paulina by a shared audition of her husband's betrayal on the radio news. This manipulation is one of the film's many innovations. While in the play the house by the sea is a summer beach home and the family plans an autumnal return to their city house, the secluded house on the cliff in the film seems to be Paulina's home, on the outskirts of society. In the play, Gerardo is merely a junior member of the president's commission, not its chair, and there is no official mention of the likelihood of him becoming minister of justice.

As feminist film scholarship has convincingly argued for decades, many conventional films identify (viewers') gazing and visual subjection (of on-screen characters) with male dominance on-screen, thus gendering all viewers and constructing them as male (Mulvey 1989). The Dorfman-Polanski construction of Paulina successfully undermines this convention. Despite her femininity, Paulina is the film's sole possessor of the gaze, inviting all viewers' identification. Despite her constant on-screen presence (and even one nonerotic nude scene), the film's camera eye does not objectify but rather empowers Paulina: the camera's clear attraction to her does not rob Paulina of her own visual power but enhances it. She is, bluntly speaking, treated by the camera—and consequently the cooperating viewer—as a male hero, without undermining her femininity and feminine point of view.

This subversive stand awards Paulina the position of an honorary man while concomitantly undermining the automatic gendering of the viewer as male. The film's unhesitant insistence on viewer identification with a crude, aggressive rape survivor, who presents a feminine concept of justice and subjects all on-screen male characters to her penetrating gaze and uncompromising judgment, is a noteworthy and scarce act of feminist resistance and defiance in mainstream, commercial cinema. It complements and enhances the film's combination of feminist approaches of care and dominance mentioned earlier, as well as the film's unique achievement in presenting a female protagonist as both victim and agent, inviting both compassion and admiration.

Viewer identification with Paulina undercuts identification with Gerardo. From Paulina's point of view, shared by the film's viewer, Gerardo is exposed as a cowardly, self-serving man, unwilling to acknowledge his wife's heroism and self-sacrifice for his sake, reluctant to confront his own unheroic, disloyal conduct, eager to promote his self-interest in the new political environment at all cost. His "objective," "unbiased," "legalistic" position concerning law and justice in times of transformation is exposed as highly subjective and self-serving, and his "ideological" preference of reconciliation over legal inquiries into the past is exposed as stemming from bad conscience and bad faith, personal guilt, a refusal to feel gratitude, and simple cowardice. Through Paulina's penetrating gaze, Gerardo's legalistic-patriarchal position is stripped of its neutral, professional facade, and behind the scenes lurk denial, silencing, and naked interests of self-preservation. Behind Gerardo's hesitation to take legal action lie his refusal to confront the past, Paulina's brutal victimization, systematic injustice, and, above all, his own role in and responsibility for her tragedy.

Sympathy and compassion for Paulina attract viewer identification with her at Gerardo's expense on yet another, deeper, emotional level. In his analysis of the therapeutic process trauma victims must undertake in order to return to life, Dr. Dori Laub stresses the crucial part played by the compassionate *other*:

> Massive trauma precludes its registration; the observing and recording mechanisms of the human mind are temporarily knocked out, malfunction. The victim's narrative—the very process of bearing witness to massive trauma—does indeed begin with someone who testifies to an absence, to an event that has not yet come to existence . . . The listener, therefore, is a party to the creation of knowledge *de novo* . . . By extension, the listener to trauma comes to be a participant and a co-owner of the traumatic event: through his very listening, he comes to partially experience trauma in himself . . . The listener has to feel the victim's victories, defeats, and silences, know them from within, so that they can assume the form of testimony.
>
> Bearing witness to a trauma is, in fact, a process that includes the listener. For the testimonial process to take place, there needs to be a bonding, the intimate and total presence of an *other*—in the position of one who hears. Testimonies are not monologues; they cannot take place in solitude. The witnesses are talking *to somebody*: to somebody they have been waiting for for a long time. (Felman and Laub 1992, 58–59, 70)

The film's viewer, drawn to Paulina's forceful plea to commence the journey to the uncharted land of horror, is urged by the film to take on that intimate and total presence as the other. Through deep bonding with and commitment to the trauma victim, the viewer participates in the making of the traumatic memory by taking an active part, and partially experiencing trauma him or herself. The viewer's commitment to Paulina, her trauma, memory, and truth, is thus profound.

At the same time, the viewer experiences resentment towards Gerardo, who has neglected—and even refused—to fulfill this role all these years, and continues to do so. In a sense, the viewer's resentment is all too real and personal: s/he blames Gerardo in that his selfish, cowardly evasion of re-sponsibility towards his wife have not merely denied Paulina salvation, but have also now burdened the viewer with the difficult task of witnessing and experiencing trauma.

To complicate things further, Dr. Laub advises us that taking the position of the compassionate listener entails negotiating hazards and unpleasant responses: "Trauma—and its impact on the hearer—leaves, indeed, no hiding place intact. As one comes to know the survivor, one really comes to know oneself; and that is not a simple task . . . To maintain a sense of safety in the face of the upheaval . . . the listener experiences a range of defensive feelings . . . These listening defenses may include . . . a sense of outrage and of anger, unwittingly directed at the victim—the narrator. The listener . . . experiences a need, an urgency to pull back, to withdraw into a safer place, a place where he can in turn protect himself" (Felman and Laub 1992, 72). Overwhelmed by such unexpected emotions, does the viewer resent Paulina and identify with Gerardo? Does she feel shame, guilt, and even more resent-ment towards Gerardo? And how does Paulina's love for Gerardo affect the viewer? Does a viewer share that love, finding him or herself more forgiving, or is the viewer infuriated by Paulina's love for her undeserving husband, begrudging him even more?

Double Identification and Self-Judgment to the Bitter End

One of the film's outstanding triumphs lies in its vehement refusal to allow its implied viewer to fully choose one of the characters over the other, that is to reject Gerardo and side with Paulina. Constantly playing the viewer's con-flicting sympathies and inclinations against each other, the film maintains intensive viewer identification with both Gerardo and Paulina throughout. At times, Gerardo seems the only reasonable, decent, stable point of reference, while Paulina appears monstrous, preoccupied with sickening vengeance, hatred, and rage. At other moments, Paulina seems courageous and truthful, a vulnerable woman in need of sympathy and compassion, while Gerardo appears weak, cowardly, and unable to love. The dialogue's quick pace invites a constant shift of emotions and inclinations, confusing, paralyzing, and frustrating the film's bewildered, torn, tormented viewer.

Identifying with Paulina, the viewer cringes in horror when, reflected in Gerardo's responses, s/he realizes the depth of vindictive, ruthless hatred one is capable of harboring. At the same time, identifying with Gerardo, seeing him or herself through Paulina's eyes, the viewer is embarrassed to acknowledge and admit the powerful attraction of peace and quiet at all cost. The film's cooperating viewer is ashamed to confront his or her difficulty to side with Paulina, to love and support her, and struggles with the secret longing to break away from the suffocating obligation and pursue a new, happier future, free of the haunting ghosts of a painful past.

The film's manipulation of viewer identification is epitomized in the film's ending. I mentioned earlier the film's choice not to deviate from the play version by not presenting the viewer with flashback shots of Paulina's rape and torture. The film's ending demonstrates an even more dramatic cinematic choice, this time in deviating from the play. In the play, in complete darkness, the viewer hears Roberto's recorded confession, the details of which were supplied by Gerardo, who heard them from Paulina. When Roberto finishes writing out the recorded confession and signing it, Paulina sends Gerardo to fetch Roberto's hidden car, and in Gerardo's absence announces to Roberto that she is now convinced that he really is her rapist, and is determined to shoot him. She says that only if he gives her a true confession, and repents, can she forgive him and let him live.

Roberto refuses, insisting on his innocence. As they converse, both characters are slowly "covered from view by a giant mirror which descends, forcing the audience to look at themselves. For a few minutes, the Mozart quartet is heard, while the spectators watch themselves in the mirror" (Dorfman 1992, 53). We do not know whether Roberto is innocent, and whether Paulina indeed shot him as she has said she would. In the final scene, when he appears in a concert hall where Gerardo and Paulina attend a concert, we cannot tell whether he is a living man or a phantom: "Roberto enters, under a light, which has a faint phantasmagoric moonlight quality. He could be real or he could be an illusion in Paulina's head" (Dorfman 1992, 55).

In the film, Paulina is not satisfied with Roberto's videotaped "confession" which, she claims, seems staged and phony. As night fades and morning lights the scene, she decides to end the charade and kill Roberto. While Gerardo is phoning Barcelona to check Roberto's alibi (Roberto claimed that he spent the relevant time in residency in a hospital in Barcelona), Paulina pushes the handcuffed and blindfolded Roberto at gunpoint to the edge of the cliff. When Gerardo, running, brings news that Roberto is indeed remembered by a woman at the hospital, Paulina discredits this evidence, saying Roberto must have arranged for the woman to supply him with this alibi, as did many of the old regime's criminals. Before pushing him into the ocean, Paulina removes Roberto's blindfold, looks into his eyes and asks: "Look at me. Isn't it bright enough to see me? Don't you know me?" In the light of day, in the open landscape, in a very long close-up shot capturing every nuance of his expressions, documenting his emotional upheaval, Roberto delivers a detailed confession:

> I was strong; I fought it so hard . . . I washed you. You soiled yourself. You told me, "I am dirty," and I washed you clean. The others egged me on: "Come on doctor, you're not going to refuse free meat, are you?" . . . And inside I could feel I was starting to like it . . . You didn't know. It was bright in those rooms. And I didn't have to be *nice* to anyone. I didn't need to seduce them. I realized I didn't even have to take care of them. I had all the power. I could break anyone. I could make them say or do whatever I wanted. I was lost. I got curious. Morbid curiosity. How much can this woman take? What's going to happen to her vagina? Does it dry out when you shock her? Can she have an orgasm afterwards? I like being naked. I would undress slowly . . . I liked you knowing what I was going to do. I was naked in the bright light and you couldn't see me. You couldn't tell me what to do. I owned you. I owned *all* of them. I fell in love with it. I could hurt you or I could fuck you. And you couldn't tell me not to. You had to thank me. I loved it. I was sorry it ended. I was very sorry it ended.

As he completes his narrative, Gerardo rushes at him, apparently attempting to push him over the cliff. After a short, pathetic struggle he lets go, confessing: "I can't do it, Pauli. I just can't." As Gerardo sits helplessly on the fence with his head bowed, Paulina unties Roberto and walks home, Gerardo slowly following. Roberto remains standing, facing the ocean, and the camera assumes his point of view, looking down at the turbulent waters below.

In the film's final scene, the camera pans from a quartet, playing *Death and the Maiden*, to a concert hall packed with a well-dressed audience. The camera zooms in on Paulina sitting tense, grave, tormented, alongside Gerardo. Sensing something, she looks up and meets Roberto's eyes, sitting in the balcony with his wife and two boys and looking down at her with a soft, longing look. Roberto's eyes meet Paulina's and then Gerardo's. A long medium shot leaves us with Paulina and Gerardo sitting very close together with paralyzed, stone-like faces.[15]

Thus the film replaces the play's open-ended last scene with a clear-cut resolution, actively preventing the viewer from dwelling philosophically on the unreachable nature of truth, a confounding endeavor, as well as the convenient evasion of judgment.[16] In the analysis of *Rashomon* in chapter 1, I suggest that that film's open end leaves the viewer pondering on the human impossibility of getting at the "real truth" of any past event, thus effectively distracting attention from the substantive issues of judgment and misogyny in the cinematic judgment process. Dorfman-Polanski's *Death and the Maiden* refuses to let its viewer off the hook.

The film's ending leaves little doubt: Roberto *did* torture and rape Paulina; Paulina *did* recognize him correctly; her narrative *was* truthful, his denial deceitful. Together with Gerardo, with whom s/he has strongly identified throughout the film, the viewer is overwhelmed by shame. S/he is ashamed at not having been able to tell truth from falsehood; at not having been able to love Paulina enough to do her justice; for siding with the aggressor, merely because it was easier, and he was more appealing. The viewer, together with Gerardo, the country's leading jurist, short-listed for the office of minister of justice, is terrified, realizing his blindness and incompetence in distinguishing true testimony from false, acknowledging how eager s/he was to dismiss Paulina's narrative. S/he feels deep guilt for doubting Paulina, accusing her of mental illness, undermining her sense of self-respect. The viewer, together with Gerardo, is horrified at how close s/he came to exonerating a man guilty of brutal rape and torture, realizing that, together with Gerardo, s/he has been actively participating in what amounts to a second rape. Like Gerardo, the viewer also feels betrayed and humiliated by Roberto, with whom s/he had bonded, howling together at the moon, now ashamed at having been so easily deceived. The viewer, together with Gerardo, feels greatly humbled; the smug, self-assured bystanding judge now sits with bowed head.

To demonstrate the applicability of the theoretical terminology presented in the introduction, let me situate this last line of thought in the larger scheme of law-and-film study. In calling its viewer's attention to the ways in which a member of any judging community, be it legal or cinematic, may be seduced to side with the aggressor at the victim's expense, *Death and the Maiden* illuminates the inner operation of a central element of the legal system. Concurrently, it points to the similarities between law and film as influential social discourses, illustrating how a film viewer, just like a member of a legal system, may be incited to participate in a victim's second (judicial) rape. My engagement with this is a film-parallels-law type of analysis.

The film's ending offers still further revelations and conclusions. The viewer's disillusioned realizations in the film's final moments call for a revised evaluation of the legalistic, masculine concept of law personified by Gerardo. Undoubtedly, the ending proves Gerardo wrong in his determinations that Paulina is too ill to recognize Roberto and that her evidence is unreliable. The film's ending reveals that the "real real truth," as Roberto would put it, is manifested in Gerardo's desperate confession: "I can't do it, Pauli, I just can't do it."

This confession echoes another memorable sentence, uttered by Paulina in one of the film's early scenes. When Roberto succeeds in tripping Paulina and causing her to drop her gun, he urges Gerardo to grab the weapon and overpower her, and is greatly disappointed when Gerardo fails to do so. "You didn't do anything. You just stood there," he accuses. "Of course he just stood there," Paulina replies. "He is the law." Embodying the law, Gerardo is inherently incapable of "taking sides" and acting on his intuition and conviction. This accusation echoes, in the viewer's mind, yet another one of Paulina's powerful lines, addressed to Gerardo: "I don't want you to be my lawyer. I want you to be my husband."

Indeed, Gerardo's confession, "I can't do it," is not merely that of a lawyer, but that of a husband as well. As a husband, Gerardo is socially expected to protect his wife and avenge her. Hearing of his wife's brutal, repeated rape from the very man who raped and tortured her, who admits he "loved it" and was sorry it ended, Gerardo can be expected to be infuriated to the extent of losing self-control. His inability to kill, or even just strike, Roberto under these circumstances may indicate that his previous inability to see Paulina's victimization derives from and facilitates a selfish need not to see what he cannot face and cannot respond to. Unable to kill Roberto or punish him in any meaningful way, Gerardo is better off not knowing of Paulina's rape, that is, he is best served by insisting that her evidence is inadmissible and her mental state too fragile to trust. Gerardo's condescending "professional" rationalizations regarding inadmissible and inconclusive evidence and unreliable witnesses are thus explicitly exposed by the film's ending as pathetic excuses, concealing incompetence and bad faith.

Throughout the film, its viewer was invited to respectfully consider, compare, and critique both presented notions of law and justice at face value. The film's ending pronounces its unreserved condemnation of the legalistic vision of law as objective, neutral, and therefore impartial and just. The film leaves its implied viewer little room for doubt that such conceptualization of law is a smoke screen, disguising personal, completely subjective fears, human deficiencies, and self-promoting interests. It is Paulina's bold, honest, courageous pursuit of healing justice, fully professing her subjective grounds, motivations, and biases, that the film celebrates and embraces, thus pronouncing its cinematic judgment. Perhaps Paulina's pursuit cannot secure a comprehensive, coherent system of objective judgment, but perhaps what it does constitute is as good as law and justice are ever likely to get.

The film seems to leave the Gerardo-identified viewer little with which to save face. But the film's implied viewer is also deeply identified with Paulina, thus also experiencing her redemption and relief. The viewer feels just in identifying with Paulina, and greatly relieved that the process of testimony creating, in which s/he actively shared, has been shown to be truthful and accurate. Further, the viewer is relieved that Paulina did not execute Roberto, that is, that her overwhelming, frightening, embarrassing vengeance, lacking any compassion or empathy for Roberto, vengeance in which the viewer may have, at times, viscerally participated, was really redeemed and transformed into the pursuit of truth and justice.

Strongly associated with both Paulina and Gerardo, the implied viewer thus forcefully applies Paulina's judgment to himself or herself as the arrogant husband-jurist who could not tell right from wrong, and who failed to love and care for his victimized wife. The film mirrors the viewer, leaving the Paulina-identified aspect of the viewer holding an unrelenting mirror to the cringing Gerardo-identified viewer's face. Celebrating Paulina's regained dignity in the face of what the film exposed as both men's false, dangerous sense of honor and respectability, the cooperating viewer is left with little doubt as to the film's uncompromising value system.

The film's ending clarifies that its most significant judgment is not the one presented on-screen for approximately one hundred minutes, nor even that experienced by the viewer during the viewing. It similarly clarifies that the film's primary defendant is not Roberto. The real judgment instigated by the film begins only with the film's last scenes, when the Gerardo-identified viewer is presented with his tormenting reflection. Only at this point can the viewer begin to reassess his or her feelings and inclinations throughout the dramatic night, and begin to scrutinize and judge them. This process of self-inspection and self-judgment, the film's enduring cinematic judgment, may last far longer than one hundred minutes.

Back to the Jurisprudential Dilemma: Law or Truth Commission?

Death and the Maiden's ending exposes and discredits Gerardo's condescending formulation of law and justice, but this does not resolve the authentic dilemma regarding the desired nature of the legal system and its appropriate role in the transition from postdictatorial regimes. Throughout the film, this dilemma was lost in the noise of Gerardo's bad-faith arguments deriving from personal weakness and selfish needs; silencing this noise does not resolve the dilemma, but merely exposes and enhances it. Should the law "take sides" and act on its intuition and conviction—or should it, indeed, merely supply the contesting sides with a stage and "neutral" rules? Is the law equipped to handle atrocities for which there is—and can be—no ordinary, conventional evidence? In a real court of law, lacking Roberto's confession, would we be able to determine his guilt? And if not, is the legal process really the right social avenue to treat Paulina's victimization and trauma?

These unresolved concerns give rise to an additional sociolegal question, which, although not confronted by the film explicitly, is subtly implied and illuminated: would Paulina's needs be better served by a legalistic trial or by a truth commission (such as the South African TRC)? The private process conducted on-screen, in which the viewer is invited to actively participate, features some characteristics of a trial and some of a truth-finding process. While Paulina initiates the proceeding with a formal accusation, stresses the importance of confronting her assailant, insists on the importance of establishing the only real truth of Roberto's crimes and her victimization, and speaks of punishing Roberto, she also promises him amnesty (his life and freedom) in exchange for his confession and remorse, and, in fact, releases him when he eventually acknowledges responsibility and confesses.

Would and should Paulina prefer the safety of the truth commission, abandoning the demand for clear-cut determination and exposure of her perpetrator? Was Roberto's confession crucial for her recovery, or was the direct confrontation more essential for her empowerment? Would giving testimony in Roberto's absence serve her therapeutic needs and sense of justice? Should she make the pragmatic choice, and prefer the more compassionate, therapeutic avenue, not risking a brutal cross-examination? Would that be a defeatist choice? And which of the options should the viewer opt for, having come to internalize and cherish Paulina's complex, acute needs?

The film does not provide a clear solution. In this respect, it elects an open ending. It does, however, invite viewer awareness of these questions. To facilitate viewer consideration, it provides the necessary background for understanding the situation, ensures the emotional involvement required for committed, attentive deliberation, and establishes the parameters and the considerations to be discussed and weighed.

Roman Polanski's Death and the Maiden

It is not a trivial choice to study and celebrate a Roman Polanski film, and a film representing a rape victim and perpetrator in particular. I therefore conclude this chapter with some reflections on the connection between the themes I have pursued and the film's "Polanski character." Writers and critics have noted *Death and the Maiden*'s place in Polanski's canon. Lawrence Weschler insightfully asserts that " 'Death and the Maiden' might have served as an alternative title for well over half of Roman Polanski's movies (for *Knife in the Water*, for instance, and *Repulsion*, and *Chinatown*, and *The Tenant* and *Tess*, and *Frantic* and *Bitter Moon* and maybe even for *Macbeth* or *Rosemary's Baby*)" (1994, 90). More specifically, Gordana Crnkovic explains that "many of Polanski's films explore the victimization of a female character which ends with death—either that of the character, or of those who persecute her . . . Polanski's films obsessively rework the motif of a woman-victim seizing power, a tool of death, and then deploying it in different ways" (1997, 39–40, 44).

Additionally, it is very evident to anyone familiar with Polanski's work that "the mood of intensifying claustrophobia, of three scorpions tangling in an ever-tapering bottle, is so distinctly Polanskian that the whole project may well have been dubbed 'Knife in the Water II,' in homage to the director's first feature film" (Weschler 1994, 90). *Death and the Maiden*'s characters' entrapment in a secluded, hellishly claustrophobic environment, where two men and a woman confront themselves and each other, does indeed seem like another take on the theme that has fascinated Polanski throughout his work. In both these respects, *Death and the Maiden* is and must be viewed as a Polanski film.

There is yet another significant element that seems most relevant to this discussion: the film's reflection of its director's (renowned) life story and personality. As many have noted, from this perspective, *Death and the Maiden* may be the paradigmatic Polanski film: "The play neatly distributes among its three characters three of the principle guises by which Polanski's life has come to be so publicly known. Polanski the guilt-ridden husband, who had to come to terms with the savage killing of his own young wife, Sharon Tate, by Charles Manson and his gang in 1969; Polanski the man himself accused, eight years after that, of statutory rape [of a thirteen-year-old girl], who, like the doctor, steadfastly continued to maintain his innocence . . . and before either of those events, Polanski, the young Jewish victim of a Fascist regime during the Nazi occupation of his native Poland" (Weschler 1994, 90). Violence, brutality, violations of human rights and dignity, insanity, victimization, and the complex relations and boundaries between victim and aggressor are central themes in Polanski's films, as in his life.[17] Murder, suffering, rape, loss, trauma, and guilt have shaped his life and art. Until his directing of The Pianist in 2003, nearly sixty years after World War II, Polanski seems never to have confronted his loss, victimization, and trauma as a Holocaust survivor. His survival strategy has been to leave the past behind without looking back, focusing solely on the future.[18] Perhaps as a consequence, it seems that the past has never ceased to inhabit his present, in life and art alike,[19] and he has found himself repeating its traumatic horrors as both victim and aggressor.[20]

Casting and editing choices surely contributed significantly to Death and the Maiden's powerful impact.[21] But I believe that it is absolute director identification with all three characters that explains, more than anything, the film's gripping hold on its viewer. This film's director did not merely instruct each of his actors how to perform the smallest of gestures (Weschler 1994, 105) but also lived each of the parts, breathing his own life into them. Directing the film, he was, in fact, each of the characters and all three, inspecting, condemning, hating, and loving each of them through the others' eyes. The film's compelling power is in Polanski, through his fictional characters, pulling away from the tormented past—and holding on to it, suppressing pain over the loss of loved ones, aching for redemption, and denying a guilt which haunts his very existence. The director invites his viewer into his own point of view by insisting that s/he identify, concomitantly and throughout the film, with victim and guilt-ridden bystander, and even, though partially, with the aggressor. The urgent, conflicting needs for justice, recovery and remembrance, forgetfulness and denial, forgiveness and reconciliation, inherently impossible to fulfill, seem to be Polanski's own, haunting the spot in which he positions his film's viewer.

In Death and the Maiden, Polanski allows us to enter his own tormented life as a trauma survivor, an aggressor, and a guilt-ridden bystander, and to experience the claustrophobic horror it entails. It is from this painful perspective that we are presented with social and jurisprudential questions regarding men and women, victimization, memory, truth, law, and reconciliation. This humbling experience invites us to reconsider fundamental notions of justice, dignity, humanity, and life itself.

Postscript: The Piano

The discussion of *Death and the Maiden* focuses on the film's unique features, highlighting issues such as trauma, memory, and conflicted societies. To conclude, let me return to the definition of the film as an alternative narration and judgment of *Rashomon*'s theme, demonstrating how differently a film can treat the theme of man, woman, and rapist confronting issues of victimization and guilt. This reading of *Death and the Maiden* can be useful in the discussion of other feminist and nonfeminist films. One such example is Jane Campion's *The Piano* (1994).

Set in nineteenth-century New Zealand, *The Piano* follows its female protagonist, Ada (Holly Hunter), as she arrives at her new husband's colonial home in the thick forest. Mute by choice, Ada lives and communicates through her beloved piano. Collecting her at the shore, Ada's new husband, Stewart (Sam Neill), decides to leave the piano by the ocean rather than have his men carry it in the slippery forest roads. Stewart's neighbor and friend, Baines (Harvey Keitel), agrees to escort Ada to visit her piano, and enchanted by her music he buys the instrument from Stewart, together with music lessons given by Ada. When the reluctant Ada attempts to teach him to play, he offers to "sell" her back her piano for private concerts in his bedroom.

During these concerts, Banes becomes increasingly sexual towards Ada, demanding physical contact and finally intercourse instead of music lessons. Acknowledging that this arrangement is prostituting her and making him miserable, he finally sends the piano back to Ada. She then comes to see him of her own free will, and the relationship takes a romantic turn. Stewart attempts to prevent Ada's adulterous relationship, locks her in the house, and finally punishes her disobedience by cutting off one of her fingers. Eventually Ada leaves with Banes, throwing her piano overboard into the ocean. In her new city home she learns to speak.

Once again, woman, husband, and sexual offender are trapped together in a secluded forest on the outskirts of civilization. A sexual intercourse between woman and sexual offender undermines the men's bonding. The woman's objectification by the men is ignored and thus sanctioned by law.

The woman's husband buys her from her father, sells her piano as well as her work and skill, locks her in, attempts to force intercourse on her, disciplines her through assault and injury—and is fully within his legal rights. As husband, he is entitled to lay down the law that she must obey; in this respect she is "married to the law." Lacking legal agency and rights to defend her subjecthood and autonomy, the woman is outside the protecting reach of the law: an "outlaw." Every expression of agency and will on her part is illegal: when she sells her body to reclaim her piano she is prostituting, and when she makes love to the man of her choice she is committing adultery. Silenced by culture and law, she embraces the only course of action open to her, choosing complete self-imposed silence. Finding a man who learns to see her as a person and listen even to her unspoken voice, she chooses to reenter society together with him.

Does *The Piano* judge Ada together with its male characters, or does it allow her to judge them? Does the film support the patriarchal legal system it depicts and the social order this system upholds? Does the film call its viewer's attention to patriarchal society and law as a means of criticizing them? Does it offer an alternative, feminine concept of justice? Does it invite its viewer to conduct a cinematic judgment? Does it present Ada's silence as powerful resistance or as a passive aggressive, manipulative means of control? Is the ending a happy, optimistic, feminist one, or does it restore and secure patriarchal order, condoning the damaging, popular fantasy of women falling in love with their sexual offenders? Reading *The Piano* against *Rashomon* and *Death and the Maiden* can illuminate these questions and many others.

In one respect *The Piano* clearly resembles *Rashomon*, *Death and the Maiden*, and all the other films discussed so far: it does not present its female protagonist with the option of creating or joining a community of women. Woman faces men, society, culture, and law all alone. Her power is solely that of an individual facing society and its institutions. The following chapters discuss films that explore relations between law, judgment, and women's communities.

Part III

WOMEN RESISTING AND SUBVERTING JUDGMENT

Beyond Conventional Feminist Jurisprudence

A Question of Silence 8

(Netherlands, 1982)

FEMINIST COMMUNITY AS REVOLUTION (READ AGAINST

"A JURY OF HER PEERS")

The Dutch film A Question of Silence (1982) illustrates how a law film can express a view alternative to that which it attributes to its fictional legal system. Marleen Gorris's Silence exposes its legal system's inadequate judgment of women and critiques it by offering an alternative, feminist cinematic judgment. Silence's critique of its fictional legal system's attitude echoes that of an earlier American short story and play: Susan Glaspell's 1916 "A Jury of Her Peers" (the play version is titled Trifles). Silence also shares with "Jury" a dominant theme: women's community as feminist revolution.

"A Jury of Her Peers": Synopsis

For almost a century, "Jury" has been a powerful, influential feminist statement. Glaspell's plea is effectively echoed and extended to contemporary audiences through the work of feminist creators who have heard Glaspell's voice and have accepted her invitation to feminine, feminist networking. "Jury" has inspired a whole subgenre of feminist writing and filmmaking, a genre which theorizes and represents the community of women so intriguingly suggested by Glaspell. *Thelma and Louise* (1991) is an important member of this subgenre, as is *Silence.*

In Glaspell's story, women's awakening, their feminine bonding, and ideological activism are inseparable from their realization of the gender discrimination and oppression inherent in the existing legal system, and their responsive creation of alternative, feminine justice and judgment. I suggest that in her 1916 short story, Glaspell anticipates both legal feminist theory that focuses on dominance, oppression, and resistance, and psychological feminist theory that focuses on an ethics of care. Further, her narrative combines the two perspectives into a coherent, comprehensive worldview. Quilting serves as a metaphor for feminine social networking as well as for women's engagement in law, thus symbolically mediating between the fundamental structures of feminine community and feminist legal thought.

The story is based on a court case that Glaspell covered in 1900 as a reporter (Ben-Zvi 1995; Hedges 1995). An abused woman, Minnie Foster Wright, strangles her abusive husband, Mr. Wright, to death in his sleep. The narrative begins when the sheriff, the county attorney, and a witness visit Minnie's home, the scene of the crime, in search of evidence and a motive. They are joined by the sheriff's wife, Mrs. Peters, and the witness's wife, Mrs. Hale, who were asked to select some clothes for the imprisoned Minnie Foster. As the men inspect the outdoors and the upper floor in search of clues, the two women bond with the absent Minnie as they explore her kitchen. Through dialogue, applying their own life experiences while closely reviewing the details of her oven, armchair, towel, and preserves, the women piece together Minnie's secluded, lonely, silenced life. (Unlike the male lawyer's invasive search in *Nuts*, the women move through Minnie's world as if afraid to contaminate a sacred ground. Apologetic, they try to disturb as little as possible in the fulfillment of the task they reluctantly execute.)

Finding an empty birdcage and the body of a strangled canary, they recognize the deceased man's dominating brutality, which had triggered Minnie's desperate, violent outburst. "No, Wright wouldn't like the bird . . . a thing that sang. She used to sing. He killed that too" (Glaspell 1996, 90). "The women reason that the strangled bird had been treasured by the desperately lonely farmwife for its companionship and killed at the hands of her husband, and must have been the proverbial last straw prompting the wife to kill her abusive husband" (West 1997, 243). Examining the stitches of the quilt Minnie was knotting, they learn of her distraction and excitement after committing the killing.

Belittling the women, the condescending men exclude them from the legal investigation. External to the official process, the women collect the evidence, analyze it, and reach their own verdict, condemning Mr. Wright and exonerating Minnie. As Linda Ben-Zvi rightly notes: "In the process of judging they become compeers, Mrs. Peters recognizing her own disenfranchisement under the law and her own potential for violence, Mrs. Hale recognizing her failure to sustain her neighbor and thus her culpability in driving the desperate woman to kill" (Ben-Zvi 1995, 34).

The women refrain from supplying the investigating men with the dead canary, and undo and replace Minnie's uneven stitches. Realizing their social position outside the legal arena as well as the law's inability to see women's lives, to hear their stories, to recognize their pain, or to try them justly, they refuse to cooperate and instead apply their own justice in a silent, collective act of defiance and disobedience. "Not waiting to be given the vote or the right to serve on juries, Glaspell's women have taken the right for themselves" (Ben-Zvi 1995, 39). Yet their disobedience is secretive and their voices remain mute. Perhaps they save Minnie Foster, but they do not attempt to change the world. Excluded from the legal process and the public sphere, their brave act of feminine solidarity and resistance remains unnoticed, as they return to their respective solitary kitchens.

Women's Community, Dominance, and Care

Glaspell's treatment of her female characters is realistic and compassionate. The three farm housewives are neither heroes nor villains, neither "virgins" nor "whores." Portrayed from a feminine point of view, Minnie Foster, Mrs. Hale, and Mrs. Peters are flesh-and-blood women, victims of varying degrees of harsh circumstances while also active, responsible agents.

Female bonding is a central theme in "Jury of Her Peers," long celebrated by feminist writers. Conversing, Minnie's neighbor and the sheriff's wife realize how difficult Minnie's work must have been at the bad stove, how shabby and humiliated she must have felt in her worn-out clothes, and how she must have longed for music. They appreciate how desperately she must have missed other women's company and their social activity, friendship, warmth, conversation, and compassion. Pausing from their daily chores to scrutinize Minnie's life, they come to apprehend their own, reluctantly admitting that: "We all go through the same things—it's all just a different kind of the same thing! If it weren't—why do you and I understand? Why do we know—what we know this minute?" (Glaspell 1996, 91). As Karen Alkalay-Gut rightly notes, the women "not only sympathize but also identify with the murderess" (1995, 75). Looking into Minnie's life they are horrified to discover it reflects their own.

Acknowledging Minnie's life as a reflection of their own lives, Mrs. Hale and Mrs. Peters recognize their distinct cultural perspective as women and find their unique, communal voice. Mutually practicing the use of this newly discovered voice, they begin to articulate their story of Minnie's life and of their own. The women's story is told with much compassion for the accused woman. Their quiet, hesitant narration focuses on emotional elements: her pain, hardship, and disappointment. Empathizing with the absent woman, the two neighbors notice the smallest details in Minnie's life, respectfully acknowledging their significance. Intuitively, "it came into Mrs. Hale's mind that that rocker didn't look in the least like Minnie Foster—the Minnie Foster of twenty years before. It was a dingy red, with wooden rungs up the back, and the middle rung was gone, and the chair sagged to one side" (Glaspell 1996, 79). Minnie's life is reflected in that chair. The women realize the hard labor that went into preparing the fruit preserves, and feel for Minnie's loss. They appreciate the sentimental value of Minnie's little box, which Minnie must have had since childhood, and understand her deep attachment to the canary she buried in it. They notice the uneven stitches in Minnie's quilt, expressive of her emotional turmoil, and carefully replace them with prettier ones. In contrasting the women's attitude with the men's, Glaspell emphasizes the distinct nature of their different voices and points of view.

Yet, while Glaspell's female protagonists speak in a different voice, the story they tell is one of patriarchal dominance and oppression. The Minnie they reconstruct is an abused, battered woman, confined and tormented both mentally and physically by a tyrannical spouse. Witnessing the men's legal investigation of Minnie's crime, the women perceive it as additional abuse of the unfortunate woman. Invading Minnie's home, the men turn it against her. Blind to the tragic circumstances of her life, they read every piece of information as testifying to her guilt. Even the dirty towel is said by the men to attest to Minnie's lack of the "home-making instinct" (Glaspell 1996, 82). Further, Glaspell subjects Mrs. Peters and Mrs. Hale themselves to male oppression. The men repeatedly belittle, patronize, and mock them, trivializing their domestic work, doubting their intelligence, and ridiculing their interest in feminine craft. "Women are used to worrying over trifles" (81), observes Mr. Hale, and wonders: "Would the women know a clue if they did come upon it?" (82). In response, "the two women moved closer together."

It is, therefore, masculine oppression and the women's awareness of it that bring about their unity, their support of Minnie, and their increasing awareness of their unique feminine identity, voice, story, and community. Nevertheless, once vocalized, this voice is unique and powerful. It is clear and brave, caring and just. It is genuinely valuable and feminine. In a paradoxical way, it is only under the tyranny of patriarchal oppression that Glaspell's women converse and find their feminine voice. But once found, their voice marks the community of women, empowering them in resistance to that oppression.

Women's Community and the Law

The law plays a crucial part in the awakening and transformation of Mrs. Hale and Mrs. Peters, both as a vehicle of male oppression and in expressing a unique feminine culture. The existing legal system manifests male domination of women. It is closely associated with male brutality, patronizing attitudes, and systematic exclusion and dismissal of women. In Glaspell's text, only men participate in the legal enterprise. The sheriff, county attorney, and farmer form the homogeneous community of men that searches for evidence, establishes the facts of the case, determines the scope of relevance, and evaluates the reasonableness of actors and behavior.

It is the men's common sense, their life experience, and point of view that underlie the entire preliminary procedure that will frame and determine the courtroom scene. From the men's perspective, John Wright was a good man: "He didn't drink, and kept his word as well as most . . . and paid his debt" (Glaspell 1996, 88). He was respectable and intelligible. Mrs. Wright, on the other hand, lacked the "home-making instinct," and looked "queer" (79). She was strange, incomprehensible, and a failure at her social and domestic duties. Neither the men nor the law can see Minnie Foster: the reality of her life with John, her hard work, her pain and frustration. Least of all can they see her victimization by her husband, nor can they apprehend her violent response as "self-defense," a desperate act of self-preservation provoked by the cruelty of the dead man. Exclusively in the hands of the men, the legal quest is aimed solely at proving the woman's guilt in the death of the man.

In "Jury," the brutal blindness of the legal investigation all but forces Mrs.

Hale and Mrs. Peters to identify with Minnie Foster. They rightly realize that they each could have been in her place, and that mere coincidence or luck has spared them this time. As Alkalay-Gut points out, "Minnie's existence and her behavior are determined by her man who makes the rules she lives by. In this respect all three women are the same. Their behavior varies only because different men motivate different behavior" (Alkalay-Gut 1984, 6). The law's patronizing dismissal of everything the women know and understand, of their life experience and point of view, leaves them no choice but to rebel. Glaspell's women realize that accepting the legal system's interpretation of Minnie would entail accepting a system of meaning in which all abused women are either evil or crazy. It is a system of meaning that excludes their perspective, obviating their "subjecthood" and status as human beings. It is a system of power that is bluntly and blatantly set against them. It is inherently unjust and dangerous to them as women. Resistance and civil disobedience are therefore acts of self-defense and self-preservation whereby the women preserve their dignity, humanity, and sanity. And since it is as women that the law challenges them, they unite against it as a community of women.

Toward the story's end, the county attorney says laughingly: " 'Mrs. Peters doesn't need supervising. For that matter, a sheriff's wife is married to the law. Ever think of it this way, Mrs. Peters?' . . . When she spoke, her voice was muffled. 'Not—just that way,' she said" (Glaspell 1996, 92). The men leave the kitchen, and the women are left on their own. "Slowly, unwillingly, Mrs. Peters turned her head until her eyes met the eyes of the other woman. There was a moment when they held each other in a steady, burning look in which there was no evasion nor flinching. Then Mrs. Hale's eyes pointed the way to that basket in which was hidden the thing that would make certain the conviction of the other woman—that woman who was not there and yet who had been there with them all through that hour. For a moment Mrs. Peters did not move. And then she did it" (93).

Mrs. Peters is reminded by the men that she is in the privileged position of being "married to the law": unlike other women, she is trusted and given a free hand to go through Minnie's personal belongings. But in this privileged legal status Mrs. Peters recognizes the men's demand that she betray her sex, her friends, herself, siding with the oppressors and serving their agenda. In order to maintain her dubiously privileged status she must disown her sisters and her own identity.[1] Realizing the full implication of her situation as a woman "married to the law," she is faced with the choice to serve the patriarchal law, as she serves her husband, or resist and be true to herself. Mrs.

Hale's active, inviting presence allows her to choose a dignified feminine existence in a community of women.

In the face of a hostile, masculine legal system, the women find their own, distinct sense of justice and judgment. They apply their own common sense, life experience, and point of view. Conducting an alternative legal process, they determine what is and is not relevant to the case, and what constitutes reasonable behavior. The women establish the existence of a "reasonable woman," determine her distinctness from the "reasonable man," and find that, placed in Minnie's situation, the "reasonable woman" could well have acted as the accused did. In this they find Minnie reasonable and exonerate her from the charge of murder. In their alternative legal proceeding, the women claim the murdered bird as crucial evidence. Within the men's legal system, this evidence would have supplied the motive for Minnie's crime, proving her wickedness, madness, and guilt. Within the women's legal system, the dead bird proves John Wright's crime and Minnie's reasonableness. Uninterested in fine, abstract legal distinctions between excuse and justification, the women simply find that Minnie has suffered enough. By claiming the crucial evidence (the dead canary) exclusively for their own legal proceeding, the women express self-confidence and faith in their alternative judgment.

Feminine legal culture is thus a clear outcome of and response to patriarchal legal dominance, yet it manifests distinct ethics of compassion and care. The two feminist perspectives, the ethics of care and dominance theories, often perceived as contrary and adversarial, seem completely coherent and mutually explanatory in Glaspell's artistic work. Patriarchal law is so deeply oppressive to women that their only rational means of resistance and survival is communal disobedience. No individual woman stands a chance in the face of the coercive, pervasive, and powerful legal system. Extending existing individual legal rights to women is irrelevant reparation. In order for women to survive the law, their collective social oppression must be acknowledged, and the reality of their social conditions must be viewed from their own, unique perspective. A resisting community of women, speaking in a different voice, is therefore imperative in the face of the hostile legal system. The other side of this argument, Glaspell's work recognizes and demonstrates, is that a genuinely feminine community, taken seriously, is inherently a resisting and civilly disobedient community.

Let me push this line of thought further. Robin West reads "Jury" as a critique of a fundamental social value and institution sanctioned by law, marriage as we know it: "Through marriage, the story suggests, young girls are separated from their communities and families of nurturance, and isolated within heterosexual relationships in which they are expected to altruistically sacrifice their own needs and subordinate their own wills, and which are often—typically?—far less emotionally nourishing than the communities from which they came . . . What it is about is the injury done to women through the rendering of their emotional attachments to their largely female communities of origin, and of friendships, and the displacement of those communities with the too often isolating, cold, and nonsustaining relationship of heterosexual marriage" (West 1997, 243–49). In our patriarchal societies, "the function of law is to validate, through the institution of marriage, the isolation of women from each other" (254). A community of women, therefore, is a direct challenge to existing law and the rule of law, comprising not merely civil disobedience but a full-scale revolution.

Quilting

Quilting is one of the central metaphors of "Jury," much discussed in feminist scholarship. I wish to emphasize that this feminine skill, ridiculed and minimized by the men in the story, serves Glaspell to define both feminine communal networking and feminine legal thought. In Alkalay-Gut's words, "Each patch has an individual entity, but its beauty (and meaning) is in relationship to the other patches formed with similar painstaking consideration. The colors are coordinated and contrasted by balance and relationship, but the general pattern is one that emerges with the quilt" (1995, 73). The art of quilting is a patient one, dignifying small details, aspiring to communal harmony, and respecting the uniqueness of each material and piece, different or "queer" as it may be. The beauty and strength of a quilt derive from the careful, collective work of women who cooperate in appreciating the diverse materials of mundane reality, patching them together into a colorful pattern that maintains their distinct colors and textures. Quilting demands long-term solidarity and caring investment, an eye for trifles and a vision of harmony. It is a practical art, gracing survival with beauty. Patiently, respectfully quilting together the small pieces of life, Glaspell's women compassionately understand and review Minnie's violent act in the full context of her chronic and prolonged victimization. In this context, their deliberation over whether Minnie was going to quilt her work or knot it is deeply significant. "Quilting is a more artistic, but time-consuming, method of in-and-out stitching. Knotting is simple, quick, single stitch. That Minnie Wright was going to knot rather than quilt the individual pieces is symbolic both of the joyless, Spartan life Mr. Wright had forced on her and her method of killing him. The story ends with the county attorney facetiously asking about the quilt and Martha Hale responding that Minnie Foster Wright was going to 'knot it, Mr. Henderson' " (Marina Angel 1997, 804). In their determination that Minnie was knotting (rather than quilting), the women pronounce judgment: John Wright's brutal restriction of her life forced his wife to "knot," i.e., it was his abusive behavior that provoked her and elicited her violence against him.

Like Mrs. Hale and Mrs. Peters, Susan Glaspell quilts her story compassionately. The text does not open with an "objective," "factual" narration of John Wright's strangulation by his wife. Such a seemingly neutral presentation of the "relevant facts" would have been damning, closing the reader's mind rather than opening it to attentive reading of details and complexity. Instead, the text opens with Mrs. Hale's unfinished work at her kitchen, and it is from her point of view that the small patches of detail slowly come together to portray the sad picture of Minnie's life and crime.[2] The patches quilted together in the making of meaning include experiences and memories from the lives of all three women, and the outcome is a colorful, communal story. As in a quilt, the crime emerges only in the context of the bigger picture of Minnie's life and of women's lives at large; it is not an isolated, objective, given fact, but an interpretation of a cluster of details within a wider context. This story's reader is invited to join Mrs. Hale, Mrs. Peters, and Susan Glaspell in quilting the story of women's lives, victimization, and consequent crimes. In this context of compassionate patching of painful life experiences, judgment takes on a whole new meaning: it is feminine, caring, nonjudgmental. The story's insights are as relevant today as they were at the beginning of the twentieth century.

A Question of Silence: Plot Synopsis

In this narrative, Christine (Edda Barends), a silenced, mentally abused housewife of thirty, confronts a boutique owner who catches her shoplifting a blouse and rebukes her with a condescending, silent look. Deprived of the stolen blouse, Christine looks the man in the eye, and deliberately grabs it back and stuffs the blouse and another garment into her bag. Two other random female shoppers notice the incident: Annie (Nelly Frijda), who is forty-seven, a hard-working, divorced waitress sexually harassed by her male customers, and Andrea (Henriëtte Tol), who is thirty-five, a bright, single secretary oppressed by her male employer. The two "watch with interest this spectacle of an obviously guilty woman refusing to act guilty. They come to her defense and then, slowly, deliberately, join in her offense, taking garments themselves" (L. Williams 1994, 433). Annie and Andrea "surround the man, stuffing clothes slowly, challengingly, into their bags. The shop owner senses the gravity of the situation, but like a terrified rabbit, he is frozen in place. The women murder him with the same slow, deliberate, ritualistic movements that they employ to steal the clothes" (Elsley 1992, 197). The scene portrays "a gradual escalation of an initial crime against property into the ritual mutilation and murder of a male scapegoat. We see almost none of the actual violence of this scene—just enough to know that hangers, clothes racks, and ashtrays serve as weapons" (L. Williams 1994, 433). Other female shoppers, young and old, rich and poor, Black and white, stand by, watching the brutal, fatal attack, and silently leave the shop.

Awaiting their trial, the three defendants (Christine, Annie, and Andrea) are interviewed by Dr. Janine van den Bos, a woman psychiatrist (married to a lawyer) assigned to determine their sanity. "The detective on the case tells Janine 'it's an open and shut case—they didn't deny anything.' Her husband, a lawyer, comments, 'It's obvious. These women are completely deranged'" (Elsley 1992, 197). Christine (the housewife) refuses to say a word, while the other two narrate fragments of their lives, pose intimate questions, and offer enigmatic comments. The bewildered psychiatrist attempts to apply detached, abstract, formal professional tools, but is co-opted by the defendants, who demand that she treat them as a woman treating women rather than as a professional examining scientific objects; they demand that she see their points of view, hear their voices, and practice empathy, compassion, and care. They demand she see herself in them as a woman.

"The only way to 'read' this crime, [Janine] learns, is to see it as proceeding from the portion of women's culture and experience that is truly not known to men" (L. Williams 1994, 434). As Janine is drawn to the women, Andrea further suggests the possibility of an intimate, erotic relationship between Janine and herself. Struggling with fragments of narratives and emotions, torn between her professional obligation (as well as her marital loyalty) on the one hand, and her new, feminist insights and perceptions on the other, Janine comes to see the gender discrimination and oppression that pervade the women's lives and triggered the violent outburst. "They're so normal," she concludes.

Her position, unacceptable to the legal system, evokes harsh responses from lawyers and judges, including her own spouse (a court spectator). As she fails to explain her professional position to the court, the prosecutor undermines her status, suggesting she is not objective, that she is expressing personal views and supporting the cruel murder. The prosecutor and judge demand that she declare the women's insanity or state a motive for their crime. Insisting on a gender-blind perspective, the court is unable to hear her suggestion that the women responded to male oppression. There is no difference, the prosecutor determines, between three women killing a man and three men killing a woman.

In response to this statement, the three accused women burst into a roar of laughter, joined by the other women shoppers who witnessed the killing and are silent courtroom spectators. Realizing laughter's power to bond and liberate, Janine joins in as her spouse leaves the courtroom. Horrified, the judge orders the accused to be taken away. The women shoppers leave, and Janine storms out of the courtroom. On the stairs leading away from the courthouse, Janine finds herself bonding in silence with the other boutique customers who stand there gazing at her. Walking away from the courthouse, looking away from her waiting husband who is nervously blowing the car horn, Janine's eyes find those of the women and she smiles.

Silence does not follow a linear narrative. The film can be read as containing five parts. Part 1 introduces the four women, featuring fragments of their lives immediately prior to and during the arrests and concluding with the three accused women signing a confession. The second part combines scenes of the accused women's routine lives before the killing with scenes of Janine's meetings with them in prison, and with episodes in Janine's life during her investigation: listening to the tapes at home, meeting Christine's husband, Andrea's boss, the pathologist. In this part, both Janine and the viewer struggle with the tormenting questions: Who are these women? Are they crazy? Why did they commit the horrifying crime? How should one think of this? It concludes with Janine's realization and determination that the accused women are completely sane and ordinary. Part 3 then features the killing itself, and moments in the killers' lives immediately following it. The fourth part features Janine's transformation, and the process of her opening up to the women, connecting with them, letting them touch her life and touching theirs. Through a series of scenes portraying Janine's meetings with the women and her nightmarish preoccupation with them at home, this part shows Janine getting personally involved, overcoming her professional distance, and expressing human, feminine feelings of compassion and care. The fifth and last part contains the courtroom scene, where Janine sides with the women, speaks up for them within the legal process using professional rhetoric, and is promptly belittled and expelled from the legal world. Leaving the courthouse, she looks away from her husband and smiles at the small group of silent, determined women.

Silence *As an Adaptation of* "Jury"

In *Silence*, much as in "Jury," an emerging community of women adjudicates women charged with the killing of a man. Examining the relevant evidence from a gendered perspective, the awakening feminine community silently faults the system, understanding the accused, identifying with and exonerating them, and defying legal authority. As in "Jury," the women in *Silence* are neither bigger nor smaller than life in any stereotypical, archetypal, or mythological way; they are portrayed as victims of patriarchal dominance and oppression, and yet fully capable and dignified active agents.[3] As in "Jury," it is their oppression that the film judges and faults, not their inherent feminine nature or desperate response to their oppression.

Like Minnie Foster, Christine is a secluded, tormented housewife who responds violently to the last straw laid on her back by someone she experiences as an oppressive man. Christine, like Minnie, is isolated and tormented by a self-centered, insensitive spouse, completely oblivious to her needs and frustration. The killing of Minnie's songbird provoked a deadly outburst, followed by silence, dramatically enhanced by her absence from Glaspell's text. A patronizing, prohibiting, and penalizing masculine rebuke triggers Christine's violent act, after which she retreats to complete silence. Both women resemble caged, delicate birds. Minnie responds violently when deprived of her bird, her sole companion, voice, and soul. Christine is deprived of a garment she picks for herself: her single little fantasy of intimate self-indulgence.

The role of Minnie's neighbors, Mrs. Hale and Mrs. Peters, is doubled and divided in *Silence*. Annie, a talkative, heavy woman, and Andrea, sharp and assertive, are *Silence*'s Mrs. Hale and Mrs. Peters. Sharing Christine's social background, they are her peers. Sensitive to the few clues about Christine's life, they recognize her oppression, identify with her, embrace her anger and violence, and commit a grave crime while siding with her and offering compassion and support. They awaken together in the face of her plight and form with silent solidarity a community of women, choosing their own set of values over the official, patriarchal one, sanctioned by law. The other silent female shoppers, present both at the scene of the crime and in the courtroom, are accessories to the murder; additionally, they withhold evidence and obstruct justice. Their behavior echoes Andrea's and Annie's, as they form an additional circle of "Mrs. Hale and Mrs. Peters"—though a more passive one. Their shadow judgment and participation is through a communal silent presence.

At the same time Janine, the investigating psychiatrist, can also be read as performing a function similar to that of Mrs. Peters and Mrs. Hale. Janine, like Mrs. Hale and Mrs. Peters, is officially summoned to the scene of the crime. Like them she encounters the accused women's silence, and is left to piece together fragments of evidence, attempting to understand the motive behind the killing. Like Glaspell's women, she enters the scene judgmental and condemning, goes through a fundamental process of awakening, comes to see herself in the accused women, bonds with them, reaches her own judgment, and undermines the legal attempt to explain, condemn, and marginalize the women as crazy or "queer."

As with Mrs. Hale, the official request to join the legal investigation disrupts Janine's "housekeeping," and like Mrs. Hale she leaves hurriedly. Like Mrs. Hale, Janine's point of view is the first and most prominent offered by the text. In the first scenes, Janine, like Mrs. Hale, is committed to a significant, intimate relationship with her spouse. As the plot unfolds, Janine, like Mrs. Hale, sees her husband move away from her to join the condescending community of men. Like Mrs. Peters, Janine is "married to the law": her husband is a lawyer, and she works in the service of the legal system, expected and trusted to cooperate with the legal proceeding and facilitate it. Like Mrs. Peters, Janine is torn between professional duty and gender loyalty, feels increasingly alienated by the masculine legal system, and chooses gender solidarity over marriage to the law.

Like "Jury," Silence indicates that when isolated, a woman is silenced and oppressed. It takes three women in compassionate dialogue and action to form a feminine community speaking in a different voice. In its insistence on three women and more, Silence follows in the footsteps of "Jury," differing from female-friendship films like Thelma and Louise that offer deep, intimate feminine relationships, but not a community of women. Like "Jury," Silence chooses to leave its (woman) viewer in the company of female protagonists who remain alive and free at the end of the narrated events to continue in the making of a feminine community. The men in *Silence*, much like those in "Jury," form an oppressive patriarchal community, are one-dimensional, self-centered, patronizing, insensitive to the women's reality and pain, and unchanging.

These narrative and thematic similarities invite exploration of the dialogue between the two texts, and the film's end-of-the-century commentary on the story's turn-of-the-century themes.[4]

Silence's Commentary

CONTEMPORARY WOMEN

Whereas the three women in "Jury" are housewives, in *Silence*, the silent and most obviously oppressed woman, Christine, is a housewife, while Annie and Andrea are a waitress and a secretary respectively. Janine is a psychiatrist. Christine is married with two young children, Annie seems to be divorced with a daughter, Andrea is single, and Janine is married with no children. The variety of women's roles in the workplace and in the family has expanded since the early part of the century, *Silence* indicates; women seem to have more options, are less confined by traditional patterns, and enjoy more opportunity and choice in both public and private spheres. In comparison with Mrs. Hale and Mrs. Peters, Annie, Andrea, and Janine seem to have gone a long way. But these differences are illusory, reveals *Silence*.

Sixty-six years later, Annie, Andrea, and Janine are as trapped, marginalized, and oppressed as Minnie Foster, Mrs. Hale, and Mrs. Peters. Annie and Andrea are reduced and confined to serving men in a restaurant and an office; their jobs are thinly disguised "housekeeping" jobs. Serving condescending, sexually harassing men, their professional lot is not much different from Christine's or that of Glaspell's women. In all spheres, their relationships with men are as oppressive, unrewarding, and damaging as in 1916. Seemingly free to compete in the public sphere, they are in fact segregated, secluded, and isolated in patriarchal restaurants and offices. The 1982 Dutch urban women are as lonely, frustrated, and unhappy as their rural American predecessors.

Janine, a seemingly happily married, successful professional, imagines that her own reality is completely different—only to discover, through involvement with other women's lives, the painful gulf that separates and alienates her from both her husband and her male colleagues. Beneath a modern disguise of equality, opportunity, and choice, contemporary women are as oppressed as ever, argues the film. But at the end of the century, separated into different professions, jobs, and family situations, it may be even harder for them to realize the common grounds that unite them, to speak a common language, share perspectives and goals, and struggle for solidarity.

DOMINANCE AND CARE

In *Silence*, the women no longer share a similar lifestyle, as they belong to different classes, and are each situated differently in the labor force. Nevertheless, the film reveals that despite these apparent differences, they all share similar marginalization, subordination, and humiliation. Christine's repression and silencing by her husband may appear to differ from Annie's humiliation by the restaurant customers, or from Andrea's subordination to her boss, but in their seemingly distinct careers they "all go through the same things—it's all just a different kind of the same thing!" (Glaspell 1996, 91).

It is that underlying shared experience of oppression, despite its many guises, that defines the women's condition, generating their shared sensitivities, point of view, ethics of care, and feminine voice. Janine, whose social position most obviously differs from the other women's, is the last to recognize her restriction and oppression within patriarchy, and hence the last to realize her feminine voice and point of view. But in *Silence*, even this happily married, successful, professional woman does not escape feminist awakening. The film clearly invites its contemporary woman viewer to accompany Janine in this process.

CLASS ACTION AND COLLECTIVE RESPONSIBILITY

Silence takes from "Jury" the themes of collective, gendered solidarity and responsibility to their ultimate conclusion. Unlike Minnie Foster, *Silence*'s Christine does not kill her husband, her immediate oppressor, but rather a male boutique owner who happens to perform one restrictive, patronizing act too many. In preventing her from stealing a blouse, the man restrains Christine in her single attempt to indulge herself. The boutique owner is not killed for his individual oppressive action, but as a willing, active member of patriarchy's dominating class. Similarly, Annie and Andrea, Christine's peers, go beyond Mrs. Peters's and Mrs. Hale's withholding of evidence and obstruction of justice as they join Christine in the killing itself, playing the part of active—and even initiating—accessories in the primary, violent crime.

Minnie's act of killing took place in the privacy of her bedroom. The site of

Christine's crime is a semipublic feminine domain. The boutique, like the well in ancient and traditional societies, like quilting societies in traditional European America, is the public zone where women assemble, share, and bond. Locating the killing in a feminine space enhances its gendered significance. As Linda Williams observes: "Showalter's first method of understanding the wild zone of female culture is to visualize it as a place—a 'no-man's-land'—where women congregate. There are few such places outside the home, but a woman's dress shop is certainly one of them. Although the psychiatrist could never argue the point in a court of law, it is clear that the crime could not have taken place in a more male-defined space . . . Only in this space could the women let out the rage and defiance they did not even know was in them, only in this space could Christine channel her rage into action, and only in this space could Annie and Andrea identify with this rage, own it, and finally share in its expression as well" (1994, 434). In *Silence*, both men and women are members of gender communities and are responsible for their peers: all men are accountable for the crimes of patriarchy against women, and women stand together as a victimized class fighting back. The killing of a man by a group of women takes place in women's public sphere. In Judy Elsley's words: "The murder, which the women never explain, is an act of reclamation. . . . The male shop owner becomes a symbol of all men and their oppressive hold over the women's lives, down to the very clothes they wear. The women are taking back what is theirs in a scene that turns stealing into a silent ritual" (1992, 197).

"MARRIED TO THE LAW"

Like Mrs. Peters, Janine is married to a member of the legal profession. Additionally, she is a psychiatrist in the service of the legal system. In this respect, Janine's marriage to the law is similar to Amanda Bonner's in *Adam's Rib*, and can be read against that character as well (see chapter 5). Amanda's dual marriage to the law amplifies her double victory: she succeeds in advancing her feminist cause both as a lawyer in court and as a married woman in her domestic relationship, paying almost no price in either sphere. In clear contrast, Janine, like Mrs. Peters, discovers the price of being married to the law and is confronted with the choice of betraying her gender and integrity or risking dual divorce, that is, losing her professional status as well as her domestic relationship.

Unlike Amanda, Janine undergoes a transformation, and learns to see the "trifles" of women's lives as only they can see them. Bonding with the women she studies, Janine develops the skills that enable Mrs. Peters and Mrs. Hale to read Minnie's dead bird the way they do. But when she attempts, Amanda-like, to bring such evidence before the court and change the system from within, she discovers the limits of her power. Janine learns that her dual marriage to the law is a double bind, trapping and confining her in the service of patriarchy. Unlike her Hollywood predecessor, the Dutch professional woman learns that she is a member of an oppressed class, and that she must choose between loyalty to that class and loyalty to the law, which symbolizes both career and heterosexual couplehood. Unlike Amanda, Janine also learns that there is an alternative: a community of women, whose lives are more similar to hers than she would have ever thought.

Silence's choice to portray Janine as a psychiatrist in the service of the court offers an insightful variation on the theme of marriage to the law. Hers is not a strictly legal voice, but one analyzing emotions and mental states for the legal system and its proceedings. Janine's profession and status within the system are "feminine" in that she deals with the irrational, subjective, disorderly aspects of human behavior. A professional, she does not approach the human condition from a uniquely feminine perspective of compassion, intuition, and respect for trifles. Her professional status demands that she translate feminine sensitivity to human pain into the patriarchal, analytical language spoken and sanctioned by law. Janine's job is to bring feminine issues into the legal discussion, while substituting the feminine voice for a legal one. In this process of translation, compassion is transformed into legal, analytical condemnation and labeling. Sensing her traitorous mission, Annie and Andrea refuse to cooperate with Janine, and Christine refuses to speak to her altogether.

Through her connections with the women, Janine realizes the nature of her marriage to the law. She recognizes her role as a professional tool, designed to bring before the legal system only very selective fragments of information, processed and organized in specific structures that do not challenge the social order. Other aspects of the human condition are not admissible into the legal discourse, including the reality of women's lives under patriarchy. Like Mrs. Peters before her, Janine turns her back on her matrimonial obligation, refusing to translate the accused women into explanatory terms that would relieve the legal system of the hazardous task of examining the roots of women's violence and confronting their oppression.

In *Silence*, as in "Jury," women are systematically silenced by men. Their silencing is a form of victimization invisible and inaudible within the law. In both texts, women's silencing brings about their violent outbursts. These outbursts, unlike the victimization that provoked them, are both seen and heard by the legal system, quick to condemn the violent women and label them "furies" and "crazy." In each text, the legal system elides the women's abuse, amplifying their criminal behavior and "abnormal," dangerous dispositions. Preventing testimony—or even verbalization—of the victimization that provoked the women's outbursts, each text's legal system facilitates the portrayal of the criminal woman as unreasonable, and her action as inexplicable and unjustifiable. In each text, in the face of the legal system, the accused woman chooses silence.

Silence is thus chosen by the accused women when victimization is translated by the legal system into their criminality and insanity. They sense that anything they say will be used against them. Silence is a passive means of withdrawal, self-defense, and resistance in the face of an overwhelming, oppressive system. Paradoxically, embracing the silence imposed on them by men is the women's only course of refusing to cooperate with the alienating legal system, the only way to preserve their sanity and dignity. Such silence is the last retreat for those who have no faith in the system and no hope for change.

In a parallel move, the women embrace the outlaw status imposed on them by the social system. Leaving the courtroom, the women literally step outside the law to the excluded place they have always already occupied. The women realize that they were never included in the legal sphere as equal members of the legal community, nor protected by the law as worthy citizens. Walking away, they resist the discriminating system, denying it obedience and pretense. Choosing silence and stepping outside the law, women choose to own their oppression, thus, through resistance, manifesting and enhancing agency and dignity. Both "Jury" and *Silence* distance themselves from the legal systems they portray by allowing the women to narrate their silencing through their own perspectives and in their own voices. The texts' compassionate narrations of the accused women's victimization expose the fictional legal systems' blindness and biased perspective.

The women's occasional laughter and smiling express the joy, bitterness, contempt, and frustration that they cannot verbalize. Annie's chilling laughter haunts Janine as she listens to the tapes of her interviews with the accused women. Andrea smiles, with great pleasure at Annie, during their collective arrest, and dismissingly in her meetings with Janine. After the killing, she is mistaken for a prostitute, and agrees to accompany a man to a hotel room and perform sexual intercourse. Fully clothed, not allowing him to touch her, she sits on top of the man, moving her body up and down. Leaving the room, she looks back and laughs at him. Christine smiles, happy, only when, immediately following the killing, she flies through the air on a merry-go-round, holding on to her child. In the courtroom she laughs again, briefly, when, following Janine's explanation of her choice of silence, the judge solemnly says to the psychiatrist: "I assume that you explained to her that the court always takes into consideration a defendant's social and psychological background. She must realize that your report is of the greatest importance in determining her sentence, and that her future depends to a large extent on . . ." Finally, breaking into roaring, collective laughter, Marleen Gorris's women move from passive retreat and hopeless, solitary self-preservation to active, collective challenge of the oppressive legal system.

Examining Janine on her professional report, judge and prosecutor demand that she either declare the accused insane or supply the court with a motive for the brutal murder. When Janine stresses that it was a man the women killed, the judge refuses to understand, and the prosecutor insists that there is "no difference between this case and, let's say, if they had killed a female shop owner, or, yes, the other way around, if three men had killed the female owner of a shop." Here, Annie breaks into hearty laughter, and is soon joined by the other accused, female spectators in the courtroom and Janine. The women laugh together until the judge orders them out of the courtroom, announcing that the case will continue in the defendants' absence. (Read against *Adam's Rib*, this scene expresses *Silence*'s view of Amanda's liberal, gender-blind feminism. The prosecutor's remark repeats Amanda's cross-gender closing argument in *Adam's Rib*; in *Silence*, this line of thought provokes the women's roaring laughter).

The women's communal laughter deprives the system of its power and authority over them, exposing its vulnerability in the face of the women's awakening, self-realization, and existential freedom. In "Laughter as Feminine Power," Judy Elsley explicates:

Their laughter in the court is the only time in the film that the women demonstrate any power within a society that has entrapped them. In the end, they are likely to be "sentenced"—torn from the safety of silence by the power of the verbal constructs of the patriarchy—so their temporary victory remains ambiguous. But for the time being, as the film closes, Gorris shows the one way these women can come to power: through laughter. Why is their laughter so disturbing, so powerful, so disruptive? First, the women wordlessly bond together. Their laughter brings defendants, psychologist and the silent witnesses of the crime into understanding and sympathy with each other. As a result of that bonding, the women gain the strength to resist and exclude the ruling male order. They refuse to be intimidated, to be controlled, to be shaped by the patriarchy any longer . . . Women's laughter dissipates the power of an oppressive culture; it brings the women closer together; and most important of all, their laughter expresses the women's growing sense of autonomy. (1992, 198)

Unlike the boutique, the courtroom is not a "feminine zone." In fact, the women experience it as a hostile, alienating, silencing territory. Collective laughter is the women's only way of claiming and occupying the public space that is denied them. In the last scene of Blackmail, Alice White, alone, trapped between two men, is chuckling as they heartily laugh at a joke made at her expense. In Silence, the joke is on men and their legal system, and women are laughing together.

"Jury" moves from Minnie's silencing to her silence in the face of the law, to Mrs. Peters's and Mrs. Hale's legal silence, leaving the reader/viewer with the stifling, hopeless silence of the awakening oppressed. Silence moves from Christine's silencing to her self-imposed silence, to her silence in the face of the law, to the other women's communal silence, to the women's collective, roaring laughter in the courtroom, ending with Janine's smile in the last shot. Having shattered the legal system's façade with the women's laughter, the film leaves its viewer with Janine's smile of awakening, liberation, and choice. It is a painful turning point, one that may demand the sacrifice of matrimonial love and professional recognition, but Janine faces it smiling at the silent community of women at her side.[5]

THE EXPANSION OF WOMEN'S COMMUNITY AND PERSONAL PRICE

Silence elaborates and extends the theme in "Jury" of woman's isolation and women's community. Adding the silent female shoppers and Janine's character, the film portrays a continually expanding community of women, highlighting the complex, multifaceted relations among its members, and offering women viewers a rich variety of feminine characters and roles to contemplate and identify with. In its exploration of feminine relationships, the film does not evade the implication that solidarity, intimacy, understanding, and compassion are only a step away from erotic attraction. Moreover, it boldly admits that in a patriarchal world, women's solidarity comes at a price.

In "Jury," no harm comes of Mrs. Peters's and Mrs. Hale's bonding with Minnie Foster, and at the end of their cathartic experience they each return home. Changed they may be, but they resume their roles as wives, housewives, and mothers. *Silence* is far less reassuring. The women's solidarity with Christine leads to a brutal, horrifying murder, costing the life of a man who did not deserve to die. Unlike Mrs. Peters and Mrs. Hale, Annie and Andrea do not return to their lives, losing their freedom, perhaps for life. Janine's exposure to the feminine community leaves her facing a tragic choice at a high, personal price. The viewer is invited to examine diverse patterns of joining a feminine community—as well as the dear individual prices they exact.

Cinematic Quilting

Discussing "Jury," I suggested that its reader was invited to join Mrs. Hale, Mrs. Peters, and Susan Glaspell in quilting the story of women's lives, victimization, and crimes. Embracing this strategy, *Silence* lends the quilting metaphor cinematic depth. The film pieces together flashes of the women's lives in a painful, colorful, pattern of oppression and humiliation.[6] Respecting the uniqueness of each woman's life, preserving the distinct character of each of their stories, the film weaves them into a coherent feminist manifesto. Christine, Annie, Andrea, and Janine create a four-faced, complex feminine identity. The scenes portray episodes that illuminate the four women's routines, combining them with moments in their lives immediately prior to the killing, during and immediately following it, immediately preceding the accused women's arrests, and in prison, when the women are awaiting trial. Only the film's last part, depicting the legal proceeding in the courtroom, offers a continuous, real-time, linear narration.

This cinematic quilting invites the viewer to piece together not merely the events that led to the killing, as in a detective story, but also the life experiences of all the film's female protagonists. Only in the big, colorful picture of women's lives can the viewer see the killing, as well as its "motive," that is its social and psychological context. In this, the film offers its (female) viewer a transformational experience similar to Janine's.

Legal Critique: Beyond Justification and Excuse

In her legal discussion of "Jury," Marina Angel presents the criminal terms *justification* and *excuse*:

> Because common law homicide was defined on the paradigm of the reasonable man and not the reasonable woman, abused women who killed were so far outside the paradigm that they often had to rely on an insanity defense. An excuse, such as insanity, finds there is something so wrong with an individual that the individual cannot be held criminally liable. Insanity excuses conduct because an individual did not understand the difference between right and wrong, because the individual was acting abnormally and/or irrationally. A justification, on the other hand, such as self-defense, looks to the circumstances surrounding a killing and finds that an act that would otherwise be murder is not morally blameworthy and therefore is not criminal. It is not clear whether provocation is an excuse or justification. At common law, the circumstances of sustaining physical blows or discovering the wife in the act of adultery provided justification that made the reasonable man less blameworthy, reducing murder to manslaughter. These circumstances also partially excuse the reasonable man for losing control (1996, 317).

Angel makes the legal argument that "if the common law . . . could partially excuse or partially justify the actions of a husband killing in the heat of passion, similarly, our law could also partially excuse or partially justify the actions of an abused woman who kills her husband" (317–8, emphasis added).[7]

"A Jury of Her Peers" wisely refrains from suggesting any relation between the case of a man killing a woman in jealous rage and that of an abused woman desperately killing her abuser. I view such comparison as misleading and damaging. "Jury" does, however, suggest that a "reasonable woman" in a given social context differs significantly from a "reasonable man," as men's and women's experiences, situations, means of communication, and fields of interest and expertise differ vastly. An (emotionally) abused woman, "Jury" exposes, experiences her oppressive husband as her executioner and responds accordingly. Patriarchal law offers such a woman no defense, as it sees her criminal behavior but not her victimization.

"Jury" indicates that other women, even those not harshly abused, recognize the abused woman's victimization and sympathize with her predicament. If they, her peers, were to structure a legal doctrine, they would partially excuse and/or partially justify her criminal behavior. They would determine that, under the circumstances, she acted as a reasonable woman, and would find that her action was in self-defense, and/or provoked by the deceased. This position questions the conceptual legal distinction between justification and excuse in a case such as Minnie Foster's. Minnie's "abnormal," "irrational" mental state is portrayed as a result of oppressive social circumstances and not as an isolated, personal problem. In fact, within the abnormal, irrational, abusive circumstances of her life, her abnormal, irrational mental state may be both normal and rational. Once a legal system learns to see women's victimization, the concepts of justification and excuse may have to be reexamined.

Silence portrays the women's refusal to be "excused," and their struggle to represent their criminal behavior as justifiable in the context of patriarchal oppression of women. The legal system's vehement insistence that Janine classify the women as insane can be read as a blunt, systematic refusal to consider the women's crime in terms of justification and to see their victimization under patriarchy. Janine's betrayal of the legal system lies in her refusal to confirm that the women's crime can be discussed only within the framework of "excuse."

Silence extends the legal argumentation of "Jury." In *Silence*, the social reality is that all women are abused by all patriarchal men. A woman may, therefore, reasonably experience any patriarchal oppression as abusing herself or another woman, and may reasonably respond in violent self-defense and/or find herself provoked. Within this feminist conception of social reality, justification and/or excuse may apply not merely to an abused woman who kills her abuser, but to women such as Christine, Annie, and Andrea when they kill the boutique owner. The distinction between justification and excuse is blurred not merely in Minnie Foster's case, but in any case of a woman killing an oppressive man. This view poses the possibility that killings such as that portrayed in *Silence* cannot and should not be treated by criminal law, as these are not individual acts of "blameworthy" violence. Perhaps such killings of men by women, viewed in the context of patriarchal oppression, should be treated as atrocities of war.[8]

Jurisprudential Critique: Beyond Conscientious Objection, Civil Disobedience, and Rebellion

In his classical treatment of the jurisprudential issue, the legal philosopher Joseph Raz offers the following summary of three distinct categories of legal disobedience:

It is convenient to follow the traditional classification of morally and politically motivated disobedience into three categories: revolutionary disobedience, civil disobedience, and conscientious objection. *Revolutionary Disobedience* is a politically motivated breach of law designed to change or to contribute directly to a change of government or of the constitutional arrangements (the system of government). *Civil Disobedience* is a politically motivated breach of law designed either to contribute directly to a change of a law or of a public policy or to express one's protest against, and diassociation from, a law or a public policy. *Conscientious Objection* is a breach of law for the reason that the agent is morally prohibited to obey it, either because of its general character (e.g. as with absolute pacifists and conscription) or because it extends to certain cases which should not be covered by it (e.g. conscription and selective objectors and murder and euthanasia). (1983, 263)

He stresses that "revolutionary acts and civil disobedience are cases of political action, they are essentially public actions designed to have a political effect. Conscientious objection is not. It is essentially a private action by a person who wishes to avoid committing moral wrong by obeying a (totally or partially) morally bad law" (264).

Raz further claims that "much intellectual effort has been invested in an attempt to articulate and justify a doctrine of the permissible forms of civil disobedience. It must be used as a measure of last resort after all other means have failed to obtain one's desired goal; it must be non-violent; it must be openly undertaken; and its perpetrators must submit to prosecution and punishment; such acts must be confined to those designed to publicize certain wrongs and to convince the public and the authorities of the justice of one's claims; it should not be used to intimidate or coerce. Such and similar conditions have been much discussed and often favored" (269).

Raz maintains that narrow definitions of civil disobedience are designed to support the claim that civil disobedience is morally justified. He himself argues that "there is no moral right to civil disobedience in liberal states; normally there is such a right in illiberal states" (272). And, "the case for a right to conscientious objection, however, even in liberal states, seems much stronger" (278). Nevertheless, "[a] right to conscientious objection should be introduced only very sparingly and only in the absence of better ways of protecting freedom of consciousness" (288).

"Jury" poses the jurisprudential question of how to categorize Mrs. Peters's and Mrs. Hale's conduct, and whether it can be justified as rightful.

Using Raz's definitions, their legal disobedience seems to resemble conscientious objection more than the other two types of illegal behavior. Mrs. Peters and Mrs. Hale refuse to obey a law that seems to them morally wrong, but do not seem to express "political" ideology, nor is their conduct publicly oriented to call for and bring about systematic change. Can such conscientious objection be justified? Given that in 1916 American women did not have the vote, nor were they allowed to serve on juries, the relevant political system may be described as "illiberal," at least regarding women. Under such circumstances, Mrs. Peters's and Mrs. Hale's fear that Minnie would not get a fair trial can be understood, and their choice to disobey the law demanding their cooperation in her prosecution may be morally justified. The story makes it clear that the women saw no alternative legal means of avoiding the immoral outcome of supplying the legal system with evidence of Minnie's crime. Their action was not violent and did not give rise to fear that it would induce additional acts of legal disobedience. "Jury" thus seems to present a case that can be accommodated by traditional categories, and even justified as manifesting reasonable conscientious objection.

Silence poses a much harder case. The women's killing of the boutique owner is public, violent, ideologically motivated conduct; it manifests political protest and aims to challenge existing, male-supremacist social order and change society's fundamental values. Is the women's conduct "civil" or "revolutionary" disobedience? Does it challenge "a law or a public policy," or "government or the constitutional arrangements"? Can it be morally justified, especially given that 1982 Netherlands is a "liberal" state? Using jurisprudential logic presented above, it would be hard to "justify" the disobedience portrayed in Silence with no moral defiance. This may account for the public uproar that the film provoked (Murphy 1986, 105; Root 1986, 219).

I suggest that Silence challenges the jurisprudential conceptual distinctions discussed above. From a feminist point of view, it rejects the nuanced distinction between "law or norm" and "constitutional arrangement," as well as that between a "liberal" and "illiberal" state. It discards the notion of "rightfully justifiable." As far as women are concerned, Silence seems to contend, patriarchy as a system, as well as every legal and social aspect of it, is oppressive. "Justifiably" or not, women cannot and will not cooperate with this oppressive system, and when pushed to the wall, they will commit hideous, violent crimes. From this perspective, all women who stand up for their rights and defy patriarchy, legally or not, take part in an ideological uprising which the film endorses unambiguously. Some such acts will be "reasonable," "understandable," "justifiable," or "excusable" from patriarchy's point of view and others will not. But Silence is not concerned with patriarchy's point of view nor with its conceptual and moral distinctions. Stepping out of the courthouse, it leaves all these behind.

Set It Off 9

(U.S.A., 1996)

MINORITY WOMEN AT THE POINT OF NO RETURN

Diversity and identity politics have been the most vibrant and transformative forces in legal feminist thought since the 1990s. As Martha Chamallas accurately recaps:

> In the 1990s, diversity among women has been the theme that has most captivated feminist legal scholarship . . . The major political impetus behind the diversification of feminist legal theory came from critiques and divisions within the feminist movement . . . Women of color argued that the movement was dominated by white women who built their organization's agenda around issues of importance to women like themselves . . . Lesbian feminists who had always been very active in the women's liberation movement and in women's studies insisted that feminist organizations change and take up issues like the legal status of domestic partnership, artificial insemination for unmarried women and other issues of greater concern to lesbians than to heterosexual women . . . The political struggle within the diffuse feminist movement formed the background against which the Diversity Stage of feminist legal theory grew. (2003, 85–86)

Of the many powerful arguments made by minority legal feminists, let me introduce, for the uninitiated, two short excerpts from two fundamental Black feminist legal essays that seem to me to capture the heart of this critique. In her 1990 article "Race and Essentialism in Feminist Legal Theory," Angela Harris clarifies that: "The result of essentialism it to reduce the lives of people who experience multiple forms of oppression to additional problems: 'racism + sexism = straight Black women's experiences,' or 'racism + sexism + homophobia = Black lesbian experience' . . . As long as feminists, like theorists in the dominant culture, continue to search for gender and racial essences, Black women will never be anything other than a crossroads between two kinds of domination, or at the bottom of a hierarchy of oppressions; we will always be required to choose pieces of ourselves to present as wholeness" (349). In a similar vein, Kimberle Crenshaw presented her notion of "intersectionality": "Black women can experience discrimination in ways that are both similar to and different from those experienced by white women and Black men. Black women sometimes experience discrimination in ways similar to white women's experiences; sometimes they share very similar experiences with Black men. Yet often they experience double discrimination—the combined effects of practices which discriminate on the basis of race, and on the basis of sex. And sometimes, they experience discrimination of Black women—not the sum of race and sex discrimination, but as Black women" (1989, 385).

Not being a woman of color, a member of an ethnic or cultural minority, nor a lesbian, it is with great hesitation that I approach minority women's unique life experiences and their implications. After years of reading and hearing personal and theoretical accounts and analyses of such experiences, I still struggle to fully grasp them, and in particular their legal implications. In the following discussion I try to walk the fine line that is neither excluding nor patronizing, neither essentializing nor universalizing, by relying on the presentation and analysis of Black and lesbian women's life experiences by Black and lesbian legal feminists. Based on their insights, I attempt to reconcile some of their critique with the feminist legal tradition of constructive deconstruction presented in the introduction. In this vein, this chapter reads the film Set It Off as a popular jurisprudential text offering a diversity-based, feminist, legal, constructive deconstruction of norms and conventions regarding poor Black heterosexual women. The chapter's last section offers a brief diversity-sensitive, feminist, legal, constructive deconstruction of the film's own presentation of poor Black lesbians.

Just as the model for feminist constructive deconstruction presented in the introduction can be sensitized to honor- and dignity-based norms and social conventions through the insertion of an "honor test," so a "diversity test" might similarly sensitize the model to diversity among women. A diversity test would scrutinize the social convention in question in search of a distinction (whether overt or covert) drawn between different groups of women based on race, color, ethnicity, class, or sexual orientation. If the social convention analyzed is found to be exclusively relevant to a specific group of women (for example, middle-class white women), the diversity test would direct us to suspect that it may be but one manifestation of a fundamental social attitude that may manifest itself differently in reference to other groups of women. In a case such as this, the diversity test may direct us to search for these diverse manifestations, so that they too may be addressed. In accordance with the findings of the diversity test, the model's fourth stage (the proposing of an alternative definition to the ruling norm), must acknowledge and challenge the social implications of diversity among women, as revealed in the analysis of the relevant social conventions.

The incorporation of the diversity test into the basic model can help maintain the female-centered scope of feminist legal constructive deconstruction, while ensuring that the analysis remains inclusive and relevant. It can do so by ensuring the analysis accounts for the many different ways that women encounter group-based manifestations of gender discrimination. The incorporation of the diversity test encourages the assessment of every group of women on its own terms, precluding the assessment of any one group of women against any other group that serves as a privileged universal standard. Further, with the diversity test fully incorporated into the analysis, the structure of feminist legal constructive deconstruction is well situated for the exposure, analysis, and critique of norms and social conventions that are uniquely oppressive to particular groups of women. Not every feminist legal argument must be relevant to the life experience and hardship of every woman; it must only signal its acknowledgment of its scope, avoiding the traps of universalism and essentialism.

To demonstrate how the incorporation of the diversity test makes the model more robust, let us return to the two feminist legal arguments used in the introduction to demonstrate the logic of the model: constructive deconstruction of the Aristotelian notion of equality and of the common-law perception of rape. The feminist analysis presented in stage two of the deconstruction of the Aristotelian equality, finds that under patriarchy women are systematically constructed as inherently different. But, as minority feminist legal scholars have shown, not all women are constructed as equally or similarly different. The "differences" of distinct groups of women have been constructed in reference to the universal standard of the ruling white man, as well as to each other. In many Western cultures in which white upper-class (heterosexual) man was defined as a rational, utilitarian, self-defining, strong, active, autonomous being, white upper-class (heterosexual) woman was often defined as emotional, intuitive, fragile, passive, and in need of manly guidance and protection. Lesbian white women were often constructed as nonfeminine, unattractive, deviant, misguided, and pitiful. In some such European cultures, Jewish and/or Roma ("Gypsy") women were constructed as dark, sinfully seductive, and dangerous. Asian women were constructed as submissive, servile, efficient, and hardworking. In the United States, Black women were often constructed as inherently nurturing, strong, domineering, simpleminded, and sexually promiscuous, lacking any inhibitions. As stated by Patricia Hill Collins, "from the Mammies, jezebels and breeder women of slavery to the smiling Aunt Jemimas on pancake mix boxes, ubiquitous Black prostitutes, and ever-present welfare mothers of contemporary popular culture, negative stereotypes applied to African-American women have been fundamental to Black women's oppression" (2000, 5).

Because diverse groups of women are constructed as different in a variety of ways, there are differences in the ways women of diverse groups are socially treated, and in how legal notions and norms are applied to them. In terms of the model's third stage, the juxtaposition of the accepted definition of the ruling norm (equality requires similar treatment of individuals similarly situated), with the diverse constructions of women as different produces distinct variations on the paradoxical result. The phrase *Black heterosexual women's equality* is differently paradoxical from the phrase *white heterosexual women's equality* or from the phrase *Asian lesbian women's equality*. Black, white, Asian, and/or lesbian women's unique type of constructed difference and its social implications are crucial for the deeper understanding of discrimination against Black, white, Asian, and/or lesbian women in specific social and legal settings. Let me offer a basic example. Based on their differently constructed differences, Black women are likely to be discriminated against, in comparison with Asian women, in interviews for positions requiring delicacy, discipline, and/or exactness. Asian women may be discriminated against in comparison with Black women in interviews for positions requiring physical strength and/or warm nurturing (gardening, cooking, and attending to children come to mind).

A detailed new definition of gender equality must study and acknowledge the vast variety of such distinct types of gender discrimination and address them. It may need to specify that gender discrimination may manifest itself in any practice that reflects and perpetuates the patriarchal social construction of any category of women constructed by the society under consideration. Consistent with this line of thought, gender equality requires the exposure and confrontation of diverse discriminatory and oppressive practices applied by the investigated patriarchal society to its diverse categories of women.

The feminist analysis presented in stage two of the deconstruction of the common-law concept of rape finds that under patriarchy, legitimate sexual intercourse is constructed as permitting the use of significant force by the man and not fully requiring the woman's freely given consent. But, as minority feminist legal scholars have been showing, legitimate sexual intercourse is conventionally constructed differently in the context of African American women. Angela Harris claims that: "the paradigm experience of rape for Black women has historically involved the white employer in the kitchen or bedroom . . . Moreover, as a legal matter, the experience of rape did not even exist for Black women. During slavery, the rape of a Black woman by any man, white or Black, was simply not a crime" (1990, 350). In other words, the social convention relevant to the life experiences of African American women maintains that any sexual intercourse with a Black woman employee is always legitimate. Clearly, the juxtaposition of this convention with the common-law definition of rape as unconsented, forceful intercourse results in a meaningless, paradoxical operative norm that is specifically relevant to the understanding of the legal treatment of rapes of African American women.

Set It Off is a mainstream film that offers a feminist legal critique focused exclusively on a single group of women: lower-class Black women. The norm investigated by the film is equality before the law, defined as including the rights to equal citizenship, equal protection of the law, and equal application of the presumption of innocence. The social conventions critically analyzed by the film construct poor Black women as inherently guilty by association (with the Black community, Black inner city, and Black men); as untrustworthy employees, fit only for lowly domestic work; as irresponsible mothers, and as "unrapeable," i.e., "inherently consenting to sexual intercourse." The film demonstrates in great detail how, given the existing social conventions, poor Black women are not protected by law, do not enjoy the presumption of innocence, and are treated as second-class citizens. In these three spheres, they do not enjoy equality before the law.

Set It Off's diversity-based feminist legal critique is intertwined with a coherent presentation of Black feminist thought, which grounds the feminist analysis of the social conventions the film presents and scrutinizes. The film's Black feminist outlook combines elements of radical and cultural feminisms, cleansing them of white biases and augmenting them with poor Black women's experiences. In Set It Off, dominance-oriented feminist critique exposes patterns of oppression unique to poor Black women, and the feminine ethic of care manifests itself in Black women's sisterhood as well as in mothering. These are the tools with which the social conventions are analyzed by the film.

In its focus on the significance of women's community building, as well as in its revolutionary frame of mind, Set It Off resembles A Question of Silence. Realizing that the social and legal systems are inherently and irrevocably set against them, the women in the film do not confront specific individuals who wronged them, but the system at large. Robbing banks, they set out to take back from a society that has systematically oppressed them all their lives. Like Nuts, Death and the Maiden, "A Jury of Her Peers," and A Question of Silence, Set It Off demonstrates how a film or story can dignify and respect its women characters by allowing the women distinct voices and points of view, avoiding stereotypical presentations, and refraining from judgment. Free of honor-based notions, the film does not portray its heroines as either guilty or objects, but as unjustly victimized agents.

Film Synopsis

Set It Off features a close-knit group of four African American young women in a Los Angeles housing project, an inner-city "hood." Having pulled herself up by her bootstraps, Frankie (Vivica A. Fox) has a job as a bank teller outside the project. (She is the only one of the four protagonists who straightens her hair, not wearing it in cornrow braids.) The film's opening sequence portrays her fall. Robbed at gunpoint by a drug addict from the project whom she recognized, she is suspected by police and her employer to have been in collusion with him, and is immediately fired.

Cleo (Queen Latifah) is a rough, heavy-looking lesbian and a petty car thief. Comfortable in her social setting, she lives in the moment, spending no time on dreams and hopes of change. Her partner, Ursula (Samantha MacLachlan), is a silent, sexually provocative noncharacter.

Since the death of her parents, Stony (Jada Pinkett) has invested her life in her younger brother, Stevie (Chaz Lamar Shepard), encouraging him to finish high school and apply to college. Learning that he did not receive a scholarship, she is determined to pay his tuition, so she accepts a sales position from Nate (Charles Robinson), a Black businessman. When she asks him for an advance, he conditions it on a sexual encounter, turning a blind ear to Stony's pleading and a blind eye to her tears. Weighing her own integrity against her brother's future, Stony complies. Meanwhile, her brother is gunned down by a police force raiding the project in search of the bank robbers. He is shot when the police notice that his haircut resembles that of one of the suspects.

Tisean, or "T. T." (Kimberly Elise), is a timid single mother, struggling to get by on the little she earns cleaning office buildings with Stony and Cleo. When her Black male employer, Luther (Thom Byrd), deducts taxes from her meager salary, she can no longer afford a babysitter for her son, and brings him with her to work. The baby swallows some detergent, and is claimed by the welfare system, represented by a middle-class Black woman. In order to regain custody, T. T. must reassure the authorities she can provide for her son.

Having all reached dead ends, feeling betrayed and victimized by Black and white systems and individuals, the four friends gradually reach a decision to rob a bank, "taking away from the system that's fucking us all anyway," as Frankie phrases it. But the money does not last, and after much hesitation and conflict they decide to commit a second robbery that would allow them to leave town and start new lives. This time the loot is sufficient. The women hide the money at work, but it is found and taken by Luther. When they confront him in an attempt to retrieve the money, Luther is accidentally shot dead. As these events take place, Stony finds herself in a budding relationship with Keith (Blair Underwood), a Black bank manager she meets scouting a downtown bank. Caring and cooking for her, Keith opens his world to her, teaching her to plan and hope for a tomorrow. (As has rightly been noted, this is "the least believable element of a fairly realistic situation" [Friedman 1997].) But Stony repeatedly chooses her childhood women friends over her new love interest.

After Luther's killing, the women are desperate to leave town, and decide to take another bank. All hell breaks loose as they are spotted and chased through the streets of Los Angeles by hoards of police cars and a helicopter. T. T. is shot to death by a guard in the bank. Cleo sacrifices her life to distract attention from the escaping Frankie and Stony. In a powerful scene she teases the police, provoking the snipers to shoot and kill her. Surrounded, Frankie similarly chooses not to give in. Continuing to run with her share of the money, she triggers the snipers to shoot her in the back. Stony alone succeeds in escaping, to board a tourist bus headed to Mexico. Mourning her friends, she shaves her head and rides her new, red jeep into the unknown, with the exotic Mexican beach in the background.

Unlike the other films presented in this book, Set It Off was overlooked and dismissed by public and critics alike. In the very pointed and accurate words of Elisabeth Friedman, who wrote an online review of Set It Off:

> F. Gary Gray's largely passed-over Set It Off slipped quietly from the screen into the Blockbuster "New Releases" section. And in this reviewer's opinion, undeservedly . . . It puts African American women squarely front and center. In doing so, it neither has them waiting to exhale nor cooking soul food, but bringing to life tragic heroines of all-too-real modern times. And they get to drive stolen cars and shoot submachine guns too . . . The film Set It Off could be considered a Black Thelma and Louise (with a twist on the no-way-out ending), or a female Boyz N the Hood. Except that in focusing on elements of African American women's experience, it reveals a less-explored set of issues which are finally making it onto the big screen. So why haven't you heard of it? Good question. (1997)

The Film's Black Feminist Thought

Asked to recall a Hollywood film presenting the sexual victimization of an African American woman and the killing of a man, many name A Time to Kill. Utilizing every known Hollywood formula, this production based on a John Grisham novel features a white Southern lawyer defending an African American father who shot and killed the two racist rednecks who brutally raped and nearly killed his young daughter. Bringing together a plotline that resonates with To Kill a Mockingbird, a courtroom drama attracting out-of-town lawyers à la Inherit the Wind, lawyerly bonding in the style of Anatomy of a Murder, and the tired theme of an "accidental lawyer" drawn into the ideology he advocates, this film focuses on two men: Black killer and white defender. Privileging the white lawyer's point of view, the film goes to great lengths to stress the analogy between Black fatherhood and white fatherhood, preaching that a Black man's murderous grief over the brutal victimization of his daughter is just as real, understandable, and justified as a white man's would have been under analogous circumstances. Simply stated, it beseeches white folk to not do unto others what they would not have done to themselves, and to excuse Black conduct where they would have excused their own. This reversal technique is popular and successful. (Its mirror image is presented by *White Man's Burden*, showing a Black-controlled society and discriminated-against, impoverished white people).

Set It Off rejects the reversal strategy, offering an unmodified Black feminist perspective. One of this film's most powerful features is its refusal to measure Black women and their plights against white women and their life experiences. Its single white woman is the prostitute hired by Luther with the money he stole from his Black women employees. *Set It Off* presents a community of Black women on its own terms and from its members' points of view. It assumes and conveys that their plight is real not because it can be viewed as resembling that of other people, but because these women *are* real people and their predicaments are all too real. To the film's feminine community, white people are the owners of the empty, soulless office buildings they spend their nights cleaning. They see white people's faces only in photographs they dust; it is mostly white people's garbage they encounter directly. These buildings are the tools enabling white people to preserve their privileges and rule the world, and it is poor Black women's job to maintain and beautify them.

Discussing Black women's traditional role as domestic workers for white families, Patricia Hill Collins notes that: "Black women knew that they could never belong to their White 'families.' They were economically exploited workers and thus would remain outsiders. The result was being placed in a curious *outsider-within* location, a peculiar marginality that stimulated a distinctive Black women's perspective on a variety of themes" (2000, 11). In an interesting commentary on this point, the film presents Frankie, the Black bank teller, as occupying the outsider-within location. For two years Frankie believed that she had succeeded in becoming an insider in her bank, that she could and did belong to her white "family." She worked hard and was rewarded with appropriate promotions. But in the film's first sequence she learns, together with the viewers, that she was never anything but an outsider-within. When her employer justifies the decision to let her go by asking how he could trust her not to be in collusion with the next Black man who plans to rob the bank, Frankie replies that her employment history should provide ample reassurance. But such treatment is reserved for the real insiders, and Frankie is stripped of her illusory position as an outsider-inside and relegated to join her domestic worker friends, cleaning white people's offices under the supervision of a Black man.

Luther's abuse of his unlimited power over the women touches on another Black feminist theme. As Patricia Hill Collins phrases it: "Black men who wish to become 'master' by fulfilling traditional definitions of masculinity—White, prosperous and in charge—and who are blocked from doing so can become dangerous to those closest to them" (2000, 158). Luther is not an abusive intimate partner, but very much a would-be "master," relishing in his imitation of a slave owner's, or at least a slave overseer's, role. An intermediary between the invisible white rulers and the poor Black women he employs, Luther's janitorial company is the women's immediate oppressor. Reprimanding the women for not remembering to recycle, Luther refers to his white clients as "good white folks" and to his employees as "bitches." Much like Nate, who sexually Blackmails Stony, and the bank robber who threatens Frankie's life, Luther shows no solidarity, consideration, empathy, or respect for his Black female employees. In fact, he openly exploits them in any way that is available to him. Set It Off poignantly reveals the irony marking poor Black women's situation: they are suspected and accused by the white system for their alleged collusion with Black men who are abusing them in ways similar to those once used by the white slave masters.

An additional central Black feminist theme masterfully presented by Set It Off is the importance of Black women's sisterhood. Stony, Cleo, T. T., and Frankie are lifelong friends, so close and intimate that they constitute a family. Their reliance on and devotion to each other are the most significant, stable elements in their lives, and they cherish them accordingly. The women nurture each other and share experiences. They smoke and get high together, dream and fantasize together, rob together, and die for each other. They constitute juries of peers for each other: condemning each other's victimization, supporting each other's conduct. Along the way, tensions and even violence arise and erupt, but the fundamental sense of unity prevails. At the same time, Set It Off's strong communality of women does not undermine, and in fact strengthens, each of the women's unique individuality, agency, and victimization. Avoiding a stereotypical presentation of Black women as a monolith and their perspectives as unanimous, the film respectfully distinguishes among the four women and their unique points of view.

Relational feminism has been criticized by Black legal feminists for emphasizing the mother-child nurturing relationship at the expense of other, race-based, interpersonal relationships. Relational feminism's model of womanhood and women's relationships is said to be biased in its exclusive reference to white women's experiences. Relational feminism is described as "gender imperialistic" in its imposition of this race-biased model on Black women (Harris 1989, 352). Set It Off effectively brings this point across, demonstrating the depth of sisterhood among poor Black women and its fundamental importance in their lives. Sisterhood may not substitute for maternal emotional urges (T. T. is devoted to her son and Stony to her baby brother), but it is no less significant for the women's well-being. It clearly replaces the nonexistent heterosexual relationships in these women's lives (Stony's relationship with Keith can hardly be viewed as more than a fantasy). The prevalence of single women in African American society is a familiar theme. Through sisterhood, Set It Off empowers its protagonists beyond the need or yearning for male partners.

Like A Question of Silence before it, Set It Off demonstrates that a real community of women is inherently revolutionary, enabling and leading women to challenge the social order and break free from their systematic collective oppression. True to its diversity-based feminist perspective, Set It Off focuses on inner-city women, asserting, specifically, that a community of poor Black women is inherently revolutionary, given these women's unique sociolegal oppression. (This message may be responsible for harsh critique of the film for portraying Black women as inherently dangerous.)

The film presents two middle-class Black women as alienated and self-distancing from the lower-class sisterhood. The strict social worker shows some understanding of and sympathy for T. T.'s predicament, but is unyielding regarding custody of her son. Keen to please her superior, a white man, the policewoman investigating the bank robberies is "tougher than a man" and "whiter than white." These two middle-class Black women are not atypical of women who succeeded where Frankie failed. Having secured good government positions, they are eager to maintain them, showing allegiance to the systems they serve, and distancing themselves from poor Black sisters. Both women are viewed exclusively from the inner-city women's points of view, which are the film's privileged and exclusive perspectives.

Set It Off's exclusive focus on poor Black women can further be read as implementing one of the most challenging claims made by Black feminist legal thinkers: that discrimination against African American women must be the starting point of the comprehensive investigation of any group-based discrimination. Discrimination against Black women necessarily sensitizes us to intersectionality, which is an important component of any group discrimination. As Kimberle Crenshaw puts it: "With Black women as the starting point, it becomes more apparent how dominant conceptions of discrimination condition us to think about subordination as disadvantage occurring along a single categorical axis . . . This single-axis framework erases Black women in the conceptualization, identification and remediation of race and sex discrimination by limiting inquiry to the experiences of otherwise-privileged members of the group. In other words, in race discrimination cases, discrimination tends to be viewed in terms of sex—or class—privileged Blacks; in sex discrimination cases, the focus is on race—and class—privileged women" (1989, 383). Set It Off establishes poor Black women as its starting point, inviting viewers to explore their intersectional discrimination.

The film's dignifying treatment of its protagonists further manifests itself in its consistent refutation of prevalent stereotypes of African American women. Not one of the four women is even remotely sexually provocative in any way that would bring to mind a "jezebel." None of them is a "mammy," "matriarch," or "domineering" type. Stony comes closest to a being a "domineering" character, actively supervising her brother's life. But her attitude is explained by the film as necessary to protect Stevie from the dangers of the rough hood. Furthermore, Stony, who took over raising her brother after the death of their parents, is shown trying to live vicariously through him the life she never had a chance to pursue for herself.

A third, contemporary, negative stereotype of Black poor women is that of the parasitic, irresponsible welfare single mother. T. T., the film's single mother, is hardworking and as responsible as the difficult circumstances of her life enable her to be. The fourth devaluating stereotype of African American women is that of the Sapphire. "Author bell hooks notes that 'as Sapphires, Black women were depicted as evil treacherous, bitchy, stubborn, and hateful, in short all that the mammy figure was not.' Postslavery, the Sapphire image evolved as a devaluation of what little independence African-American women had through their labor force participation, predominantly in domestic service. Most importantly, 'the Sapphire image of African-American womanhood [. . .] necessitates the presence of an African-American male. When the Sapphire image is portrayed, it is the African-American male who represents the point of contention, in an ongoing verbal dual between Sapphire and the African-American male'" (Springer 2001, 175).

Unlike Kimberly Springer, who feels the film poses the potential threat of the latent Sapphire in every Black woman, I suggest the film supplies its Black women (with the possible exception of Cleo) with abundant good reasons to lose their temper and abandon good manners. Given the circumstances the film creates for them, Stony, and even more so, T. T., are remarkable in their resistance of the violent urge, showing impressive moral fiber and consideration of potential innocent victims of violent acts. Frankie, less "feminine" than T. T., does not restrain her outrage at the wrong done to her. Yet her rage is proportionate enough to be likely understood and accepted by a reasonable viewer. At the film's end, when holding a gun to the head of the police officer who was responsible for her dismissal, she merely wants to teach him a lesson, and is not tempted to pull the trigger, even as she chooses her own death.

Not restricting them to stereotypes, the film allows its characters to undergo significant transformations. The women's growth (with the possible exception of Stony's) is futile, leading them nowhere. But Set It Off does not attribute fault to the women. It presents their paths as leading to dead ends through no fault of their own. The women are never judged or blamed. They are constructed as victimized subjects, who, under very difficult circumstances, struggle to the best of their ability to survive and maintain their dignity. Yet their struggle, the film shows, is against all odds, as the social cards are stacked against them.

Though the film refuses to use a reversal technique and present its Black women as dark-skinned white women, it does find an alternative way of suggesting a comparative reading of its protagonists' lives. It does so through explicit and generic reference to Thelma and Louise. A turning point in popular cinematic treatment of (poor, white) women and their abuse, Thelma and Louise has become a point of reference. Many of Set It Off's features are so reminiscent of Thelma and Louise that it is hard to not view the former as engaging in a dialogue with its predecessor. In case the resemblance is lost on an inattentive viewer, the film brings the point home by having Stony address Cleo by saying, "All right, Louise. You take Thelma over there and y'all go rob another bank." Thelma and Louise, the mythologized working-class white women pushed beyond a point of no return, are thus present in the viewer's conscience, enabling her or him to read Set It Off in a wider context.

Read against Thelma and Louise, Set It Off is a vivid reminder that the oppressive lives that lead the working-class white women to rebel and leave are beyond the realm of inner-city Black women's dreams. Thelma's suburban home and middle-class lifestyle and Louise's job as a waitress, frustrating as they may be, are beyond the reach of Stony, Cleo, T. T., and even Frankie. Thelma's husband is controlling and verbally abusive, but he seems to provide her with a stable, safe life. Louise's partner neglects to cater to her romantic needs, and occasionally gets violent, throwing things around, when he loses his temper. Though such relationships certainly impose hardships, the hardships endured by Set It Off's women seem to be of a different magnitude.

Particularly telling is the comparison of the two films' cinematic allusions. As has been noted by many, Thelma and Louise signals women's daring, rebellious fantasy of appropriating the most manly of all American genres, the western. Two outlaws traveling through the western landscape in avoidance of the law, Thelma and Louise seize the right to join a long line of American (cinematic) outlaw heroes. Driving through the wild, wild West, they enter the sacred domain of American mythological masculinity. Discovering the freedom of the open, never-ending American countryside, they awake to a new life, more thrilling and challenging than they ever imagined possible. Although their road leads nowhere, the ride itself is a victory in its own right. In contrast, Set It Off's Black heroines never leave the confines of the urban setting. The film genre they explicitly cite and associate themselves with is the gangster movie. Discussing the commission of their second bank robbery, they impersonate characters of "dons," members in The Godfather's fictional Italian Mafia. Unlike Thelma and Louise, Stony, Frankie, Cleo, and T. T. cannot envision themselves roleplaying traditionally cherished American outlaw heroes. Their point of reference is the fictional world of immigrant, minority outlaws, confined to big cities' urban settings.

In its final sequence, Set It Off evokes the dramatic ending of Thelma and Louise, but in doing so, powerfully foregrounds the importance of a diversity analysis. Much has been said of the white outlaw women's leap into the Grand Canyon, and about the cinematic choice to leave them hanging, frozen, above the abyss, sparing the viewer the vision of their destruction. Set It Off brings its women to the same dead end, but shows no such concern for its viewer's sensitivities. Like in Thelma and Louise, Stony, Frankie, and Cleo are chased by dozens of police cars and a helicopter. Frankie and Cleo, like Thelma and Louise, choose not to surrender, preferring to die free. But unlike the white women, they do not make it easy on society, each forcing the authorities to actively shoot her to death. The brutal, overwhelming scenes of their killings spell out the truth about their lives and deaths. They were cornered into a situation of no exit, and gunned down by a society that viewed them as a menacing threat. Frankie was appropriately shot in the back.

Frankie's and Cleo's choice, like Thelma's and Louise's before it, expresses the women's ultimate lack of trust in society and its legal system. The women know beyond reasonable doubt that the judicial system cannot and will not hear their voices, see their victimization, nor do them justice. They know there is no future for them within society, and no hope for change. If they cannot live as outlaws, they cannot live at all. Once they embarked on a revolution, there is no turning back. Like *A Question of Silence*, *Set It Off* has a feminist message of complete disenchantment with society and its legal system, and total abandonment of hope for (Black) women within it.

But unlike *Thelma and Louise* or *A Question of Silence*, *Set It Off* allows one of the characters, Stony, to survive and remain free. I agree with Kimberly Springer's critique of this ending's heavy-handed morality. "Do Stony's hopes for middle-class mobility and heterosexual alliance save her? Perhaps, as demonstrated by her desire to send Stevie to college and her adoption of Keith's rhetorical question ('Where do you see yourself in five years?'), Stony is worth saving because she aspires to be more than a 'hood rat. As Cleo noted, Stony cannot accept that fate, and her denial of poverty turns out to be the key to her cage" (Springer 2001, 194). Nevertheless, the image of Stony driving her red jeep, having shaven her cornrow braids, compels viewers to reflect on her future. Where can she go? What can she do? What should she do? *Set It Off*'s viewer accompanied Stony throughout the experiences that transformed her and forever changed her life. Having experienced some of that transformation herself, the viewer finds herself involved in worrying about Stony's possible future. In some respect, contemplating Stony's future, the viewer is invited to rethink her own.

Equal Treatment of the Law

Following closely the daily lives of four poor African American women, *Set It Off* portrays how no discrimination, abuse, or injustice inflicted on them is socially or legally defined as a breach of any law. At the same time, every breath they take seems to be constructed as breaking the law. The film presents a sociolegal system that is incapable of identifying harm done to poor Black women, while feeling threatened by every move they make. The film pointedly reveals that underlying this sociolegal blindness and overreaction is the construction of the poor Black woman as guilty by association, untrustworthy, fit for lowly domestic work, an irresponsible mother, and "unrape-able." Again, this image of the poor Black woman renders her a second-class citizen, who is guilty until proven innocent.

Luther's Janitorial Services is an abusive employer, preying on the help-lessness of poor Black women. Luther patronizes the women, offends them, pays them a meager salary they cannot live on, and threatens to lay them off when they try to negotiate their work conditions. Stony, T. T., Cleo, and, as it turns out, even Frankie are "captive employees." Their life conditions and the educational system provided them by the state did not equip them with skills required for any other employment. If, by some miracle, they overcome these obstacles and manage to get a job outside the confined Black ghetto, they are likely to lose it, like Frankie, due, in one way or another, to their perceived affiliation with the Black community.

In reference to these women, Luther enjoys an employers' market. This unjust advantage is facilitated by direct government policy (level of education) complimented by the state's failure to address racial discrimination in the employment market outside the Black ghetto. Despite the state's alleged commitment to and responsibility for every citizen's education and equal employment opportunities, no law is available to the women to help them confront Luther's abuse of their vulnerability, which is an outcome of their systematic group discrimination.

Similarly, no law protects Frankie against her employer's decision to fire her based on his suspicion that she may be in collusion with the man who robbed the bank, merely because they both live in the project. "I can't help who I know," Frankie reasons, but her employer is legally entitled to hold her acquaintances against her. As long as the bank does not lay off every Black employee, Frankie cannot bring forth a claim of race-based discrimination. The fact that she was fired based exclusively on her racial affiliation with the robber is not legally sufficient; the law would identify discrimination only in the unlikely event of collective dismissal of every employer who is racially affiliated with the robber.

Much as Frankie's guilt by racial affiliation led to her termination, Stevie's guilt by racial affiliation led to his killing at the hands of the police. Stevie was spotted in the housing project, leaving the home of a Black man known to the police. Associating his hairstyle with that of the robber, the police ordered him to lie on the ground, and when he reached for a bottle stashed inside his coat (so as not to lie on it), the police assumed he was reaching for a gun and shot him dead. The whole scene resembles a battlefield more than a police search and arrest. Stevie was treated like an enemy rather than a citizen. But no law was broken. Given the neighborhood's violent reputation, the police's interpretation of Stevie's move would likely be found reasonable by any investigation or court of law. Consequently, Stony, an American citizen, would not be entitled to compensation, apology, or acknowledgment of the wrong done to her brother and her. It seems likely that in a middle-class, white neighborhood, Stevie's killing would never have happened. If it had, an investigation and a legal procedure would have found the police conduct unreasonable, leading to disciplinary chastisement and/or criminal punishment, and serving as grounds for compensation for the unjust killing.

In presenting the women's captive employment by Luther's Janitorial Services as discrimination, Set It Off identifies a pattern of discrimination that is largely race- and class-based, but tends to also be gender specific. In the other instances, the film depicts poor Black women's racial discrimination, which is comparable to that of poor Black men. The only distinction is that the women are punished through no fault of any Black women, whereas the men are punished for the (alleged) criminal conduct of other Black men. Additionally, the film calls attention to two patterns of discrimination that are unique to African American women and address the unique combination of their race and gender.

Asking Nate for an advance on her salary, Stony is faced with the choice to allow him sexual gratification or not accept the advance. No law would consider this as rape or sexual assault. No physical force was used, no life-endangering threats were uttered or intimated, Stony did not resist, and she willingly participated, thus conveying consent. Stony is presumed to be an adult woman in her right mind and an autonomous decision maker. Through legal eyes, her conduct is at best a contract that was freely entered into, and at worst self-prostitution.

But, as shown by Black feminist legal scholars, Black women's paradigmatic experience of rape involved a white master (or later employer) using his victim's economic dependency to have her submit to his sexual demands. Such rape did not necessarily involve the use of physical force, severe threats, the Black woman's utmost resistance, or her explicit objection. The master or employer did not use force or threats because he did not need to, and the Black woman did not resist or object because she could not afford to. This was a pattern of rape distinct in its particular details from some rapes within the white, hegemonic world. It was even more distinct from the archetypal rape as envisioned by the hegemonic society and prohibited by its law: the sexual attack of a virtuous (white) woman by a (Black) stranger lurking behind the bushes. The paradigmatic rape of an African American woman (analogous to typical rapes of many lower-class, working women of all races) did not satisfy any of the legal requirements to qualify as rape. It was, thus, not acknowledged as rape. It was deemed consensual conduct, conveying the woman's choice.

Since the paradigmatic rape of Black women was not rape, then Black women were "unrapeable." Since any sexual conduct was constructed as chosen and desired by them, they were naturally voluptuous, whores. Since they were naturally voluptuous, they perpetually "got to have it," no sexual encounter with a Black woman could possibly be rape.

Set It Off suggests that, given its specific context, Stony's sexual encounter with Nate differed from Black women's paradigmatic experience of rape only in that her abusive employer was a Black, not a white, man. The sexual encounter during which Stony cried, and after which she showered thoroughly, was a typical rape of a Black woman, viewed by the law as conveying her "choice" and "free will." Interestingly, in the context of rape, Stony enjoys equal treatment of the law and is constructed by it as an autonomous, self-governing individual. If she participated in a sexual encounter that was not physically forced on her, then she must have chosen and willed it, and the law must protect her right to choose and implement her will. Any other approach would, God forbid, undermine her individuality and human dignity. The same law that treats her as a second-class citizen and finds her brother and best friend guilty by racial affiliation is adamant in protecting Stony's choice to sell her body to an abusive employer.

The legal treatment of T. T. as a mother exemplifies a pervasive form of discrimination practiced against African American women. Her status as a young, Black, single mother marks her as suspect, and her poverty is held against her, interpreted as testimony of her neglectful mothering. The same system that invested little in T. T.'s education, did little to equip her with the skills necessary to earn a living, and turns a blind eye to her exploitation by Luther Janitorial Services, holds her to norms of motherhood befitting middle-class economic means. Rather than viewing T. T. as heroic because of her efforts to support herself and her son, rather than seeing her as a good mother because of her decision to bring her child with her to work (rather than leaving him alone at home), rather than seeing her immediate attendance to his medical needs as signs of responsibility and caring, the system interprets her efforts as testifying to T. T.'s incompetence.

Like Stony, T. T. is presumed by the law to be a fully autonomous, self-governing, decontextualized individual. If she had a child she must have wanted to, and must be held accountable; if she is not earning enough to employ a baby-sitter she must not be trying hard enough; if her child swallowed poisonous cleaning materials she must not have been caring for him properly. The facts that she may not have fully planned to give birth and that she uses her resources to the best of her ability under difficult circumstances she does not control, are simply deemed irrelevant. "The good of the child" is used to terrorize T. T., to control and punish her for being a Black single mother.

Set It Off does not supply specific formulas for alternative definitions of legal norms that would acknowledge and challenge pervasive, discriminatory social conventions. It seems to suggest that the system is hopeless and Black women have no chance of amending it, or surviving within it. But it does an extraordinary job of fleshing out the meaning of the systemic discrimination of Black women. It reveals harms done to Black women, conveys the meanings of these harms, and points to the legal sites that ignore these harms, dismiss and deny them. Through narrative, characters, and visual images, it brings to life Black feminist legal arguments. For anyone hoping to implement change, this must be a starting point.

Lesbian on the Side

In the same vein as Thelma and Louise, Boys on the Side (1995) features an abused (white) woman's homicide of her abusive male partner, and the consequent all-woman journey west. In this variation, one of the two white women is dying of AIDS, and the other, impregnated by the man she killed, falls in love with a police officer and surrenders to the authorities. Interestingly, these two successors of Thelma and Louise are reinforced by a third female character, who is both Black and a lesbian (played by Whoopi Goldberg). This character is the one who encourages the abused woman character to stand up for herself and confront her violent partner, whose outraged response leads to his death. The Black lesbian is, thus, the promoter of the abused woman's assertiveness, but also the instigator of a woman's violence that leads to the death of a man.

Set It Off similarly presents Cleo, the Black lesbian, as the one who stands up for her friends and encourages them to not yield to abusers. When Luther picks on T. T. and humiliates her, it is Cleo who speaks out in protection of her friend. When Frankie is unjustly dismissed, it is Cleo who suggests robbing a bank, and she is the one most committed to the idea until it materializes. Her outraged attack on Luther, confronting him after he stole the women's loot, leads to his killing. Cleo is, thus, also a promoter of women's assertiveness and an instigator of violence which leads to a man's death. But the portrayal of Cleo is not nearly as nuanced as that of Goldberg's analogous character. In fact, it is stereotyping and stigmatizing in every way. In her review of the lesbian in law films, Jenni Millbank notes that cultural conventions construct lesbian sexuality as signifying "aggression, irrationality and carnality" (1996, 472). She observes that "true stories of jolly nice, non-murdering, or even heroic lesbians don't tend to appear in film and, if they do appear, the character's lesbianism is almost always muted or erased. Whereas when lesbians are killers, or killers are presumed to be lesbian, the story is told and retold and their sexuality is always central to the tale" (1996, 472–73). She shows that this is also true for feature films not based on fact. Against such social and cinematic conventions, Cleo reaffirms every negative stereotype.

Queen Latifah's character is powerful, convincing, and human. Her Cleo is a loyal friend, brave and resourceful. But she is also depicted as very different from her friends, and that difference is of a very specific nature. Unlike the others, Cleo has no long-term plans or aspirations whatsoever. She does not pursue a career, raise a son, or provide for a brother. She lives the moment, irresponsibly spending money without thinking ahead. Most notably, Cleo is a manly woman, who spends her life fixing cars and stealing them, just like the boys in the hood. Like a man, she drinks, curses, supplies the women with drugs, and spends her money on car gadgets and sexy outfits for her woman. Her character is the only one that does not undergo transformation of any kind. Significantly, she is the only woman the film does not supply with a clear, immediate motive for the outbreak of violence. At the same time, she is the only one with a criminal record. Cleo seems content with her life in the hood, and violence simply seems to be a way of life for her, as for the young African American men around her. In her daily interactions she easily loses her temper, on one occasion pointing a gun at Stony's head, triggering a brawl and a (short-lived) tension among the friends. Springer rightly notes that Cleo "is depicted as a stereotypical 'bulldagger' with violent tendencies. While Stony acts as the moral conscience of this group of women, Cleo has the dubious privilege of being all 'id' and aggression" (2001, 187).

Cleo's manliness and natural aggression go hand in hand with her lesbian sexuality. Cleo is the only one of the four friends who has a stable relationship. But it is a stereotypical, overtly sexual, butch-femme relationship with the tall, skinny (bleached) blonde, Ursula, who never speaks. Ursula takes no part in the women's sisterhood. She mostly ignores their presence as they look at her disapprovingly. She is not "one of the women-guys" but a sexual mate "on the side," appropriately dressed in short, provocative outfits. The film offers no information about her life. Cleo's lesbian sexuality is, therefore, not portrayed by the film as a part of her Black womanhood or of the sisterhood. It is an unpleasant addendum the other Black women accept with dismay.

Critical and observant as it is regarding discriminatory social conventions and legal norms applied to heterosexual, poor, Black women, Set It Off is neither critical nor self-reflective regarding discriminatory social conventions and legal norms applied to poor, Black lesbians. From a feminist legal perspective, the film offers no deconstruction, constructive or otherwise, of Cleo's and Ursula's construction by society or by law. Both women are presented as "naturally" being what they are: a violent, manly "butch" and a nonperson "femme." Cleo's violence is presented as natural "lesbian criminality," to use Millbank's phrase (1996, 454). In Set It Off, no sociolegal constrictions seem to have restricted Cleo or Ursula, and no laws are exposed as discriminating against them. The film leaves untouched the other women's silent rejection of the lesbian relationship. It creates no situations that could give rise to critical viewer consideration of lesbian-focused social and legal issues, such as legalization of lesbian relationships, parenthood in lesbian families, sexual-orientation-based harassment, and employment discrimination. The film's sharp critique of damaging social conventions regarding Black women highlights its uncritical presentation of (Black) lesbians.

10 High Heels

(Spain, 1991)

ALMODOVAR'S POSTMODERN TRANSGRESSION

In a comprehensive article, "On Postmodern Feminist Legal Theory," Maxine Eichner rightly notes that "the postmodern impulse has been far more muted in the field of feminist legal theory than in other areas of feminist studies. This may be because of the difficulty of deriving a positive program from postmodern principles, which have been interpreted as primarily critical and deconstructive, and largely framed on a metatheoretical rather than political level. Such framing comports poorly with feminist legal theory's focus on developing concrete, positive legal projects . . . Law, itself, is so closely associated with the vision of modernity against which postmodernists are reacting; those feminists who subscribe to postmodern tenets may, accordingly, avoid considering legal solutions" (2001, 4).

In fact, postmodernism has provoked deeply hostile responses from the most serious feminist legal theorists. Robin West argues in no uncertain terms that "the four central ideas of postmodern social theory that have proven to be of most interest to critical legal theorists—ideas that center around the nature of power, of knowledge, or morality and of the self—will not further our understanding of patriarchy, and will frustrate rather than further our attempts to end it" (1997, 259). Catharine MacKinnon is just as explicit and unhesitant about her objection to postmodernism: "According to postmodernism, there are no facts; everything is a reading, so there can be no lies. Apparently, it cannot be known whether the Holocaust is a hoax, whether women love to be raped, whether Black people are genetically intellectually inferior to white people, whether homosexuals are child molesters" (2000a, 152). From her dominance-focused perspective she asks: "Can postmodernism stop the rape of children when everyone has their story and everyone is presumably exercising sexual agency all the time? . . . How can you oppose something that is always only in play? . . . If the subject is dead and we are dealing with deeds without doers, how do we hold perpetrators accountable for what they perpetrate?" (155). She concludes: "I do know this: we cannot have this postmodernism and still have a meaningful practice of women's human rights, far less a women's movement" (159). Given such strenuous objections, can a postmodern film like Pedro Almodovar's High Heels be read as contributing to the feminist project?

High Heels, although not as universally acclaimed as some of the director's later works, was a huge box-office success (Almodovar 1996, 121; P. J. Smith 1994, 131). It continues to be available in video-rental stores around the world. Like many of Almodovar's films, it eludes classification within any defined film genre. It combines motifs of melodrama, film noir, detective thrillers, musicals, and films of female friendship.[1] More than anything else, it seems to fit the definition of a postmodern comedy: "The notion of postmodern comedy arguably resists any clear definition as a discrete filmic style or practice precisely because of its ostentatiously hybrid, cross-generic character and its contempt for established filmic aims as well as other cultural and social boundaries and hierarchies. Its humor tends to arise as much from the willful disruption of the spectator's reading expectations as from narrative and generic incongruities and the juxtaposition of the bizarre and the banal . . . Almodovar was deliberately and willfully engaging in generic confusion, mixing and juxtaposing aspects of cine[ma] verite, melodrama, situation comedy, pornography, advertising, pop music, zarzuela (operetta), etc. into a unique melange, which would become an unmistakable Almodovarian trademark" (Jordan and Morgan-Tamosunas 1998, 81–83).

High Heels is clearly a postmodern text, extravagantly celebrating fluidity, impersonation, imitation, and the inherent lack of authenticity. It could be, and indeed has been, read as conveying antifeminist messages (Fischer 1998,

212–14; P. J. Smith 1994). And yet, another prevalent approach presents Almodovar as a profeminist creator (Jordan and Morgan-Tamosunas 1998, 115). One way in which Almodovar's films can and have been perceived as feminist is in the portrayal of strong women (Jordan and Morgan-Tamosunas 1998, 143). Almodovar's films are also feminist in portraying women as sexually desiring subjects (137), in presenting female support networks (133), in allowing female characters access to the powerful cinematic gaze, in offering sympathetic treatment to difficult subjects, such as women who kill, and in undermining patriarchal gender roles. "Films by Pedro Almodovar have been particularly instrumental in introducing and promoting the fluidity of traditional gender attributes in particularly challenging ways" (152). Even his choice of genre, that is his respectful treatment of melodrama, can be considered a feminist attitude. As Rikki Morgan observes, "Strongly associated with 'women's films,' and consequently devalued, melodrama has only recently been reconsidered as a result of feminist attention. Almodovar's reprise of the form is typical of his indifference to critical snobbery . . . Time and again he returns to *family* melodrama as both a narrative form and a thematic focus, a typical example of his characteristic disregard for critical and social propriety" (1992, 29). She further asserts that in his melodramas, including *High Heels*, Almodovar challenges the conventional family unit while "retain[ing] a strong sense of the supportive role his alternative families play." Such subversion of patriarchal norms can clearly be read as feminist.

Fully aware of the legitimate concerns regarding postmodernism, I nevertheless read *High Heels* as both postmodern and feminist. In her concluding remarks in the article "Feminism, Postmodernism and Law," Robin West suggests that feminism can and should have it "both ways" with regard to postmodernism. Feminists should embrace and celebrate some postmodern insights, while rejecting others: "A skepticism toward particular claims of objective truth, a particular account of the self, and any particular account of gender, sexuality, biology, or what is and is not natural, is absolutely necessary to a healthy and modern feminism. But that skepticism need not require an unwillingness to entertain descriptions of subjective and intersubjective authenticity, claims of a pervasive and cross-cultural patriarchy, various accounts of the female self, promises of a nurturant or caring morality" (1997, 292). I suggest that, combining deep skepticism with fresh imagery and interpretation of "subjective and intersubjective authenticity," as well as with "promises of a nurturant or caring morality," *High Heels* offers a brilliant example of one such possible combination of postmodernism and feminism.

The film's postmodern, carnivalesque character facilitates its bold rejection of traditional, patriarchal structures and symbols, and the playful, fantastic search for imaginative alternatives.

Treating the familiar theme of a sexual woman committing adultery and then killing a man (in this case her husband), High Heels, very much like "A Jury of Her Peers" and A Question of Silence (both discussed in chapter 8), focuses on what led to the killing—the systematic mental oppression of the woman. Adopting the woman's perspective, and that of those who love her, the film all but ignores the criminal act and the dead man. Inviting the viewer to adopt a nonjudgmental point of view of the woman's fatal action, the film allows her to convey the pain caused by her mother and her husband, who have wronged her all her life. Like "A Jury of Her Peers," A Question of Silence, Death and the Maiden, and Set It Off, High Heels transcends the apparent dichotomy between feminist thought focused on an ethic of care and "radical" feminism, focusing on patriarchal oppression and dominance. Combing the two perspectives, the film portrays an oppressive, patriarchal social reality, while promoting the notion of justice of care. High Heel's advocacy for a justice of care is most apparent in its image of the investigating judge.

In Caring for Justice, Robin West offers a notion of justice that closely links it with care and compassion. She argues that "the 'ethic of justice' and the 'ethic of care' are in fact much more interrelated and interdependent than [the] widely accepted dualism suggests" (1997, 24). She further argues that "the zealous pursuit of justice, if neglectful of the ethic of care, will fail not just as a matter of overall virtue, but more specifically, it will fail as a matter of justice." In her discussion of justice and care, West focuses on cultural images. She presents several traditional images of justice, concluding that "the plumb line, the cupped hands,[2] the blindfolded judge and the scales of justice, as well as the values of consistency, integrity, and impartiality that they represent—do indeed constitute foundational elements of what James Boyd White calls our 'legal imagination'" (1997, 30). The legal imagination reflected in and refracted by traditional images does not promote the association of justice with care. To bring about change in the legal imagination and in public notions of justice and law, to reconceptualize justice and law not merely in terms of "objectivity" and impartiality, but also in terms of compassion and care, new images are needed—images as powerful, memorable, and attractive as traditional ones.

In accordance with West's line of thought, I suggest that cinema is a rich source of contemporary imagery—popular, familiar, and imaginative. Postmodern cinema, such as Almodovar's, may be a particularly rich source of fresh, uninhibited imagery. Interdisciplinary, feminist law-and-film analysis can identify imagery of "caring justice" in movies like High Heels.

Unlike any of the other films discussed in this book, High Heels focuses on the judiciary and the system of justice, rather than on lawyers and adversary dueling. Clearly, the film's European origin accounts for its interest in the judge, as well as for its inquisitorial logic and temperament. Whereas the Anglo-American legal system is adversarial, focusing on the combating parties according to the deeply held belief that the best man will win, the European one is inquisitorial, focusing on the judge's search for truth and justice. The binary, dueling nature of the Anglo-American legal system suits the patriarchal social order and its zero-sum mentality, which is also a central component of honor-based societies. As such, the adversarial precludes imagery with subversive feminine potential. With its spotlight more often on the judiciary, European cinema is more likely to facilitate reconsideration of fundamental elements of the judicial system and exploration of possibilities of feminine concepts of justice.

Read in its cultural context, High Heels offers a radical and feminist alternative to the patriarchal image and ideal of Solomonic justice, which dominates our Judeo-Christian heritage, and the notion of good judging in particular. The traditional imagery is replaced by imagery that links ethics of justice with ethics of care. As mentioned earlier, in the process of linking the notions of justice and care, High Heels also links the feminist perspective focusing on care with the radical one highlighting dominance and oppression. The film's fresh, postmodern imagery of justice is thus feminist in a variety of ways worthy of investigation and acknowledgment.

As in the biblical story of Solomon's judgment, in High Heels two "mothers" compete over the love of a female "child" (who is also a character accused of murder in the film's detective subplot). But in this contemporary image, the law, represented by and embodied in the character of the transsexual investigating judge, is one of the competing mothers. This law is deeply and emotionally involved in the lives of both the accused child-woman and her "real" mother, who are both oppressed by patriarchy. Moreover, the law is caring, compassionate, and loving. Justice is achieved through caring involvement. Care, compassion, law, justice, and judgment are interdependent, as are masculinity and femininity, and many more traditionally contrasted categories. The film's compassionate treatment of almost all characters, judging and judged alike, invites the viewer to adopt the caring/just/ dignifying attitude of the law/mother, transcending judgment as we know it.[3]

Film Synopsis

The film opens with the image of Rebecca (Victoria Abril) in Madrid's airport, nervously awaiting her mother's arrival. The mother, Becky (Marisa Paredes), a dazzling—if aging—pop star, has been absent from Rebecca's life for fifteen years. Waiting, Rebecca recalls painful childhood scenes of parental neglect and desertion. On Becky's arrival, the viewer learns that Rebecca has married Manuel (Fedor Atkine), once Becky's lover and now the head of the television channel where Rebecca works as a news broadcaster.

That night, after a tense dinner party (during which, as she'd done years earlier, Rebecca intentionally eavesdrops on her mother's conversation with Manuel, overhearing his refusal to say that he loves his wife), the three go to the last show of a drag performer, Letal (Miguel Bosé), who imitates Becky in performance. Rebecca discloses that, missing her mother, she often went to watch Letal perform. Imitating the younger Becky, Letal delivers a breathtaking performance in what has been called "the most brilliant sequence in the film . . . When the camera cuts to a reverse shot of the spectators, we see that Becky watches the performance with narcissistic fascination, Rebecca with erotic desire, and Manuel with hostility and contempt" (Kinder 1995, 151). After the performance, Letal joins their table, asking for Becky's earrings as a token of bonding. While Manuel makes a pass at Becky, Rebecca follows Letal to his dressing room. Letal confesses that he wishes to be "more than a mother" to her, and a lengthy sex scene takes place.[4]

In the following scene, Judge Dominguez is shown spending a domestic evening with his mother, who collects newspaper clippings of Becky. Next, a shot is heard, and Judge Dominguez is seen investigating the death of Manuel, whose body was found in his summerhouse. The investigating judge performs a pretrial investigation, aimed at determining whether or not to press criminal charges, and if so against whom. In the judge's chambers, Rebecca learns that Manuel was not only sexually involved with another newswoman, but also with Becky. All three women confess to having visited Manuel on the night of his death, but all deny having committed the murder. That night, delivering the news on a live television broadcast, Rebecca confesses that she murdered Manuel, showing the audience photographs she took of her house after committing the crime. The judge, who (with his mother) is watching her broadcast, orders her arrest.

Insisting that he wishes to help, Judge Dominguez convinces Becky to see her daughter and arranges a meeting. Rebecca passionately accuses her mother of desertion and, in a lengthy allusion to Bergman's film *Autumn Sonata*, expresses her feelings of inadequacy, revealing that she has tried to imitate Becky all her life, that she married Manuel in the hope of defeating her mother, and that she was the one who instigated her stepfather's death (by causing him to take sleeping pills before a long night drive). She explains that she was trying to protect her mother from the dominating stepfather and to help Becky lead her own life. She then denies having killed Manuel. On the way back to prison, Rebecca breaks down in heartbreaking weeping. On-stage, in her comeback performance (attended by Judge Dominguez), Becky, too, breaks down and sheds a genuine tear when she dedicates the opening song, "Think of Me," to her imprisoned daughter.

After discovering that she is pregnant, a desperate Rebecca is mysteriously released from prison. Back home, she retrieves Manuel's gun, the murder weapon, from the television set. Judge Dominguez, who arrives on the scene unexpectedly, advises her to see Letal who, that same night, performs for her the song "Think of Me." In his dressing room after the performance, Rebecca learns, together with the viewer, that Judge Dominguez and Letal are one and the same man. Without the drag costume, Letal becomes Eduardo, who puts on a fake beard and dark glasses to become the judge. He proposes marriage, saying that she must have come to see Letal because he is the father of her child. If not for that, he continues, Rebecca would have preferred to spend the evening with her mother. Strange as it may be, he argues, they have formed a family.

As they speak, Becky appears on the television screen, singing "Think of Me," and the news broadcaster reports that she has collapsed and been hospitalized. Rebecca and the judge rush to the hospital, where Rebecca confesses to her mother that she did, actually, shoot Manuel. On the night of his death, Rebecca narrates, she offered to kill herself, asking Manuel whether he preferred that she use the gun or sleeping pills. Manuel replied that he couldn't care less, to which Rebecca responded by shooting him. Becky sighs, "Men," and decides to take responsibility for Manuel's death. She confesses to the judge that, as he had suspected from the start, she was the one who committed the murder. Dominguez, suspicious, considers disqualifying himself, but Rebecca dissuades him.

The final scene takes place in Becky's renovated basement apartment after Becky plants her fingerprints on the gun that Rebecca has brought her for this purpose. It is in that basement apartment that she was raised by her poor, janitor parents, watching the high heels of women passing by in the street above and fearing that they had come to take her away. As mother and daughter watch these passing heels together, Rebecca recalls how, as a child, she waited for the sound of her mother's heels every night before falling asleep. "At the end of the film the two women's regressions merge" (Fischer 1998, 208). Becky then dies and Rebecca is left weeping at her bedside. "The final fade has Rebecca embracing her dead mother as if the two 'form[ed] one body' " (P. J. Smith 1994, 132).

Solomon's Judgment

I read High Heels, and the image of Judge Dominguez, against the ancient story of the Solomonic judgment, and image of King Solomon, the archetypal good judge. The Book of Kings contains the familiar story of two unnamed harlots who came before King Solomon, each claiming to be the real mother of a single child (each additionally claiming that the other woman's newborn died due to the mother's negligence). "And the king said Bring me a sword. And they brought a sword before the king. And the king said Divide the living child in two, and give half to the one and half to the other. Then spake the woman whose the living baby was unto to the king, for her bowels yearned upon her son, and she said O my lord, give her the living child, and in no wise slay it. But the other said, Let it be neither mine nor thine, but divide it. Then the king answered and said, Give her the living child, and in no wise slay it: she is the mother thereof. And all Israel heard of the judgment which the king had judged; and they feared the king: and they saw that the wisdom of God was in him to do judgment" (1 Kings 3:24–28 King James). The structure, rhetoric, and narration of the story, its location in the chronology of King Solomon and its significance in the historical context of the ancient Hebrews' fierce attack on the worship of the great goddess have invited careful feminist analysis (Ashe 1991; Althouse 1992). Here I wish to focus only on the imagery of law and justice as it is constituted by this classic text that "has long been accepted as a paradigmatic account of 'justice' and of 'wisdom' " (Ashe 1991, 81).

In the text of Kings, the judge is portrayed as a man, a king, son and heir to God's chosen King David, and himself blessed and embraced by God. He is the story's single protagonist. At his feet, the two adversaries are wretched, anonymous women, both portrayed as whores, in conflict over the issue of motherhood. The male judge reveals the truth, determines justice, and pronounces the law through the swift, masculine drawing of a phallic, deadly sword. The legal process is detached, quick, violent, and efficient. It is deaf and blind to the women's identities, predicaments, and narratives, as well as uninterested in a consideration of the child's best interest. The legal process, as well as the narrative depicting it, caters to the male judge's honor, expressing complete disregard of the dignity of the women.

A whole set of issues is not raised and thereby deemed irrelevant: the socioeconomic structure that reduces women to wretched "harlots," the culture that evaluates them in exclusive reference to their sexual behavior and motherhood, the responsibility of unmentioned fathers (Who were they? Did they have the women's consent to impregnate them? Did they support their offspring?), and the responsibility of the women's families and society at large. Only the women's immediate behavior before and during the trial is relevant, calling for judicial scrutiny. In order to reach good and just law, the judge outsmarts the women, uses their bodies and instincts against them, and treats them as objects. Their lifestyle, of course, renders them inherently guilty objects. This judicial process manifests the judge's superiority over the women. In deciding which of the women will receive the child, the male judge, by virtue of his sword, also determines the essence of true motherhood. Only one of the women can be the real, true, good mother. Motherhood is, therefore, exclusive, excluding, and recognized on the basis of man's all-or-nothing logic.

In its presentation of this scene of judgment, the biblical text distinguishes between judging male and judged females, establishing the first as subject, king, and lord, the latter as whores and mothers. True motherhood is identified with care, compassion, and sacrifice; wise and just judgment with extravagant, violent, external, zero-sum allocation of goods. The child, totally objectified, attracts no subjective attention. The text's own impartial indifference towards the judged women and the child, along with its determination that the winner is, indeed, the child's real mother, invites the reader to identify and side with the judging man. It constitutes its reader as a male judge.

Themes and elements of this biblical story are so deeply embedded in our notions of law, justice, and the legal process that they have become fully transparent and taken for granted. They underlie judicial decisions, lay concepts, and contemporary cultural imagery, including complex, sophisticated works widely acknowledged as works of genius. Moving to the cinema, recall Alfred Hitchcock's treatment of motherhood and law in *Marnie* (1964). Motherhood is a major theme throughout the Hitchcockian canon, *Marnie* being Hitchcock's most powerful treatment of the mother-daughter relationship. Marnie's young single mother is a prostitute who nightly removes her daughter from her bed to entertain sailors. When one of her clients fondles the little girl, the mother attacks him and, rushing to her rescue, the girl kills the assailant.

Protecting her daughter, the mother assumes responsibility for the killing and is released on the basis of self-defense. The girl completely suppresses the memory. Although refusing to offer her daughter for adoption, the mother, turned pious, is cold and distant, unable to show affection to her daughter. As a result, Marnie (Tippi Hedren) matures into a frigid woman and a thief. She resorted to stealing, the film explains, in order to compensate for the lack of mother love, as well as to support her mother and buy her attention with valuable gifts. Enter rich, masculine, educated, forceful Mark (Sean Connery) who outsmarts Marnie, catches her stealing, and decides to reform and cure her of both frigidity and thieving despite her expressed will. Threatening to turn her in to the police, he blackmails her into marrying him, rapes her, and confronts her with her mother. Forcing Marnie's return to the memory of the night of the suppressed childhood trauma, he exposes the mother, thus curing the young woman of her obsessive attachment to the cold woman and taking the mother's place as the young woman's true savior.

In this twentieth-century treatment of ancient themes, the manly Connery character steps into Solomon's majestic shoes. Empowered by both law and psychoanalysis, in swift, clean moves, this superior man pronounces judgment on the whoring mother and motherhood at large, rescuing the child from the harmful custody of a cold mother and paving her safe passage into mature heterosexuality where she will fulfill a domestic role at the side of a powerful man. Although the mother's act of self-sacrifice seems to complicate the distinction between good and bad motherhood, it does not, in fact, undermine the clear patriarchal judgment reached and executed by the film's male protagonist and fully endorsed by the film. Good motherhood is associated with warm compassion, the law is fearsome, and the distinction between the two upholds the social order. The social issues disregarded in the biblical story are similarly disregarded in the film.[5] High Heels shares many of Marnie's plot elements, but against the background of Marnie's perpetuation of Solomonic morality, High Heels's treatment of the same issues is clearly and dramatically different.

Fact Finding, Relevance, Conflict Resolution, and the Law

In any proceeding within the Anglo-American legal world, two parties play the roles of adversaries. A judge reviews, supervises, and referees, distinguishing between relevant arguments, which are permitted to be included in the proceeding, and irrelevant ones, which are excluded. Based on the parties' relevant arguments, the judge finds the facts of the case, applies the relevant law, arrives at a judicial (and judicious) decision, and imposes it on the parties and their conflict. Parties, in this world, are adversaries; judges and their judicial resolutions are distinct from parties and their conflicts; relevant is distinguishable from irrelevant as are facts from law and law from justice.

In High Heels, none of these distinctions applies in the making of just law. The law is not addressed by two adversaries but merely confronted with a story to be thought through and worked out. The inquisitorial investigating judge does not referee. He actively searches for truth and justice. In his investigation, he does not distinguish relevant from irrelevant, fact from law, or law from justice. The facts are not determined separately from, or prior to, doing justice, nor is the law indifferent to justice. Every source of information may be legitimate, every aspect of life may be relevant, every emotion, impression, and insight are meaningful, if they serve the goal of reaching the right decision. Furthermore, the judge does not reach and impose a resolution, but empowers the parties (Rebecca and Becky) to negotiate and determine both the nature of the conflict and its just resolution.[6] The judge accepts and respects their resolution despite his suspicion and better judgment.

Such lack of clear, standard legal norms and procedures to be applied uniformly in all cases invites the obvious concern about arbitrary discrimination and personal bias. The film's reply to this concern is that its justice is not arbitrary; it is profoundly caring and compassionate. These values ensure that every person who comes before the law will receive equal, compassionate treatment. Care and compassion for the individuals before the judge and the law determine the relevance of facts, emotions, and laws alike—guaranteeing a just outcome. Such care and compassion presuppose a great deal of trust, humanity, and maturity. They are also the signature traits of motherhood.

High Heels goes a long way to position Letal as Rebecca's surrogate mother. Letal is first mentioned when Rebecca tells her mother that when longing for her, she goes to watch Letal's performance. He first appears on screen in the context of Rebecca taking Becky to see this mother image. Letal's appearance, gestures, and style are all an imitation of Becky. The voice that comes out of his lips is hers.[7] Becky looks at him as a person would at her own distant reflection. Rebecca looks at him with longing and joy that she cannot express towards her mother.[8] After the performance, Becky and Letal perform a bonding ritual in which they exchange "body parts" (Becky's earrings for Letal's fake breast), sealing their bond with this exchange.

Rebecca herself is portrayed as a woman-child. Our first and lasting impression of her, in a long flashback recounting her childhood memories, as she awaits Becky in the airport, is as a little girl: receiving earrings from her mother, degraded by her, worrying over her mother, and deserted by her. Throughout the film we see her in reference to her mother: imitating her (through her choices of a performing career and of Manuel as a partner), seeking her company (through both Manuel and Letal), helping her (by killing Becky's oppressive husband), and above all feeling abandoned, neglected, and rejected by her. The compassion, longing, hurt, and resentment Rebecca feels for her mother are so overwhelming that they leave her no room or energy for other emotions. Rebecca is completely preoccupied with her conflicting feelings for her mother. Letal, also known as Judge Dominguez, is a surrogate mother because Rebecca's need for a mother is so deep. Because she transfers her love for her mother to him, he reciprocates and loves her in turn. Because she loves him as a child, he sees and bonds with the child in her.

But things are far more complicated, since Becky, the "original" mother whom Letal imitates, is herself not a loving, caring, compassionate mother. On the contrary, busy being a sex symbol as well as a successful career woman, she is the "bad," deserting mother. Self-centered, individualistic, and irresponsible, she is far from any conception of a good mother. Further, as a sexy pop star, she is a personification of a sexual fantasy. As she herself admits, it is hard to tell whether there is anything there other than this superficial, inauthentic image. If Letal were an imitation of this mother, s/he would hardly be a good, caring one her/himself, and yet s/he is.

So, is he, the law, also the real mother? Not quite. High Heels does not offer either-or, zero-sum solutions. Through her relationship with Judge Dominguez, Becky undergoes a transformation. Outgrowing her artistic narcissism, she matures into a caring person and a loving mother. In the confrontation with Rebecca, initiated and supported by the judge for Rebecca's sake, singing for her imprisoned daughter under the judge's watchful eye, Becky takes on the responsibilities of a good mother.[9] In a sense, she imitates her double, Letal, the judge, absorbing the caring qualities s/he developed earlier while performing Becky's motherly role. It seems that when the law performs a mother's role, a bad mother can become good. When the fake mother (the judge) becomes a real one through compassion and care, the real but bad mother can grow, with the law's assistance and support, into a loving one. Thus, distinctions between real and fake or good and bad fade away, as do legal rights (of motherhood). Similarly, motherhood and femininity are not biological, essentialist traits. They are human frames of mind, transcending and undermining any simple binary opposition of the sexes.

In a central and important sense, Becky and Letal are adversaries. They compete for Rebecca's love as well as for the right to protect and save her. Ironically, they each attempt to save her from the other: Becky from the law, and Judge Dominguez from her painful, distorted existence in the shadow of her uncaring mother. On arrival in Madrid, Becky sees Letal's poster announcing that he is the "real Becky." "I thought I was the real Becky," she responds in dismay. It is when Becky arrives on the scene that Letal first consummates the sexual desire between him and Rebecca. This is one thing the real Becky cannot offer Rebecca, and he can.

It is after Rebecca has been imprisoned by the judge that Becky sings to Rebecca "Think of Me" and "My Life is Yours"; such complete support and self-sacrifice only she, not the law, can offer. In turn, Judge Dominguez releases Rebecca from prison and brings Letal back to life. This time Letal is dressed as the older Becky and, sitting at Rebecca's table, he sings the same song, promising, in a mother's voice, that his life is hers. Additionally, he reveals himself as the father of Rebecca's child, and the person through whom she will herself become a mother. In this, Rebecca's ultimate imitation and replacement of her mother, Letal is her supportive partner, not Becky.

Further still, he offers her truth, sincerity, and trust. Revealing his true identity to her, he entrusts her with his deepest secret. Not surprisingly, this is the exact moment when Becky's image appears before Rebecca (on the television screen) singing "Think of Me" and collapsing. The sick Becky becomes completely vulnerable, and is in immediate need of Rebecca's presence, care, and forgiveness. Following Letal's appearance as the father of

Rebecca's child, Becky offers Rebecca forgiveness, compassion, and the ultimate sacrifice: she accepts responsibility for Manuel's death. In so doing, she also accepts responsibility for her part in Rebecca's unhappiness. This false confession is the only thing that can really set Rebecca free, and Rebecca accepts it with gratitude. Mother and daughter conspire together, presenting the law with the version of truth and justice they have agreed upon. Then Becky dies, leaving Rebecca with the judge.

If there is indeed competition between the mothers, it is hard to determine which of the two wins her case. Unlike in Solomon's judgment, winning does not seem to be the main issue. Comparison with that story makes it clear that in High Heels, the child, far from being an object in dispute before the law, is in a significant sense the judge of both mothers.[10] The competition is not for legal rights but for the child's love, a love that can be gained only through motherly love and devotion. Further, in the course of the competition, both mothers improve in response to the needs of the child, becoming more caring and more compassionate. They also become closer to each other, less readily distinguishable. Above all, in High Heels, fierce as the competition may be, there is room for both mothers to love and be loved. (In Marnie, the Connery character seems to replace the young woman's mother.)

Confronting her mother, Rebecca discloses that all her life she has felt judged by her mother and found inadequate. Rebecca experiences motherhood as uncaring, hurtful judgment. Through the encounter with Judge Dominguez, judgment becomes motherly, and both the maternal and the judicial become caring and compassionate. In Caring for Justice, Robin West argues a reciprocity of care and justice. Just as justice depends on caring, so compassion must include justice. "The pursuit of care, if neglectful of the demands of justice, will turn out to be, in the long run, not very caring"(West 1996, 24). High Heels's coupling of motherhood and law represents this delicate balance. The film's last scene presents an image of a reverse pieta with Rebecca mourning over the body of her dying mother. In taking the mother's position, pregnant Rebecca matures into a caring mother herself.

Law as Son, Lover, Father, and Man

In addition to being Becky's double, Eduardo (Judge Dominguez) is also portrayed as his mother's son, as the deserting boyfriend of a woman named Paula (Cristina Marcos), and as the father of Rebecca's unborn child. The law is thus not exclusively maternal; neither is compassion.

Judge Dominguez lives with his mother, a narcissistic hypochondriac who has not left her bed in ten years. Investing all her emotional energy in her collection of newspaper clippings of other people's (celebrities') lives, the judge's mother deserted him many years earlier, leaving him a vulnerable child. Like Rebecca, Judge Dominguez is loyal to and protective of his neglectful mother, as well as hurt and angry. Through his relationship with his own mother he understands Rebecca's pain, as well as Becky's. Significantly, an old newspaper clipping that his mother supplies him with, showing Becky with Manuel, informs him of the relationship between these two. This gives him insight into Rebecca's relationship with Manuel and leads him to suspect Becky of Manuel's murder. It is as his mother's son, then, that he learns to see deeper into the relationships he investigates. It is through his reading of Becky against his own mother that he sees deeper into her character, and through his identification with Rebecca as a hurt child that he understands her.

In another subplot, Rebecca (and the viewer) meet Paula, a warm-hearted woman in search of her disappearing boyfriend. Adding up the clues, Rebecca realizes that Paula's vanishing boyfriend is no other than Letal/the judge. He then admits this and explains that while investigating a case, he secretly went undercover as a drug addict. It was under this (false?) identity that Paula fell in love with him and tried to rehabilitate him. When his investigation concluded, he simply disappeared.

In this incident, the judge treated Paula as an object, using and degrading her. This aspect of his personality, this experience in his past, makes him guilty of dehumanizing a fellow human being and abusing a woman. This, too, is a part of the law. This aspect of Judge Dominguez's character associates him with Manuel, whose death he investigates. After their single encounter at the drag performance, Letal refers to Manuel as a "monster." This personal, emotional stance conveys his feelings not merely as Rebecca's lover, but also as a man who recognizes Manuel's inhumanity. In High Heels, the judge's very personal antipathy to the victim of murder is no reason to disqualify him from sitting in judgment. On the contrary, it contributes to his ability to reach a just legal decision.

As Rebecca's lover and an expectant father, Judge Dominguez is deeply concerned for Rebecca's well-being. This personal concern blinds him to certain aspects of the situation, rendering him incapable of seeing Rebecca's guilt. Like the judge's other personal biases, this loving blindness, too, is portrayed as legitimate and helpful in the pursuit of justice. All these complex, personal elements of his human experience are inseparable from Judge Dominguez's role as judge, from his professional investigation, and from his truth and justice. His insights, intuition, and emotional responses to characters and situations are relevant professional tools and sources of information. They assist him in collecting data, assessing it, and arriving at conclusions. Most importantly, in High Heels, the data he collects and the conclusions he reaches based on his personal experience are true, right, and just precisely *because* they rely on his personal experience as mother, son, man, and father-to-be. Subjective experience and personal involvement are essential judicial tools in High Heels. So much so that Judge Dominguez does not limit himself to his own personal experiences, but impersonates other characters to accumulate more human experiences. Equality before the law means that each individual deserves to be seen, understood, and treated for who s/he is. The notion that a just legal decision must be reached through objective, impartial, analytic reasoning is subverted. The traditional image of the blindfolded goddess of justice is replaced by that of Judge Dominguez.

Compassionate Cinematic Judgment

Enacting a cinematic inquisitorial pretrial process parallel to the fictional legal one presented on-screen, High Heels supports its fictional legal system, illustrating how investigation and judging (of women, of a woman accused of killing a man, and of a mother) can be conducted with compassion and care. Through its cinematic judging process, High Heels constitutes its viewer as a compassionate judge who, together with the fictional judge on-screen, investigates, determines relevant facts, and reaches a just legal decision: not to prosecute Rebecca. Like the fictional judge, the viewer judges two women through shifting personae and points of view, through identification with the involved parties, and through caring for them. Like the judge, the compassionate judging viewer cannot find the women guilty, despite the obvious facts that they did commit the crimes ascribed to them (killing a man and being a selfish, neglectful mother).

In her essay on equity and mercy, Martha Nussbaum suggests: "The novel's structure is a structure of *suggnome* [judging with forgiveness]—of the penetration of the life of another into one's own imagination and heart. It is a form of imaginative and emotional receptivity, in which the reader, following the author's lead, comes to be inhabited by the tangled complexities and struggles of other concrete lives" (1999, 170). This description of narrative fiction can be extended to dramatic fiction, and well describes the film *High Heels* (as well as Almodovar's *All About my Mother* [1999]). Above all, *High Heels* invites its viewer to practice "participatory identification" with Rebecca. It does so in several connected ways: by giving Rebecca a point of view, by closely aligning the viewer's point of view with hers, by positioning her as the most dominant, sympathetic on-screen character, by continuously presenting the child within her, and by looking at her through the eyes of the two mothers who love her and seek her love in return. The viewer's carefully orchestrated sympathetic identification with her mediates and shapes the process of judging.

The viewer's association with Rebecca's point of view, however, is not complete. The viewer does not know whether or not Rebecca shot Manuel until she reveals the truth to her mother on Becky's deathbed. Here, as in the confession of Rebecca's first killing, it is Becky's point of view that the viewer shares. In other words, the viewer learns of Rebecca's crime while identifying with her mother, who has finally taken on the loving role of a good mother. When she tells Becky of the events that led to the killing, Rebecca narrates Manuel's cruel indifference and her own pain and humiliation. Becky, identifying with her daughter, sighs, "Men," supporting Rebecca's characterization of Manuel as unfeeling and uncaring while offering a generic verdict of her own. Learning of the killing in this context, the viewer is influenced by the dying, remorseful mother's attitude. The viewer joins her in the impulse to protect Rebecca, save her, and compensate for the emotional abuse she has suffered all her life. This, of course, influences the viewer as Rebecca's judge, inviting the viewer to enact its alternative vision of justice.

Further still, the film has Rebecca testify five times, offering a different version of Manuel's death each time. Interestingly, the testimonies, some of which are confessions to the crime, do not build tension nor do they lead to a dramatic revelation of the "real" truth. On the contrary, they lull the viewer into nonjudgmental indifference to the actual details. As all accounts seem plausible and sincere, the quest for real truth and real guilt loses its edge.

On her deathbed, Becky reassures Rebecca that Rebecca is not the only culpable party. In this, Becky clearly voices the film's stand that Rebecca is not the only character scrutinized and examined. Becky herself is, throughout the film, far more judged than her daughter. She is accused of being self-centered, of neglecting and deserting her daughter, and of not caring enough. Eduardo is similarly accused of abusing Paula and disregarding her feelings. But as with Rebecca, here, too, the film invites the viewer to see the hurt child inside each of these characters, to accept their sincere remorse and to see them in reference to Rebecca's forgiving love and vulnerability. In this, the film chooses the least judgmental and most compassionate perspective in presenting them to the viewer. Doing justice with these characters includes caring for them, seeing them for who they are, and understanding them through their life experiences and vulnerabilities. It is on this point that *High Heels* differs most significantly from both *Autumn Sonata* and *Marnie*. Read against the earlier films' judgment of their mother characters, *High Heels*'s compassionate generosity is fully apparent.

Manuel is the only character not allowed a childhood, a point of view, or remorse. Manuel remains a selfish, uncaring man who objectifies women and causes them pain. Not surprisingly, his death arouses little sadness in the viewer; it does not invoke a need to see "justice done" by punishing Rebecca.

In its own nonjudgmental attitude, in constructing its viewer as a compassionate judge of Rebecca, Becky, and Eduardo/Letal/Judge Dominguez, *High Heels* supports its fictional judge. In demonstrating how cinematic judgment can be caring, compassionate, and nonjudgmental, it offers a vision of a caring and compassionate legal system, a legal system free of honor-based notions, fully respecting all parties and their human dignity.

Conclusion: But Is It Really Feminism?

The film's advocacy in support of a justice of care can be read as promoting a feminine worldview—or as essentializing femininity while supplementing women with men. I suggest that the film's advocacy of a justice of care should be read together with two other elements. First, the caring judge, Dominguez, is a man who chooses to take on a feminine identity *in addition* to his own. Care is thus portrayed as neither biologically female nor appropriated by men. It is, rather, a human trait, socially associated with women, that can and should be acquired by men—particularly those in positions of power who wish to improve themselves as well as the public functions they fulfill. This combination of justice of care with transsexuality is highly subversive and feminist.[11]

Second, the justice of care and compassion is practiced in *High Heels* on a woman accused of killing a man. In our patriarchal culture judges sometimes feel compassion for men who abuse women.[12] It is harder to find sympathy for women who kill men—especially if the killing woman were not raped and battered in an outrageous way immediately prior to the killing. Applying a justice of care to Rebecca is thus a subversive move that can be seen as feminist. Making this move, *High Heels* follows in the footsteps of feminist texts, such as "A Jury of Her Peers" and *A Question of Silence*.

Interestingly, the film's feminist themes do not point towards a unique feminine culture, but rather portray the reality of patriarchal oppression and its tragic outcomes. Both Becky and Rebecca are oppressed by the men in their lives (Rebecca's stepfather and her husband) and molded by the men's desires and expectations of them. If Becky spends her life impersonating a sex fantasy, it is because men expect it of her and her livelihood depends on it.[13] If Rebecca is driven to commit murder (twice) it is because men objectify women, exchanging one for another, undermining human dignity. Becky and Rebecca do come to form a kind of feminine community, as do the women prisoners, but this community hardly speaks a language of its own—it has yet to liberate itself, discover its identity, and speak in its true voice.

In other words, Almodovar's film does not present an ethics-of-care feminist vision so much as one that rejects and deconstructs patriarchal oppression and dominance. It is a feminism that understands a woman's need to kill men who abuse her. Violent feminine resistance is acknowledged and condoned. Nevertheless, as this chapter has shown, this same film constructs elaborate images of compassionate law and the justice of care, thus escaping, transcending, and combining distinct categories of feminist theory. *High Heels* combines rage at, and violent response to, women's oppression with a human search for compassion—acknowledging social constraints, yet subverting them in pursuit of love and joy. Generously, the film portrays the law as a major character in pursuit of this vision. Its unique, vital contribution lies in the fact that "seeing is believing," as well as in the film's ability to spread its viewpoint among millions of viewers worldwide.

Perhaps because it does not restrict itself to feminist analysis of dominance and oppression, *High Heels* can offer a hopeful ending, away from the depth of the Grand Canyon. Perhaps because it does not conform to feminist notions of ethics of care, it escapes the traps of essentialism and trivialism. Compassion and care, although portrayed as maternal, are not portrayed as feminine in a confining, repressive sense. Human beings, men and women alike, can, do, and are encouraged to find the maternal within them, and to combine it with their pursuit of justice. They are invited to apply this justice of care to women who kill in distress. They are invited to transcend rigid distinctions between femininity and masculinity and liberate themselves from the constraints of patriarchy. Maternity in *High Heels* is not a biological trait; it is a human resource, feminine yet universal, essential for the operation of law and justice.

The image of Letal/Judge Dominguez, the caring mother-judge is, of course, a fantastic one. But so is the image of King Solomon with his sword of justice. I suggest that in the process of expanding the legal imagination and the imagery of law and justice, the colorful, postmodern image of the caring judge should take its place in a pantheon of images of justice and law.

Notes

Preface

1 For collections of law-and-film essays see Denvir 1996; "Symposium: Picturing Justice" 1996; "A Symposium on Film and the Law" 1997; "Symposia: Law and Popular Culture" 1998; "Symposium: Law and Popular Culture" 2001; and Machura and Robson 2001. For monographs see Black 1999; Sherwin 2000; Kamir 2001; Greenfield, Osborn, and Robson 2001; and Chase 2002. Anthony Chase, Peter Robson, Richard Sherwin, Rebecca Johnson, Austin Sarat, Susan Silbey, and William MacNeil have each published numerous particularly noteworthy articles. For a presentation of the discipline of law and film see my article "Why Law and Film, and What Does it Actually Mean?: A Perspective" *Continuum*, February 2005.

2 For a contemporary collection of essays on the topic, and an exhaustive bibliography, see Cartmell and Whelehan 1999.

3 To be exact, the texts I have been teaching in my feminist law-and-film class, titled "Law and Film: Women as Victims and Villains," are *Rashomon*, *Pandora's Box*, *Blackmail*, *Anatomy of a Murder*, "A Jury of Her Peers," *Adam's Rib*, *Thelma and Louise*, *A Question of Silence*, *Set It Off*, *The Piano*, and *High Heels*. Two other law-and-film classes I taught relied on other films but were as exciting and pleasurable to the students.

Introduction

1 I first introduced this presentation of honor and dignity cultures in "Honor and Dignity Cultures: The Case of *Kavod* (Honor) and *Kvod ha-adam* (Dignity) in Israeli Society and Law," 2002. Several of my recent publications develop this theme. See in particular Kamir 2004b and forthcoming.

2 See, for example, Herzfeld 1980. The literature on honor cultures, mostly anthropological, is too voluminous to survey here. Much of the literature I rely on is cited in W. Miller 1993. For some of the most classic writing see Peristiany 1966 and Pitt-Rivers 1977.

3 The discussion of dignity manifests much ambiguity in crucial points: Is dignity inherent and equal in all persons under all circumstances? Does a person's moral behavior influence his or her dignity? Is a person's dignity dependent on social recognition? Can a person be deprived of human dignity, and if so how? (Gewirth 1992, Fletcher 1984). I do not address these ambiguities here.

4 Peter Berger and Charles Taylor each pursued Bourdieu's line of comparison between honor and dignity. Berger suggests that an honor culture reduces a person to his or her social roles, whereas a culture based on human dignity highlights the intrinsic self. Based on this distinction, he defines honor cultures as premodern, and cultures based on human dignity as modern ones (1983, 177). Taylor similarly perceives cultures based on human dignity as more modern in spirit than honor cultures. He argues: "With the move from honor to dignity has come a politics of universalism, emphasizing the equal dignity of all citizens and the content of this politics has been equalization of rights and entitlements" (1994, 37). On the whole, I accept much of their analysis.

5 For a full, methodical development and presentation of this argument (not in the context of honor), see Coughlin 1998.

6 I pursue this issue in great detail elsewhere, in a Hebrew publication analyzing existing rape law and suggesting a new, dignity-based conceptualization of both rape and consensual intercourse (Kamir 2004a). Based on the principles put forth in this article, a draft law has been prepared and placed on the table of the Israeli House of Representatives, pending further consideration.

7 This section refers more accurately to chapters 6 and 7. The film discussed in chapter 5, *Adam's Rib*, shares many of the features described here, but also some of those attributed to the films discussed in part 1. Unlike the other films in this part, *Adam's Rib* does not fully reject honor-based values in favor of dignity-based ones, does not fully succeed in expressing coherent feminist perspectives, and does engage in some amount of judgment of its woman protagonist.

1. Rashomon

1 Analyzing the film's reviews is a fascinating project yet to be undertaken. One telling comment is George Barbarow's observation that "the bandit's narration [is] the longest because it includes the encounter along the forest road" (1987, 145). Interestingly, Barbarow did not notice that Tajomaru's is also the only narration that includes the sexual encounter.

2 "A man commits rape when he engages in intercourse (in the old statutes 'carnal knowledge') with a woman not his wife; by force or threat of force; against her will and without her consent. That is the traditional, common law definition of rape, and it remains the essence of even the most radical reform statutes" (Estrich 1987, 8). Similarly, Japan's penal code (Law No. 45, 24 April 1907), defines (in article 177) that "a person who by violence or threat, obtains carnal knowledge of a female person . . . shall be guilty of rape." Additionally (according to article 178), "a person who, by taking advantage of loss of reason or incapacity to resist . . . obtains carnal knowledge of a woman" is similarly punished as if he committed rape.

3 Much has been written about the bias that the influential myth of woman's deceitful sexuality generates within the legal system and the public discourse surrounding it, and its harmful consequences in the treatment of women who suffer sexual offenses. For some fundamental works, see, e.g., H. Benedict 1992; Brownmiller 1975; Estrich 1987; and MacKinnon 1987.

4 Yukiko Tsunoda argues that these traditional patriarchal values continue to underlie Japanese society and culture, as well as its law. She argues that Japan's criminal prohibition on rape was historically intended to protect woman's chastity, that is, to punish the man who robbed the woman's husband's property and honor. Similarly, the criminal prohibition on adultery was designed to protect woman's chastity by punishing consensual illicit intercourse. Tsunoda claims that these notions continue to dominate social and legal attitudes, and that judicial attitudes reflect them openly and explicitly (private conversation).

5 Carmody offers an example of model feminine behavior: "Compromised by a powerful noble, one Lady Kesa promised to submit to his advances if he killed her samurai husband. He agreed, and she told him to steal into her bedchamber and kill the sleeper who had wet hair. Then she made sure that her husband drank enough to sleep soundly, washed her hair, and lay calmly awaiting her death" (1989, 118).

6 In David Medine's article on the legal aspects of this film, he states that "we simply do not know who should be convicted for the woman's rape and the man's death" (1992, 59). I can think of only one explanation for this opaque sentence: The sentence originally referred to the death alone and, as a last-minute

gesture, the author added the reference to the rape. Indeed, the film clearly invites this forgetfulness.

7 To better understand the specific cultural context, it is interesting to note that in early periods of Japan's history, women performed central religious and ritualistic functions. In the Middle Ages they were stripped of all such roles. Nevertheless, "rural Japan has never lost the presence and impact of shamanesses. Working with a blend of folk beliefs, Shinto and Buddhism, these women have continued to function as mediums and diviners . . . Traditionally, the shamanesses tended to travel in bands of five or six, walking a regular rounds of villages. They would tell fortunes, pray for the sick, contact the dead . . . The bands no longer travel, in part because the authorities, who always resented them, and often defamed them as prostitutes, finally tended to prevail" (Carmody 1989, 119). In *Rashomon*, the medium, a debased female priestess suspected of illicit sexual behavior, is reduced to serving the patriarchal authorities and a husband who accuses his wife.

2. *Pandora's Box*

1 In Wedekind's play, *Earth Spirit*, Lulu shoots Schoen five times in the back, in a wordy, melodramatic scene (1972, 98).

2 The courtroom scenes are the film's addition. Wedekind's first Lulu play, *Earth Spirit*, ends with Schoen's killing and Lulu's arrest; the second, *Pandora's Box*, opens with the countess's plot to smuggle Lulu out of prison.

3 Five years was the minimum incarceration prescribed for manslaughter (whereas the death sentence was the obligatory penalty for murder).

4 In Wedekind's text, Lulu serves her sentence in prison, and is rescued from jail by the self-sacrificing countess.

5 The Christmas theme and the Salvation Army are the film's innovations.

6 For extensive discussion see Kamir 2001, chapters 2 and 3.

7 The image of Medusa, the snake-coiffed Gorgon whose hideous gaze turned men to stone, is adorned with menacing teeth, a protruding tongue, and fangs. Hesiod's version of her story states that Medusa had been a beautiful young maiden who was seduced (i.e., raped) by Poseidon in Athena's shrine. As punishment, Athena transformed Medusa's hair into snakes and gave her look its fatal effect. With Athena's help, Perseus decapitated Medusa as she slept, using a mirror to avoid looking directly at her face. The severed head was then placed in the center of Athena's shield, where Medusa's staring eyes maintained their deadly power, now in the service of the Olympian goddess (Tripp 1974, 364).

8 Wedekind claimed that the tragedy of this "human being burdened with the curse of abnormality" was the central dramatic theme of the Lulu plays (1972, 104).

9 In Wedekind's play, *Earth Spirit*, Lulu was associated with Lilith not merely through

her name, but also through the image of the snake. In Jewish kabbalah, Lilith was referred to as "the snake." In the prologue to *Earth Spirit*, an actor playing the part of an animal tamer, armed with a whip and a gun, places the actress playing Lulu's character in front of him and, presenting her to the audience as a snake, he announces: "She was created for every abuse, To allure and to poison and seduce, To murder without leaving a trace . . . Sweet innocence. My treasure all of grace!" (1972, 10–11).

10 In Wedekind's play, *Earth Spirit*, having deliberately shot Schoen to death, Lulu grieves: "The only man I ever loved!" (98). In the film she loves no one and says nothing.

11 The allusion to fire offers a subtle link between Lulu and Pandora, implying their corresponding tragic passivity. Pandora was sent by the gods in revenge for men's appropriation of the gods' sacred fire. Similarly, Lulu was smuggled out of the courthouse in the guise of the public panic that ensued when her friends cried, "Fire." She was later killed when the candle's flame caught Jack the Ripper's eyes, causing him to lose self-control.

12 This is a mirror image of the portrayal of woman in *Rashomon*: There, the woman's guilt is related to her attempt to step out of her role as obedient wife, a role that requires her to kill herself in protection of her husband's honor.

13 Although I use concepts relevant to Anglo-American criminal law, the German legal system at the time consisted of analogous notions. Most importantly, self-defense was viewed as a full defense against criminal culpability. The defense allowed a person to fight any unlawful, aggressive act against himself or another person, and was wide enough to encompass a situation in which the person defending himself, out of fear or terror, overstepped the boundaries of defense.

14 In Wedekind's play, *Earth Spirit*, as Schoen demands that Lulu shoot herself, she says: "You may have sacrificed the evening of your life to me, but you've had my whole youth in exchange" (97). We also learn that, over the years, Schoen prostituted her to other men. In the play *Pandora's Box*, referring to his first encounter with Lulu, Schigolch says: "That's right, have a good cry, a really good cry. It took you like this once before, fifteen years ago. No one has ever screamed sin the way you managed to scream then. In those days . . . you had neither boots nor stockings on your legs" (144).

3. Blackmail

1 For a fascinating, detailed discussion of the production of the film's talking version, comparing it with the film's silent version, see C. Barr 1999. For an earlier discussion of this point, see Spoto 1992.

2 Compare with Claudia's dream in *Nuts*, discussed in chapter 6. Dreaming of the

attempted rape that led her to kill her assailant, Claudia envisions only her victimization, not her "guilty," fatal action.

3 For an Anglo-American history of self-defense, and feminist critique, see Donovan and Wildman 1981.

4 This is so because most treatises refer to published cases, and there are almost no such relevant cases.

5 *State of Missouri v. Robert James Thorton*, App., 532 S.W. 2d 37 (1975); *State of Nebraska v. Mark Schroeder*, 261 N.W. 2d 759, 199 Neb. 822 (1978); *State of Main v. Leland B. Philbrick*, 481 A. 2d 488 (1984). Similarly, provocation arguments (reducing murder charges to manslaughter) are made—and accepted—when the defendant kills a man who attempted to sodomize him. See Lee 2003, 67. Given the same-sex character of these situations, which is perceived as significantly different from that of heterosexual sexual relationships, it is not possible to deduce from these cases women's right to defend themselves against rape.

6 Durgnat, who dedicates much of his discussion to the question of Alice's guilt, states, "I wouldn't think it abnormal of a woman to threaten to stick a knife into a man who tried to rape her, and then do it" (1974, 87). He claims that according to other critics, Chabrol and Rohmer, "a girl's virtue isn't worth a man's death" (ibid.).

7 For further discussion of *Marnie*, together with *High Heels*, see chapter 10. Other Hitchcock guilty-woman films that do not feature obvious elements of cinematic judgment (films such as *The Man Who Knew Too Much*, *Rebecca*, *Notorious*, *Strangers on a Train*) can be read as echoing the essence of its sociolegal logic of condemnation.

4. Anatomy of a Murder

1 Abby McFarland-Richardson publicly accused her husband, McFarland, of continuous abuse, and it seems clear that Evelyn Nesbit Thaw suffered some abuse at the hands of her husband (who shot her seducer, Stanford White). "Similarly there is evidence that 'Little Phil' Thompson, Edward Johnson and George Cole verbally abused their spouses before they 'fell' to the seductive allure of libertines" (Ireland 1989, 35).

5. Adam's Rib

1 See Sheffield 1993, 73, 92–93; Shapiro 1995, 955, 962–63; Tushnet 1996, 244, 247–49; Bailey, Pollock, and Schroeder 1999, 180, 189; and Caplow 1999, 55, 62–63. Representing a unanimous feeling among these writers, Shapiro summarizes that "as a film portraying women lawyers, [*Adam's Rib*] has still not, more than 40 years later, been surpassed" (963 n. 36). Graham and Maschio (1995–96) stand

out in arguing that "the movie . . . is not only ambiguous in its attitude toward equality for women, but it paints an ambiguous image of the lead character, Amanda Bonner, as a woman lawyer" (1034).

2 To this day, common-law systems condone, to varying degrees, the "provocation" that infuriates a man, catching his wife in an act of adultery, and leads him to kill her. Such provocation is recognized, in most jurisdictions, as a "partial defense," mitigating charges of murder to manslaughter. Unlike the unwritten law, this partial defense is an excuse, not a justification, and it does not exonerate the defendant but mitigates his crime and sentence (Horder 1992).

3 Robert Ireland reports a case of a woman who killed her husband's mistress in 1877. She was found guilty of murder and sentenced to hang. "A national campaign of protest that highlighted the inconsistencies of the unwritten law that forgave wayward husbands but punished faithful wives eventually prompted Georgia's governor to commute Kate's sentence to ten years, only a partial redress of the inequity" (1989, 34). Martha Umphrey argues that "though killings by women may be understood as 'crimes of passion,' the unwritten law is . . . a specifically male (and perhaps American) variant of the more general category" (forthcoming).

4 The same is true of the partial defense of "provocation," which is still used by husbands who kill their adulterous wives. Referring to this "partial defense," Horder suggests that "from a feminist perspective the existence of such mitigation simply reinforces in the law that which public institutions ought in fact to be seeking to eradicate, namely, the acceptance that there is something natural, inevitable, and hence in some (legal) sense to-be-recognized forgivable about men's violence against women, and their violence in general" (1992, 194).

5 In *Love Among the Ruins* (1974), the next courtroom drama she participated in, she is reduced to the character of an aging vain lady sued by a young lover for breach of marriage agreement.

6 *Woman of the Year* (1942); *Keeper of the Flame* (1942); *The Sea of Grass* (1947); *State of the Union* (1948); *Adam's Rib* (1949); *Pat and Mike* (1952); *Desk Set* (1957); *Guess Who's Coming To Dinner?* (1967).

7 On this point, it is interesting to compare *Legally Blonde* with *Anatomy of a Murder*. Elle, Brook, and the manicurist are each a version of *Anatomy*'s bimbo-blonde. But in *Blonde*, Elle takes Jimmy Stewart's place as the hero-lawyer, Brook, though highly sexual, is independently wealthy and independent, and the manicurist is a moral, motherly, good woman. Unlike *Anatomy*'s Laura, these women are no longer guilty.

6. Nuts

1 For mixed reviews see, for example, Brode 1987; Benson 1987; Siskel 1987; and Lyons 1988.

2 In an interview, Streisand expresses a similar view: " 'It's a strange phenomenon that our society is not ready for a Renaissance woman. It is only ready for a Renaissance man,' she says, referring to the fact that the critics become particularly acerbic every time Streisand takes on more than one role—such as when she produces and directs the movies in which she also acts. 'Society still wants to keep women in their place. It's too threatening somehow to most people, women as well as men' " (Cullen 1988). Eight years later, she admits, "I used to be embarrassed and defensive about it . . . Now I say 'What, are you kidding? Of course I want utter and complete control over everything I do!' And the audience buys my products because I do control it, because I am a perfectionist, because I care deeply. I think it's a sexist attitude, definitely" (Stoynoff 1996).

3 This whole scene, as well as the characterization of Levinsky and his relationship with Claudia, are uniquely cinematic, and do not originate in Topor's play. The play begins at the competency hearing itself when Levinsky, a pricey, private lawyer, represents Claudia as he sees fit. Claudia, a law student, offers her input, but does not control the proceedings, and remains silent much of the time.

4 The flashbacks constituting Claudia's memories, and the whole theme of attempted rape and murder, are cinematic and do not originate in the play version.

5 In the play version, Claudia willingly discloses her stepfather's childhood molestation to her lawyer, and Levinsky relies on her testimony when cross-examining Kirk on this point.

6 The mother's drunken corroboration does not exist in the play version.

7 In its flashback support of Claudia and refusal to leave open the option that she may be lying or falsely remembering, the film takes the exact opposite stand to that discussed in the reading of *Rashomon*. For a further discussion of this point see chapter 7.

8 As in *Anatomy*, Levinsky's western-hero persona is clearly the film's making: none of the features discussed here appear in Topor's play. See chapter 4.

9 Clint Eastwood's 1994 *Unforgiven* positions the western hero in a very similar and just as awkward situation. Despite Eastwood's multiple roles as producer, director, and star performer, the film was met with (deserved) tremendous box office and critical success. (For feminist readings of the film see Johnson and Buchanan 2005 and Kamir forthcoming).

10 Jeffrey Lyons (1988) rightly remarks that "although they have never worked together before, Streisand and Dreyfuss establish the kind of instant communication few actors can create. Her acting rhythms really coincide with his; her defiance meshes perfectly with his grim determination to get through to this iron-willed, deeply troubled woman."

11 In *Adam's Rib*, Amanda's egalitarian worldview undermines and ridicules Doris's

old-fashioned one. The film's sensible liberal stand undermines Amanda's liberal feminist one.

12 For further development of this theme see discussion of *High Heels* in chapter 10.

7. Death and the Maiden

1 For Claudius's lyrics and a presentation of the "Death and the Maiden" theme—and its deep misogyny—in German art, see Luban 1998, 123–30. For discussion of the theme in Schubert's music and in contemporary art, see Wolff 1993.

2 For a different reading, which deliberately does not distinguish between play and film and treats them as a combined narrative, see Luban 1998.

3 The film implies that the South American country could be Chile, Dorfman's homeland. For discussion of Chile's history of human-rights violations, transformation from dictatorship to democracy, and truth and reconciliation commission, see Ensalaco 1999 and Roninger and Azanjder 1999.

4 The doctor joins them on the pretext of assisting Gerardo with a flat tire, presenting himself as a good Samaritan.

5 Gerardo's line of thought is taken to its logical end in Mark Osiel's (1997) extensive sociological-legal study on mass atrocity, collective memory, and the law.

6 Professional literature reveals that Paulina's response is typical of trauma victims and makes perfect survival sense in the context (Herman 1992, 42).

7 "Robert Jay Lifton found 'survivor guilt' to be a common experience in people who had lived through war, natural disaster, or nuclear holocaust. Rape produces essentially the same effect: it is the victims, not the perpetrators, who feel guilty" (Herman 1992, 53).

8 "Shame is a response to helplessness, the violation of bodily integrity, and the indignity suffered in the eyes of another person" (Herman 1992, 53).

9 Catharine MacKinnon perfectly captured the essence of the connection between rape and genocide-rape in a succinct formulation: "The rapes in the Serbian war of aggression against Bosnia-Herzegovina and Croatia are to everyday rape what the Holocaust was to everyday anti-Semitism: both like it and not like it at all, both continuous with it and a whole new departure, a unique atrocity yet also a pinnacle moment in something that goes on all the time" (2000, 74). See also Card 1996.

10 Two of the film's many painful moments are that in which Paulina says to Gerardo, who wants to hold her as she narrates her rape: "I love you; I don't trust you," and that in which she admits to having given him a false detail about her torture, in expectation that he would betray her and provide Roberto with the details of her intimate confession. Paulina is, of course, correct in her antici-

pation. (This episode turns out to be one of the film's dramatic moments. Roberto's deviance from the information provided him by Gerardo, which turns out to have been false, indicates that his acquaintance with the details of Paulina's torture does not rely merely on Gerardo's tips. Paulina's trick tips the scale in her favor.)

11 Many male viewers surely identify with the familiar complaint Gerardo later refers to his wife: "I am always in the wrong, and I am sick of it."

12 Signourney Weaver's Paulina is chillingly violent and almost savage, provoking the viewer's great unease, and even repulsion. Paulina's crude savagery is unique to the film. The play's character is more delicate and fragile, and hardly the vicious Amazon Polanski's Weaver presents. As Gordana Crnkovic rightly puts it, Polanski's Paulina is "much 'uglier' and less feminine (or not feminine at all) than in Dorfman's play" (1997, 43). Paulina's character and conduct have been criticized as "provocative": "It's clear that the director has confused sexual assault with sex, the only possible explanation for Paulina's provocative behavior" (Monahan 1995, 18). I believe my discussion makes it clear that I disagree with this reading.

13 A dramatic moment occurs when Paulina relates to Gerardo that she remembers her rapist's habit of quoting Nietzsche. "At least I think it was Nietzsche," she says, and imitates a man's voice and intonation. In this scene Roberto is not present. But in an earlier scene, in which Roberto and Gerardo were alone, Roberto did, indeed, refer to Nietzsche in exactly the manner imitated by Paulina. The viewer recognizes with Gerardo the damning phrase, realizing, together with Gerardo, that this may be a significant clue, processing it, and hesitating over what to make of it. This brief realization bonds the viewer with Gerardo through a common point of view.

14 This, of course, is a result of gender expectations. Dirty Harry's crudeness and aggression would never compromise his heroic position. In Paulina's case it threatens to render her repulsive, "unfeminine," and "crazy."

15 Aurea Maria Sotomayor asserts that Paulina is doomed to eternal victimhood, as there is no liberation from victimization and "there are no ex victims" (1997, 29).

16 Polanski's choice to tighten, or "close," the play's open ending was conscious and deliberate. In an interview he states: "In the play, he's definitely guilty, I think. It gives an answer, but then somehow it doesn't manage to give an answer. It's ambiguous, and it seems to me to a certain extent to be a cop-out. But I think we managed to make it more satisfying" (Thompson 1995, 8).

17 "When Polanski discusses the violence that occurs in his films, he often asserts that, far from being a sensationalist, he is a pure realist" (Weschler 1994, 91). "The membrane between victim and victimizer is unusually porous throughout Polanski's films, as it has been throughout his life" (95).

18 All his life, "he saw everything in front of him and nothing behind him, his eyes

firmly fixed on a future he already seemed to be hurtling toward, at maximum speed . . . Roman was hurtling forward like a rocket, but it wasn't so much toward the future as away from the past" (Weschler 1994, 93).

19 "All Polanski films . . . have been about the war and, in particular, about the simultaneous combination of claustrophobia and agoraphobia that characterized the ghetto experience" (Weschler 1994, 94).

20 Dr. Laub claims that survivors who do not look back to know and grieve for their victimization and loss doom themselves to relive it repeatedly through tragic life occurrences that constitute their "second holocaust." "Through its uncanny reoccurrence, the trauma of the second holocaust bears witness not just to a history that has not ended, but, specifically, to the historical occurrence of an event that, in effect, *does not end*" (Felman and Laub 1992, 67).

21 Editing choices have been discussed throughout the chapter. The film's casting has received much praise. See James 1995, 40; Dowell 1995, 26; Crnkovic 1997, 41, 44; Weschler 1994, 90.

8. A Question of Silence

1 Compare with Alice White's realization at the end of Blackmail, that being married to Frank, the law, she will forever be silenced, isolated, blackmailed, and controlled by patriarchy. See discussion in chapter 3.

2 Compare with Adam's Rib's opening scene, discussed in chapter 5.

3 Further, Silence can be read as commenting on women's archetypal images and offering alternative explanations for them. Christine, the "good Eve," the perfect mother, is, the film shows, an abused, catatonic housewife. Andrea, "Lilith," tempting men and having her way with them, is a frustrated, talented woman, discriminated against in the workplace.

4 For discussion of the differences between the texts see L. Williams 1994, 436–39.

5 In Nuts, too, Claudia moves from being silenced (by her stepfather who puts his hand on her mouth), to self-silencing, to subversive laughter at the psychiatric and legal systems, to a happy smile on the streets of New York. But Claudia remains without a feminine community, as does Paulina in Death and the Maiden, who similarly experiences silencing, self-silencing, and laughter. In the film's last scene, seated by Gerardo in the concert hall, Paulina does not even smile.

6 Silence can be read as containing five parts. The first part introduces four women, featuring fragments of their lives immediately prior to and during the arrests and concluding with the three accused women signing a confession. The second part combines scenes of the accused women's routine lives before the killing with scenes of Janine's meetings with them in prison, and with episodes in Janine's life during her investigation: listening to the tapes at home, meeting Christine's husband, Andrea's boss, the pathologist. In this part, both Janine and the viewer

struggle with the tormenting questions: Who are these women? Are they crazy? Why did they commit the horrifying crime? How should one think of this? It concludes with Janine's realization and determination that the accused women are completely sane, normal, and ordinary. The third part of the film then features the killing itself, and moments in the killers' lives immediately following it. The fourth part features Janine's transformation and her process of opening up to the women, connecting with them, letting them touch her life and touching theirs. Through a series of scenes portraying Janine's meetings with the women and her nightmarish preoccupation with them at home, this part shows Janine getting personally involved, overcoming her professional distance, expressing human, feminine feelings of compassion and care. The fifth and final part contains the courtroom scene, where Janine sides with the women, speaks up for them within the legal process using professional rhetoric, and is promptly belittled, undermined, and expelled from the legal world. Leaving the courthouse, she looks away from her husband and smiles at the small group of silent, determined women.

7 This is very close to Amanda's line of reasoning in *Adam's Rib*.

8 In conversation with her lawyer spouse, Janine indeed tries to compare the killing to war atrocities.

10. *High Heels*

1 For a presentation of the female friendship film, see Hollinger 1998.

2 The cupped hands represent the judge's personal integrity, which is at stake when he sits in judgment. West quotes Robert Bolt's Thomas More explaining that "when a man takes an oath . . . he's holding his own self in his own hands. Like water. And if he opens his fingers then—he needn't hope to find himself again" (West 1997, 26).

3 Unlike *High Heels*, *Talk to Her* (2003), Almodovar's most acclaimed film to date, expresses a deeply disturbing, objectifying, and disrespectful attitude to women, featuring unbelievable feminine characters and nonjudgmental acceptance of rape and its perpetrator (such acceptance of rape is already apparent in earlier films, including *Kika* and *High Heels*).

4 The sex scene is highly confusing, and I hesitated to define it. It begins with Letal forcefully imposing himself on Rebecca, who asks him to let her go. This, of course, looks very much like rape. Yet, in typical Almodovar style, the scene hardly feels like rape, ending not merely with Rebecca's pleasure, but with her expression of gratitude and statement that she needed the encounter. Additionally, as Kinder notes, the sexual encounter "is simultaneously very erotic and hysterically funny, a combination that is very difficult to achieve but that Almodovar consistently masters" (1995, 152). This scene may, of course, be viewed as

the representation of rape as adultery. In the context of the whole film, I do not stress this aspect of the scene.

5 For general discussion of *Marnie*, see Wood 1989, 173; Spoto 1992, 339; and Samuels 1998, 93. See also chapter 3.

6 Although, of course, not the official parties to the film's criminal proceeding, the two women are clearly treated by the judge as the parties to the real issue at the heart of the offense.

7 Of course, both Letal and Becky impersonate the "real" singer, Luz Casal, a similarity that associates them even further. Casal, in turn, imitates Chavela Vargas's version of this song (Almodovar 1996, 115).

8 A comparison of this scene with the one Rebecca mentions in Bergman's *Autumn Sonata* is revealing. In both instances the dinner reunion between mother and daughter is followed by a performance. But whereas in Bergman's film daughter and mother each perform and watch the other performing, here, rather than looking at each other, they both look at the performing Letal, the judge, the law, Becky's mirror image, Rebecca's image of her mother. In the performing law figure they both see Becky; he is therefore a mediating image.

9 Judge Dominguez respectfully pleads with Becky to see her daughter, and, having arranged the meeting, leaves the women to conduct it themselves. It is interesting to compare this facilitating behavior with that of Connery's character in *Marnie*. There, the male protagonist physically forces the women into confrontation; participating in their meeting, he actively runs the show.

10 During the first investigation in the judge's chambers, Becky addresses her daughter, who repeatedly reminds her that it is the judge whom she needs to convince, and not her (Rebecca). Clearly, it is her daughter that Becky rightly feels judged by. Later, Rebecca scolds the judge for his uncaring, deceitful behavior towards people, and he promises to change his ways.

11 Chris Straayer suggests that "the rebellious effect of a drag queen depends on a disguise which appropriates and manipulates gender conventions, and on the purposeful breakdown of that disguise into essentially contradictory levels of information. This leaves the viewer unsure about sexual identification and rules for sexual determination, and thereby offers the most radical conclusions" (1992, 52).

12 For one list of United States judicial decisions that manifest such judicial compassion for men who batter or murder their spouses see Wiegand 1997, 46–49.

13 As Lucy Fischer rightly notes, "Letal's simulation also reveals what many theorists have observed about 'femininity' within patriarchal culture: that it requires a masquerade even of biological women—a performance not at all different from drag" (1998, 206).

Bibliography

"A Symposium on Film and the Law." 1997. *Oklahoma City Law Review* 22.

Akutagawa, Ryunosuke. 1952. *Rashomon and Other Stories*. New York: Liveright.

Alkalay-Gut, Karen. 1984. "*Jury of Her Peers*: The Importance of Trifles." *Studies in Short Fiction* 20:1–9.

——. 1995. "Murder and Marriage: Another Look at *Trifles*." In *Susan Glaspell: Essays on Her Theater and Fiction*, edited by Linda Ben-Zvi, 71–81. Ann Arbor: University of Michigan Press.

Almodovar, Pedro. 1996. *Almodovar*. Edited by Frederic Strauss and translated by Yves Baigneres. London: Faber and Faber.

Alster, Laurence. 1988. "Nuts." *Films and Filming*, February, 38.

Althouse, Ann. 1992. "Beyond King Solomon's Harlots: Women in Evidence." *Southern California Law Review* 65:1265.

Ashe, Marie. 1991. "Abortion of Narrative: A Reading of the Judgment of Solomon." *Yale Journal of Law and Feminism* 4:81.

Anderson, Benedict. 1985. *Imagined Communities: Reflections on the Origin and Spread of Nationalism*. London, Verso.

Angel, Marina. 1996. "Criminal Law and Women: Giving the Abused Woman Who Kills A Jury of Her Peers Who Appreciate Trifles." *American Criminal Law Review* 33:229–348.

——. 1997. "Susan Glaspell's *Trifles* and *A Jury of Her Peers*: Woman Abuse in A Literary and Legal Context." *Buffalo Law Review* 45:779–844.

Asimov, Michael. 1996. "When Lawyers Were Heroes." *University of San Francisco Law Review* 30:1131–38.

Bailey, Frankie Y., Joycelyn M. Pollock, and Sherry Schroeder. 1998. "The Best Defense: Images of Female Attorneys in Popular Films." In *Popular Culture, Crime and Justice*, edited by Frankie Y. Bailey and Donna C. Hale, 180–95. Belmont, Calif.: West/Wadsworth Publishing.

Baker, Frederick M., and Rich Vander Veen. 2000. "John D. Voelker: Michigan's Literary Justice." *Michigan Bar Journal* 79, no. 5:530–31.

Barbarow, George. 1987. "*Rashomon* and the Fifth Witness." In *Rashomon*, edited by Donald Richie. New Brunswick, N.J.: Rutgers University Press.

Barnet, Hilaire. 1998. *Introduction to Feminist Legal Studies*. London: Cavendish Publishing.

Barr, Charles. 1999. "The Conversion to Sound: Charles Bennett; *Blackmail*." In *English Hitchcock*, 78–97. Moffat, Scotland: Cameron and Hollis.

Barr, Judith A. 1999. *Our Lives Before the Law: Construction of Feminist Jurisprudence*. Princeton: Princeton University Press.

Barsky, Robert F. 1997. "Outsider in Literature: Construction and Representation in Death and the Maiden." *Sub-stance* 84:66.

Bass, Gary Jonathan. 1992. "International Law: War Crimes and the Limits of Legalism." *Michigan Law Review* 97:103.

Bazin, Andre. 1971. *What is Cinema?* Berkeley: University of California Press.

Beck, Marilyn. 1998. "Box-office Woes for Nuts." *St. Petersburg Times*, 4 January 1988.

Benedict, Helen. 1992. *Virgin or Vamp: How the Press Covers Sex Crimes*. New York: Oxford University Press.

Benedict, Ruth. 1989. *The Chrysanthemun and the Sword: Patterns of Japanese Culture*. 1946. Reprint, Boston: Houghton Mifflin.

Benson, Sheila. 1987. "*Nuts* Puts an Ethical Issue on the Stand." *Los Angeles Times*, 20 November.

Ben-Zvi, Linda. 1995. " 'Murder, She Wrote': The Genesis of Susan Glaspell's *Trifles*." In *Susan Glaspell: Essays on Her Theater and Fiction*, 19–47. Ann Arbor: University of Michigan Press.

Berets, Ralph. 1998. "Lawyers in Film: 1996." *Legal Studies Forum* 22:99–108.

Berger, Peter. 1983. "On the Obsolescence of the Concept of Honor." In *Revisions: Changing perspectives in Moral Philosophy*, edited by Stanley Hauerwas and Alasdair MacIntyre, 172. Notre Dame: University of Notre Dame Press.

Black, David A. 1999. *Law in Film: Resonance and Representation*. Urbana, Ill.: University of Illinois Press.

Bluestone, George. 1971. *Novels into Film: The Metamorphosis of Fiction into Cinema*. Berkeley: University of California Press.

Bourdieu, Pierre. 1966. "The Sentiment of Honor in Kabyle Society." In *Honor and Shame: The Values of Mediterranean Society*, edited by J. G. Peristiany. Chicago: Chicago University Press.

Brill, Leslie. 1988. "Do Not Presume: Irony." In *The Hitchcock Romance: Love and Irony in Hitchcock's Films*. Princeton: Princeton University Press.

Brode, Doug. 1987. "Streisand Guilty in *Nuts* of Uneven Performance." *The Post-Standard* (Syracuse), 25 November.

Broeske, Pat H. 1987. "Barbed." *Los Angeles Times*, 29 November.

Brownmiller, Susan. 1975. *Against Our Will: Men, Women and Rape*. New York: Simon and Schuster.

Buckley, Michael. 1988. "Nuts." *Films in Review*, February, 100.

Camilleri, Marijane. 1990. "Lessons in Law from Literature: A Look at the Movement and a Peer at Her Jury." *Catholic University Law Review* 39:557.

Campbell, J. K. 1966. "Honor and the Devil." In *Honor and Shame: The Values of Mediterranean Society*, edited by J. G. Peristiany. Chicago: Chicago University Press.

Caplow, Stacy. 1999. "Still in the Dark: Disappointing Images of Women Lawyers in the Movies." *Women's Rights Law Reporter* 20:55–71.

Card, Claudia. 1996. "Rape as a Weapon of War." *Hypatia* 11:5.

Carmody, Denis Lardner. 1989. *Women and World Religions*. New Jersey: Prentice Hall.

Cartmell, Deborah, and Imelda Whelehan, eds. 1999. *Adaptations: From Text to Screen, Screen to Text*. New York: Routledge.

Cavell, Stanley. 1981. *Pursuits of Happiness: The Hollywood Comedy of Remarriage*. Cambridge: Harvard University Press.

Chamallas, Martha. 2003. *Introduction to Feminist Legal Theory*. New York: Aspen Law and Business.

Chase, Anthony. 1999. "Civil Action Cinema." *Law Review of Michigan State University–Detroit College of Law* 1999:945.

———. 2002. *Movies on Trial: The Legal System on the Silver Screen*. New York: The New Press.

Clover, Carol. 1998. "God Bless Juries!" In *Refiguring American Film Genres: History and Theory*, edited by Nick Browne. Berkeley: University of California Press.

Collins, Patricia Hill. 2000. *Knowledge, Consciousness, and the Politics of Empowerment*. New York: Routledge.

Connerton, Paul. 1989. *How Societies Remember*. Cambridge: Cambridge University Press.

Cooke, Jennifer. 1987. Calendar Desk. *Los Angeles Times*, 13 December.

Coughlin, Anne M. 1998. "Sex and Guilt." *Virginia Law Review* 84:1.

Crenshaw, Kimberle. 1989. "Demarginalizing the Intersection of Race and Sex: A Black Feminist Critique of Antidiscrimination Doctrine, Feminist Theory and Antiracist Politics." In *Feminist Legal Theory: Foundations*, edited by D. Kelly Weisberg, 383–95. Philadelphia: Temple University Press.

Crnkovic, Gordana. 1997. "*Death and the Maiden*." Film Quarterly 50:39.

Cullen, Jenny. 1988. "Streisand: From Fanny Brice to 'Miami Vice.'" *St. Petersburg Times*, 8 July.

Culligan, Lawrence J., and Milorad Nikolic. 1990. *Corpus Juris Secundum: A Contemporary Statement of American Law as Derived from Reported Cases and Legislation.* St. Paul, Minn.: West Publishing.

Davidson, James F. 1987. "Memory of Defeat in Japan: A Reappraisal of *Rashomon.*" In *Rashomon,* edited by Donald Richie. New Brunswick, N.J.: Rutgers University Press.

Denvir, John. 1996. *Legal Reelism: Movies as Legal Texts.* Urbana, Ill.: University of Illinois Press.

———. 2000, "Law, Lawyers, Film and Television." *Legal Studies Forum* 24:279.

Doane, Mary Ann. 1991. "The Erotic Barter: *Pandora's Box.*" In *Femme Fatales: Feminism, Film, Theory, Psychoanalysis.* New York: Routledge.

Donovan, Dolores, and Stephanie Wildman, 1980–81. "Is the Reasonable Man Obsolete? A Critical Perspective on Self-Defense and Provocation," *Loyola L.A. Law Review* 14:435.

Dorfman, Ariel. 1992. *Death and the Maiden.* New York: Nick Hern Books.

Dowell, Pat. 1995. "Maiden America." *In These Times,* 20 February, 26.

Durgant, Raymond. 1974. "Blackmail." In *The Strange Case of Alfred Hitchcock, or The Plain Man's Hitchcock,* 85. Cambridge: MIT Press.

Eichner, Maxine. 2001. "On Postmodern Feminist Legal Theory." *Harvard Civil Rights–Civil Liberties Law Review* 36:1.

Eisner, Lotte H. 1969. "Pabst and the Miracle of Louise Brooks." In *The Haunted Screen: Expressionism in the German Cinema and the Influence of Max Reinhardt,* 295. Berkeley: University of California Press.

Elsaesser, Thomas. 1986. "Lulu and the Meter Man: Pabst's Pandora's Box (1929)." In *German Film and Literature: Adaptations and Transformations,* edited by Eric Rentscheler. New York: Methuen.

Elsley, Judy. 1992. "Laughter as Feminine Power in *The Color Purple* and *A Question of Silence.*" In *New Perspectives on Women and Comedy,* edited by Regina Barreca, 193. Philadelphia: Gordon and Breach.

Ensalaco, Mark. 1999. *Chile Under Pinochet: Recovering the Truth.* Philadelphia: University of Pennsylvania Press.

Erens, Patricia. 1979. *Akira Kurosawa: A Guide to References and Resources.* London: George Prior Publishers.

Estrich, Susan. 1987. *Real Rape.* Cambridge: Harvard University Press.

Everson, William K. 1994. *Hollywood Bedlam: Classic Screwball Comedies.* New York: Citadel Press.

Eyuboglu, Selim. 1991. "The Authorial Text and Postmodernism: Hitchcock's *Blackmail.*" Screen 32:58.

Felman, Shoshana, and Dori Laub. 1992. *Testimony: Crisis of Witnessing in Literature, Psychoanalysis, and History*. New York, Routledge.

Fischer, Lucy. 1998. "Modernity and Postmaternity: *High Heels* and *Imitation of Life*." In *Play It Again, Sam: Retakes on Remakes*, edited by Andrew Horton and Stuart Y. McDougal. Berkeley: University of California Press.

Fletcher, George P. 1984. "Human Dignity as a Constitutional Value." *The University of Western Ontario Law Review* 22:171.

——. 1996. "Domination in the Theory of Justification and Excuse." *University of Pittsburgh Law Review* 57:553.

Friedman, Elisabeth. 1997. "*Set It Off*." http://www.usfca.edu/pj/articles/set_it_off.htm.

Frug, Mary Joe. 1992. *Postmodern Legal Feminism*. New York: Routledge.

Gewirth. Alan. 1992. "Human Dignity as the Basis of Rights." In *The Constitution of Rights: Human Dignity and American Values*, edited by Michael J. Meyer and William A. Paret. Ithaca, N.Y.: Cornell University Press.

Gilligan, Carol. 1982. *In a Different Voice: Psychological Theory and Women's Development*. Cambridge: Harvard University Press.

Glaspell, Susan. 1996. "A Jury of Her Peers." In *Women in the Trees: U.S. Women's Short Stories about Battering and Resistance, 1839–1994*, edited by Susan Koppelman, 77–93. Boston: Beacon Press.

Goodwin, James. 1994. *Akira Kurosawa and Intertextual Cinema*. Baltimore: John Hopkins University Press.

Gordon, Ruth, and Garson Kanin. 1949. *Adam's Rib: A Viking Film Book, Screenplay*. New York: Viking.

Graham, Louise Everett, and Geraldine Maschio. 1995–96. "A False Public Sentiment: Narrative and Visual Images of Women Lawyers in Film." *Kentucky Law Journal* 84:1027–73.

Graham-Yooll, Andrew. 1991. "Dorfman: A Case of Conscience." *Index Censorship* 6:3.

Grant, Judith. 1996. "Lawyers as Superheroes: *The Firm*, *The Client*, and *The Pelican Brief*." *University of San Francisco Law Review* 30:1111–22.

Greenfield, Steve, Guy Osborn, and Peter Robson. 2001. *Film and the Law*. London: Cavendish Publishing.

Griffith, Richard. 1959. *Anatomy of a Motion Picture*. New York: St. Martin's.

Harrington, Curtis. 1987. "*Rashomon* and the Japanese Cinema." In *Rashomon*, edited by Donald Richie. New Brunswick, N.J.: Rutgers University Press.

Harris, Angela P. 1993. "Race and Essentialism in Feminist Legal Theory." In *Feminist Legal Theory: Foundations*, edited by D. Kelly Weisberg, 348–58. Philadelphia: Temple University Press.

Hartog, Hendrick. 1997. "Lawyering, Husbands' Rights, and the 'Unwritten Law' in Nineteenth-Century America." *The Journal of American History* 84:67.

Hedges, Elaine. 1995. "Small Things Reconsidered: A Jury of Her Peers." In *Susan*

Glaspell: Essays on Her Theater and Fiction, edited by Linda Ben-Zvi, 49–69. Ann Arbor: University of Michigan Press.

Herzfeld, Michael. 1980. "Honor and Shame: Problems in the Comparative Analysis of Moral Systems." *Man* 15:339.

Herman, Judith. 1992. *Trauma and Recovery: The Aftermath of Violence—from Domestic Abuse to Political Terror*. New York: Basic Books.

Hoff, Timothy. 2000. "Anatomy of a Murder." *Legal Studies Forum* 24:661.

Hollinger, Karen. 1998. *In the Company of Women: Contemporary Female Friendship Films*. Minneapolis: University of Minnesota Press.

Hom, Sharon K., and Eric K. Yamamoto. 2000. "Collective Memory, History and Social Justice." UCLA Law Review 47:1747.

Horder, Jeremy. 1992. *Provocation and Responsibility*. Oxford: Clarendon Press.

Imwinkelried, Edward, J., Paul C. Giannelli, Francis A. Gilligan, and Frederic I. Lederer. 1998. *Courtroom Criminal Evidence*. Charlottesville: Michie.

Ireland, Robert M. 1988. "Insanity and the Unwritten Law." *The American Journal of Legal History* 32:157.

———. 1989. "The Libertine Must Die: Sexual Dishonor and the Unwritten Law in the Nineteenth-Century United States." *Journal of Social History* 23:1.

James, Nick. 1995. "*Death and the Maiden*." *Sight and Sound* 4:40.

Johnson, Rebecca. 2002. *Taxing Choices: The Intersection of Class, Gender, Parenthood and the Law*. Vancouver: UBC Press.

Johnson, Rebecca, and Ruth Buchanan. 2002. "Getting the Insider's Story Out: What Popular Film Can Tell Us about Legal Method's Dirty Secrets." *Windsor Yearbook of Access to Justice* 20:87–110.

———. "The Unforgiven Sources of International Law: Nation-Building, Violence, and Gender in the West(ern)." In *International Law: Modern Feminist Approaches*, edited by Doris Buss and Ambreena Maji, 239. Oxford: Hart Publishings.

Jordan, Barry, and Rikki Morgan-Tamosunas. 1998. *Contemporary Spanish Cinema*. New York: Manchester University Press.

Kamir, Orit. 2000. "Judgement by Film: Socio-Legal Functions of *Rashomon*." *Yale Journal of Law and the Humanities* 12:39.

———. 2000a. "X-Raying *Adam's Rib*: Multiple Readings of a (Feminist?) Law-Film." *Studies in Law, Politics & Society* 22:103.

———. 2000b. "Feminist Law and Film: Searching for Imagery of Justice in Popular Culture." *Chicago-Kent Law Review* 75:899.

———. 2001. *Every Breath You Take: Stalking Narratives and the Law*. Ann Arbor: University of Michigan Press.

———. 2002. "Honor and Dignity Cultures: The Case of *Kavod* (Honor) and *Kvod ha-adam* (Dignity) in Israeli Society and Law." In *The Concept of Human Dignity in Human Rights Law*, edited by David Kretzmer and Eckart Klein. Amsterdam: Kluwer.

———. 2003a. "Dignity, Respect and Equality in Sexual Harassment Law: Israel's New Legislation." In *New Directions in Sexual Harassment Law*, edited by Catharine MacKinnon and Reva Segal. New Haven, Conn.: Yale University Press.

———. 2003b. " 'The Queen's Daughter is all Dignified Within' (Ps. 54:14): Basing Israeli Women's Status and Rights on Human Dignity." In *Men and Women: Judaism and Democracy*, edited by Rachel Elior, 31. Tel Aviv: Urim Press.

———. 2004a. "A Different Kind of Sex: Rape Law Between Equality, Dignity, and Honor" (in Hebrew). *Mishpat Umimshal Law Journal* 7:669.

———. 2004b. *Israeli Honor and Dignity: Social Norms, Gender Politics, and the Law* (in Hebrew). Jerusalem: Carmel Press.

———. 2005a. "Why Law-and-Film and What Does it Actually Mean?—A Perspective." *Continuum: Journal of Media and Cultural Studies* 19:255.

———. 2005b. "Anatomy of Hollywood's Hero-Lawyer: A Law-and-Film Study of Western Motifs, Honor-Based Values, and Gender Politics Underlying *Anatomy of a Murder's* Construction of the Lawyer's Image." *Studies in Law, Politics, and Society* 35:67.

———. Forthcoming. "Honor and Dignity in the Film *Unforgiven*: Implications for Sociolegal Theory." *Law and Society Review*.

Kauffmann, Stanley. 1987. "The Impact of *Rashomon*." In *Rashomon*, edited by Donald Richie. New Brunswick, N.J.: Rutgers University Press.

Kehr, Dave. 1987. "Streisand Carries 'Playhouse 90' into '80s in *Nuts*." *Chicago Tribune*, 20 November.

Kernan, Thomas J. 1906. "The Jurisprudence of Lawlessness." Report of the Twenty-Ninth Annual Meeting of the American Bar Association, 29–31 August, St. Paul, Minnesota, 450.

Kinder, Marsha. 1995. "From Matricide to Mother Love in Almodovar's *High Heels*." In *Post-Franco, Postmodern: The Films of Pedro Almodovar*, edited by Kathleen M. Vernon and Barbara Morris, 145. Westport, Conn.: Greenwood Press.

Kurosawa, Akira. 1969. *Rashomon*. New York: Grove Press.

———. 1987. "Something Like an Autobiography." In *Rashomon*, edited by Donald Richie. New Brunswick, N.J.: Rutgers University Press.

LaFave, Wayne R. 2000. *Criminal Law*. 3rd ed. St. Paul: West.

Lee, Cynthia. 2003. *Murder and the Reasonable Man: Passion and Fear in the Criminal Courtroom*. New York: NYU Press.

Levensque, John. 1991. "Nolte Marvellous in Moving *Prince of Tides*." *Hamilton (Ontario) Spectator*, 26 December.

Liebman, Stuart. 1995. "Weimar Cinema's Greatest Hits." *Cineaste* 21:50.

Linderman, Deborah. 1990. "The Screen in Hitchcock's *Blackmail*." *Wide Angle: A Film Quarterly of Theory, Criticism and Practice* 4:20–28.

Littau, Karin. 1995. "Refractions of the Feminine: The Monstrous Transformations of Lulu." *MLN* 110, no. 4:888–912.

Luban, David. 1998. "On Dorfman's *Death and the Maiden*." *Yale Journal of Law and the Humanities* 10:115.

Lumenick, Lou. 1987. "*Nuts*: A Triumph of a Film for All Involved." *The Record*, 20 November.

Lyons, Jeffrey. 1988. "*Nuts*." *The Washington Post*, 17 July.

MacKinnon, Catharine. 1987. *Feminism Unmodified*. Cambridge: Harvard University Press.

——. 1989. *Toward a Feminist Theory of the State*. Cambridge, Mass.: Harvard University Press.

——. 2000. "Turning Rape into Pornography: Postmodern Genocide." In *Mass Rape: The War Against Women in Bosnia-Herzegovina*, edited by Alexandra Stiglmayer, 73–81. Lincoln: University of Nebraska Press.

——. 2000a. "Points Against Postmodernism." *Chicago-Kent Law Review* 75:687.

——. 2001. *Sex Equality*. New York: Foundation Press.

Machura, Stefan, and Stefan Ulbrich. 2001. "Law in Film: Globalizing the Hollywood Courtroom Drama." In *Law and Film*, edited by Stefan Machura and Peter Robson, 117. Bristol, UK: Blackwell Publishers.

Machura, Stefan, and Peter Robson, eds. 2001. *Law and Film*. Bristol, UK: Blackwell Publishers.

Mael, Phyllis. 1989. "*Trifles*: The Path to Sisterhood." *Literature/Film Quarterly* 17:281.

Maree, Cathy. 1995. "Truth and Reconciliation: Confronting the Past in *Death and the Maiden* and *Playland*." *Literator* (South Africa) 16:25.

Maslin, Janet. 1987. "Streisand in *Nuts*." *The New York Times*, 20 November.

Mathews, Jack. 1988. "Laughing Their Way to the Bank." *Los Angeles Times*, 6 January.

McDonald, Kieko I. 1987. "The Dialectic of Light and Darkness in Kurosawa's *Rashomon*." In *Rashomon*, edited by Donald Richie. New Brunswick, N.J.: Rutgers University Press.

Medine, David. 1992. "Law and Kurosawa's *Rashomon*." *Literature Film Quarterly* 20:55.

Mellen, Joan. 1976. *The Waves at Genji's Door: Japan Through Its Cinema*. New York: Pantheon.

Millbank, Jenni. 1996. "From Butch to Butcher's Knife: Film, Crime and Lesbian Sexuality." *The Sydney Law Review* 18:451.

Miller, Carolyn Lisa. 1994. " 'What a Waste. Beautiful, Sexy Gal. Hell of a Lawyer.': Film and the Female Attorney." *Columbia Journal of Gender and Law* 4:203–32.

Miller, William Ian. 1993. *Humiliation: And Other Essays on Honor, Social Discomfort and Violence*. Ithaca, N.Y.: Cornell University Press.

——. 1998, "Clint Eastwood and Equity: Popular Culture's Theory of Revenge." In *Law in the Domains of Culture*, edited by Austin Sarat and Thomas R. Kearns. Ann Arbor: University of Michigan Press.

Milne, Tom. 1988. "*Nuts*." *Monthly Film Bulletin*, February, 48.

Minow, Martha. 1998. *Between Vengeance and Forgiveness: Facing History after Genocide and Mass Violence.* Boston: Beacon Press.

Modleski, Tania. 1989. *The Women Who Knew Too Much: Hitchcock and Feminist Theory.* New York: Routledge.

Monahan, Julie. 1995. "Rape and Death and the Maiden." *off our backs: a women's news journal* 25:18.

Morgan, Rikki. 1992. "Dressed to Kill." *Sight and Sound* 12:28.

Mulvey, Laura. 1989. *Visual and Other Pleasures.* Bloomington: Indiana University Press.

———. 1995. "The Myth of Pandora: A Psychoanalytical Approach." In *Feminisms in the Cinema*, edited by Laura Pietopaolo and Ada Testaferri, 3. Bloomington: Indiana University Press.

———. 1999. "Visual Pleasure and Narrative Cinema." In *Feminist Theory: A Reader*, edited by Sue Thornham, 57. New York: New York University Press.

Murphy, Jeanette. 1986. "A Question of Silence." In *Films for Women*, edited by Charlotte Brunsdon, 99–108. London: British Film Institute.

Mustazza, Leonard. 1989. "Generic Translation and Thematic Shift in Susan Glaspell's 'Trifles' and 'A Jury of Her Peers.'" *Studies in Short Fiction* 26:489.

Nevis, Francis M. 1996. "Through the Great Depression on Horseback: Legal Themes in Western Films of the 1930s." In *Legal Reelism: Movies as Legal Texts*, edited by John Denvir, 44. Urbana: University of Illinois Press.

Nussbaum, Martha. 1999. *Sex and Social Justice.* New York: Oxford University Press.

Osborn Jr., John Jay. 1996. "Atticus Finch—The End of Honor: A Discussion of *To Kill A Mockingbird.*" *University of San Francisco Law Review* 30:1139.

Osiel, Mark. 1997. *Mass Atrocity, Collective Memory and the Law.* New Brunswick, N.J.: Transaction Publishers.

Ozieblo, Barbara. "Rebellion and Rejection: The Plays of Susan Glaspell." In *Modern American Drama: The Female Canon*, edited by June Schlueter. London: Fairleigh Dickinson University Press.

Pawelczak, Andy. 1995. "*Death and the Maiden.*" *Films in Review* 46:54.

Peristiany, J. G., ed. *Honor and Shame: The Values of Mediterranean Society.* Chicago: Chicago University Press.

Peukert, Detlev J. K. 1971. *Shame and Guilt: A Psychoanalytic and Cultural Study.* New York: Norton.

———. 1989. *The Weimar Republic.* New York: Hill and Wang.

Piers, Gerhart, and Milton B. Singer. 1971. *Shame and Guilt: A Psychoanalytic and Cultural Study.* New York: Norton.

Pitt-Rivers, Julian. 1966. "Honor and Social Status." In *Honor and Shame: The Values of Mediterranean Society*, edited by J. G. Peristiany. Chicago: Chicago University Press.

———. *The Fate of Shechen or the Politics of Sex: Essays in the Anthropology of the Mediterranean.* Cambridge: Cambridge University Press.

Prince, Stephen. 1991. *The Cinema of Akira Kurosawa: The Warrior's Camera*. Princeton: Princeton University Press.

Rainer, Peter. 1988. "Streisand Saves It." *Connoisseur*, February, 19.

Raitt, Fiona E., and M. Suzanne Zeedyk. 2002. *The Implicit Relation of Psychology and Law: Women and Syndrome Evidence*. Philadelphia: Routledge.

Ramanathan, Geetha. 1992. "Murder as Speech: Narrative Subjectivity in Marleen Gorris' *A Question of Silence*." *Genders* 15:58.

Ray, Robert. 1985. *A Certain Tendency of the Hollywood Cinema, 1930–1980*. Princeton, N.J.: Princeton University Press.

Raz, Joseph. 1983. "A Right To Dissent? I. Civil Disobedience, II. Conscientious Objection." In *The Authority of Law: Essays on Law and Morality*, 262–89. Oxford: Clarendon Press.

Reynolds, Kimberley, and Nicola Humble. 1993. *Victorian Heroines: Representations of Femininity in Nineteenth-Century Literature and Art*. New York: NYU Press.

Richie, Donald. 1996. *The Films of Akira Kurosawa*. 3rd ed. Berkeley: University of California Press.

———, ed. 1972. *Focus on Rashomon*. Englewood Cliffs, N.J.: Prentice-Hall.

———, ed. 1987. *Rashomon*. New Brunswick, N.J.: Rutgers University Press.

Rimmon-Kenan, Shlomit. 1983. *Narrative Fiction: Contemporary Poetics*. New York: Methuen.

Robinson, Marilyn. 1998. "Collins to Grisham: A Brief History of the Legal Thriller." *Legal Studies Forum*, 22:21.

Robson, Ruthann. 1998. *Sappho Goes to Law School*. New York: Columbia University Press.

Roniger, Luis, and Mario Aznajder. 1999. *The Legacy of Human Rights Violations in the Southern Cone: Argentina, Chile, and Uruguay*. Oxford: Oxford University Press.

Root, Jane. 1986. "Distributing 'A Question of Silence'—A Cautionary Tale." In *Films for Women*, edited by Charlotte Brunsdon, 213–23. London: British Film Institute.

Rostovsky-Halperin, Sarah. 1991. *'Zaner ha-Rashomon ba-Siporet ha-Yisrae'elit* (The Rashomon Genre in Israeli Narratives). Jerusalem: Reuven Mas.

Ruether, Rosemary Radford, ed. 1974. "Misogynism and Virginal Feminism in the Fathers of the Church." In *Religion and Sexism: Images of Women in the Jewish and Christian Traditions*. New York: Simon and Schuster.

Ryal, Tom. 1993. *Blackmail*. London: British Film Institute.

Ryan, Cheyney. 1986. "Print the Legend: Violence and Recognition in The Man Who Shot Liberty Valance." In *Legal Reelism: Movies as Legal Texts*, edited by John Denvir, 23. Urbana: University of Illinois Press.

Salem, Rob. 1987. "You'll go Nuts for Barbra." *The Toronto Star*, 20 November.

Samuels, Robert. 1998. *Hitchcock's Bi-Textuality: Lacan, Feminisms, and Queer Theory*. Albany: State University of New York Press.

Sarat, Austin. 2000. "Imagining the Law of the Father: Loss, Dread and Mourning in *The Sweet Hereafter*." *Law and Society Review* 34:3–46.

Sarat, Austin, Lawrence Douglas, and Martha Merrill Umphrey, eds. 2005. *Law on the Screen*. Stanford: Stanford University Press.

Sarat, Austin, and Thomas R. Kearns, eds. 1999. *History, Memory and the Law*. Ann Arbor: Michigan University Press.

Sartre, Jean-Paul. 1966. *Being and Nothingness: A Phenomenological Essay on Ontology*, translated by Hazel E. Barnes. New York: Pocket Books.

Sato, Tadao. 1987. "*Rashomon*." In *Rashomon*, edited by Donald Richie. New Brunswick, N.J.: Rutgers University Press.

Schachter, Oscar. 1983. "Editorial Comment—Human Dignity as a Normative Concept." *American Journal of International Law* 77:848.

Shapiro, Carole. 1995. "Women Lawyers in Celluloid: Why Hollywood Skirts the Truth." *University of Toledo Law Review* 25:955–1011.

Sheffield, Ric. 1993. "On Film: A Social History of Women Lawyers in Popular Culture 1930 to 1990." *Loyola of Los Angeles Entertainment Law Journal* 14:73–114.

Shehan, Katherine C. 2000. "Caring for Deconstruction." *Yale Journal of Law and Feminism* 12:85.

Sherwin, Richard K. 2000. *When Law Goes Pop: The Vanishing Line between Law and Popular Culture*. Chicago: University of Chicago Press.

Siskel, Gene. 1987. "Serious Girl Streisand is Weighted Down by a 'Message' Movie." *Chicago Tribune*, 22 November.

Smith, Beverly A. 1982. "Women's Work—*Trifles*? The Skill and Insight of Playwright Susan Glaspell." *International Journal of Women's Studies* 5:172.

Smith, Paul Julian. 1994. "*Tacones lejanos (High Heels, 1991)*: Imitations of Life." In *Desire Unlimited: The Cinema of Pedro Almodovar*, 121. London: Verso.

Smith-Khan, Cheryl. 1998. "African-American Attorneys in Television and Film: Compounding Stereotypes." *Legal Studies Forum* 22:119–32.

Sokolow, David Simon. 1991. "From Akira Kurosawa to (Duncan) Kennedy: The Lessons of *Rashomon* for Current Legal Education." *Wisconsin Law Review* 1991: 969.

Sotomayor, Aurea Maria. 1997. "[To be] Just in the Threshold of Memory: The Founding Violence of the Victim in Diamela Eltit's *Lumperica* and Ariel Dorfman's *Death and the Maiden*." *Nomada: Creacion, Teoria, Critica* (Puerto Rico) 3:23.

Spoto, Donald. 1992. *The Art of Alfred Hitchcock: 50 Years of His Motion Pictures*. New York: Anchor Books.

Springer, Kimberly. 2001. "Waiting to Set It Off: African American Women and the Sapphire Fixation." In *Reel Knockouts: Violent Women in the Movies*, edited by Martha MacCaughey and Neal King, 170–99. Austin: University of Texas Press.

Straayer, Chris. 1992. "Redressing the 'Natural': The Temporary Transvestite Film." *Wide Angle*, January, 36.

Strickland, Rennard. 1997. "The Cinematic Lawyer: The Magic Mirror and the Silver Screen." *Oklahoma City University Law Review* 22:13–23.

Stoynoff, Natasha. 1996. "The Beauty Myth." *The Toronto Sun*, 10 November.

"Symposium: Picturing Justice: Law and Lawyers in the Visual Media." 1996. *San Francisco University Law Review* 30.

"Symposia: Law and Popular Culture." 1998. *The Legal Studies Forum* 22.

"Symposium: Law and Popular Culture." 2001. 48 UCLA Law Review 48 (August).

Taslitz, Andrew E. 1996. "Patriarchal Stories I: Cultural Rape Narratives in the Courtroom." *Southern California Review of Law and Women's Studies* 5:387.

Taylor, Charles. 1994. "The Politics of Recognition." In *Examining the Politics of Recognition*, edited by Amy Gutmann, 125. Princeton: Princeton University Press.

Thompson, David. 1992. "*Tacones Lejanos (High Heels).*" *Sight and Sound* 12:81.

——. 1995. "I Make Movies for Adults." *Sight and Sound* 4:6.

Thornham, Sue. 1999. *Feminist Film Theory: A Reader*. New York: NYU Press.

Tompkins, Jane. 1992. *West of Everything: The Inner Life of Westerns*. Oxford: Oxford University Press.

Toppor, Tom. 1980. *Nuts: A Play in Three Acts*. New York: Samuel French.

Traver, Robert. 1959. *Anatomy of a Murder*. New York: Dell.

Tripp, Edward. 1974. *The Meridian Handbook of Classical Mythology*. New York: Meridian.

Tushnet, Mark. 1996. "Class Action: One View of Gender and Law in Popular Culture." In *Legal Reelism: Movies as Legal Texts*, edited by John Denvir, 244–60. Urbana: University of Illinois Press.

Tyler, Parker. 1987. "*Rashomon* as Modern Art." In *Rashomon*, edited by Donald Richie. New Brunswick, N.J.: Rutgers University Press.

Umphrey, Martha. 1999–2000. "Media Melodrama! Sensationalism and the 1907 Trail of Harry Thaw." *New York Law School Law Review* 43:715.

——. Forthcoming. "*Dementia Americana*": Culture and Responsibility in the Trials of Harry Thaw. Chapel Hill: University of North Carolina Press.

Walters, Margaret. 1988. "Tart with a Heart." *The Listener*, 11 February, 32.

Weinstein, Jeremy D. 1986. "Adultery, Law and the State: A History." *Hastings Law Journal* 38:195.

Wedekind, Frank. 1972. *German Expressionism: The Lulu Plays and Other Sex Tragedies*. London: Calder and Boyars.

Weschler, Lawrence. 1994. "Artist in Exile." *The New Yorker*, 5 December, 88.

West, Robin. 1993. *Narrative Authority and Law*. Ann Arbor: University of Michigan Press.

——. 1997. *Caring for Justice*. New York: NYU Press.

Wexman, Virginia Wright. 1993. *Creating the Couple: Love, Marriage and Hollywood Performance*. Princeton: Princeton University Press.

Wiegand, Shirley A. 1997. "Deception and Artifice: Thelma, Louise, and the Legal Hermeneutic." *Oklahoma City University Law Review* 22:25.

White, James Boyd. 1973. *The Legal Imagination.* Boston: Little, Brown.

——. 1984. *When Words Lose Their Meaning.* Chicago: University of Chicago Press.

——. 1999. *From Expectation to Experience.* Ann Arbor: University of Michigan Press.

Williams, Linda. 1994. "A Jury of Their Peers: Marleen Gorris's *A Question of Silence.*" In *Multiple Voices in Feminist Film Criticism,* edited by Diane Carson, Linda Dittmar, and Janice R. Welsch, 432. Minneapolis: University of Minnesota Press.

Williams, Patricia J. 1991. *The Alchemy of Race and Rights.* Cambridge: Harvard University Press.

Wolff, Janet. 1993. "*Death and the Maiden:* Does Semiotics Justify Murder?" *Critical Quarterly* 35:38.

Wood, Robin. 1989. *Hitchcock's Films Revisited.* New York: Columbia University Press.

Wright, Will. 1975. *Sixguns and Society: A Structural Study of the Western.* Berkeley: University of California Press.

Index

divorce, 120, 163, 232

Dolores Claiborne, xv, 182, 183

domain, 99, 169, 201, 256; cultural, xvii; feminine, 232; legal, 40, 193

domesticity, 81; guilty, 97; patriarchal, 78

dominance, xv, 11, 14, 146, 197, 202, 218, 219, 223, 248, 265–268, 282; male, 202; patriarchal, 156, 220, 228

domination, male, 221

Dorfman, Ariel, xv, 187

doubt, 26, 27, 58, 59, 124, 127, 144, 169, 171–173, 177, 195, 207, 209; feminist, 153; reasonable, 55, 114, 126, 171, 189, 193, 257

drag queen, 297 n.11

Eden myth, 60–65, 72

emancipation, 13, 18, 26, 74, 119, 176

empathy, 9, 31, 34, 81, 189, 193, 209, 226, 252

employee, female, 252

employer, male, 226, 249

employment discrimination, 146, 263

empowerment, xiv, 189, 200, 210

encounter, sexual, 33, 37, 45, 55–59, 88, 95, 101, 102, 105, 121, 125, 126, 180, 249, 260, 287 n.1

environment, feminine, 98

equality, 4, 5, 10, 12, 19, 21, 140, 144, 152, 153, 231; Aristotelian notion of, 245; before the law, xi, 39, 136, 177, 247, 248, 279; gender, xii, 14–16, 21, 25, 247; norm, 138; racial, 2; sex, 71, 141, 156; social, 79; women's, 246

essentialism, 12, 244, 245, 282

ethics, feminist, 193; of care, 133, 218, 223, 231, 248, 267, 268, 282; of justice, 267, 268

event, traumatic, 186, 191, 203

evidence: criminal, 54; hearsay, 59; inconclusive, 208

excuse, legal, 114

exoneration: legal, 104, 107; social, 107

experience, traumatic, 97, 168, 180, 190, 191, 192

family: lesbian, 263; melodrama, 266; values, 121, 129, 142, 149, 150, 156

fantasy, sexual, 275

father figure, 70

fatherhood, 4, 251; Black, 251

Felman, Shoshana, 191

femininity, xiii, 8, 19, 24, 70, 78, 79, 81, 84, 147, 152, 153, 202, 268, 276, 281, 282, 297 n.13; malignant, 84

feminism, xiii, 11, 12, 156–158, 235, 253, 266–282; of care, xv, 12, 202; cultural, 39, 146, 181, 248; gender-blind, 235; liberal, 39, 156; minority legal, 244; modern, 266; optimistic, 158; radical, 39, 146, 155, 156, 158, 181; relational, 253

femme fatale, 32, 33, 64, 73, 79, 84, 88, 93, 108, 129

film: as jurisprudence, 1; feminist, theory, xiv, 11, 13, 25, 110; noir, 265; paralleling law, 1; popular fiction, xii; viewing, 22, 24

fire, sacred 289

force, use of, 17, 19, 20, 102

forgiveness, 6, 52, 72, 164, 212, 276, 277, 279

fornication, 20, 35–37, 106

freedom, 21, 27, 28, 99, 103, 104, 106, 119, 125, 127–129, 150, 151, 162, 165, 194, 196, 210, 235, 237, 240, 256

friendship, female, 265

frigidity, 109, 273

functions, social, xiii, xvii, 12, 34

gangster movie, 256

gaze, 22, 28, 30, 31, 47, 80, 100, 101,

violence (*continued*)
295 n.17; domestic, 32, 120, 121, 127–
129, 145, 180; sexual, 11, 33, 95, 195
voice, 12, 46, 48, 50, 58, 62, 64–66, 68,
72, 83, 97–99, 104, 107, 110, 111, 121,
126, 139, 163, 171, 175, 180, 188, 193,
200, 201, 214, 217, 220–223, 228,
229, 231, 233, 275, 276, 282
voluntariness, 35, 85

war atrocities, 296 n.7
Wayne, John, 152
Wedekind, Frank, 73, 74, 83, 85, 88, 89,
288, 289
Weimar Republic, 74, 88, 89
West, Robin, 12, 223, 264, 266, 267, 277
White, James Boyd, xvii, 3, 267
wife: abuse, 120; battered, 114, 127;
dependent, 142; maltreated, 140
wisdom: common, 44, 51, 52, 57; conventional, 50, 51, 53, 56, 57, 60
witness, unreliable, 56, 57, 128, 167,
189, 208
womanhood, 12, 62, 69, 77, 143, 158,
253, 254
women: allegorical, 35; Asian, 246; bio

logical, 297 n.13; Black/African
American, 40, 244, 246–248, 251–
263; blonde, 91; as different, 246;
good, 64, 142, 292; guilty, 34, 38, 91,
106, 109, 131, 226; heedless, 76; heterosexual, 243, 244, 246; inner-city,
253; lawyer, 143, 149; lesbian, 12, 244,
246; manly, 262; minority, 243, 244;
modern, 73, 94; new, 78, 91, 94, 100,
108, 137, 142, 149, 173; objectification
of, 30; of color, 243; outcast, 96;
poor, 254; prostituted, xv, 94, 180;
reasonable, 223, 238, 239; remote,
73; revered, 78; sexual, xiii, xiv, 56,
57, 74, 82, 91, 95, 129, 130, 157, 267;
silenced, 71, 72, 97, 108, 110, 112, 128,
138, 163, 174, 175, 180, 189, 195, 214,
218, 225, 229, 234; single, 253; treatment of, xiii, 12, 33, 34, 130, 165, 173,
179, 287 n.3; unattractive, 78; unmarried, 63, 243
world: legal, 51, 58, 109, 140, 141, 153,
228, 274; masculine, 143
worldview, 3, 51, 128; honor-based, 19

zone, feminine, 236

Orit Kamir is a professor of law and gender at the
Hebrew University in Jerusalem and a visiting
professor at the University of Michigan Law School.

Kamir, Orit.
Framed : women in law and film / Orit Kamir.
p. cm.
Includes bibliographical references and index.
ISBN 0-8223-3636-7 (cloth : alk. paper)
ISBN 0-8223-3624-3 (pbk. : alk. paper)
1. Women in motion pictures. 2. Sex discrimination
in motion pictures. 3. Legal films (Drama)—
History and criticism. I. Title.
PN1995.9.W6K235 2006
792.082—dc22   2005025675